# VITA

# VITA

## The Life of
## V. Sackville-West

## Victoria
## Glendinning

Quill
New York

Library of Congress Cataloging in Publication Data

Glendinning, Victoria.
Vita : the life of V. Sackville-West.

Includes bibliographical references and index.
1. Sackville-West, V. (Victoria), 1892–1962—
Biography.   2. Authors, English—20th century—
Biography.   I. Title.
PR6037.A35Z68   1985     823'.912 [B]     84-62075
ISBN 0-688-04111-6

Printed in the United States of America

First Quill Edition

1 2 3 4 5 6 7 8 9 10

*For Paul*

# ACKNOWLEDGEMENTS

MY principal thanks are to Nigel Nicolson, Vita Sackville-West's younger son and literary executor. He invited me to write the life of his mother, and put a vast mass of family papers at my disposal. He left me alone to write the book, yet was always ready to answer queries. Most of the photographs come from his family albums. His generosity and patience at every stage have been extraordinary.

Many other people have helped me in different ways. I should like to mention in particular Shirley Beljon, Dorothy Church, Ursula Codrington, the Hon. Sonia Cubitt, Simon Glendinning, John Gross, Evelyn Irons, Eardley Knollys, Mitchell Leaska, Edie Lamont, Alvilde Lees-Milne, James Lees-Milne, Lady McAlpine, John Phillips, Lady St Levan, Dame Janet Vaughan, Luisa Vertova, Michael Wishart, Francis Wyndham and, last but first, Terence de Vere White.

I am grateful to Peter Cranham for permission to use the phrase 'The Enclave and the Tower', which is the title of his own unpublished work on the world of V. Sackville-West.

I would also like to thank the following libraries and their librarians: the Berg Collection, New York Public Library; the Humanities Research Center, University of Texas at Austin; Yale University Library; the University of Sussex Library. For permission to quote from the published letters and diaries of Virginia Woolf, I am grateful to the trustees of the author's estate and to the Hogarth Press.

My final thanks are to my agent, Bruce Hunter, and to my editors at Weidenfeld & Nicolson in London and at Alfred A. Knopf in New York for their support.

# CONTENTS

# ILLUSTRATIONS

WE should ourselves be sorry to think that posterity should judge us by a patchwork of our letters, preserved by chance, independent of their context, written perhaps in a fit of despondency or irritation, divorced, above all, from the myriad little strands which colour and compose our peculiar existence, and which in their multiplicity, their variety and their triviality, are vivid to ourselves alone, uncommunicable even to those nearest to us, sharing our daily life. . . . Still, within our limitations it is necessary to arrive at some conclusions, certain facts do emerge.

V. Sackville-West,
Introduction,
*The Diary of the Lady Anne Clifford*
(1923)

---

THE only thing is to know and realize that Vita has got blanks in herself and these blanks are blank. If I find a blank, I get a plank and bridge it and I don't look down, lest I get vertigo.

Edwin Lutyens,
quoted by Vita's mother in her diary,
10 April 1931

# Family Tree
## of Sackvilles and Nicolsons

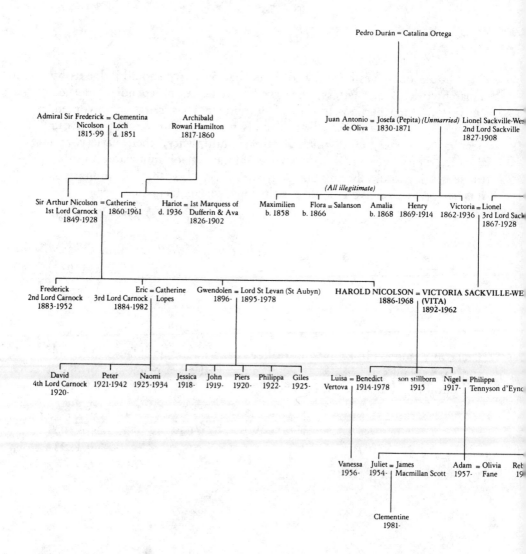

Pedro Durán = Catalina Ortega

Admiral Sir Frederick = Clementina    Archibald        Juan Antonio = Josefa (Pepita) *(Unmarried)* Lionel Sackville-Wes
Nicolson   Loch      Rowan Hamilton     de Oliva   1830-1871           2nd Lord Sackville
1815-99   d. 1851      1817-1860                                       1827-1908

*(All illegitimate)*

Sir Arthur Nicolson = Catherine    Hariot = 1st Marquess of     Maximilien   Flora = Salanson   Amalia   Henry     Victoria = Lionel
1st Lord Carnock   1860-1961    d. 1936   Dufferin & Ava    b. 1858   b. 1866       b. 1868   1869-1914   1862-1936   3rd Lord Sack
1849-1928                   1826-1902                                           1867-1928

Frederick           Eric = Catherine   Gwendolen = Lord St Levan (St Aubyn)     HAROLD NICOLSON = VICTORIA SACKVILLE-WE
2nd Lord Carnock   3rd Lord Carnock   Lopes    1896-   1895-1978           1886-1968     (VITA)
1883-1952      1884-1982                                                1892-1962

David     Peter     Naomi    Jessica   John   Piers   Philippa   Giles     Luisa = Benedict   son stillborn   Nigel = Philippa
4th Lord Carnock   1921-1942   1925-1934   1918-   1919-   1920-   1922-   1925-    Vertova   1914-1978     1915     1917-   Tennyson d'Eync
1920-

Vanessa   Juliet = James           Adam = Olivia    Reb
1956-   1954-   Macmillan Scott   1957-   Fane     19

Clementine
1981-

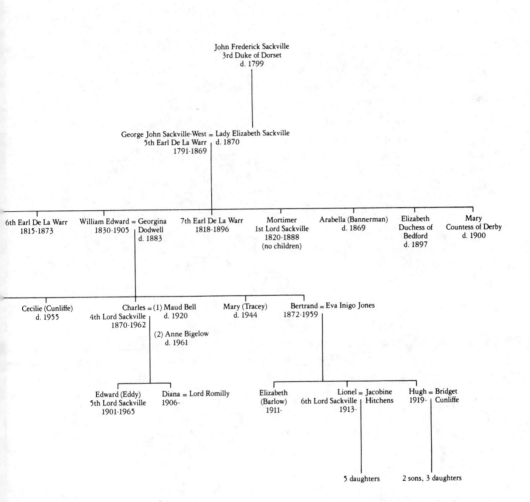

John Frederick Sackville
3rd Duke of Dorset
d. 1799

George John Sackville-West = Lady Elizabeth Sackville
5th Earl De La Warr ╷ d. 1870
1791-1869

6th Earl De La Warr
1815-1873

William Edward = Georgina
1830-1905 ╷ Dodwell
d. 1883

7th Earl De La Warr
1818-1896

Mortimer
1st Lord Sackville
1820-1888
(no children)

Arabella (Bannerman)
d. 1869

Elizabeth
Duchess of
Bedford
d. 1897

Mary
Countess of Derby
d. 1900

Cecilie (Cunliffe)
d. 1955

Charles = (1) Maud Bell
4th Lord Sackville ╷ d. 1920
1870-1962

(2) Anne Bigelow
d. 1961

Mary (Tracey)
d. 1944

Bertrand = Eva Inigo Jones
1872-1959

Edward (Eddy)
5th Lord Sackville
1901-1965

Diana = Lord Romilly
1906-

Elizabeth
(Barlow)
1911-

Lionel = Jacobine
6th Lord Sackville ╷ Hitchens
1913-

Hugh = Bridget
1919- ╷ Cunliffe

5 daughters

2 sons, 3 daughters

# PREFACE

THIS is Vita Sackville-West's story. One of the 'lies' of all biography is in that fact. (Another is that any story can ever be the whole story.) The people around Vita are in shadow except where their stories touch hers. They are distorted or diminished by this effect, especially as Vita's personality is unusually strong. Important aspects of the personalities and careers of Violet Trefusis and Virginia Woolf, for example, are not touched on, but there are plenty of books about these two, at least, in which they themselves are in the spotlight. I am more concerned about the lessened impact of Vita's husband Harold Nicolson. Because he was more conciliatory and, to use her term, 'mild', and because he tended to write about himself in a humorously deprecating way, the diminishing effect is the more marked. But Harold Nicolson's story too has been told, in two volumes, by James Lees-Milne. The only secondary character to whose ghost I need make no apology is Vita's mother, who threatened to take over her daughter's biography with the same tragi-comic bullying charm that she exercised in life.

There are other ways in which this book is less than comprehensive. It is a biography and not a work of literary criticism, though I have characterized and quoted from V. Sackville-West's prose and poetry. She was first and foremost a writer. The first great sorrow of her life was that, by an accident of gender, Knole could never be hers; the second, the realization that she was not a 'great' writer. As a poet, she came to feel that she had failed. Her reputation rests uneasily on *The Land*, which came early in her career and was a resounding success. But I think that her second long poem, *The Garden*, and some of her short lyrics now stand up to scrutiny better than *The Land*, and that her poetry as a whole deserves to be rescued from the relative obscurity into which it has fallen.

The divisions and conflicts of Vita's temperament caused her unhappiness and produced neurosis which she could sometimes use creatively. Distrusting amateur psychiatry, I have not attempted it, nor have I ventured to interpret her strange animal dreams. But an analytical study based on the evidence in this book would, I believe, be of interest and value.

The marriage between Vita and Harold was not in itself so extraordinary. There is no need to bow the knee. This predominantly masculine woman and this slightly feminine man, as James Lees-Milne has observed, were themselves obsessed by its unorthodoxy. Many marriages are, in one way or another, as strangely and finely balanced as theirs; many marriages are as close, and in commonplace ways closer. Some readers may feel that the Nicolsons' relationship was not a marriage so much as a friendship. What is extraordinary is how much, through their letters and diaries, is known about it. It must be one of the best-documented marriages in history. The evidence – of their actions as well as of the written word – poses a hundred questions about that institution, and if some of them are disturbing, so much the better.

Some of Vita's behaviour was indefensible. I am aware that while to some readers she will be an inspiration, to others she may seem unlikeable. I would like her story to be read as an adventure story. I think she would like that too.

Graveley, 1983.

# VITA

# PROLOGUE

VICTORIA Sackville-West was thirty when she went into labour for the first and last time at midday on 8 March 1892. She had been having what Mrs Patterson the nurse called 'spurious pains' for two days; she had been weepy and depressed, making her will and writing a farewell letter to her husband Lionel in case she died. Lionel and Mrs Patterson sat with her now as the day faded. 'I was suffering so much that I begged them to kill me. It was a hundred times worse than I had expected,' she wrote in her diary in French (which was still her first language).

In the small hours of the morning of 9 March she asked for chloroform – 'I was frantic' – but Lionel couldn't get the bottle open. 'Ma chère petite Vita' was born at 4.15 a.m., healthy, weighing in at 7½ pounds, with a fine head of dark hair. Although a son would have inherited Knole, the great house in which the baby was born, and also a title (Lionel was heir to Lord Sackville, who was his uncle and his wife's father), Victoria at least was not disappointed that she had a daughter. She had been expecting a girl and had referred to the unborn child as 'Vita' – a contraction of her own name – for the past six months.

Lord Sackville, Victoria's father, elsewhere in the vast complex of ancient buildings that is Knole, was not informed of what was going on until his granddaughter was safely born: he was not to be worried. 'Papa and I loved each other very dearly,' wrote Victoria. 'I reminded him very much of Mama whom he *adored*.... I was very fond of my dolls and a good little mother to them – how I loved afterwards my live Doll Vita.... I had the deepest gratitude to Lionel, who I was madly in love with, for giving me such a gift as that perfect baby.... Lionel was perfect to me in those days.'

On 3 May, when the baby was christened Victoria Mary in the chapel at Knole, the doctor pronounced the new mother not well enough to leave her room. So Victoria was absent from her daughter's christening

– '*si terriblement* disappointed' – as she was to be absent from Vita's wedding. During her long convalescence Lionel, to whom Victoria had given the loving nickname 'Tio', was attentive. He read Thackeray's *Vanity Fair* aloud to her. 'Becky Sharp interests me so much,' she noted in her diary. It was not surprising : they had a lot in common.

Victoria's background was romantic, mysterious, even disreputable.[1] She was born in Paris in 1862, the second child and eldest daughter of the humbly born Josefa Durán, better known as Pepita, the beautiful and internationally famous Spanish dancer. Victoria was registered as 'fille de père inconnu', even though Pepita was still legally married to her former dancing teacher, Juan Antonio de Oliva. The 'père inconnu' was an unmarried English diplomat, Lionel Sackville-West, who had been faithfully attached to Pepita for ten years by the time Victoria was born.

Lionel established his mistress and her two sons and three daughters – all assumed to be his – in a house she called the Villa Pepa in Arcachon in south-west France. Here Comtesse West, as she styled herself, lived with her children in a seclusion partly dictated by discretion and enforced by the ambiguity of her position. Papa, adored and adoring, visited them as often as his profession allowed. Other familiars of the house were Catalina Ortega, Pepita's mother (a barber's widow from Málaga, who had supported her daughter in early days by taking in washing and peddling old clothes) and the Vicomte de Béon, the assistant station master at Bordeaux, who took a benevolent interest in the family.

This odd but happy *ménage* was shattered in 1871 when Pepita died. The following year Lionel was *en poste* in Buenos Aires ; old Catalina, penniless, was in Málaga, and the motherless family was taken over by M. de Béon and his wife. Lionel was not being irresponsible. He wanted Max to go to Stonyhurst, the English Roman Catholic public school (the children had been raised in their mother's religion), and arranged for Victoria and her sisters to attend a convent in Paris, in the rue Monceau. Mme de Béon deposited Victoria there when she was eleven, and there she stayed until she was eighteen. She hated it.

And then, in 1880, Lionel Sackville-West acted with decision and courage. On his instructions, a Mrs Mulhall took his illegitimate family over to England. On the boat, she broke the news to Victoria that her parents had never been married, then she took the bewildered, French-speaking children to meet their two aristocratic paternal uncles – the Earl de la Warr at Buckhurst, and Mortimer, the first Lord Sackville, at Knole. They met their father's sisters too – Elizabeth, the Duchess of Bedford, and Mary, the Countess of Derby. This last was the kindest.

She had them to stay at Knowsley and took steps to transform them into young English ladies and gentlemen. Aunt Mary advised the children, for the moment, to continue to call themselves 'West' rather than the unequivocal 'Sackville-West'.

What was to become of Victoria, who at eighteen was virtually grown-up and ought to be 'out'? Her father had been appointed British Minister to Washington. Discreet liaison between Aunt Mary Derby and influential ladies on the other side of the Atlantic led to assurances that Victoria would not be cold-shouldered by Washington society. Within two years of emerging from the French convent, Lionel's illegitimate and inexperienced daughter was a diplomatic hostess presiding over his parties and making a huge success of it.

Victoria was exceptionally pretty with big blue eyes and the thick dark hair, hip-long, that she had inherited from Pepita. And she was a gift to society journalists. A Washington newspaper cutting of 1882 preserved in her scrapbook says that as a hostess she showed 'the grace and self-possession of a married woman, and a youthful gentleness that adds to the charm'. The 'sweet and winning charm of her manners' was enhanced by contrast with 'the grave and Chesterfieldian bearing of her distinguished father'. At the races in Ivy City it was observed that, as everywhere else, Miss West was 'very popular, and surrounded by her gentlemen friends'.

She claimed that twenty-five of these gentlemen friends proposed to her – she made a list later for Vita. Among the most pressing were Baron Bildt, *chargé d'affaires* at the Swedish Legation, whom she nicknamed 'Buggy'; a Frenchman, the Marquis de Loÿs Chandieu; several American millionaires, and two young men later to be distinguished in British diplomacy but then young secretaries on her father's staff, Charles Hardinge and Cecil Spring Rice.

She flirted but she did not marry. Five years after her arrival the Washington columnists were wondering why not. Miss West was still 'the most beautiful woman in diplomatic circles' but, as they delicately put it, 'no longer "a bud"'. Her younger sisters had joined the family at the Legation and it was Flora who got engaged first – to Gabriel Salanson, a third secretary at the French Legation.

It was on the family's return from Paris, where the Salansons were married in autumn 1888, that a minor political indiscretion put an end to Lionel Sackville-West's diplomatic career. As *New York Truth* put it on 1 November, he 'committed the unpardonable diplomatic sin of having a small private opinion which he expressed privately and which the un-scrupulous political temper of the moment made public'. Nevertheless, it was felt that he should be recalled over the incident, which was known as the Murchison Letter affair. There was a humiliating sale of the family's private effects at the British Legation, scene of so many glittering parties and personal triumphs for Victoria. It was said that 'persons high in the circles of society trampled on one another to get in their bids.'

The Sackville-Wests left Washington on 23 November. The following day Victoria wrote in her diary : 'I am so worried about the future.' But they did have something to go back to. During the Murchison Letter crisis, Lionel's elder brother Mortimer had died childless. Victoria's father was now the second Lord Sackville and the inheritor of Knole. She was to be hostess of one of the largest, oldest and most famous of the great country houses of England.

Among the relations who came to Knole in those first bewildering months of Victoria's administration was a young man of twenty-two who bore the same name as her father : Lionel Sackville-West. He was the elder Lionel's nephew – the son of his younger brother William and of Georgina Dodwell of County Sligo in Ireland – and thus Victoria's first cousin. He had been educated at Wellington and had recently taken his degree in modern history at Christ Church, Oxford. He and Victoria lost no time in falling for one another.

Victoria was five years older than Lionel and much more experienced, after her Washington conquests, in the ways of flirtation. She was in love for the first time and not averse to liberties being taken. They kissed in the garden at Knole, kissed again and spoke of marriage by moonlight in the King's Bedroom ; and she tortured him with talk of his chief rival, the Marquis de Loÿs Chandieu, who had followed her to England. She was still trying to make up her mind what to do when Lionel went away to Weimar to learn German. They corresponded almost daily. Lionel's letters were naive, sincere, very young. 'Tell me again my darling that you did not think I was wrong in all we did together – you, my own pure-minded Vicky, I *know* did nothing wrong, but for me somehow it is different.' He had no very high opinion of himself as a match for Victoria. 'I am not what people could call good or religious. I am not good-looking enough or clever or amusing.' But he was attractive. Their daughter Vita described him in youth as being 'a good-looking young man, with trustful hazel eyes, and a charming gentle smile. A quiet and faithful person, easily hurt by an unkind word.'[2]

When Lionel came home in early 1890 they broke their marriage plans to their respective fathers. (Lionel's mother, like Victoria's, was dead.) The wider family, having already had to adjust to the very existence of Victoria and her brothers and sisters, now had to face the fact that she had captured the heart of the boy who would inherit Knole and the title after his uncle died. Aunt Mary Derby wrote to Victoria that 'your letter rather took my breath away'. There was the 'great objection' of their being first cousins, and 'Lionel's youth frightens me.' But she ended up on the lovers' side, seeing 'a hundred thousand advantages to set against objections which might be raised'.

In the event the only serious objection to the cousinship was raised by Victoria's confessor. But Lionel went to see Cardinal Manning and obtained a dispensation. There was also anxious discussion about the religion of the children of the marriage. (Vita was not brought up as a Roman Catholic: she was confirmed in the Church of England at sixteen.)

Victoria continued to excite and be excited by Lionel. On an April evening she let him come into her room to say goodnight to her when she was in her petticoats, and a few nights later she allowed him to see her bare foot. She used all the titillation that late Victorian costume and custom provided. 'We love each other more every day.'

For her part, she was learning the social attitudes and the private language of her new-found family, to be passed on to her own child when the time came: a wedding present of a bracelet from a Mrs Dodgson was, she noted in her journal, '*un peu* Bedinty'.* The Prince of Wales sent a diamond and pearl brooch. Life had indeed changed for the uneducated little girl with no future. 'Quel roman est ma vie!' as she was to say and write many times in the coming years.

They were married in the chapel at Knole on 17 June 1890, only eighteen months after Victoria's return from Washington. The bride headed her diary entry for that day with the Sackville motto, '*Jour de ma vie*'. '*J'ai dit "Obey"*', she noted.

She and Lionel embarked on a sexual idyll. At Knole they followed the custom of their class and generation in having separate bedrooms, which occasioned delicious visits night and morning. By day they made love on the library sofa, in the bath, in the park and on a fur rug that excitingly charged Victoria with static electricity. She recorded it all in her diary – where, when, how and how often. Being away from home brought its compensations too; the December after their marriage, in London, Tio was '*si content . . . à cause de* spring mattress'.

Tio did not get into the Foreign Office (for which he had learnt German) but it hardly mattered. He was heir to the great property in which he now lived with his entrancing wife and which she, with her innate talent for organization, was already running with little help either from him or from her father. Extrovert and vital, she put the neighbouring ladies in the shade. Adored by both her gentle Lionels, she was queen of a kingdom.

---

*Bedint: Sackville family word for 'servant'; by extension, anyone or anything not of the upper classes; common, vulgar.

The only cloud on the horizon was her own family. Amalia, her unmarried younger sister, had perforce to make her home at Knole too to start with – ungraciously and enviously. But then Victoria had perhaps got a bit above herself. When one of Amalia's rare admirers came to luncheon, Victoria dismissed him as a *'pauvre garçon, très intimidé, très très* bedint, counter-jumper'. Her married sister, Flora Salanson, wrote from Paris asking for money, which Victoria sent, but 'I can't get over my sisters' bad behaviour'. M. de Béon also felt he had a claim on her changed fortunes and asked for cash in consideration of services rendered to the family in the past. Victoria called this 'blackmail'. There was worse to come.

In summer 1891, while they were at Henley for the regatta, Victoria suspected that she was pregnant. It was confirmed. 'I can't think of anything else,' she wrote on 10 July.

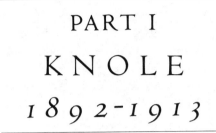

# PART I
# KNOLE
# 1892-1913

# CHAPTER 1

VICTORIA recorded her daughter's first word – 'Dada' – and her first steps, as she staggered at eighteen months across the Green Court with Alfred the footman hovering behind her. As the months passed her little legs carried her further around the extraordinary place where she had been born, but which, owing to her sex, would never belong to her.

The Green Court leads into the Stone Court with a Jacobean colonnade down one side; there is also the Water Court and four other courts, making seven in all. There are alleged to be fifty-two staircases in the house and 365 rooms, corresponding to the weeks and days of the year; but not even Vita verified this. The complex of stone buildings, largely fifteenth-century, was built over an even older house and covers more than six acres. The Great Hall, where one hard winter Vita came face to face with a stag sheltering from the cold and where her mother distributed presents to the estate children every Christmas (the scene is immortalized in Vita's novel *The Edwardians*), was built by Archbishop Bourchier in about 1460. He also built the Brown Gallery and probably the chapel, which in Vita's childhood was hung with Gothic tapestries. It was Queen Elizabeth I who gave Knole to her cousin Thomas Sackville, Vita's ancestor.

The house is set in a great park, dramatic with slopes and gullies and the great beeches about which Vita wrote a poem. The main gates of the park open into the high street of the small town of Sevenoaks. Seen from across the park, Knole seems not so much a house as 'a mediaeval village with its square turrets and its grey walls, its hundred chimneys sending blue threads up into the air,' as Vita wrote in *The Edwardians*. 'The house was really as self-contained as a little town; the carpenter's shop, the painter's shop, the forge, the sawmill, the hot-house.' For fifty servants, rigidly observing their own hierarchy – their number often augmented by the maids and valets of the Sackville-Wests' visitors – Knole was also home, even though Lord Sackville and Lionel might never know the faces of some of them, let alone their names. The great kitchen itself was as wide and high as a cathedral.

The library – lined with unread bound volumes, but comfortable, informal and warm – was the family sitting-room in Vita's childhood. Her own children, when staying at Knole, were scared by the long journey from the library through corridors and up dark stairs, past the watchful eyes of family portraits, on their way to the nurseries. But it was what Vita had known from the beginning and she was not easily scared.

The family sitting-rooms, bedrooms and, during Victoria's reign, increasing numbers of bathrooms were constantly reallotted, rearranged and redecorated. Victoria liked entertaining and she fitted up the spare bedrooms lavishly, each with its little brass frame on the door into which a card with the occupying guest's name was slotted. This was useful not only for administrative but also for amorous purposes: '*chacun à sa chacune*', as Mrs Keppel is said to have remarked.

The Sackville-Wests' dining-room was the Poets' Parlour where Pope, Dryden, Congreve, Wycherley and Rochester had dined and drunk with the poetic sixth Earl of Dorset, Charles Sackville. Still more impressive were the ballroom, the Cartoon Gallery, the Brown Gallery, the Leicester Gallery – and the three great state bedrooms which, even in Vita's day, had not been slept in for 200 years. These were, and still are, the 'show rooms'. These show rooms are cold, but nothing there rots, sealed within the great stone walls. They 'preserved their ancient furnishings, their gildings and velvets', gleaming in the light of candles that Vita and her mother held as they walked through with admiring visitors.

The King's Bedroom – 'where the great four-poster of silver and flamingo satin towered to the ceiling and the outlines of the famous silver furniture gleamed dimly in the ray of the moon'[1] – had been prepared for the reception of King James I and scarcely touched since. (Vita later thought the suite of solid silver furniture and fittings a little vulgar.) It was in the King's Bedroom that Vita's parents had kissed and petted in their courting days; it was in the King's Bedroom, under a different name, that Sebastian in *The Edwardians* tried to seduce the infatuated little doctor's wife; it was in the King's Bedroom that Vita was first properly kissed by the man she would marry, and where she would subsequently bring other lovers.

Then there is the Venetian Ambassador's Room, tapestried in dusty pink, green and gold with a bed big enough for three, and the Spangled Room. But for a little girl there are other equally magical things at Knole, closer to her line of vision and her imaginative life: ancient carved bosses, grotesque faces in the woodwork ; a door-stopper called 'Shake-speare', a square little man of a size to look at a three-year-old eyeball to eyeball, but who seems older than the playwright ever was; and above all the heraldic leopards. At Knole there are stone leopards silhouetted all along the roofline, on pinnacles, rampant. There are spotted leopards on the newels of the Great Staircase, and saucy black and white leopards on the *trompe l'oeil* frescoes of the staircase wall. Vita wrote a poem, 'Leopards at Knole' :

> Leopards on the gable-ends,
> Leopards on the painted stair,
> Stiff the blazoned shield they bear,
> Or and gules, a bend of vair,
> Leopards on the gable-ends,
> Leopards everywhere.[2]

At the top of the great house, right under the vast acreage of roof and chimneys, are the Retainers' Galleries, where long ago the servants would sleep as in dormitories, beneath a ceiling of plaster decoration still elegant though now crumbling. In Vita's childhood these long attics, which give access to the roof, were stacked with discarded paintings, statues, furniture and carvings, stowed away there by successions of Sackvilles as they imposed the taste of their own generation on the house. Here Vita would retreat, to play and prowl and dream and rummage in trunks and chests. It was here that she found a Roundhead drum, which she brought downstairs. She kicked off her shoe into it, splitting the stretched vellum that had lain upstairs undisturbed for more than three centuries.

Her other private place, as soon as she could read and write, was the little fretted summer-house in the garden, overlooking the Looking-glass Pond. History spilled over from the house into the garden :

> The white rose which was planted under James 1's room has climbed until it now reaches beyond his windows on the first floor . . . the magnolia outside the Poets' Parlour has grown nearly to the roof, and bears its mass of blossoms like a great candelabra. . . . The soil is rich and old. The garden has been a garden for four hundred years.[3]

But the Vita who loved her heritage and was to write those words was still only a tiny girl, falling on the slippery polished floors indoors and grazing her knees on the gravel walks in the garden – 'she won't go on the grass'.

When Lionel was away the child slept in her mother's bed: 'She hugs me so sweetly in the mornings.' Victoria heaped on Vita the dolls she herself had loved as a child ; there were nineteen of them before Vita was two.

The one she liked best was a small wooden doll she called Clown Archie. In January 1897 her father photographed her with all the dolls lined up beside her, outside the long reception room they called the Colonnade (because it was a glassed-in arcaded walk). Vita – aged nearly five – had just been bridesmaid at the wedding of Lionel's brother Charlie to Maud Bell. Her hair was curled for the occasion, she wore white satin, and Uncle Charlie gave all six bridesmaids 'muff-chains of pink coral and turquoises'. When the married pair came down the aisle at the end Vita, the smallest bridesmaid, ran forward and clutched the bridegroom by the leg – 'Oh! Uncle Charlie!'

In June of that year there was a party of fifty at Knole in honour of the Chinese delegation to Queen Victoria's Golden Jubilee. The sixteen Chinese visitors were led by Tsang Yen Hoon, 'gorgeous in deep pink', who had been a diplomatic colleague of Lord Sackville's in Washington. 'They all sat in the Colonnade along the windows, Vita peacocked up and down in front of them; she struck up a great friendship with the son of Marquis Tsang,' noted her mother approvingly.

The following month the family had even grander visitors: the Prince and Princess of Wales. 'I went to receive them at the wicket with Vita,' Victoria recorded. 'I felt desperately shy and Vita nearly burst into tears.' While the party were in the garden for a tree-planting ceremony and the inevitable photograph, Princess Alexandra held Vita's hand. Her mother, however 'desperately shy', was no respecter of persons. The Prince of Wales had requested that his current favourite, Lady Warwick, should be invited to Knole that day 'and also his new friend, the Hon. Mrs G. Keppel. But I told him I preferred to ask some of the County Ladies.... He acquiesced and was v. nice about it.' Victoria was already formidable. And she was delighted with the social performance of her five-year-old. 'I am so afraid of Vita getting spoilt; everybody tells her she is so pretty. She can entertain people very nicely.'

Vita learned early to take parties of visitors round the house, opening up the show rooms for them. Her grandfather refused to perform this office 'for he shared the family failing of unsociability'. Vita's favourite piece of decoration in the house was the frieze in the ballroom 'with its carved intricacies of mermaids and dolphins, mermen and mermaids with scaly, twisting tails and salient anatomy'.[4] The small chatelaine felt contemptuous towards those visitors who ignored these glories and preferred to look at the paintings.

But there were a great many days when no visitors came, when the grown-ups in her family were away and the servants busy elsewhere. Then the only child wandered through the great house and courtyards and gardens, imagining :

Pictures and galleries and empty rooms !
Small wonder that my games were played alone ;
Half of the rambling house to call my own,
And wooded gardens with mysterious glooms.

My fingers ran among the tassels faded ;
My playmates moved in arrases brocaded ;
I slept beside the canopied and shaded
Beds of forgotten kings.
I wandered shoeless in the galleries ;
I contemplated long the tapestries,
And loved the ladies for their histories
And hands with many rings.[5]

When she was six she went absent without leave. 'She went to Sevenoaks with Ethel [the nursemaid] and ran away from her; Ethel could not find her anywhere. Vita came home alone! after having been to buy a balloon and a cricket ball. I have punished her by having her dinner upstairs and no fresh cherries which I bought for her yesterday.'

Vita was a greedy child. 'That naughty Vita has stolen and eaten all my Xmas sweets! She confessed it and I spoke very gently to her showing her how little confidence I could have in her if she does these things. She has such a dear soft nature and understands everything so readily – and is so affectionate.'

The Easter that Vita was seven Victoria bought some tinsel material to be made up into 'a fairy dress for Vita who loves playing at fairies'. This fairy Vita was the child that Victoria Sackville-West had dreamed of. While Vita was very small she could ignore the fact that her daughter's sweetly curled hair was, by nature, uncompromisingly straight, and that beneath the tinsel dress beat a fierce and uncompromising heart, however loving.

Vita mixed very little with other children. Almost the only one she knew at first, apart from the servants' children with whom she was sometimes allowed to play, was her little cousin Lionel Salanson, to whom she prattled in French. When Vita was seven, Victoria organized a weekly dancing class for local children to be held in the dining-room at Knole. Vita was alleged to be 'delighted' by this, but after a while there were complaints from Lady Winchester that 'Vita had been so rough with little Mountjoy.... ' Nor was she altogether reliable when left with her other baby cousin, Eddy Sackville-West, the son of Charlie and Maud and probable heir to Knole. He was a frail and sickly child and Vita, to whom the dynastic implications of his existence had been explained, did not take to him. She did not really approve of other children coming to Knole at all; she had the territorial instincts of a cock robin.

As an adult, Vita was unsentimental about childhood. 'The normal child, if not an insufferable prig, thoroughly enjoys being unkind to something.' Even to animals :

A theory exists among grown-ups that children are fond of dogs and take an interest in them. I distrust this theory. Children like dogs only in so far as they can pull their tails or poke their fingers into their eyes : their attitude towards dogs is neither humane nor anthropomorphic. One should not senti-mentalize about children. Realists themselves, it is the last thing they would desire, if they knew enough about their feelings to put them into words. The natural instincts tend towards pugnacity and bullying – which is one of the reasons why the Nazi training met with so terrifying a success among the young.[6]

Vita as a child was so tough with any children invited to Knole that soon none of them would come to tea 'except those who had acted as my allies and lieutenants'. Regular visitors were the little Battiscombes from Sevenoaks :

There were five of them, four girls and a boy. The boy and I were allies ; the four girls were our victims. The boy and I made a practice of tying the four girls up to trees and of thrashing their legs with nettles. Also, we stuffed their nostrils with putty, and gagged their mouths with handkerchiefs.[7]

No real hostility was implied, wrote Vita airily, long after. 'The girls enjoyed it masochistically, as much as the boy and I, sadistically.' Whether they did or not, none of them ever breathed a word to their own mother or to Vita's about the torture that went on behind the rhododendrons after tea at Knole.

What did this clever, solitary, watchful girl make of her parents? She wrote three versions of her view of them : the first shortly after her marriage in 1913, in an unpublished manuscript called 'Marian Strangways'; the second seven years later, unpublished in her own lifetime, and the third in *Pepita*, published in 1937 after her mother's death. The three accounts are often contradictory, but what they add up to is an uncomfortable ambivalence towards her mother who 'loved me when I was a baby, but I don't think she loved me as a child, nor do I blame her'.[8]

Her father, Vita said, used to take her for long walks and talk to her about Darwin, 'and I liked him a great deal better than Mother, of whose quick temper I was very frightened. I don't even remember thinking her pretty, which she must have been – lovely, even.'[9] (Later Vita was to write that her mother had been a 'truly beautiful woman'.) Victoria was unpredictable in her moods and volubly critical of the growing girl's appearance, her untidiness and her silences. She used to 'hurt my feelings,' wrote Vita, 'and say she couldn't look at me because I was so ugly.'[10]

Victoria's quick temper meant that there was always a rapid turnover of nurses and governesses. There was Nurse Brown and then Nurse Grey and then Nurse White. 'At the age of four or five I had seen my own loved Nannie torn from me because three dozen quails having failed to arrive in time for a dinner-party my mother insisted that Nannie had eaten them.'[11] Then there was Miss Bennett, who was dismissed for discipline problems. Vita, then aged ten, was upset. She was taken to the pantomime with Rosamund Grosvenor to get over it, but Miss Bennett held on : 'We are much annoyed with Bentie,' wrote Victoria, 'who writes pages to Vita, asking her to beg me to take her back. She does want in tact and makes the child miserable.' Vita was schooled early in the strategy of women's emotional warfare. Miss Scarth succeeded Miss Bennett but did not last, and Vita finally settled down with Mademoiselle Hermine Hall, and a nursemaid, Jane Gay (whom her mother rechristened 'Giovanna'), to look after her outside 'school' hours.

It was under Miss Bennett's tutelage that Vita, then aged eight, embroidered a mauve and yellow footstool cover for her mother. This hideous but loving piece of work was the inspiration for a telling unpublished sketch that Vita later wrote called 'The Birthday'. In it a wealthy woman of taste subtly rejects the ugly antimacassar her little daughter has so proudly made for her and hurts the child – who has 'ugly' straight hair – to the quick, at the same time managing to convey that she herself, the mother, is heartbreakingly misunderstood and exploited by all the family.

One great source of tension between mother and daughter was Knole itself. It was Vita's secret world, but it was Victoria's hobby. 'Mother made all the capital she could out of the house ; to hear her talk about it you would have thought she had built it, but she had no real sense of its dignity, as Dada had, who worshipped in his bones, but would rather die than say so.' Victoria loved showing visitors round, explaining everything in her quick light French-accented voice ; she 'got all the credit for everything, because she was the kind of person who always came in for quite a lot of flattery from everyone.'[12]

But this was not the whole story. Victoria enslaved her daughter as she enslaved others. 'How my mother puzzled me, and how I loved her! She wounded and dazzled and fascinated and charmed me by turns.' When Victoria sweetly forgave Vita for something she had never done 'I felt she had conferred an inestimable grace on me. . . . I loved her the more for it; my love for her mounted ever higher and higher, as one mounts the rungs of an endless ladder.'[13] Writing of Victoria as she was in the early 1900s, Vita said: 'My mother was adorable at that time of her life. She was tiresome, of course, and wayward, and capricious, and thoroughly spoilt; but her charm and real inward gaiety enabled her to carry it all off.' But Victoria was also materialistic and acquisitive, and morally untrustworthy.

Lionel used to try to put his daughter right with little axioms of his own. 'I fancy that my father, discreet and loyal as he was, watched with a far shrewder eye than I ever gave him credit for.'[14] Some of his little axioms were literary. As a middle-aged woman, Vita was never able to disregard them without a sense of guilt. Always write a letter long enough to turn over the page, he told her; never begin a letter with the word 'I' because it gives an immediate impression of egoism, and never write as many as ten monosyllables in succession.

But Mother was the dominant parent. She was also the dominant spouse. Her husband, peace-loving by nature, suffered from her much-vaunted Latin temperament, as did Vita and old Lord Sackville. 'She trampled on the wincing sensitiveness of the three . . . who all shrank from the foreign scenes she made.' She took little interest in Lionel's public service activities for the local education committee, the grammar school, the hospital, or the West Kent Yeomanry which he commanded. And yet, 'if ever the phrase "turn one's heart to water" meant any-thing,' wrote Vita, it meant 'when my mother looked at you and smiled. . . . No wonder I loved and wondered,' she said. 'No wonder my father loved, and got hurt.'[15] He got hurt beyond healing, and then he began to hurt his wife in return.

# CHAPTER 2

By the time Vita was seven or eight her parents' pleasure in one another was over. Victoria's defensive diary entries in March 1900 show the way the wind was blowing. 'Of course, I let Tio do just what he likes and he enjoys it so much.' She was going to be modern : physical fidelity was not greatly valued in the marriages of the British upper classes. Lionel's new friend was young Lady Camden. Victoria called the affair 'a mild flirtation' for as long as she could and tried herself to take an interest in Joan Camden's unhappy marriage. 'I feel so sorry for poor little Joan Camden. How different my darling husband is to me.' There is a *voulu* air about her diary that suggests she thought – or hoped – that Lionel would read it.

When Vita was an elderly woman, an equally elderly gentleman rushed up to her at a party. It was Joan Camden's eldest son. 'I did remember him, though I hadn't seen him since he was a schoolboy, and I wondered whether he knew that my Dada had loved his mother.

Victoria never protected her daughter from the complexities of her own married life. But in public she maintained the same control she observed in her married women friends in similar circumstances. She observed too, over the years, the dignified demeanour of Queen Alexandra in regard to Mrs Keppel. She even gave Lady Camden and Lionel advice about being discreet, which Lionel did not appreciate.

It was Victoria who put the stop to marital sex. Lionel had wanted a second child ; she did not, so they took the unsatisfactory precautions available at the time. At the end of 1904 Victoria found medical justification for abstinence. Dr Ferrier 'found my circulation extremely slow and my nervous system out of order'. He prescribed iron and valerian and 'said things that won't please my darling husband, but my nervous system *must* be left in peace'. She was then forty-two.

Lionel was already moving on again – to Lady Constance Hatch. Vita, by then in her early teens, did not like Lady Connie at all: 'a stringy, wispy, French-music-hall Englishwoman with whom Dada was for years most inexplicably in love'.[2] In his retreat from Victoria, Lionel chose gentle women. Victoria highly approved of wispy Connie, who wrote her grateful letters.

Vita, who was later to be regarded a pioneer of 'open marriage', was in fact behaving as much like an Edwardian as like a mid-twentieth-century woman. In her own parents' marriage she had a highly evolved model, albeit one that finally broke down. Victoria's one sorrow was that Lionel grew ever colder and more distant with her. Simple-hearted and highly sexed, he was a man whose affections followed his desire closely. In order to preserve appearances, however, Victoria continually cajoled him into accompanying her to balls and dinners so that they might be seen together in society.

But Victoria had found some consolation too. At about the time when Lionel first began to stray she met Sir John Murray Scott, a fabulously wealthy bachelor about fifteen years older than herself. He had inherited a lease on Hertford House in London – from Sir Richard and Lady Wallace – with its valuable collection of pictures and furniture, now known as the Wallace Collection. Scott had been the Wallaces' secretary and they had also left him a large amount of money; land in Ireland and in Suffolk; a first-floor Paris apartment situated on the corner of the boulevard des Italiens and the rue Laffitte (it had twenty windows along both streets and was crammed with art treasures); and Bagatelle, a 'pavilion' in sixty acres in the Bois de Boulogne that had once belonged to Marie Antoinette.

Sir John was entranced by Victoria Sackville-West. It is said that the day after he showed her around Hertford House he added a codicil to his will leaving her £50,000. That was only the beginning. Lionel approved of the friendship; it released him, somewhat, to pursue his own. If anyone was to restore the Sackville fortunes it was Sir John Murray Scott. Victoria was by no means unusual among married women of her class in accepting protection – and large sums of money – from socially acceptable admirers. This aspect of the friendship was also understood by Lionel who did not discourage it. When Sir John paid for Victoria's house at 34 Hill Street, Mayfair, for example, he dealt directly with her husband.

As early as 1900 Victoria was noting with satisfaction that Sir John treated the eight-year-old Vita 'like a daughter'; he had just given her a cricket set. This became one of the child's most treasured possessions and when, the following summer, she sat down to draw up a childish will of her own, she bequeathed it to Dada, along with her football, her

Mama. A quarter of my bank money. My Diamond V.

Dada. A quarter of my bank money. My pony and cart. My cricket set. My football.

Seevy. My Larke. my minatura. my Claret jug. my whip

pony and cart, and a quarter of her 'bank money'. Mama was to get
another quarter of her bank money and 'My Diamond V'. Bentie – the
emotional Miss Bennett – was left the remaining half of the bank money,
'My Pearl V' and 'my ships'. To Ralph Battiscombe, her youthful partner
in crime, she appropriately left 'My Armar. My swords and guns, my
fort my soldiers, my tools. My bow and arrow my pocket money my
target.' (The collection of dolls had by now been forgotten.)

Sir John's French servants pronounced his name 'Seer John'; Vita
reduced this to Seery, and Seery he became to Victoria as well and all her
circle. To Seery, Vita willed 'my miniature, my claret jug, my whip' –
and her khaki soldier-suit, though it would hardly have fitted him. His
relationship with her mother was ambiguous. After both Seery and
Victoria were dead, Vita tried to fathom it : 'I do not mean that Sir John
was "in love" with my mother. I do not believe that he was, and during
the many years that I was constantly in their company I had ample
opportunity for observing them. She most certainly became, however,
the centre and pivot of his life.'[3]

He was a huge person, 6 feet 4 inches tall and weighing over 25 stone.
To Vita the idea of such a creature being in love in the ordinary sense
was 'too grotesque'. Victoria speculated freely to her child about the
precise nature of Seery's feeling for her. Certainly Vita well understood
one important aspect of their relationship : admiring her mother's smart
stationery, she wrote : 'I like your new paper very much, did the good
Seery give it to you? I suppose he is on the generous tack just now, as
you say you have no rows.' There were many rows, mostly engineered
by Victoria, although Seery always came back for more. The scene
described by Vita in her autobiographical manuscript of 1920 encap-
sulates the relationship :

When I think of Seery I see him sitting before an immense writing table,
rattling a bunch of keys and trying every key in every lock in turn. . . . Then
when he had got a drawer open, Mother would come and make a pounce at
his stamps, and he would cry, 'Go away, you little beggar', or 'You little
Spanish beggar', but of course he worshipped her and let her have whatever
she wanted. (At times she wanted a good deal.) . . . Mother became absolutely the light and air of his life.[4]

Watching her parents, and their relations with one another, and with
other people and with her, Vita became too knowing, while remaining
childishly innocent. Her trouble as a child was that she had a fiercely
ardent, romantic temperament, and what she saw and experienced
made her cynical; the conflict caused her to withdraw even further into
herself.

Vita first went to Bagatelle, Marie Antoinette's playground, when she was nine. It now belongs to the city of Paris; but driving out from Paris every afternoon in the hot summers at the turn of the century, Seery and his guests had the great gardens to themselves. 'In the shady garden I could wear an overall only and could run barefoot over the cool grasses.' She played, like a princess, round the grottos, lakes, bridges, islands, caves, statues and ornamental urns. (These last were to end up in her own garden at Sissinghurst many years later.)

Seery's vast apartment on the corner of the rue Laffitte was more intimidating. It was an anachronism even in the early 1900s. There was no telephone, no electricity, and there were long vistas through communicating rooms with golden floors and ivory woodwork, filled with priceless objects.

> Small and clean, with painfully frizzed hair, I would stand by, very bored, while visitors marvelled at the furniture.... Louis quatorze, Louis quinze, Louis seize, Directoire, Empire – all these were names, half meaningless, which I absorbed till they became as familiar as bread, milk, water, butter. Empire came last on the list; for the life of the house seemed to have stopped there.[5]

Lionel and Grandpapa generally came too on the annual visits to Paris with Seery, closely followed by Lady Connie. She and Lionel would go off together every day, while Vita increasingly became her mother's confidential companion. Without her daughter, Victoria would spend dull evenings in the rue Laffitte 'between Seery snoring and Papa [old Lionel] coughing'.

When both the odd couples – Lionel and Lady Connie, Victoria and Sir John – were out, Vita had the apartment more or less to herself. She would whizz through the long sequence of golden rooms in Seery's wheelchair, bumping the precious furniture. Or she would light all the candles in all the rooms and prowl about. 'Sometimes I used to go into the big gallery and cry bitterly over a stuffed spaniel in a glass case that I imagined was like a spaniel of mine that had died.... I must have been very sentimental, but, as I never let anybody know, it didn't matter.'[6] (When her own loved spaniel was run over, her mother was astonished by Vita's calmness. 'It is a pity she has so much self-control; it frightens me for the future. She never speaks of what she feels, or never answers any questions relating to herself.')

When Vita was eleven, Victoria observed that she 'is beginning to know a great deal about furniture etc. She is intelligent.' Victoria was training her daughter in her own preoccupations – it mattered to her that Vita should learn the difference between Directoire and Empire –

and developing her taste. She was pleased when she took Vita to
Fabergé and the child 'told them that she liked their shop even better
than a sweet shop! She is wonderfully artistic for one so young.' But in
London, when she sent Vita to Mr Morland for drawing lessons, it was
not a success; Vita could not draw.

Another of Seery's benefactions was Sluie, the shooting lodge he took
every year in the Scottish Highlands, near Banchory. Here Vita, her
mother and her grandfather – and sometimes her father – would join Sir
John for yet another holiday. Vita ran wild with the dogs and the local
children and fished – alone or with her father: 'I shall never forget the
enchantment of those evenings.... He was a pleasing man, my
father.'[7]

It was at Sluie that Vita learnt the facts of life. The summer that she was
eleven, the local farmer's son Jackie 'told me a great many things he
oughtn't to have told me'. (Her mother, so communicative about so
many unsuitable matters, was careful with Vita over the physical facts of
sex; she even stopped Vita reading *The Woman in White* and *The Count of
Monte Cristo* for fear of awkward questions.) Vita said later about Jackie's
revelations that 'as I had always lived in the country I took most things
quite for granted, and was neither excited nor interested by them'. But
Jackie did not only tell her, he demonstrated. One day by the ghillie's
hut he said 'Miss Vita, Miss Vita, Vita, Vita, I love you' and put his hand
on her thigh. 'But because of his inborn respect, his sense of class, he
didn't rape me,' Vita wrote long after. He masturbated instead. And he
made her take hold of his dog's penis and work it backwards and
forwards until 'the dog reached the point where he came and squirted
his semen all over my shoes, and I was alarmed by this manifestation.
.... I think that there was nothing wrong about what Jackie or I did.' It
was a curious introduction to male sexuality. Jackie's adolescent passion
for Vita was not ended by this episode. Two summers later she wrote to
her mother from Sluie that 'Jackie made protestations of eternal love and
fidelity and confided that after I had gone, he went away by himself *and
cried*!'

She was amused, then pleased with her power. At thirteen, she was
already taller than her mother, who was 5 feet 7 inches. That same
summer her mother noted that 'She is getting quite fond of clothes and
hats, and I am glad to see her getting a little more coquette and tidy.' In
London, Vita started attending day classes at a small school run by Miss
Woolff in South Street, off Park Lane. Rosamund Grosvenor and the
Keppel girls, Violet and Sonia, were among the other pupils. Vita's
governess, Mademoiselle Hermine, stayed on to help Vita with her
homework and to act as chaperone.

Vita's first real friend had been Rosamund Grosvenor, a little older and as neat and clean as Vita was untidy, who was invited to stay to cheer her up when Dada went away to the Boer War. Later Rosamund shared an early governess of Vita's for morning lessons. 'Vita likes her lessons with Miss Moss very much, especially sums and drilling.'

When Vita was twelve she made a more exciting friend. Violet Keppel was two years younger than Vita and the elder daughter of the Mrs George Keppel whom Victoria had once forbidden to Knole, and the mistress of the former Prince of Wales, King Edward VII. The children met at a party in London. Violet saw a girl 'tall for her age, gawky, dressed in what appeared to be her mother's old clothes'; she thought her 'nice, but rather childish'.8 Violet was an exceedingly precocious child.

Vita was invited to tea with Violet at the Keppels' house in Portman Square. They sat in the dusk in Mr Keppel's study and talked, boastingly, about their ancestors. Vita, finding someone who found history as romantic as she herself did and who furthermore was enthusiastic about all her favourite books (they both knew Rostand's *Cyrano de Bergerac* by heart and loved Walter Scott and Dumas), was for once neither secretive nor silent. 'I've got a friend,' she sang that night in her bath.

They had more than books in common. Violet's life, like Vita's, was dominated by the personality of her charming mother. They both had fairy-tale childhoods spent in great houses, they both had sweet-natured fathers, they were both young francophiles. Knole – and the idea of Vita at Knole – seemed glamorous to Violet. Likewise, the discreet visits of the King to the house in Portman Square appealed to Vita. She went to tea there very often; she used to see a little one-horse brougham waiting outside, 'and the butler would slip me into a dark corner of the hall with a murmured "One minute, miss, a gentleman is coming downstairs."' If Vita ever actually met the gentleman, the prevailing discretion kept her quiet. All there is in her diary is a laconic 'Went to tea with Violet, and stayed to dinner. The King was there,' in December 1908.

The Keppels spent much time abroad and the Sackville-Wests were more often at Knole than in London, at least until Victoria acquired her Hill Street house in 1907. Violet kept up a flow of fanciful correspondence, half in French, half in English: 'I bombarded the poor girl [Vita] with letters which became more exacting as hers tended to become more and more of the "yesterday-my-pet-rabbit-had-six-babies" type.'9 Animals and books interested Vita at twelve and thirteen more than human relations. She had ridden a pony since she was four and had dogs of her own. The summer after she made friends with Violet she was keeping a copy book as her 'Animal Record Book': at that time she had one black pony, one Irish terrier called Pat, six rabbits, one barn owl, three Japanese bantams, one Aberdeen terrier called Pickles and then three more rabbits. In this book she also wrote down useful things such as 'How to make a False Bruise' : 'Rub any small cut all round with a lead pencil, then rub with an orange or walnut rind. Chew up some grass and rub well with this. The result will be like a bad buise [*sic*].' When her mother was away, Vita wrote to her : '*Maintenant j'ai une énorme faveur à te demander*. The other day, in London, Dada and I both went to Bumpus [the Oxford Street bookshop] and I saw a lovely book there called *The Dog, all about him, his ills and how to cure them* for 2/6. . . . It's quite *convenable* and I should so love it.'

This was not the sort of thing little Violet Keppel was interested in at all. 'Violet was never young', recalled her sister Sonia nearly seventy years later. And although in the spring of 1907 when she was fifteen, Vita went with her governess to Florence, and went sightseeing there with Violet and fell in love with Italy and everything Italian in Violet's company, it was still Rosamund Grosvenor (whom she called Roddie or Rose) on whom she depended in her ordinary life at home. After she came back from Italy it was Rosamund's turn to go away on holiday and Vita wrote in her diary, in the simple but effective code she used for her private thoughts, 'After Roddie had gone I cried because I missed her. What a funny thing it is to love a person as I love Roddie.'

She could not write sophisticated, allusive letters like Violet's, but she did write – all the time, from the age of twelve onwards. She always had a work in progress, written neatly with very few crossings out, in exercise books and folio notebooks, in the small, square, plain handwriting that hardly changed all her life. She wrote ballads and plays and historical novels : 'pretentious, quite uninteresting, pedantic, and all written at unflagging speed : the day after one was finished another would begin. . . . I had flaring days, oh yes, I did ! when I thought I was going to electrify the world.'[10]

But it was all, she thought when she was grown-up, 'leaden stuff'. It was. Her writing comprised her day-dreams given fluent expression in the sententious style of Scott and Dumas. The day-dreams were those of a highly literate, romantic adolescent, fired by her environment ; a fully realized fantasy life.

The fantasy was Knole, her ancestors and herself. History at Knole was continuous, personal and tangible. Her spotted rocking-horse had belonged to the fourth Duke of Dorset, one of the little boys in the painting by Hoppner and later Byron's fag at Harrow ; with her hair just cut, at three Vita looked exactly like him. ('*Ravissante*', according to her mother.) The child noticed that Thomas Sackville, Lord Buckhurst and first Earl of Dorset in Elizabeth's reign, looked exactly like her grand-father; both had the great heavy-lidded Sackville eyes that she too had inherited. She was sometimes allowed to play with the 'diamond and ruby dingle-dangle' that Gainsborough had painted in the lace jabot of John Frederick, the third Duke of Dorset, whose eighteenth-century elegance she much admired. As she grew older she was allowed to rummage in the Muniment Room with its records of centuries of Sackvilles – letters, wills, marriage settlements, accounts, menus of feasts, estate records, diaries, inventories of furniture, glass, plate and armour. Her earliest poems were ballads about long-gone members of her family: Herbrand de Salkaville, who came over with William the Conqueror; Sir Roger West, henchman of the Black Prince; Thomas Sackville, who brought from Queen Elizabeth to Mary Queen of Scots the news of her coming execution. So tactful was Thomas that Mary gave him her carved Calvary – still on the altar in the chapel at Knole. As a child Vita used to take sanctuary there when she had been naughty. 'They never found me, sulking under the pulpit.'

Her favourite ancestor was Edward Sackville, fourth Earl of Dorset, 'the embodiment of Cavalier romance'. His portrait by Van Dyck hung in the hall. In the attics were the nail-studded trunks from which the Roundheads had broken the locks. She could touch them, open them, imagine the scene and then go down to luncheon in the room where Cromwell's soldiers had held their Court of Sequestration, for in 1642 Cromwell's troops had ransacked the house and briefly occupied it. 'The past mingled with the present in constant reminder; and out in the summer-house, after luncheon, with the bees blundering among the flowers of the Sunk Garden ... I returned to the immense ledger in which I was writing my novel.'[11] This was 'The Tale of a Cavalier'. Small wonder that self-consciousness crept in as, with an arch reference to her 'only 14 years', she composed her Author's Note: 'This book has been a great amusement to me. I wrote it in the old house where Buckhurst and Edward and Mary played together ... where his children romped and shouted in the long corridors, as I have romped myself.' And she wondered if the seventeenth-century Earl could see her and if he knew 'how I love to recall his feats and his life and wish to be like him.'

Between 1906 and 1908 she also wrote three plays in French, one of them, 'Le Masque de Fer', a full-length five-act drama in alexandrines. A novel in French, 'Richelieu', as neat and well organized as all her others, exactly fills and fits the 370 pages of a folio manuscript book. She was very methodical – some of her governesses must have taught her well – and wrote out rhyme schemes for her poems, and detailed chapter summaries for her novels.

In July 1907 she was co-winner in an *Onlooker* competition for completing a limerick and collected a prize of one pound. She wrote in her diary: 'This is the first money I have got through writing; [in code] I hope as I am to restore the fortunes of the family that it will not be the last.' This triumph turned sour. Four days later she noted sadly in her diary, again in code: 'Mother scolded me this morning because she said I write too much, and Dada said he did not approve of my writing. I am afraid my book will not be published. Mother does not know how much I love my writing.' (The book in question this time was 'The King's Secret', a romance about Charles II and the sixth Earl of Dorset.) Vita's parents knew only too well how much she loved her writing, and this obsessional private activity disturbed them. They did not want an eccentric daughter. Nevertheless her mother recognized her quality. Vita read part of 'The King's Secret' to Victoria, who wrote in her diary that it was *'very* good'.

But if Vita was going to be clever she must also shine socially. That summer she went to stay at another great house with her parents: 'Vita was a great success. . . . It was her first house party; everybody was so nice to her, especially old Mr Shuttleworth. She goes on writing snatches of her Charles II book. I think Lionel is very proud of his daughter.' Victoria was continuously preoccupied with Vita's personality, her development, her appearance. There was no one closer to Victoria's heart than Vita – her 'little Mar' as she called her – other than Victoria herself. Her self-centredness made her incapable of conceiving of a daughter who was not an extension of herself, and she nagged and reproached Vita for her shortcomings in this regard – that is, for her individuality. Vita's picture of herself, and her defences, were shaped accordingly: 'I see myself . . . plain, lean, dark, unsociable, unattractive – horribly unattractive! – rough, and secret. Secrecy was my passion; I dare say that was why I hated companions.'[12]

Vita's first school report, in the form of a letter from Miss Woolff to Victoria, was very creditable, especially – and not surprisingly – with regard to English history and literature. 'She does extremely well for her age – being so tall one is apt to forget how young she is.' But she was not popular at Miss Woolff's, or felt that she was not. 'I set myself to triumph at that school, and I did triumph . . . if I couldn't be popular, I would be clever.' She felt the other girls thought her 'a prig and a pariah'.

Miss Woolff and her largely male staff taught academic subjects unusually well; they also 'finished' the young ladies and reinforced the necessary attitudes and values. The concept of social class exercised Vita, at fourteen, obsessively:

My darling Mama. . . . On Wednesday I was *first* in Geography and I got a prize : Shelley's *Adonais*. O'Mann [her grandfather] is grumbling about coming to Paris all the time ; he says it is an uncomfortable house and that it will be too cold etc. . . . Il neige. Is Winifred Gore a bedint or not ? Yesterday we drew a mar* of four years. . . . It was rather a nice mar, a little bedint of course.

She already knew which of her schoolfellows were Jewish, and 'the little Gerard Leghs are not bedint, are they ?' As Vita wrote later, these pre-occupations were in her youth 'commonplaces of well-bred thought' : 'genealogies and family connexions, tables of precedence and a famili-arity with country seats formed almost part of a moral code.'[13]

Vita and Violet Keppel shared private Italian lessons with a Signorina Castelli. Before Violet left for Florence as usual in the spring of 1908 'she told me she loved me, and I, finding myself expected to rise to the occasion, stumbled out an unfamiliar "darling".' In May Vita too was in Florence again, sightseeing with Violet and their respective governesses. Violet's romantic attachment had not abated. On Vita's last afternoon they went for a farewell tea at Doney's. 'RING', Vita wrote in her diary, in special writing : Violet had given her the Doge's lava ring she had wheedled from art-dealer Joseph Duveen when she was six. Vita kept it for the rest of her life. From Milan Vita wrote to her mother : 'I am still regretting Florence ; I don't think I was ever more sorry to leave any place. . . . Violet Keppel seemed very sorry to say goodbye to me ; at least, she cried very much.'

On her return Vita went to a party at Kensington Palace in a pink check dress and a pink and blue hat from Woollands, a sapphire and pearl bracelet her mother had bought her at Cartier's, and her long hair tied back with a big black bow. The Queen asked after Victoria's 'little girl' and was surprised to find that she was now nearly six feet tall. This grown-up Vita, doing her best to be the conventional *jeune fille*, spent a lot of time with her mother that summer, since Lionel was preoccupied with Connie Hatch. It was at this time that Vita was intrigued by her mother's list of her twenty-five proposals of marriage and, at a society wedding they went to, expressed the pious hope that she might have 'a very smart wedding like this'.

Her mother was surprised and pleased by this development ; but what Victoria did not know was that her sixteen-year-old daughter had already been the focus for male attention of an unpleasant kind. The Hon. Kenneth Hallyburton Campbell was a man of Victoria's own generation, who had known the Sackvilles for over twenty years. He was a stockbroker, a great crony of Seery's – Victoria called him 'Kenito'

---

*'Mar', Victoria's pet-name for Vita, came to be used for any child, or anything young and small.

– and he was also Vita's godfather. To Vita he was almost one of the family and when he was at Knole, she used to be in and out of his bedroom in a natural, childish way. And it was in his bedroom at Knole that their relationship changed dramatically. Vita wrote to Harold years later:

> How abominably he behaved to me, *tout de même*, – trying to rape me when I was sixteen, and frequently after that, when I was fortunately better able to deal with the situation. I always think I had a narrow escape at sixteen, – a housemaid came along the passage carrying a can of hot water. What would Dada have said, if I'd told him?[14]

On another occasion Vita was unwise enough to agree to dine alone with her godfather. 'We were to have gone to a restaurant (which I thought safe) but at the last moment he said he couldn't get a table or something, and got me to his house. Pfui. That was another narrow escape, even narrower, and nothing but great presence of mind saved me.'[15] Telling this story to a friend in later life, she stressed the impression it had made on her: 'Perhaps it accounts for much.'

Victoria, knowing nothing of this, enjoyed recounting her own romantic past to her daughter and the course her life had taken. Vita took everything she said at face value. 'Mother told me some things about her life this morning,' she wrote in code. 'I think she is a very remarkable woman ... she would have become very famous, I am sure, had she not been so hampered by Grandpapa and Dada.'

Vita, in turn, confided in her mother in her own oblique way. She gave Victoria the completed manuscript of her novel 'The King's Secret'. In her Chapter xv Vita described the boy Cranfield Sackville as sensitive, in-communicative, more interested in writing than in people, and more interested in Knole's past than in the present. 'Nothing matters, that is my motto.' She told her mother that she meant Cranfield to be a portrait of herself. This prompted Victoria, in her diary, to a consideration of her daughter's character and personality:

> I should like her to be more open, less reserved. She *seems* indifferent, too much so, and is inclined to be rather selfish, although she is not conscious of it; it is her life as an only child which is responsible for it. She is so wrapped up in her writings that it is apt to make her forget things.

Many of those who were to love Vita in the future could echo her mother this far.

> She is a good child on the whole, but with a tendency to be too sure of her own self, and a little bit hard, not soft-hearted enough to please me. She has changed enormously since her 'things' [monthly periods] have come on. She is

*very* clever, and I really think she is devoted to me, but she does not let herself go enough.

Victoria as always related everything to herself. She went on to reproach the two Lionels for their equally inadequate demonstrations of affection towards her. The bleak Sackville reserve was very real: Vita had her share of it. But however much her mother impressed her, her father was never permanently diminished in her heart.

Grandpapa – 'O'Mann' – was more problematic. Since childhood Vita had been thrown into his company a good deal; she had lunched alone with him when her parents were away and knew him 'as intimately as a child of that age could ever know a very reserved old man of nearly eighty'. He was almost totally silent, with sudden outbursts of face-tiousness. 'Rosamund Grosvenor', he would suddenly bark out, 'got nearly run overner.' Once, when Vita came into the room hanging on to the ends of her mother's long hair, he sprang up and said: 'Victoria, never *never* let me see that child doing that again.' It had reminded him painfully of how Victoria as a child had played with her own mother's hair; it was the nearest Vita ever got to old Lionel's feeling for Pepita. Vita did not dine downstairs, and every night after dinner since she was very young her grandfather had filled a plate with fruit and deposited it in a drawer in his sitting-room which he had labelled 'Vita's Drawer' in coloured chalks. He was hurt if she forgot to go to the drawer the next morning, as he was hurt if she did not come down and play draughts with him after tea.

He dragged out his life with increasing depression and lack of pur-pose. In September 1908, Victoria sent Vita to Scotland to stay with Seery and his sisters, and was alone with her father when he died. Vita was told the news by one of Seery's sisters and she was more struck by the grotesque appearance of Miss Scott in her dressing-gown than by grief for her grandfather. Poor Seery himself produced an even stronger impression. 'I found him sitting in front of his dressing-table, clad only in a suit of Jaeger combinations. He was sobbing uncontrollably, and his sobs shook his loose enormous frame like a jelly. ... He was just over-come by the fact that "the dear old man" was no more.'[16] Vita did not go home for the funeral. Victoria arranged for her to go on to stay with Violet Keppel at Duntreath, the fifteenth-century baronial castle be-longing to the Edmonstones, Mrs Keppel's family. It was an exciting meeting with an exciting friend in a romantic place. She remembered later 'how Violet had filled my room with tuberoses, how we dressed up [Vita was 'La Bella Spagnuola'], how she chased me with a dagger down the long passages of that very ancient Scotch castle and concluded the day by spending the night in my room. It was the first time in my life I ever spent the night with anyone.'[17] It was a night of girls' talk – they never went to sleep – 'while little owls hooted outside'.

Vita was back at Knole a week after old Lionel's death. Victoria wrote in her diary : 'I told Kidlet last night all about Grandpapa's death and could not help crying and showed her my journal of that day. . . . I have been busy all day buying her black clothes at Marshall & Snelgrove. I am also arranging my boudoir at the back of drawing-room. I shall spend little on it.' All that Vita recorded of this was that her Aunt Amalia had come to the funeral and had apparently 'walked in front of Dada, which shocked everybody fearfully'. Not inappositely, in view of what was to come, she began writing (in French) a novel about the French Revolution, 'The Dark Days of Thermidor'. It amused her to see how seriously 'Lord Dada' took his new role, for on the death of old Lionel, he became Lord Sackville.

A threat had been hanging over the *ménage* at Knole since soon after Vita was born. Her father, as old Lionel's nephew, inherited the title on the assumption that old Lionel had no legitimate male heir. Victoria's brother Henry had at first contented himself, like Amalia, Flora and his brother Max, with querulous requests for money. Very soon he started claiming his 'rights' as heir. Unlike Victoria, he had been registered as Lionel Sackville-West's child. He contended that old Lionel had been secretly married to Pepita, which would make him legitimate. He was supported in his claim by other interested parties. Amalia and Flora had each received £365 a year from their father, while Henry and Max had been set up as farmers in South Africa. Now they were all out for more than money. Through Henry, they were looking to Knole itself, and the peerage.

To prove his legitimacy Henry had to show not only that his parents were married, but that Pepita had never been legally married to her dancing teacher, who was still alive when her children were born. Victoria and Lionel had to prove him wrong on both counts. The legal costs, and the costs of searches in French and Spanish record offices, mounted yearly. By late 1904 Victoria and Lionel had already spent £20,000. Seery rose to the occasion, lending money for the next round at three per cent (he 'lent' the Sackville estate over £18,000). The cost in anxiety and insecurity to the family at Knole was incalculable. The weekend parties, the royal and diplomatic visits, the guided tours round the show rooms, had all been taking place with this shadow in the background.

Vita had been taken away by her nurse once when she was six years old as Henry forced his way into the house, hysterically demanding to see his father. But if Victoria – from now on Lady Sackville – had tried to keep the details of the dispute from her before, she no longer could.

After her grandfather's death Vita started coming down to dinner even when there were visitors, her hair now 'up' behind the big black bow. Dada did not approve: 'People ask us many questions about the case; it is so awkward before Vita.'

The case did not come up before the courts for two more expensive, precarious years, during which the Sackvilles were never sure whether their home and their way of life were to be taken from them. Vita listened to the talk. In November of the year her grandfather died she went with Violet to see a new play called *The Marriages of Mayfair*, obviously based on the Sackville situation. 'It was amusing because it so closely resembles the story of my own case; peer who married a *dancer* while her husband was still alive, etc.'

In 1909, with the case pending, Vita 'came out'. She went to Lady Jane Combe's dance in January in white lace trimmed with mauve ruched ribbons. They could not give a dance for her at Knole because its revenues were frozen in the hands of the trustees. In April her mother took her to Dover for the sea air. Lady Sackville wrote that 'She and I have long talks on the pier about her views on life. I don't want her to get in the mood of asking herself about everything: à quoi bon!' But Vita, at seventeen, took a keen interest in the ambiguous history of her family.

She was fascinated by the story of Pepita and identified with the Latin side of her inheritance. The scandal made her a romantic figure in the eyes of her schoolfriends: the tone of Rosamund's letters changed. She had a crush on Vita. Many were the masochistic, sentimental notes scribbled that year to the apparently imperious 'Carmen' or 'Princess', as she addressed Vita. Vita began to carry not only her own romantic fantasies but those of other girls. Notes were passed in class at Miss Woolff's:

> Princess, why do you make one so sad? . . . It is a good thing you are living in a civilized time because there is no knowing what you might not do if anything roused your Spanish blood – is there? I should like to have you here alone one day, I don't live in the seventh heaven at all surrounded by a lot of other girls. . . . Promise *not* to sit next to me tomorrow. It is not that I don't love you being near me, but that I cannot give my attention to the questions, I am – otherwise engrossed.

In the spring Vita was off to Florence again, where Signorina Castelli, who had connections, introduced her into Florentine society. One young man she met was Orazio, the Marchese Pucci, who fell for the tall, dark English girl. He followed Vita and Signorina Castelli to Rome, where they came under the protection of Lady Sackville's old beau, Baron Bildt. When Vita came back to England in June, Orazio Pucci was on the same Channel boat. Lady Sackville was amused: 'It does seem funny that Vita has already got an "admirer". She told me all he had said to her, and he certainly meant business when in Italy. Poor little man !'

In the circumstances, they could do no less than invite him to Knole, half-closed as it was. On his first visit Vita showed him around the house and gardens. 'Mother swears that he is in love with me, and I am disposed to believe it. Poor Pucci !' The second time he came, he took photographs – Vita at her writing table, Vita in her room, Vita in her summer house. Lady Sackville was in her element. 'I let him see, in a lot of little ways, that he could never marry Vita. She said that he was on the point of "telling her some things he ought not to", but that she felt she had been a good girl. I strongly advised her not to flirt and deny herself the satisfaction of a proposal.' Vita did not in the least want to marry him, Lady Sackville felt, 'she knows he should be too masterful for her and the life too quiet.'

On the third visit Pucci had a long private conversation with Lady Sackville, walking in the garden up to the King's Beech. She conveyed to him 'the futility of his caring for Vita as we did not want her to marry'. Very wretched he left for Italy that night. (Lady Sackville herself had just embarked on a new *amitié amoureuse* with William Waldorf Astor, at nearby Hever Castle, and Lord Sackville was still 'playing golf' regularly with Lady Connie.)

Rosamund, alarmed that her 'Princess' was moving out of her reach, wrote to Vita begging for letters. 'We will always be the same to each other as we are now, won't we ?' Her plaintive missives followed Vita on a trip to Russia with her mother and Seery in the autumn of 1909. 'The case' was left far behind. They stayed with Count Joseph Potocki, a Polish nobleman, in his great *château* at Antoniny on the Ukrainian steppes, an estate 100 miles square between Warsaw and Kiev.

They were met at Shepetovka station by a pair of enormous canary-coloured Mercedes motors ; in the castle, they had Cossack servants sleeping across the threshold of their bedrooms at night ; there were 'hereditary dwarfs to hand cigarettes, a giant, and Tokay of 1740'. Lady Sackville hoped that their wealthy host did not admire Vita too much. 'That dear girl tells me everything and it is lucky I have brought her up in the way I have – although she is very innocent, she understands how to behave properly with men.'

Vita understood too the nature of the society they were glimpsing, to an extent that 'made me quite unsurprised when the Russian Revolution came eight years later'. She saw the hovels in which her host's peasants lived. 'I saw them grovelling up to their master and being slashed at carelessly with a dog-whip for their pains.'[18]

Like every mother who says her daughter 'tells me everything', Lady Sackville did not know what went on in Vita's emotional life, particularly not in its self-absorbed and passionate aspect. One of Vita's friends in Sevenoaks, Irene Hogarth (whom Vita always called by the Italian form of her name 'Pace'), analysed Vita's personality, at Vita's request, later that autumn :

> I think you are *very very pasionate* [*sic*] and *loyal* and *generous*! but that you can hate as much as you can love! You are emotional in a great many things especially where you are concerned – you are very easily hurt by unkindness. You are *very* ambitious and always want to be first.... You are frightened of being laughed at.... You like compliments. You are *very* jealous but you try and hide your feelings as much as possible. You have a great longing for sympathy, and at times you can be very sympathetic yourself.

Irene Hogarth had it right. Vita added, in a sketch of herself at seventeen in the unpublished 'Marian Strangways', that although she intimidated strangers by her aloofness she was not conceited, 'rather, diffident and humble about herself socially'.

Her defences grew ever higher. Even her private poetry was about places, historical characters or nature ; she wrote – or preserved – no adolescent lyrics about her feelings. Her attempts at humour were heavy ; the only spontaneous joking, ever, was with her father. She continued to write novels in polysyllabic Latinate English, never to be published – usually set in Italy and involving symbolic wayfarers, with casts of popes, Medicis, painters and poets.

Before the meeting with Pucci, she had completed a verse drama on the life and death of Chatterton and had left it with her mother to read. En route to Italy she sent a frantic note home : 'I forgot something this morning which I meant to ask you : don't show my play to Dada, *please please* ; to Seery if you like, but not Dada and still less Lady Connie.' Vita was, as 'Pace' said, 'frightened of being laughed at' and she well knew that some of the things she did would certainly be laughed at, if they became known. She set great store by *Chatterton* and acted it out for herself in the attic at Knole, 'moved to tears every time by my own performance'. She had devised a special costume for this role : black breeches secretly made for her by her maid Emily, buckled shoes and a white shirt. *Chatterton* was the first of her works that appeared in book form. She paid for 100 copies, printed and bound by Messrs Salmon of Sevenoaks at a cost of five pounds, saved from her pocket-money over the year. She gave a copy to her mother for her birthday.

Her solitary impersonation of Chatterton is an indication of the intensity of her fantasy life at the age of seventeen. She wrote of her heroine's girlhood in *All Passion Spent* : 'For the thoughts which ran behind this delicate and maidenly exterior were of an extravagance to

do credit even to a wild young man. They were thoughts of nothing
less than escape and disguise : a changed name, a travestied sex, and
freedom in some foreign city.'

# CHAPTER 3

THE succession case opened on 1 February 1910. Two days later Vita attended the court for about five minutes after her classes at Miss Woolff's. It was the day that Henry, his affairs going badly, opted to conduct his case himself. Lord Sackville had not wanted Vita to be there at all but Victoria smuggled her in. 'Look at your relations,' she said scornfully to her daughter, 'like plumbers in their Sunday best.' Vita noticed only that Henry looked very worried. The papers could not get enough of the case; the Sackvilles and their romantic past were wonderful copy. Vita was bewildered but excited; she accepted her mother's new dogma that Pepita, the gypsy's daughter, had been fathered by a Spanish duke and not by an obscure barber. 'I think my maternal ancestry is hard to beat for sheer picturesqueness.'

Henry lost, and Lord and Lady Sackville and their daughter returned home to Sevenoaks in triumph. The town welcomed them with presentations and addresses. Lionel found it 'an abominable nuisance' but, apart from 'an awful tea party' in the Sevenoaks Drill Hall, Vita thought it great fun. The processional return to Knole itself was even better: there was a reception committee of the staff waiting for them and Vita was presented with a box of chocolates by the head coachman's daughter. 'Never, before or since, have I felt so much like royalty.' When Vita came to write about this in *Pepita*, she said that the three of them then went inside to a quiet family dinner, but in her diary for that day she wrote that 'we motored back to London, and dined with the Hays.'

But they were in possession again, with a security they had not enjoyed for many years. Vita was allotted a new room in the tower that had been occupied by her grandfather, overlooking the tiny Pheasants' Court. Her personal maid, Emily, slept in the room above, known as the Little Duke's Nursery. Lady Sackville had Vita's room all done up in pink, but her daughter had ideas of her own. Her room was soon full of herself and of Italy, 'the strong, luxuriant, cruel Italy of the Renaissance'. She wanted it to be 'stern and austere, not the bedroom of a young girl' : no carpet, and the walls decorated with Italianate frescoes done by herself.

She had had her own portrait painted for the first time while the case was in progress. Lady Sackville was particularly flattered that the artist, the fashionable Philip de Laszlo, seemed so struck by Vita that 'he wants to paint her at once for nothing'. (Vita was a girl very much in the news.) Lady Sackville wanted Vita done wearing a big hat and a fur. De Laszlo thought that such a costume 'would detract somewhat from her youthful appearance' ; he sent a sketch – loose hair, a bonnet off the face, *décolletage* and floating gauzes. Lady Sackville won the day. 'Mother and he got on all right when she did not criticize his half-finished picture,' wrote Vita.

Her love affair with Orazio Pucci (or rather, his with her) was not over, but it came a poor second to her love affair with Italy : 'This is worth waiting for a whole year ... I am shivering with excitement and joy at my beautiful, beloved Florence.' She went this year with Rosamund Grosvenor and an old governess, Fie ; they stayed at the Villa Pestellini in Fiesole. 'We went to the races at the Cascine, with Pucci, this afternoon ; he was very surprised to get my letter, saying that I was coming.' He sent her roses and escorted them everywhere. Rosamund was disapproving. Fie forbade him to accompany them to Venice, but allowed him to go with them as far as Bologna. Vita wrote in her diary the night before they left : 'I suppose I ought not to have come here, because of him ; he has got it really badly!'

She was flattered ; she recorded every meeting, every compliment. This experience was too interesting to lose. She learnt how to flirt and tested out her power. She was not quite sure why she did not love him. Perhaps, she thought, it was because he was shorter than she was. 'In the evening, sitting down, I almost loved him.' And in the carriage in the dark after a performance of *Aida*, as he whispered his love in Italian, she almost loved him again.

He turned up in Venice in spite of Fie's prohibition and stayed four days. 'We packed him off to another hotel, as he proposed to stay here.' Vita, taking over the leadership of the ladies' party, was becoming a competent and lordly traveller : 'The pension where I hoped to get rooms had none, so we slept at Hotel Britannia, and went to Pension Visentini, but it was so bad' that they repaired to the much grander Danieli. She felt *blasée* in Venice, 'but Florence still is Florence, and I hope always will be.' Back at home, she tossed off another of her monumental, unpublishable Florentine novels, 'The City of the Lily', set in the fifteenth century.

Before going to Italy she had completed a full-length contemporary novel, 'Behind the Mask', about a modern girl with a worldly mother, thrown, like the young author, into the 'matrimonial fishpond' in which she is meant to present herself as bait. 'She hated the whole business : it seemed to her coarse and vulgar.' The heroine finally marries a dull, devoted Frenchman whom she does not love ; the man she loves but will not marry is first and foremost a playmate, clever and gay, with whom she feels an effortless affinity. Everyone, wrote Vita in this prophetic novel, conceals his or her true feelings behind a mask. 'Is there anyone without the mask ? . . . Not the husband, not the wife, not the son whose every secret the mother thinks she knows.' The heroine, married, does not give up her playmate-lover and forces each of the two men in her life to accept her feelings for the other, thus facing up to the reality 'behind the mask'. 'She dominated them', and Vita's morality, as expressed here, is that 'everything is right to the innocent conscience'. In essence, and *mutatis mutandis*, before she was eighteen Vita had written out the scenario of her own life. In life, her playmate was also her devoted husband, and it was passion that formed the third side of the triangle.

'Behind the Mask' shows Vita to be deeply disillusioned about marriage. The picture of the null, embittering relationship between the heroine and her husband is sophisticated and well observed. She had watched her parents. That year – 1910 – she had also observed the worsening rows between her mother and Seery. In March she had witnessed a particularly horrible one :

> I thought they would quarrel for good, but he became apologetic and they have half patched it up, though it can't ever be as before. It was all very unpleasant, and they called each other names, and I hated it. . . . I am awfully sorry for Seery ! After all, we were the only interest he had in his life, and he is old ; he cried this afternoon.

It was not edifying for Vita. Small wonder that as an only child, with these complex multiple models of adult 'love' presented to her daily, she should fantasize about a light-hearted companion-playmate who would be in complete sympathy with her and make few demands.

She met him very soon after, on 29 June, when she and her parents were at a London dinner party which was going on to see a play, *The Speckled Band*. Harold Nicolson arrived late, 'very young and alive and charming, and the first remark I heard him make was "What fun !" '[1] Dark and grave at the dinner table she watched, and she liked what she saw.

Vita – six years younger than Harold – was the one who made the first move : she asked him down to Knole four days later for a Shakespeare masque that was being staged in the park in aid of the Shakespeare Memorial Theatre Fund. It was performed by a mixture of professionals and amateurs: Ellen Terry was in it, but so was Lady Eileen Wellesley (to whom Harold Nicolson was very unofficially engaged), Venetia Stanley, Elizabeth Asquith, Mrs Winston Churchill, Vita herself and many of her debutante friends. Vita took the part of Portia and Ellen Terry lent her her own costume. The great actress seemed a romantic figure to Vita, who wrote of her –

> She was all woman to me, all the rhymes
> Hung by the young Orlando on the oak[2]

– but that was long after; and on the day of the masque it poured with rain. There was luncheon in the Great Hall for everyone (Mr Asquith, the Prime Minister, was there) and several people stayed on for the weekend – among them Harold, and Rosamund Grosvenor.

In the weeks that followed Vita and Harold coincided at parties in London. He came down to Knole for several more weekends during the summer, and in November she wrote the first extant letter to him, asking him to a dinner and dance for which she had been asked to 'bring a man'. She also asked after the health of his little motor car, which he called Green Archie. (The other Archie in Harold's life was Archie Clark-Kerr, like himself in the diplomatic service – his closest friend, as Rosamund was Vita's.) Harold's recurring visits to Knole do not necessarily mean that Vita was making the running. It was the debutantes' parents who gave the entertainments for the young people, the girls being bait in the matrimonial fishpond, as Vita had put it. All an eligible young man had to do was to answer his invitations.

Vita's 'coming out' had been less intensive than it might have been because of the court case, and then the death of King Edward VII put a damper on society life. She went with her father to the old King's funeral service in Westminster Abbey. 'The German Emperor talked all the time to the King [George V] which everyone thought in very bad taste.' Soon after Edward VII's death, his unofficial widow, Alice Keppel, discreetly went away with Violet and her younger sister Sonia for a protracted visit to Ceylon, and Vita went to Duntreath to see Violet before they left. Violet made the visit as romantic as before, writing afterwards to Vita, 'Don't you remember the purposeless, incessant tick-tick of pigeon-feet upon the roof, and the jackdaws flying from tower to tower? And the star that twinkled down on us from the armoury window, and the desultory cries of the night-owls?' The intense emotional atmosphere created by Violet infected Feridah, another girl staying there. Feridah described in a letter how she and Violet had discussed Vita 'for *hours*' after she had left :

> My summary of you was that you would reach Perfection when you married someone who would make you miserable.... But you must not marry an *Englishman* ! – he would not make you unhappy enough. And then I told Violet that I was proud of knowing someone in the chrysalis stage who in years to come would have her life written.... You will sit on the top of Cleopatra's needle and the needle will be forgotten.

Vita and Violet said a final goodbye in London, driving around and around Hyde Park while Violet tried to persuade Vita to join her in Ceylon. In the car she kissed Vita. It was 'extremely disturbing'.

But Vita's plans were already fixed : a persistent summer flu had threatened to become pneumonia and Lady Sackville wanted to take her to the sun during the winter months ; they were going to the Château Malet, a large white villa outside Monte Carlo. 'Do try not to get married before I return,' Violet wrote to her in one of her numerous flamboyant letters from Ceylon. 'After all, I'm only a girl. I ought to have foreseen that perhaps at your age a masculine liaison would come about. ... I feel I'm about to say improper things. You won't laugh, promise that you won't laugh.'

The six months in the south of France were 'a perfection of happiness' for Vita. The complexity of her emotional life increased and with it the need for secrecy. Their first visitors, on New Year's Day 1911, were Harold and Archie Clark-Kerr. Harold and Vita fell into 'a rather childlike companionship' and she was rather hurt when he left without apparent regret after ten days. She missed him – 'cosa tristissima', she wrote in her diary – 'he was the best actual *playmate* I had known.'

A week later Orazio Pucci turned up and proposed again. 'My God, how unhappy I'd be with him !'

The next visitor was Muriel, Archie's sister, a pale, fair young woman of twenty-five, who made Vita her confidante : she had never been in love and never wished to marry. Vita had not known her well before, but when Muriel left after three weeks she wrote of her new friend in her diary, 'I love her really very very much.' The two had talked and written letters in the villa garden, and made excursions further afield with siestas under the olive trees. Vita's lifelong association of the sun and scents of the south with the excitement of love dates from this time. 'I don't want to write descriptions but I don't think I have been so happy for a long time.' From Lower Sloane Street in London, Muriel wrote to Vita : 'I shall not be "frigid" in London – why should I be ? for I, too, care very much. I hated saying goodbye and did not half tell you enough how I loved being at Palais Malet, or how glad I am we both embarked on the "risk". Those two days in the hills ! How happy we were.'

While Muriel was still at the villa, Violet Keppel had turned up. The Keppels were now staying at San Remo. 'Still a bit mad, but fascinating,' was Vita's verdict on Violet, who had brought her a ruby from Ceylon.

With both Muriel and Violet at her side, Vita was receiving hectic letters from Irene Hogarth – 'Pace' – in Sevenoaks : 'I *do* love you – *de tout mon coeur* – and more every day, if that is possible – but I don't think you know how *frightfully* difficult it is to throw off the mask I have to wear here. . . . Scold me as much as you like – it's good for me and I like it as then I know you still care – but don't give me up.' To elicit such replies, Vita's letters to Pace must have been sufficiently demanding : the verbal equivalents of nettle-lashing, perhaps.

The next arrival was Joseph Potocki, flatteringly flirtatious, 'come from Warsaw, he said, specially to see me !'

Lord Sackville visited, which made Lady Sackville edgy ; she took her daughter on innumerable gambling trips and shopping sprees to Monte Carlo and, once, to have tea with the eighty-five-year-old Empress Eugénie. It was Lady Sackville who invited Rosamund Grosvenor to the villa, after Violet had left for Munich to learn German. 'Rosamund is very nice and sensible,' Lady Sackville wrote hopefully in her diary.

'I love her so much,' wrote Vita in hers, the night Rosamund arrived. The sentimental Rosamund took Muriel's place in the siestas under the olive trees. But when, after three weeks, Rosamund left, Vita wrote : 'Strange how little I minded, she has no personality, that's why.' And from Munich, Violet, who had a great deal of personality, wrote long, provocative, flattering, rhetorical love-letters in her wild mixture of French and English. She challenged Vita to reply on the same level or not at all ; even though she was two years younger, Violet wrote, she would always be fifty years older 'moralement'.

The Sackvilles returned home in April 1911 via Florence. Lady Sackville did not know Italian (which was why Vita wrote large sections of her diary in that language) and was impressed by her daughter in Italy. 'V. speaks Italian quite beautifully. . . . She looks and acts as if the whole of Florence belonged to her.' Yet again, Orazio Pucci proposed marriage and was turned down.

Back in England, Vita went with her father to the Coronation of King George v – she was to exploit her memories of the occasion in the closing pages of *The Edwardians* – and continued the round of parties and dances. It puzzled Lady Sackville that 'she likes these silly entertainments, as she is so serious – and most of the young men she meets are so uninteresting.' She did in fact feel alienated; she still felt, as she had at Miss Woolff's, that no one liked her. As a middle-aged woman she was to have a recurring dream about being at a party where she was very popular, very much in demand. 'Everybody likes me, and clusters round me, and makes a fuss of me. I can very easily interpret this dream: it goes right back to when I came out and nobody liked me.' In describing Sebastian's feelings about the London season in *The Edwardians* she was describing her own: 'He liked it, and he hated himself for liking it. He liked himself for hating it, and hated himself for submitting to it.' She was to write that during the months she was 'out' she was living 'a sort of false life that left no impression on me.'³

Even her relationship with Rosamund, who spent days and nights at Knole with her – they were painting Vita's new room in mock-Italian style, with a scarlet dragon, white lilies and 'vaguely architectural towers' on a background of blue and gold – was, she said, superficial. 'I mean that it was almost entirely physical, as to be frank, she always bored me as a companion.'⁴

In May Kenneth Campbell renewed his unsuitable pursuit of her. He escorted her to a ball, where he made a formal declaration of his feelings for her. She was appalled. 'Good God, he is in love with me!' she wrote in her diary. 'Is friendship impossible, then, really? What if I married him? Impossible!' She decided to tell no one about this distressing episode.

If Vita had doubts about her powers of attraction, this year of wholesale and diverse conquests should have dispelled them. But her alienation was apparent. Her father wrote to Victoria that 'although I can't help being sorry she doesn't like more normal and ordinary things ... I see that it's no good trying to force her and I am very much afraid she will end up marrying a "souly" [i.e., a 'Soul', or in Lord Sackville's terms, an intellectual – not his cup of tea].'

There were some 'ordinary things' Vita enjoyed. She learned to drive a motor car and preferred – unconventionally for 1911 – to drive herself rather than be driven. She enjoyed the Russian bear cub that was given to her by one of her dancing-partners, Ivan Hay; she kept it in a cage in the garden, and took it for walks on a chain. She gave her first ever press interview ('Lord Sackville's Daughter Talks of her Pet') to a journalist of the *Evening Times*: 'The Hon. Vita Sackville-West was interrupted in a game of tennis, wearing a simple white dress with a picturesque silk scarf curled in Corsican fashion round her head.' She reminded the reporter that the house and grounds could be visited by the public only on the last three days of each week.

Harold Nicolson, *en poste* at the British Embassy in Madrid, had been ill with a venereal infection, 'the effect of Andalusia and a desire to establish my sex'.[5] He was home in the summer of 1911. His illness was public knowledge, though not its nature, and he walked slowly round the garden with Vita, well wrapped up. When he took her and Rosamund to *Macbeth* in London, Vita did not come home to the Hill Street house until morning, and Lady Sackville was frantic with worry. Her lateness was not because of Harold, but because of Rosamund, in whose house she had slept. 'Men did not attract me in what is called "that way". Women did. Rosamund did.... Oh, I dare say I realized vaguely that I had no business to sleep with Rosamund, and I should certainly never have allowed anyone to find out, but my sense of guilt went no further than that.'[6]

She and Rosamund shared a diffuse and sentimental sensuality, but never, then or later, did they technically 'make love'. They did not think of it.

Vita stayed in great houses, often with Rosamund : they were both at the Château Laversine at Chantilly in the autumn, whence she sent her mother brittle little bulletins : 'Robert de Rothschild is a beastly little Jew. Bendor [the Duke of Westminster] is charming ... Lord Rocksavage is dim to a degree.' She went to Hill Hall, the house of Mrs Charles Hunter, in a party that included J. S. Sargent, Henry James, Percy Grainger and the artist Helleu : 'A very arty party. Dada is well out of it !' At a hunt ball in Hampshire her main partners were Lord Gerald Wellesley and Lord Lascelles. At Knole, during a weekend in mid-November when Harold Nicolson was among the guests, Lady Sackville noted that he seemed to be in love with Vita. He was back at the Foreign Office awaiting a new posting as a third secretary on a salary of £250 a year.

The question of money was exercising Lady Sackville more than usual. Seery was ill and irritable and threatening to change his will. Lady Sackville wrote in her diary, 'Vita and Lionel have been so nice about it and quite understand I can't go on as things are now.' She saw herself as the martyred breadwinner, obliged to put up with Seery's tiresomeness for her family's sake. As his will stood, she was to get £150,000 plus all the French furniture from the rue Laffitte apartment. Part of the quarrel was over Seery's dislike of Speall's, the interior decorating shop that Lady Sackville had opened in South Audley Street, Mayfair. It took up too much of her time and he was lonely. Vita was sent to Seery on peacemaking missions and brought back the invalid's missives to his dominating 'little Spanish beggar'.

When Harold was at Knole for Christmas 1911 and Lady Sackville observed again how much in love with Vita he seemed, it was his lack of money that worried her. 'He is very *sympathique* to me and L. and everybody likes him. Vita might like living abroad in an Embassy, but she often says she hates being poor, unless she was madly in love.'

At Knole over the New Year, Harold learned that he was to be sent to Constantinople. Vita vaguely hoped he might propose before he left. He helped her with the painting of her room, he played golf with Lord Sackville and Walter Rubens (Rubens's wife, a professional singer, was a new friend of Lord Sackville's), and then, back in London, he continued his light-hearted philandering with a young man friend. It was Lady Sackville, not Vita, who kept testing the temperature and Harold answered her ambiguously: 'No: I shan't find anyone in Constantinople. I fear I have an uncomfortable faculty for only admiring people who are far above me and whom I can't marry. Perhaps it is lucky that I *am* going abroad.' And Vita swung back into the dance, writing to her mother on 12 January 1912: 'I enjoyed Taplow quite *enormously*. . . . Diana Manners is staying here, I did not dislike her quite so much this time. There is also Lord Lascelles, who is rather dull, and Mr Shaw-Stewart, who is supposed to be brilliantly clever, and I should think he is, and Mr Chichester, a pretty mar boy, very effeminate.' Her hostess, Lady Desborough, had been 'very amiable', and she liked the son of the house, Julian Grenfell, 'who is enormously tall, and danced with me lots, and took me into supper'. Ivan Hay, who had given her the bear cub, was there: 'He got a little silver bear for me at Christmas, and did not send it because he thought you might not like it, which was nice of him, but he is going to send it now.' Lord Lascelles was heir to the Earl of Harewood and he was falling in love with Vita. The brilliant Patrick Shaw-Stewart had been at Balliol College, Oxford, with Harold, and was a Fellow of All Souls; he was managing director of the bankers Baring Brothers by the time he was twenty-five. Lady Sackville advised her daughter to enjoy herself: '*J'ai confiance en toi, que tu n'excéderas jamais ce qu'une "lady" peut se permettre.*'

There was a ball at Hatfield House on 18 January; Vita and Harold were to be staying at the same house-party for it. Two days before, Seery called on Lady Sackville at her shop in South Audley Street.

> He talked to me about the possibility of Vita marrying H.N. who he likes enormously and he promised vaguely to give her £ [amount deleted in diary] a year, which would be £100 per month. He also told me he would alter his will if I was not nice to him, and called me several times: *You little Rascal* and went away on those words.

The next day, Seery died.

Vita, with the self-concern of the young, was worried that she might not be allowed to go to the ball at Hatfield. But that evening she, Harold and Lord Sackville travelled to Hertfordshire as arranged.

# CHAPTER 4

AT THE ball Vita, in a new dress, hardly saw Harold until after midnight. He hated dancing. Then he came to find her. She wrote a dramatized account of what happened next in 'Marian Strangways'. They left the party, and went upstairs. There were two green travelling boxes on the landing, on which they sat. 'He looked at her in a new way', and she chattered to avoid the danger. 'She would not meet his eyes, and he tore one button after another deliberately off his white gloves.' Then 'walls crumbled between them', and he said, 'I love you, – I love you!' and all she could think was 'Now I'm for it', and all she could say was, 'Don't, oh don't', and she gave him her hand, and he almost crushed it.

The next day, back at Knole, she wrote up her diary. 'I asked him to wait, a year at least, because I didn't know. I feel as if I dreamt it. Because at the bottom of my heart I know I'll marry him. ... I told him that I didn't love him, I don't know why.' He had not kissed her; 'We sat rather bewildered over supper afterwards, and talked excitedly and rather vaguely about the flat we would have in Rome.'

Harold came to Knole and had long talks with Lady Sackville alone. 'He is such a dear boy ... so I want to know him better and talk to him like a Mother.' Later Vita sat in her mother's room in Bourchier's Tower 'trying on my jewels and talking all the time of Harold and how she would like to help him in his career.' When Lord Sackville and Lady Connie arrived they were less than enthusiastic, telling Lady Sackville she saw the sentimental but not the practical side. 'Naturally [Lionel] is disappointed that she is not making a great match with a great title.'

So in a final 'great talk' with Harold in her Chinese Room Lady Sackville told him that they could not possibly be officially engaged for over a year; that Vita must be 'absolutely free', and that 'they must not correspond as engaged people and no words of Dearest or Darling can be used !'

Thus the two young people parted as ordinary friends, in front of Dada and Lady Connie. 'I don't understand myself, I'm absolutely stunned,' Vita wrote that night. She and Harold had spent most of the day together walking very fast over the wet grass of the park, *'per bisogna di movimento'*.

As soon as he had left – he would not be back from Constantinople for six months – Vita took to her bed. 'Mother used to come to my room once or twice a day holding a little green bottle of disinfectant to her nose and saying that there were 300 steps between her room and mine and what a bore it was feeling one had to go and see someone who was ill and waiting for one, so that after she had gone I used to sob with depression.'[1] Lady Sackville had no notion of the lowering effect she produced ; she noted only that during her 'mild attack of Flue' Vita had confessed she loved Harold, as she lay in her great bed in her dim frescoed bedroom. 'It was like a scene out of a play.'

Vita had written Harold one farewell note – 'I love you. Goodbye.' Then, in her diary on 24 January : 'I don't remember ever having been so unhappy. Only today have I begun to understand that I do not love him.' She was hopelessly confused. She wrote to 'My dear Harold' every five days or so, and he to her. He also wrote once a week to her mother, knowing that she was a key supporter of his suit.

Lady Sackville met Harold's parents, Sir Arthur Nicolson (later Lord Carnock, and in 1912 a distinguished diplomat and Permanent Under Secretary of State for Foreign Affairs) and Lady Nicolson. She thought them 'both very ugly and very small and unsmart looking', though she found Sir Arthur 'a dear'. Lady Nicolson, to whom Harold was deeply devoted, seemed 'deadly dull and gênée ; most unattractive ; but une brave femme. I said nothing to her.'

Lady Sackville could afford to be condescending. Although trouble over Seery's will, under which she was chief beneficiary, had blown up immediately after his death – the Scott family solicitors advertising desperately for evidence of codicils or later wills – she felt buoyant. For one thing, her new wealth would give her a hold over her errant husband : 'I have promised him no fixed income, as I don't think I should approve of the way he'd spend it.' She bought a Rolls-Royce, costing £1,450. Vita told Harold that 'Mother has been buying chefs, and gardeners, and people, it is such fun. Yes, she is a splendid person, and I told her you had said so. She is more wonderful every day.'

Vita, accompanied by her maid Emily, went away from every Saturday to Monday (the word 'weekend' was thought to be common) for hunt balls, charity balls, amateur theatricals, fancy-dress dances. ('Are you going to be at Burghley ?' the young men and girls asked one another – or at Queen Anne's Mead, Eridge, Taplow, Coker, Sutton Courtney, Compton Beauchamp, St Fagan's, Crichel, Crewe, Elvedon, Houghton.) They referred always to the house, never to the family who lived in it ; that went without saying, for this was a closed circle.

The reality of Harold receded. He became 'a boy who lived worshipping her in a beautiful distant city'. Her romance with Rosamund, who still spent most of her time at Knole, deepened. She acquired new male admirers. Only a month after the Hatfield ball she was writing to Harold about a dinner party where

> there were queer untidy artist people, with a sprinkling of 'clever' young men like Patrick Shaw Stewart. . . . Then there was Lord Granby, who is a curious rather morose person. I don't think I altogether like him. And there were playwrights and sculptors and novelists and painters, and it was fun. . . . My erratic friend Violet Keppel is coming home in April, so you will know her ; I am so glad. She will amuse you more than anybody.

Lady Sackville was adding Patrick Shaw-Stewart's name to the list of young men who were 'rather fond of V.'. By August 1912 he was coming frequently to Knole, teaching Vita Greek and playing tennis.

At Mrs Alwynne Greville's ball Ivan Hay proposed to her. She turned him down. He cried. 'He has a diabolical character,' Vita wrote in her diary. 'I wouldn't marry him if he were 30 times a duke with 30 million pounds.' The morose Marquess of Granby, heir to the dukedom of Rutland, was another serious admirer. Her mother meditated : 'I'd not encourage her either way. Of course I'd love her to remain in England and she would do so if she was married to Ld Granby ; and she would love doing up Haddon.' In June, at Sutton Courtney, Vita was floating with the said Lord Granby in a canoe among the bullrushes in the moonlight, 'and he bored me, and I thought of Green Archie, and other things', she reassured Harold.

Lady Sackville did not think much of the 'wooden carved dismal looking saint' which Harold had given Vita for her twentieth birthday. It was a worm-eaten figure of St Barbara that he had bought in Spain ; Vita cherished it all her life. Lady Sackville was concerned because Vita would not discuss Harold at all. But her daughter could write about her feelings when she could not speak about them, and told her mother in a letter : 'H. is all my life, it's the only thing that really matters in the world. I care for H. like that.' To her mother, this did not seem to tally with Vita's behaviour.

Violet returned from Munich 'crazier than ever' in Vita's opinion. Violet, on the other hand, found Vita transformed. At twenty, she was lovely :

No one had told me that Vita had turned into a beauty. The knobs and knuckles had all disappeared. She was tall and graceful. The profound, hereditary Sackville eyes were as pools from which the morning mist had lifted. A peach might have envied her complexion. Round her revolved several enamoured young men. . . . [2]

But it was with Rosamund that Vita escaped to Florence as usual in the late spring of 1912, chaperoned by an elderly ex-governess. They stayed again at the Villa Pestellini, where the girls and their Miss Graham slept in a little annexe in the garden. 'How happy I am here with R. whom I love so much.' Yet she disingenuously discussed Rosamund in her letters to Harold; they referred to her in code as 'the Rubens lady' because of her appearance. Vita told him she was trying to make a match between the Rubens lady and Henry ('Bogey') Harris, a family friend who spent much time in Florence. They discussed Rosamund's subservient attitude to Vita, who wrote: 'It is a pity and rather tiresome. But doesn't everyone want *one* subservient person in their life? I've got mine in her. Who is yours? Certainly not me!'

So she set the stage for her complex marital relationship with Harold. She did not conceal from him how happy she was – 'it is hot, and the *grilli* sing, and I love the Rubens lady, and somewhere in the world there is you' – and asserted her right to her private friendships: 'Don't let's hate each other's friends, and anyhow we can give and take about it can't we? What were you doing here when you went to restaurants in the Piazza Sta Croce?'

This is not so worldly-wise as it sounds. Her instincts were sophisticated, but her knowledge was limited. She knew that there were 'effeminate' men (and Harold was not effeminate) but she did not know the physical realities of male homosexuality. Neither did she know that there was a name for the love she and Rosamund felt for one another, or that the Rosamund affair was to pale into insignificance beside the Violet affair. Half a century later, recalling troubled times, she told Harold that everything was 'partly your fault':

You were older than I, and far better informed. I was very young, and very innocent. I knew nothing about homosexuality. I didn't even know that such a thing existed – either between men or between women. You should have told me. You should have warned me. You should have told me about yourself, and have warned me that the same sort of thing was likely to happen to myself. It would have saved us a lot of trouble and misunderstanding. But I simply didn't know.

Oh, what an unexpected letter to write to you suddenly. You won't like it, because you never like to face facts. [3]

Characteristically, Harold in his reply made no comment on this in 1960. Nor could he have explained himself to her in 1912. His generally light-hearted homosexual friendships with young men of his own background were something he took for granted but did not examine too deeply. His instinct was not to talk about it – for psychological reasons, as well as because homosexuality was against the law – but in his heart he did not think it was wrong. Nor did it have any bearing on his love for Vita.

Similarly Vita, in her 1920 autobiography, said it did not strike her as wrong that 'I should be more or less engaged to Harold, and at the same time so much in love with Rosamund.' The two feelings were unrelated. Harold was her dream 'playmate': 'Our relationship was so fresh, so intellectual, so unphysical, that I never thought of him in that aspect at all. . . . Some men seem born to be lovers, others to be husbands; he belongs to the latter category.' Harold was to be cast as lover as well; for the moment, Rosamund filled the role. 'It was passion that used to make my head swim sometimes, even in the daytime, but we never made love.'

Vita affected total frankness with Harold. 'It's a good thing we can always talk about anything without minding, quite brutally.' But she was not candid about her feeling for Rosamund. Neither was he candid about his feeling for Pierre de Lacretelle, who appeared in Therapia, the Constantinople legation's summer quarters, that June. Pierre, an employee of the Ottoman Bank, was 'one of the men in Harold's life with whom he was undoubtedly infatuated for a time'.[4]

When Vita came home from Italy she found that her mother had a new rich friend, Pierpont Morgan. 'L[ionel] encourages me in this wonderful friendship,' Lady Sackville wrote in her diary. 'I can think of nothing else . . . I shall be frightfully discreet in connection with him.' The brilliant young Edward Horner was pursuing Vita, while Violet Keppel, installed in a studio at the top of her parents' grand new house in Grosvenor Street, was entertaining in the style of the Ballets Russes.

Vita went to the races at Ascot, staying at Adair Place with her father. Her photograph, with Lord Lascelles, appeared in the *Daily Mirror*; the caption was 'Headdress which attracted much attention'. Lord Sackville reported to his wife: 'I think the mar enjoyed herself. Lascelles is being very nice to her and took her to luncheon and I believe is going to do so again today. She looked very nice and I think her hat was a success.' (The attention-getting hat was flat-crowned, Spanish in style, worn on the side of her head.) The consequence of the photograph was that at dinner with Lord Granby's parents, and again at Sutherland House, she was congratulated on her engagement to Lord Lascelles. 'Patrick [Shaw-Stewart] and Edward [Horner] both said thanks be to God that it wasn't true! They thought it was all over!'

Four days after this, at Knole, Lord Lascelles did propose as he walked with Vita round the garden before luncheon. 'I can't think how he found the courage to say it, for he is very timid. Lunch was difficult, but he behaved very well. He has every virtue, but he is not *simpatico*. He is tall, and not too ugly, but he has a silly laugh. He will be very rich. He always looks terrified.' She did not turn him down definitely, but told him she could not answer him yet. And then :

> Harold wrote today, begging me to marry him this autumn. I found the letter as soon as I left Lord L.
>
> In the evening Kenneth [Campbell] came. He made a scene with me too. Then I had a letter from Pucci at the war in Tripoli, saying he was always thinking of me.
>
> What a day !

She told Harold that she felt she had only just begun to live and to make friends, and 'if I let you take me away this year it will all end – after all, I'm only 20 !' If he let her be selfish for a bit, 'I'll spend the rest of my life being unselfish for you.' Meanwhile, 'let us be unspeakably happy.'

She saw Lord Lascelles again at Mells, where she was staying with the Horners, and played tennis all the time so as not to have to talk to him, with the result that he went straight to Knole where Lady Sackville had one of her 'long talks' with him. 'He told me his father had £31,000 a year from his land alone, plus plenty of cash. . . . He seems a nice fellow.' Vita's attachment to Harold now seemed foolish to her, a 'mad passion'.

Harold was due back from Constantinople on leave in mid-August, and was to come straight to Knole for the weekend of the 17th. On the 12th, Lascelles was writing to Vita: 'You have no idea what castles-in-the-air I have been building upon a foundation which you have laid.' He too had been invited for that weekend. Vita wrote to Harold :

> I can't meet you with hundreds of people there. Drive Green Archie round to the stables . . . and then come to my room the back way, through the stables and the Great Hall, and the ballroom. Don't be solemnly conducted to the Colonnade where you will meet all the people staying in the house, and I shall have to come down and say Hello Harold how are you ?

As well as Harold and Lord Lascelles, Patrick Shaw-Stewart and Rosamund were to be there. Lord Sackville, away in Canada, had written a serious letter to his daughter : 'Mar, I suppose Harold will be with you soon . . . of course I shall never stand in your way but don't say "yes" unless you are *quite quite* sure that he counts for you more than anything else in the world.'

Vita did not know what she wanted. She paid more attention to Patrick than she did to Harold, who 'behaved very well and hardly *looked* at V. who was handsomer than ever.' Everything was in abeyance, as it was the next weekend when the cast of guests was the same, and Rosamund and Vita acted *The Miracle*, with Rosamund as the Nun and Vita as the King's Son. Lord Lascelles had more long talks with Lady Sackville in her Chinese Room in the small hours. 'He is not nearly so afraid of me as he is of V.'

Harold did not press. In between the two weekends, after an exchange of telegrams, he rushed off to Paris where he was met by Pierre de Lacretelle. Vita clung to Rosamund and refused to make up her mind about Lord Lascelles. She told her mother she would like 'to live alone in a tower with her books', then she threw up her arms and said, 'Oh! Mama, I really don't know what I want!'

The cluster of characteristics that were always to be hers had already developed: a distaste for the idea of marriage; an apparent candour with her intimates that was not candour at all; a capacity for sustaining multiple relationships; the division in her mind between passionate and companionate love; her fantasy – to be realized – of 'living alone in a tower with her books'; also, her disinclination to let anyone who loved her go – keeping them on a string, rebuffing them if they asked too much of her, but drawing in the line sharply if they showed signs of straying.

'Playing about' with Harold and Rosamund – always the three of them together – she grew more sure. Her parents said that she and Harold might consider themselves engaged and write freely to one another. Lord Lascelles tempted her from magnificent Harewood in Yorkshire: 'You don't know what a perfect place this could be made with a little of your taste and a little money which I hope in course of time I shall be able to spend on it.... I cannot bear to think of you transplanted into a small house in a dirty street in Constantinople, and I know you will hate it.' Vita continued to write to him, and he still had reason to hope.

The last weekend in September of 1912, Vita and Harold finally faced one another. On the Saturday it rained. In the wet garden 'he kissed me for the first time', and called her his 'wife'. On the Sunday they talked in her room, 'and I went with him through the show rooms, and he kissed me and kissed me. I love him.'

Vita and Rosamund were off to Italy yet again. Harold, en route to Constantinople, travelled as far as Bologna with them, with the little dog Mikki II that Vita had given him. The parting upset both of them. But Pierre was in Constantinople, and Rosamund and Vita, staying this time at the Villa Medici, resumed their customary idyll in Florence.

Lord Lascelles turned up the day after their arrival, a coincidence that could only have been engineered by Vita. She gave him, however, a rough time, scorning his failure to get taxis and nicknaming him 'M.' for 'Misère'. 'The M. is too splendid in shops, frightfully extravagant!' One night there was a fancy-dress dinner at the Villa Medici: Rosamund went as a Rubens lady, Vita as a fourteenth-century Florentine boy, and as for the abused Lord Lascelles: 'Dada, I wish you could have seen him last night ... he was a Viking, and had on a fur mat and a very small towel by way of a sporran, and when he sat down he sat very much on the edge of his chair nervously trying to draw it more round him. And he had two long plaits made out of the stuffing of the sofa.' Vita's eye was hurt by a firework, and the 'Florentine boy' looked even more handsome, wearing a bandage round his head. 'I hate writing this, but I must ... I was never so much in love with Rosamund as during those weeks in Italy and the months that followed. ... I seem to be incapable of fidelity.'[5]

On her return home, the predatory Kenneth Campbell was at Knole with his new wife ('awful woman'). At once, Vita was involved in middle-aged lusts and discontents. 'Kenneth told me he couldn't bear life any more; he asked me lots of questions about whether I was engaged and I didn't want to tell him. I would so much like to go back to Florence instead of this life I dislike so much. It's impossible to say just how much I miss R[osamund] every moment.' She went to a *tête-à-tête* luncheon with Harold's mother, who reminisced fondly about Harold as a little boy and showed Vita old photographs. This made her feel claustrophobic and she went straight to see Rosamund: 'Talked to her very frankly about Harold, and I don't think I love him enough to marry him. Before this talk I don't think I knew my own mind. But I'm going to let everything be for a bit. Perhaps something will happen!!'

There is nothing peculiar to the modern mind about a vivid, clever, attractive, complex girl of twenty being unwilling to tie herself down for life. Rather the reverse. The only happiness she trusted was the happiness she knew in her fugues with Rosamund, 'where nothing was boring and everything was easy'. In England, even Rosamund made problems, was jealous and possessive. She was wounded because Vita had gone to a party in her 'King's Son' costume: 'Have you no respect left for the byegone sacredness of the Miracle and the moonlight?' Patrick was writing her unhappy letters as well; she told her mother to invite him to Knole for Christmas. Lord Lascelles sent a Christmas present of a garnet cross, but was not invited.

Staying with the Wellesleys at Ewhurst in Hampshire just before Christmas, she sat in her room and fretted in her diary: 'Would it have been better, I wonder, if Harold had stayed in love with Eileen [Wellesley] and married her?' She could see nothing but trouble ahead. 'I can't, I can't, give up everything for him, at least I don't think so. ... If I didn't love him at all it would be so easy.' Why then had she not refused him straight away at Hatfield? 'Because he is so sweet, and so young, and he loves me, and we are happy together. I don't want to lose him, at least not yet. I am selfish and despise myself for it.'

And then, on Christmas Day, came a letter from Harold saying that he wanted to announce the wedding the next April (1913) and marry her in September. She showed the letter to her mother, who 'was nice about it'. 'Now it doesn't all frighten me so much, and I think I will marry him quite happily.'

Quite apart from the question of whether she should be marrying at all yet, perhaps her indecision was not only a reflection of her own temperamental ambivalence but, without knowing it, a response to Harold's: she always, on the occasions when Harold took positive action, responded almost gratefully, as if that was what she had been waiting for.

# CHAPTER 5

VITA played the young Caliph with a blacked-up face in the 'Persian Play' performed in the Great Hall over the New Year of 1913. Rosamund was Zuleika, a dancing girl, Violet a slave girl. Dada, Olive Rubens and Muriel Clark-Kerr were in it too. The audiences were 'horribly swank', consisting of peers and Cabinet ministers invited by Lady Sackville, plus their ladies – and Patrick Shaw-Stewart and Edward Horner.

Harold had left his car, Green Archie, with Vita and she made great use of it with Patrick and Rosamund. Her father gave her a room on the Green Court to use as a 'studio'; decorating it gave her great pleasure. 'I have absolutely no wish to leave Knole to go to Vienna!' she wrote on the day she took over her new room. In her letters, she did not try to conceal from Harold her distaste for the diplomatic life: 'And of course I shall hate diplomacy!... But I love you, little Harold, so what are we to do about it?'

Her girl friends fussed around her possessively. Rosamund, jealous of both Violet and Muriel, deluged Vita with letters when she left Knole. 'My sweet darling ... I *do miss you* darling one and I want to feel your soft coc! face coming out of that mass of pussy fur like I did last night.' Vita was irritated when her mother told her that Mrs Keppel had lamented she was so much with Rosamund that she could not find time for her own Violet.

Relations between Vita's parents were worsening. 'Mamma does not see that there can be faults on both sides. I talked to her very frankly, and she was angry.... Really this business makes me very unhappy.' What with her parents' troubles, the impending law case over Seery's will, Vita's vacillation over her engagement and the jealousies among the satellite girls, the emotional temperature at Knole was dangerously high. At a ball in February, Ivan Hay proposed for a second time. Rosamund's attitude to Vita's male admirers was simple: 'Darling I like to think that "Men may come and men may go, but I go on for ever", which is what it amounts to isn't it ?'

Meanwhile Vita and Harold in their letters were revealing aspects of their uncertainties – Harold seriously, Vita teasingly. Vita to Harold, 15 February 1913 :

And you know I'm not 'cultured' (how dare you !) but essentially primitive ; and not 1913, but 1470 ; and not 'modern' ; and you know that I am nicer than anyone else, and you love me more than anybody in the world – you know you do . . . and you know that if I leave my beautiful Knole which I adore, and my B.M.* whom I adore, and my Ghirlandaio room which I adore, and my books and my garden and my freedom, which I adore – it is all for you, whom I don't care two straws about.

She described to him a party she had given with Violet, 'the success of the year'. She told him – concealing the identity of Lord Lascelles – about an admirer who was 'a swank, more swank than you could ever dream of, the swankiest thing there is to be. And it chucks public dinners to come here . . . '

He wrote her a miserable letter. 'He says that I haven't written for 10 days, that I never go and see his mother, that I don't love him. I don't know what to reply.' When, for her twenty-first birthday on 9 March, she was given the valuable pearl necklace that Seery had left to her, Harold commented sadly that it was worth half of what he himself owned in all the world.

All Vita's admirers except the absent Harold were at the fancy-dress party for her birthday. Kenneth Campbell proposed the toast. 'I have been happy today,' Vita wrote in her diary. 'Vita was hideous, alas ! as an Italian beggar,' was her mother's verdict. Lord Lascelles was a pier-rot, and Patrick a Fellow of All Soles, with slippers hung all over his red domino.

The real emotional drama excluded the men. 'This jealousy between R[osamund] and V[iolet] will end badly,' Vita noted darkly. Two days later, in London, she walked in the park with Violet. 'She is mad ; she kissed me as she usually does not, and told me she loved me. Rose does not know that I went out with V. this evening.'

Lord Lascelles, encouraged by the invitation to the party, renewed his attack : 'You know quite well that you do not want the "poor little boy" to come back and make a fuss. . . . It is absurd to condemn yourself to Turkey and Rio for *pity*.' And two days later : 'We must be married in the

*B.M. for Bonne Maman – Harold's name for Lady Sackville, adopted by Vita.

summer and the whole thing must be settled when you get back from Spain.' Vita continued to play for time.

Spain, because of the wildly fantasized Pepita connection, was a place of high romance for Vita. 'It is my own country, you know, Harold, and my relations live there, and are swank, and poor, and proud, and descend from Lucrezia Borgia, as I do – Spain and Italy rolled into one.' She was taken to Spain by Mrs Charles Hunter, with whom she had often stayed at Hill Hall. Mary Hunter, the sister of the composer Ethel Smyth, entertained artists and musicians extravagantly, until in 1931 the money ran out and she had to sell up everything she had.

Vita was seen off by Rosamund and by her maid Emily, both of whom wept. At the Spanish frontier, Vita noted, 'I miss Rose terribly. I wouldn't have thought it possible.' Rosamund sent a letter ahead to the Ritz in Madrid : 'I certainly do not think H. could have been all this to you my little Mar and I feel still more certain that no one could be to me – I think we could do worse than spend our lives together Mar, I mean in days to come if neither of us have found something which can destroy what we have.'

Mrs Hunter's scandalous conversation and ostentatious habits made Vita stare; decades later she had not forgotten her liberality with the elbow-length white suede gloves she always wore: 'whenever they started to get dirty she peeled them off, rolled them up, and threw them out of the window.'[1] Once in Spain, Rosamund was forgotten and so was Harold; she could not even write to him. In Madrid she was bowled over by the dancing of Pastora Imperio. They were taken about by the linguist and future man of letters Maurice Baring, 'really a very charming man', and, in Seville, by the young diplomat Claude Russell, who intrigued her – 'mean and selfish, and most destructive, but still most attractive', as she told Harold when she felt able to write to him.

Claude took her to bullfights; she saw the great Belmonte. He took her to see the gypsies dancing and singing, and she was entranced. 'God, how free and happy I feel!' They ate with the dancers and were invited back to their house. 'I so much like this sort of Bohemian life.' Rosamund, in receipt of similar rhapsodies, wrote disapprovingly. Vita was dismissive. 'She is a stupid little thing, and her conventionality drives me mad. I suppose one is born either a free spirit or a prisoner.'

They went on to Granada, and thence to Algeciras, where Vita got a most unexpected letter from Rosamund, who was at Dartmouth Naval College, suddenly a free spirit herself and enjoying a romance with a naval instructor, Commander Reggie Raikes.

Vita took instantaneous revenge in a stinging letter designed to hurt Rosamund as much as possible. She was sarcastic and cold, saying she had decided to take Violet to the Villa Pestellini in Florence, and that she was afraid she would not have time to write. She ended, 'Oh, if I could cut you with the nib of my pen, as with the blade of a sword, I would do it!' This was blatant play-acting, but Vita believed in the roles she played.

She did indeed go home via Italy, and stayed with the Keppels in Ravello at the villa of Lord Grimthorpe (who was most probably Violet's natural father); and when she got home, Rosamund was engaged to her thirty-eight-year-old officer – but without much conviction. She wrote to Vita: 'Oh my sweet you do know don't you? that nothing can ever make me love you less whatever happens, and I really think you have taken all my love already as there seems very little left and I am so cold and heartless.'

Alone at Knole in May, in the anticlimax of her Spanish adventure, Vita felt that 'almost I want to marry Harold this year and get it over.' Depression made her hit out on the reverse tack: she sent him 'a letter that will make him jump', calling off the engagement. She identified with her mother, who was so unhappy; they were both unbroken horses, she decided. But she loved her father too. '"Nicer"! him, poor love; he's always nice, an absolute angel, but too simple to find his way about in the labyrinth of her mind.'

Could Harold, who was also 'always nice', find his way about in the labyrinth of Vita's mind? Could Rosamund? Or Violet? This last came to Vita's room at night 'and stayed till I don't know when; she has not re-pented of our last farewell, and loves me even more. She is fascinating, and will go a long way.' She never mentioned Harold to Violet at all.

Vita was playing tennis with her father when Harold's telegram arrived. He asked simply whether he was to take her letter seriously. She wired back 'No' – 'and then I scarcely knew what happened in my heart: something snapped, and I loved Harold from that day on.' It was his 'energy' in sending her a telegram that impressed her; it showed her how much he cared. She followed up her telegram with a reassuring letter. 'But I continued my liaison with Rosamund.'

She slipped back into the London season, enjoying herself at the Duchess of Marlborough's ball 'mostly with Claude [Russell]'. She lunched at the Ritz with the sculptor Rodin, the painter Sargent, and Mrs Astor:

I love that sort of party, it is such a relief after the little silly pink and whites one sits by at dinner parties for balls. After two days I am sick of it, except a very fine ball at Sunderland House, *un bal un peu propre*, not one of those scrimmages at the Ritz, but powdered footmen announcing duchesses. *N'est-ce pas dégoûtant d'être snob à ce point-là?*

Vita liked very grand parties – what she called 'touf-touf' parties – and she liked raffishness and Bohemia. What she didn't like was the middle ground.

Violet gave a birthday party, 'thé dansant! That's really very original.' At Mrs Sassoon's ball in June some people were saying that Vita was engaged to Harold Nicolson (who was coming home the following month), others that she was engaged to Bogey Harris, who paid her marked attention at an oriental evening at Mrs Carpenter's. 'He says there's no one like me, that I'm Roman, Sicilian, Greek, Venetian, I don't know what else! . . . After, we danced like lunatics, it was one of the best evenings.'

But around this time she was writing in her diary, 'These days I think so much about Harold that I can't sleep. I've got a mad longing to see him again, and I can't let him go out of my life. I shall marry him.' Irene Hogarth had married, and was now Mrs Pirie. 'Marriage suits her.' Even Violet had got engaged – to Lord Gerald Wellesley, while he was on leave from Constantinople, where he was a colleague of Harold's at the British Legation. He had given her a ring; Harold had not given Vita one. 'Do you know it has never once entered my head to give you one?' he wrote. 'Don't you think that's rather a good sign?'

The social activity of June 1913 culminated in the highly publicized court case in which the Scott family contested Seery's will. A few days before the case opened Vita was dining at Knole alone with her parents discussing the only subject, and Lady Sackville, after having been 'reasonably contradicted' by her husband, stormed out of the dining room saying she would leave him. Vita wrote: 'I'm frightened she'll do this when I'm gone. . . . Oh God I'm so upset.'

This was the family atmosphere in which the case opened. Lady Sackville rose to the occasion and emerged triumphant. Harold was on his way home when he saw reports of the case in the French newspapers. He hurried back and attended the second week of the hearing with the Sackvilles and Rosamund.

It was a titillating case: the Scotts were out to prove that Lady Sackville had exercised undue influence over Seery, implying all kinds of unpleasant things about her sexual and commercial morals and those of her husband. Society women, bringing cushions, filled the public seats. Each day's proceedings was reported in the papers, Vita being familiarly referred to as 'Kidlet', one of Seery's pet names for her. Lord Sackville was cross-questioned by F. E. Smith, for the Scotts, about his golf-playing with Lady Connie. Vita was called by Sir Edward Carson, Lady Sackville's defence counsel, to refute evidence given by a Major Arbuthnot that on an evening in July 1911 he had seen Lady Sackville surreptitiously going through Seery's private papers. Vita testified, with dignity, that she herself had been unwell that day, and that her mother had been at home and dined upstairs with her.

She wrote afterwards that she had felt like a coconut in a coconut shy; she took the whole thing, defensively perhaps, in a frivolous spirit – the papers noted how Kidlet whispered and laughed with Harold and Rosamund during the proceedings – and only realized afterwards how deeply humiliating and painful the case was for her father. After this, he sought comfort in the arms of Olive Rubens.

Lady Sackville's performance on the stand was, as Vita wrote in her diary, 'marvellous, a revelation'. She described her mother's virtuosity in 'Marian Strangways':

> Her evidence was miraculous in its elusiveness; she held the court's attention, charmed the judge, took the jury into her confidence, routed the opposing counsel, wept at some moments, looked beautiful and distressed, and bound Marian [Vita] more passionately to her. She wore blue, which matched her lovely eyes.... Marian knew storms of devotion to her mother. She criticized nothing.

Thus for Vita an immediate result of the case was 'a new worship for Mother, which had been incipient for several years'. Among Vita's manuscript papers are five pages of infatuated analysis of her mother's personality, written after the case – which ended in triumph and vindication for Lady Sackville on 7 July 1913. She now had the income from £150,000 to spend (the capital, by the terms of her marriage settlement, went into the Sackville Trust), plus all Seery's valuable French furniture from Paris. This she sold *en bloc* to the dealer Jacques Seligmann for £270,000: some of it ended up in the Frick Collection in New York. (Seery had left over £1,000,000: there was, in fact, plenty left for his resentful brothers and sisters.) Lady Sackville lost no time in letting her extravagant tastes run riot. 'How she flung money about that year!'

Vita's reunion with Harold had been without too much awkwardness, cushioned by the drama of the case. A week later their engagement was 'announced' in a gossip column in the *Daily Sketch*, which brought letters of outrage from Lord Lascelles. Vita had, at last, to admit to him her firm intention of marrying Harold in October.

She wrote two poems, 'The Prodigal' and 'Joy', alone at Knole with Harold and her mother. 'We're so happy, the three of us, as if we had been together always!' The engaged pair went to the Hunters at Hill Hall for a Saturday-to-Monday; it was a grand house-party, which included the Duke of Alba, the Princesse de Polignac, Bernard Berenson, Edith Wharton, Ethel Smyth ('horrible woman'), Lady Cunard and

Thomas Beecham. The two young ones kept apart. 'After lunch I talked to Harold again, on the grass; we were happy.' They were happy like children, like 'mars', as they often said; Vita wrote in her poem 'MCMXIII', celebrating this wonderful relief from the heavy emotionalism that had surrounded her :

> I followed him into the sun,
> And laughed as he desired,
> And every day upon the grass
> We play till we are tired.[2]

Back at Knole she wrote up her diary. 'I love him so much. Now there's no doubt; at first, I loved him one day and not the next; but now I think of nothing but him; I would go away with him tomorrow, even to Vienna; nothing frightens me.'

Yet they did not draw too closely together; they expressed more, and were equally happy, in their letters when apart. 'The nectar between them crystallized in the letters, became a durable thing; a glimpse of Paradise permitting a return.'[3] Thus they set up, so early, this parallel relationship between their different, letter-writing selves. It was to be the chief support of their marriage, a communication unbroken when not only geography but temperament and other people came between them. Harold could write to Vita the lover-like things he could never say :

> But darling I do feel so funny inside about Oct – oh my darling darling Vita who will be so absolutely mine one day – mine in a way that possession has nothing to do with – and which will be a sort of fire-fusion darling – and there are such wonderful, terrifying abysmal things that will happen in our amazing marriage ... oh my darling you don't know how passionate I am – and how it frightens me – and how glad I am of it.

For August Bank Holiday weekend they drove with B.M. in her Rolls to Somerset to stay with Mrs Heneage at Coker Court, 'buying furniture all the way'. Lady Sackville helped them choose a diamond and emerald engagement ring, and the forthcoming marriage was formally announced in the *Morning Post*. Vita and her mother went to the couturier Reville to discuss wedding dresses. (Lady Sackville was sick at heart over her husband's passion for Olive Rubens; she diverted herself by shopping with wild extravagance for Vita.)

The announcement brought forth floods of tears from Rosamund, who found her decent sailor to be a very poor consolation prize. Vita was 'cold as ice' to Rosamund now, which Harold, who liked her, could not understand. Violet, on the other hand, he thought 'a vulgar little girl'. Harold also thought Vita might try to be nicer to his mother and his schoolgirl sister Gwen: 'she is such a passionately affectionate personality, and she *has* a personality.' Vita could never summon up more than a token enthusiasm for Sir Arthur Nicolson and still less for Lady Nicolson. She was fond of Harold's great friend Archie Clark-Kerr – 'the only one of my friends', as he told Vita, 'that I am really sentimental about.'

At the end of August they went on a trip with B.M. to Interlaken in Switzerland, where they were joined by William Waldorf Astor. He took Lady Sackville off on her own, thus leaving the young pair with more freedom than they had expected: Vita's diary betrays some surprise, even some dismay, that her mother left them so much to themselves. (B.M.'s dynamic presence was a support to their still rather tentative relationship.) They remained companions rather than lovers; when Vita was unwell, 'Harold pulled my bed over to the window and we watched the sunset on the snow on the mountain. . . . We were so happy together.'

Rosamund's despair reached her by mail. 'It is only Harold, Harold, and I know now that you will sacrifice me and everything to him.' While Vita was abroad, the first poem of hers ever to be published appeared in *The English Review*. 'A Dancing Elf' was about Rosamund at the Villa Pestellini; it was dedicated to 'R.G.' and dated 'Florence, 1912'. The *Daily Sketch*, picking this up, asked coyly 'Who is the lucky R.G.?' and telegraphed to Knole to find out. Dada wrote to Vita saying that he supposed she did not particularly want the *Sketch* to know who 'R.G.' was; he took the opportunity to say more:

You know how bad I am about saying things but I am glad to see you so happy as I think you now are, and it is rather nice being fond of someone, isn't it? and you know that I like Harold awfully and I have never minded in the least his not being a Duke . . . you owe an awful lot to Harold for being so fond of you, as for a man to give you all his love is a big thing and takes a lot of paying back.

Rosamund, so far from being flattered by the publication of 'A Dancing Elf', was furious. 'How *dare you* put *my* very own beautiful poem in an ordinary magazine for all the eyes of the common public to gaze on?'

Vita returned via Paris with her mother, whom she found 'lavish' and 'adorable' as they shopped for her trousseau. On impulse, Lady Sackville took her daughter to Chaumet the jeweller and 'suddenly bought a string of emeralds and diamonds and gave it to me. It is magnificent, and I'm stunned. She really is an incomparable creature.' Vita went alone to see Rodin in the rue de Varennes, as she had arranged when she met him in London, and he gave her a small signed bronze of a walking man as a wedding present. Harold could not compete ; he felt put on one side :

> I feel so dreadfully that you do not care nearly as much for me. .... I don't mind really, as all I want is for you to let me adore you – and then, when we are married, perhaps you will get to care for me too. I mean really care – not just like. Except that I know you care more than just like already – but it is not that absolute abandonment of self that I feel.

The wedding was only a fortnight away. Harold's perceptions were accurate. Vita was taken up with, and taken over by, her mother in her most glamorous manifestation, giving her daughter all her attention and approval for the first time in years and loading her with gifts. Vita's conception of love was 'un poison mortel dont on demande encore'.[4] In 'Marian Strangways' she described how during her engagement she found little of the *poison mortel* in Harold or in her relations with him, but a great deal of the 'merry guide' :

> Behold a youth that trod
> With feathered cap on forehead
> And poised a golden rod,
> With mien to match the morning
> And gay delightful guise [5]

– a poem, she wrote, not intended as a love poem 'yet perhaps adaptable as the truest love poem of all'. She and he were 'more than lovers, they were friends ... and seriously predicted a world happier in the future for marriages based on such friendly sincerity.' What she loved in Harold was his gaiety, his optimism, his tolerance, his intelligence and his honesty. Whether all this made them as she said 'more than lovers' or less than lovers is a matter of opinion.

One effect of his honesty and simplicity was to make her see her mother, at a time when they were closer than ever before, in a less golden light. 'Already a slight wonderment at her mother's methods was awakening in her ; she saw now that Basil [Harold] was simple and easy ... confusedly she puzzled over the difference between him and her mother, but rather pathetically she drew back when she feared to blunder upon some revealing truth inconsistent with her loyalty.'[6]

The wedding took place in the chapel at Knole on 1 October 1913. The preceding days were tense. Rosamund made scenes about her brides-maid's present from Harold, but then pulled herself together. More than 600 wedding presents were put on display in the Great Hall, the

star exhibits being the jewels, mainly emeralds and diamonds, that
Lady Sackville had given Vita, arranged in show-cases. Lord Lascelles
sent a crystal and diamond hat-pin; Orazio Pucci sent a tortoise-shell
box; Violet Keppel sent an amethyst and diamond ring, but did not
come to the wedding.

'I'm dead tired,' Vita wrote in her diary the night before her wedding, 'and I cried for an hour this evening thinking of Knole. Rose
cheered me up, she is a good kind friend, and I appreciate her. – The
last night . . . ' She dated her poem 'To Knole', 1 October 1913:

> I left thee in the crowds and in the light,
> And if I laughed or sorrowed none could tell.
> They could not know our true and deep farewell
> Was spoken in the long preceding night.[7]

Her mother, that evening, had announced that she was too unwell to
attend the ceremony next day. There was general murmuring of sympathy and regret – and general relief.

On the wedding morning Harold and Vita had a 'sharp impersonal
altercation' about the arrangement of their presents. But in the chapel
their eyes met 'and it flashed into their minds simultaneously that
this was the most tremendous lark out of which they must get the
most fun possible.'[8] Rosamund and Harold's sister Gwen were the
chief bridesmaids. The Bishop of Rochester married them; Walter
Rubens played the organ and Olive Rubens, in 'chestnut-red velvet
trimmed with skunk', sang. Vita's dress was natural-coloured silk encrusted with gold. There was room for only twenty-six people in the
chapel; but hundreds, headed by four duchesses and including all
the jurymen from the Seery case (invited by Lady Sackville) were at
the reception.

Here Harold, if Vita's account in 'Marian Strangways' is to be
believed, behaved oddly: 'he wouldn't stand beside her to shake
hands in the Great Hall, but disappeared into the library to read a
book.' Perhaps he did, just for a moment. More chilling is the account
of their going away. She, in her new leopard furs – another lavish gift
from her mother – started off alone towards a back door. 'They
hauled her back and said, "Not that way. And you've forgotten
something." She looked mystified. "Your husband." They got her
husband from somewhere . . . and somebody had her dog on a lead.'
If this has not historic truth, it may have something of Vita's poetic
truth.

In the train they ate sandwiches and drank champagne from a
thermos. Vita felt shy – 'quite happy, and so gentle and darling', as

Harold reported to B.M. – and went to sleep. It was nine o'clock in the evening before they reached Coker Court, which Mrs Heneage had lent them for the start of their honeymoon.

What Vita wrote in her room at Coker that night – they had communicating rooms – was very simple.

> Today I married Harold. Mama did not get up. . . . Towards midday I went to get dressed, all in gold, it was a great success. Then I went into Mama, with Rose, Gwen, and the two children, Diana [Sackville-West] and Rosemary Stanley, and then I joined Dada in the ballroom to go to the chapel. The corridor was lined with soldiers. At the service, I felt very pleased, then after there were so many people. . . . There were letters and telegrams here, and we had dinner in the tiny room next to the dining room.
>
> *Dunque si è culminato così!*

She expanded that enigmatic comment in 'Marian Strangways'. After dinner, Harold had sat on, talking to her at great length about his uncle Lord Dufferin and Ava, who had been Viceroy of India. She listened silently, thinking that 'this, then, was the culmination of these months, this the immediate result of those words spoken when they sat on ludicrous hat-boxes at a ball; into this had resolved itself for her the secret of life.'

And so, at last, to bed.

# PART II
# CHANGE AND
# CHALLENGE
## 1913-21

# CHAPTER 6

THE next morning they sat in the garden and wrote letters. Vita to her mother: 'I can't tell you what Harold has been, so full of tact and gentleness and consideration, and I could not have believed that such happiness was possible. I will tell you a great deal I cannot write.' And in her diary the same day: 'Now everything seems more true to me. I never dreamt of such happiness.'

When they went back to London two days later, Vita slept at Hill Street and Harold with his parents at Cadogan Gardens, 'a regrettable arrangement' as he said. Vita went for a long walk with her mother in St James's Park.

Vita in 'Marian Strangways', written not long after her marriage, described her sexual initiation in the most positive and welcoming way – and in somewhat florid language.

> Then, rapidly, overwhelmingly, everything changed, and she knew nothing save that she lay crushed in his arms in the fierce night. . . . She knew that at last an irresistible cosmic force of nature, no longer to be denied, had flung their two lives together and shattered them into one. . . . She now knew the truth of all voids in her life, and they were plenteously filled as with the rush of many springing rivers. Her companionable love for Basil [Harold], half-friendship, half-playfellowship, had not sufficed. She lost all reason save of her primitive instincts . . . he was her man and her master, and in her awakening womanhood she desired nothing but that she might yield to him the most abased subjection.

Though romanticized and filled out, maybe, with a certain amount of wishful thinking, 'Marian Strangways' is the manifesto of Vita's conventional, heterosexual development; the manuscript of 1920, published in *Portrait of a Marriage*, is the record of the other side of her nature and of her love for a woman, written with some remorse and some pride, and a little distorted by the fact that she was still involved with Violet. In 'Marian Strangways' she overvalued her sexual relationship with Harold, but in the 1920 manuscript she undervalued it. There she wrote that the early years of her marriage were unparalleled 'for sheer joy of companionship'. 'Harold was like a sunny harbour to me. It was all open, frank, certain; and although I never knew the physical passion I had felt for Rosamund, I didn't really miss it.'

Vita saw Rosamund that night at Hill Street, to say goodbye, 'which bored me very much', she wrote in her diary, 'as I couldn't live up to the level of her emotion'. Harold and Vita set out next morning on the honeymoon proper, in Florence. Elaborate precautions had been taken to prevent Rosamund from knowing that they were staying in the cottage at the Villa Pestellini. 'Poor Rose!' Vita wrote in her diary, 'she doesn't know we are here, she thinks we are at the hotel.' She and Harold had been up to the Belvedere at sunset: 'Oh God, thank you for the sun, for the cypresses, and for our youth.' Later, she felt ashamed of bringing Harold to the little house she had shared with Rosamund so recently. 'Besides being disloyal to Rosamund, it was a dreadful *manque de délicatesse*.'[1]

However happy she was with Harold, and however bored with Rosamund's sentimentality, Vita wrote to her from Florence all the time: 'I believe you have not minded half so much as you thought you would. For me, I have minded more. ... I think our letters cannot be natural for a week or two – neither yours nor mine. There has been too much earthquake. Oh Lord I can't talk about it.' She told Rosamund that constraint between them was inevitable, 'unless one was willing to embark on abysmal depths, and I feel at present they are too abysmal to be sounded by a plumb-line, or that if the plumb-line did reach the bottom it would be hauled up again with tears and a little bit of torn heart sticking to it. I think perhaps it will be better when I am no longer in Florence.'

Yet she was patently happy in Florence, happy with Harold. Was she deceiving herself, and her diary, or was she deceiving Rosamund? With Vita, both were possible. She was a person who saw both sides of a coin at the same time.

They moved on eastwards on their way to Constantinople and Harold's work as third secretary. At Brindisi they were joined by Vita's maid Emily and Harold's valet Wilfred Booth (whom they called Wuffy) and their heavy luggage. On the boat to Alexandria, Vita wrote archly to Rosamund that 'it seemed wrong that I should be travelling alone with Harold, who isn't even a relation.'

They stayed at the British Agency in Cairo with Lord Kitchener for ten days. This had been fixed by the 'grown-ups' and Vita hated the idea. But she was impressed by her first glimpse of her young husband in action : at dinner 'Harold and K[itchener] talked Oriental politics ! I like it very much when he talks like that.' She saw the Pyramids, but in Luxor got sunstroke and lost her voice, and the formal dinners became an ordeal. 'Six or eight speechless, intimidated officers sat round the table ; Kitchener's bleary eyes roamed over them ; my own hoarse whisper alone punctuated the silence. Egyptian art came up as a topic. "I can't", growled Kitchener, "think much of a people who drew cats the same for four thousand years." '[2] When she was better Harold took her sailing on the Nile : 'He is a love ; I didn't know that such goodness existed.'

She wrote to her mother – who was cheering herself up in Paris, being sculpted by Rodin – as their boat neared Constantinople : 'We have awful suspicions that Emily and Wuffy share a cabin, but don't like to investigate any further.' She and Harold on the other hand, patrician and fastidious, had a three-berthed cabin each. They had been travelling too long for it to be fun any more : 'At present we are both rather sulky and cross – not with each other though.'

They had been married a month when they reached Constantinople. 'All sorts of people came to meet us' – Harold's colleagues Gerry Wellesley and Eddie Keeling, and her Uncle Bertie Sackville-West, who was inspector of the Ottoman Public Debt Office in Constantinople, 'and people in beautiful clothes who kissed Harold's hands'. She was impressed by how popular he was with everyone. She was still astonished by his consistent sweetness, and wrote to her mother on arrival that 'living with Harold is like living with a sort of very human and very merry angel, and it gets more so every day ; I never knew people could have such natures . . . I don't honestly think it is because I happen to be in love with him that makes me think him so loveable.'

To Rosamund (to whom, to her chagrin, she found she was writing much more often than Rosamund was to her), Vita described her first married home. 'It is a wooden Turkish house, with a little garden, and a pergola of grapes, and a pomegranate tree covered with scarlet fruit, and such a view over the Golden Horn, and the sea, and Santa Sophia ! And on the side of a hill, a perfect suntrap.' Having expected Constantinople to be 'beastly', she said, 'I find it lovely.'

At the back of the house, the hill sloped down to the Bosphorus, with Scutari and Asia on the further shore. Their living quarters included an upstairs sitting-room for each of them, plus a drawing-room and a smoking-room ; downstairs were their adjacent bedrooms and the dining-room. Vita was excited by everything. To her mother, the day they moved in :

> We have got a beautiful Montenegrin as a footman, and a chef like a Greek god, he is really, I tremble for Emily. . . . Harold's Persian room is going to be blue like the blue of my bedroom walls at Knole. . . . This is an extraordinary place for white jade. I bought a lump six inches long and nearly as thick as my wrist for 12 francs and it is now going to be the handle for pulling our door-bell. I find an alarming reputation for originality and 'art treasures' has pre-ceded us, and we are both racking our brains to know how to live up to it.

This was the first of their successful collaborations in creating an en-vironment. As it always would, it drew them close. Harold, knowing Vita's antipathy to diplomatic life, was anxious about her reactions, noting always in his diary whether she seemed bored or amused by the many teas, dinners, dances and receptions that as members of the diplo-matic community they were expected to attend. Indeed she was some-times bored by them but she liked Sir Louis Mallet, Harold's chief, she liked Harold's special friends, Pierre de Lacretelle and Reggie Cooper, and domestically she was happy. She wrote in her diary after three weeks in Constantinople: 'My hesitations of last year about Harold seem incredible now. But I do understand it; I didn't know him, he was always away, in fact it is surprising that I was so faithful to him. Now he seems perfect to me, and truly he is – so gay, so funny, so clever, so *young*. I've never really known him until now.' But still she fretted because Rosamund wrote so infrequently. Vita wrote her pleading, plaintive letters, cruel hectoring letters and a poem, 'Disillusion'. Vita did not like anyone who loved her to stop loving her, ever. Not that Rosamund had stopped. B.M., who saw her in London, noted that she was 'very dismal about Vita'. But Rosamund had her pride.

The need for contact with Rosamund was more, for Vita, than emotional imperialism. Her old friend was part of the home world. B.M. sent them out plum puddings and mince pies for Christmas and there was a shipment of pictures and personal belongings from Knole. Vita wrote to Rosamund on 6 December: 'I sometimes get quite humanly homesick when I am with Uncle Bertie, for instance, and see the old familiar crest on their silver; and when I was unpacking my things from Knole, and came across everything which was part of everyday life. . . . I have the 2 watercolours of my room hanging up in the sitting-room here, and they give me a lump in my throat.'

The following day Vita went for a consultation with Dr Maclean at the English Hospital. It was not for another two weeks that he was able to confirm her suspicions. Vita was pregnant. It was the week before Christmas.

'I was pleased,' wrote Vita later, 'but Harold was most pleased. His slightly medical attitude was the only thing that annoyed me. ... He wrote a letter to my mother about it which I tore up in a fury, which he couldn't understand at all.'[3] She wrote to her mother herself; the baby was due in early August, and they arranged to come home on leave for the birth. B.M., characteristically, wrote in her diary: 'Poor little girl! How I should love to be with her now and have great talks.'

Consulting no one, B.M. asked Lord Astor to be godfather to Vita's baby. Lionel was furious: 'He said it looked *intéressé* and what would the world say! I told him he did not realize what good friends we were.' Nevertheless she wrote to 'Tom' Astor retracting the invitation. Then, suffering from severe menopausal discomforts, she went off to Paris to see Rodin and Renoir, and thence to her old flame Buggy – Baron Bildt – in Rome, whose loyal affection comforted her for the loss of Vita, and of Lionel, who kept 'trying to like me but even physically is absolutely unable to do so'.

Lionel and Olive Rubens, and Olive's husband Walter, went to visit the young Nicolsons in Constantinople in April 1914, and Rosamund arrived a few days later. Vita was delighted to have them all, and gave a big party. She was in a matchmaking frame of mind. Rosamund had broken off her engagement to Reggie Raikes, and Vita thought Reggie Cooper might do nicely for her. Another broken engagement was that between Gerry Wellesley and Violet Keppel; in March Vita and Harold had met Gerry's new fiancée, who came out to see him. She was Dorothy – 'Dottie' – Ashton. 'She is very rich,' Vita noted in her diary. (Dottie, the stepdaughter of the Earl of Scarborough, had inherited a fortune and an estate in Cheshire from her brother.) The couple were married that summer.

Lord Sackville and his party sent favourable reports to B.M. in Rome. 'Lionel says Vita's touf-touf party was most successful. ... Her figure is still normal; Olive says they adore each other and are radiantly happy.' B.M. herself was thinking of staying on in Rome, pathetically manufacturing a parallel idyll between herself and Buggy: 'We are so happy together and he is with me what Harold must be with Vita.' The only flaw in this arrangement was Baroness Bildt, Buggy's 'unreasonable wife', who made difficulties, 'stupid woman'. It might not be practicable, after all, to settle in Rome.

Nor was she being encouraged to see her daughter and have great talks. Lionel said the journey would make her ill, and 'Harold writes to me I shall have to be careful with V. she has become so irritable on account of her state. It is so unlike my sweet child.' It was hardly worthwhile making the trip anyway since in mid-June, Harold and Vita came home. They left the dog Mikki II with a friend, and locked up their house, full of their wedding presents and recently acquired treasures. They would be back soon, or so they thought.

Vita was reunited with her mother at the Hotel Edouard VII in Paris. Lady Sackville, who had just heard that her litigious brother Henry had committed suicide, was emotional, but thrilled to see Vita. 'She hardly shows she is *enceinte* and she is looking beautiful; they are undoubtedly much in love.' Vita, for her part, found her mother quite unchanged: 'the same chaos of letters and parcels; Rodin on the telephone; Spealls business; what a personality!' She noticed, after this long absence, her mother's strong French accent when speaking English.

Three days after the reunion Lady Sackville was already finding cause for complaint: 'They are so wrapped up in each other and so happy. I feel I don't count any more.... She is very reserved about herself.... Naturally H. is everything to her now and the baby, and I feel I am hardly wanted. No confidences, nothing but general talk.'

Back home, Knole had 'never seemed so lovely' to Vita. Harold went for a short holiday on his father-in-law's new yacht *Sumurun* (nobly paid for by Lady Sackville). 'I miss him horribly,' wrote Vita. Her mother missed Harold less. 'Vita and I had such a nice talk, *intime*, at last.' It was still not so *intime* as she would have liked; she commented that 'Vita is very innocent still!'

While Harold was away, Vita saw her old friends – Rosamund (who was agitating to be the baby's sole godmother), Muriel Clark-Kerr, Violet – and read Harold's uxorious letters from *Sumurun* to 'my own darling wife'. She herself wrote him a letter, a supplement to her will, to be opened in the event of her dying in childbirth. He was to give Rosamund some of her jewels, and anything else she wanted; other jewels were earmarked for Irene ('Pace') Pirie and for Muriel, and 'my small sapphire and diamond ring' for Violet. She requested him to keep his first present to her, the wooden figure of St Barbara, always in his own room: 'she knew us both so well from the very beginning.' And then she wrote:

> Darling, I suppose I must say goodbye, because if ever this letter comes to you it will be after a bigger goodbye than we have ever said. Anyhow we shall have had nearly a year of absolutely unmarred perfect happiness together, and you know I loved you as completely as one person has ever loved another. ... If I could have these months over again I would not alter a day of them, – would you? I don't think many people could say as much.

The birth was imminent; war in Europe was imminent. Vita's father was mobilizing his West Kent Yeomanry. Also imminent was the publication of Vita's first book of poems. John Lane of the Bodley Head had accepted it, and came down to Knole for luncheon. War with Germany was declared five days later; Lord Sackville was telephoned during dinner to join his regiment. Harold was to be kept for the moment at the Foreign Office and they were not to return to Constantinople. Two days after, Vita had pains in the evening; she went into labour at ten o'clock.

At three o'clock in the morning Lady Sackville was still sitting outside Vita's room. Doctors and nurses went in and out. The baby – a boy – was not born until half past four the following afternoon, and at seven o'clock Vita's mother was allowed to go in.

She started to make trouble at once. She took offence because Vita did not ask to see her a second time that evening and because Harold had asked Olive Rubens to be a godmother. As a result, in the morning she went off to London in a rage. All Vita recorded was: Thursday 6 August 'Today at half-past four my son was born.' Friday 7 August 'Mama went to London and refused to see me.' Lady Sackville came back, fulminating against Harold for taking Vita away from her, as she put it. Vita lay upstairs and wrote her poem 'Convalescence', about how she would always recall

> Those all too leisured hours as they went by
> Stamped as a heritage upon my thought
> The memory of a square of summer sky
> Jagged by the gables of a Gothic court.[4]

Harold, spending the week-day nights in London, wrote to her twice a day. Her mother rarely saw her except to make scenes. Her father, stationed in Gravesend, advised her to take no notice. 'Anyhow you have got Harold and your mar, and you and I always hang together, don't we?' (He discreetly enclosed a letter to Olive, who was staying at Knole.)

Three weeks after the baby was born, B.M. 'came in the evening to scream at me, and after dinner ... she refused to see me. I think she is crazy and try to excuse her. I'm still very weak, and she's making me ill. Harold isn't here.'

But his letters were loving, referring to their happy times, giving a glimpse of a moody Vita in Constantinople: 'I long to see my darling – and be soundly snubbed when I come in – like you used to do at Cple. do you remember? You used to go on writing with your pretty little head over your table and refusing to turn round. Darling ... ' And two days later: 'Oh my darling please don't snub me tomorrow. Vita I simply worship you my own saint.' He was cheered up by a visit from Pierre de Lacretelle, and Rosamund came to join the motley occupants of Knole.

('I hate to think of you and Rose talking shut-outs [secrets] together,' wrote Harold.)

Lady Sackville's resentments were justifiably fuelled by the almost permanent presence of Rosamund and Olive at Knole, both of whom were nursing at the local hospital. 'I get sick of them always here.' But a major snub was Vita and Harold's decision to call their baby 'Benedict Lionel' instead of 'Lionel Benedict'. Lionel himself did not mind in the least, but she chose to see it as an unforgiveable insult. Rosamund sent up a note to Vita: 'She says "if she prefers the name Benedict to her mother's love she is welcome to it". . . . I almost advise you to give in . . . I really think she was almost mad this evening.'

The baby was christened Lionel Benedict, according to his grandmother's wishes, on 20 September. Rosamund, Olive and Violet – 'at her own sarcastic request' – were the godmothers, Kenneth Campbell and Baron Bildt the godfathers. Nevertheless, Lady Sackville was unappeased, and stormed off to London again. The cause now was that Vita and Harold were not going to *call* the baby Lionel (they referred to him when he was tiny as 'Detto', short for 'Benedetto'). Vita drafted several letters to her mother, veering between defiance and conciliation, and showing how shocked and shaken she was by this stupid quarrel.

> So much strife and discord have passed over his little head, and though I have struggled to keep him mine, the only thing I owe to nobody but Harold, I must give him up. After all, he was absolutely mine for nine months, and I suppose I must not expect more than that. . . .
>
> I know now you don't love me, and that at the very first strain I put upon your love you are ready to fling me aside like an old glove. I always knew you were unlike other people, and could make yourself as hard as granite, but I did think that me at least you really loved. . . . You have given me your lavish generosity, it is true, but the generosity of the heart which I should have valued infinitely more you have denied me. . . . It is hard to lose faith in that which one has idolized.

Vita's relationship with her mother was often more like a stormy love affair than anything else.

She and Harold did the sensible thing and moved out of Knole; they rented a house in London – 182 Ebury Street, Pimlico – and life became normal again. 'I became quite sociable,' Vita wrote later. This was 'the only period of my life when I achieved anything like popularity. I was no longer plain, I took adequate trouble to make myself agreeable, Harold was loved by everyone that met him. . . . I was so happy I even forgot to suffer from *Wanderlust*.' With hindsight, under the influence of her passion for Violet, she was to add, 'Oh God, the horror of it.'[5] But there was no horror at all, at the time. And by December 1914, when her first baby was only four months old, she was pregnant again.

They spent that first Christmas of the Great War at Knole. On 28 December, the household heard that a tree had fallen on a car approaching the house. Vita was waiting for Harold to arrive – 'never, no *never* have I been so anxious.' But it was only poor Rosamund, returning from the hospital, with a cut head and a broken nose. Vita's anxiety about Harold was also allayed in a graver matter : he had been given complete exemption from military service for work at the Foreign Office.

So their happy domesticity was not to be disturbed. Vita stayed on at Knole over the New Year of 1915 ; on 5 January Harold wrote to her that their little Detto was 'an unconscious and eternal pledge of all those early months of such love as we have had my sweetest. Detto is, is not he, a little repository – an ostensory almost – of all our fugitive moments when we have been nearest to each other.'

# CHAPTER 7

WHILE AT Knole Vita finished a play, 'The Amber Beam', that she had begun in Constantinople, never to be performed or published. It was about womanly, self-sacrificial Beatrice, who for thirty years had supported and tended the genius of a great sculptor. There is no suggestion that Beatrice resents this life of service and subservience. Undemanding devotion is presented as the ideal. Happy marriage, for Vita, was standing out in blessed relief from her mother's deranged emotionalism. There was another bad row that January in London : 'I was meant to have lunch with her before a matinée, but I went away and had lunch with Harold in an Italian restaurant; so what does it matter, when I have him ?' But it always would matter, to Vita.

A few weeks later she saw a house called Long Barn for sale in Weald village, only a couple of miles from Knole. 'It would do very well indeed.' She took Harold and then her mother to see it and they both approved. From that moment relations with her mother were 'much better, more normal and peaceful'. The house was bought in March 1915 for £2,500 ; on 10 April, Harold and Vita and the baby and his nurse, and Emily and Wuffy, and the servants, moved in. 'I'm thrilled with everything! Dada came to tea. Harold came home early.'

Long Barn is a very old house. The tradition is that Caxton, the father of English printing, was born there. A coin of 1360 was found behind the plaster when the Nicolsons were renovating it. Vita loved the house for its antiquity, for its associations and because it belonged to her and Harold. She wrote in her diary on the last day of May :

The weather this May has been magnificent; I work in the garden, I work several hours a day on my history of Italy, I pick up Harold in the evening at the station with Archie [the motor-car] – warm, sweet, spring evenings – I play with Detto, I think of his sister who will be born in September, and I am very

happy. We are more in love than ever. I thank God that I have known absolute happiness.

H. goes at 9 in the morning and all day the thought of his return is like a ray
of sunshine. But I feel guilty seeing other people's misery in this time of war.

A friend who came to luncheon told her that 'the doors of our house are
like glimpses of paradise. Which indeed it is.' To complete the harmony,
Emily and Wuffy got married in mid-June.

Although Vita and Harold had loved their wild garden in Constantinople, they had not had time to develop it. That summer, Vita
began to garden seriously. She knew almost nothing about it. Their very
first planting had been a clump of primroses that they had dug up in the
woods and replanted on the bank in the garden. She wrote her first
garden poem :

> We waited then for all to grow,
> We planted wallflowers in a row.
> And lavender and borage blue, –
> But love was all that ever grew.[1]

One day at the end of June she handed Harold a note to read in the
train ; she had been looking at his letters to her from their engagement
period and saw how all their dreams had come true. 'There is a great
warm enveloping radiance, and Detto stands for wonderful things ...
and every evening when you come back our minds and our hands rush
together and merge.' She did not love him morbidly, she told him, 'but
strongly, and passionately, and every way.'

An affectionate routine was even established with B.M., who wrote
that summer that 'I see her and her darling baby nearly every day. I
seldom go there when H. is there, as I know they prefer to be alone
together.'

B.M.'s own problems were not resolved. Lionel had converted and
furnished the old laundry at Knole as an apartment for Olive and Walter
Rubens ; Walter was away at the war and Olive was installed there on
her own. 'I found out by mere chance that when L. came here, he had
even his breakfast alone with Olive in the Laundry.' She was ordering
marmalade for his breakfast when the maid blurted out the truth of his
arrangements, 'and I pretended I knew it and had forgotten it.' It was
horribly humiliating. There was talk and B.M. received a few anony-
mous letters. Walter Rubens was complaisant, referring to 'our dear little
home'. Lady Sackville struggled with herself. 'I want to be happy and
radiate happiness and have "Peace within".' She gave Vita and Harold
a Rolls-Royce, and they engaged a driver called Bond. B.M. was

glamorous and wonderful again in Vita's eyes. Harold's mother, who came to stay at Long Barn, could not match her: 'I got angry with her old-fashioned ideas.'

In late September Lord Sackville went away with his regiment to the Dardanelles and Gallipoli. Vita was upset saying goodbye to him; she was unwell and her second baby was due. Before he left, her father wrote to her:

> I am thinking of you, Mar dear, and all the trouble and pain before you and it strikes me how selfish I was today as we talked of nothing but me, when you have so much before you. You seemed to think that I didn't know or appreciate your love for me which is just wrong, Mar dear, because you and I are so alike and are not always able to show these things. But I know you have always been more to me than perhaps I have ever quite realized, and probably you have felt the same.

Her father saw that he and she were 'so alike'. Vita was also uncomfortably like her mother. Since her parents had proved so incompatible, it is no wonder that the temperamental heritage each gave Vita caused conflict within her and sometimes total war. Her father never failed Vita in spite of his reserve and in spite of the quiet ruthlessness with which he fought to free himself from Vita's mother. Her mother on the other hand failed Vita constantly, like an unpredictable female deity.

Vita's baby was weeks overdue. She did not go into labour until 1 November. Twenty-four hours later the doctor realized that the baby, still unborn, was dead. He summoned a colleague. Vita was anaesthetized for five hours while the 9-pound baby boy was extracted with instruments. 'I had to go to London, to the Bank,' wrote Lady Sackville blandly in her diary. 'Saw Harold very dejected in the evening. ... He said she was black and blue all over, as the doctors had had to squeeze her terribly, especially over the stomach.'

Vita was in bed until the end of November, during which time Detto learnt to walk by himself. One night towards the end of that month, she scribbled a desperate letter to Harold in London on the back of a letter from Messrs Marshall & Snelgrove.

> Harold, Mar is sad, she is thinking of that little white velvet coffin with that little still thing inside. ... I can't help minding and I always shall, I mind more when I see Detsey how sweet and sturdy he is, and the other would have been just the same. It isn't so much that I grudge all the long time or the beastly end, as everybody thinks, I mind him being dead because he is such a person. ... Detsey makes it worse as well as better. I can't bear to hear of

people with two children. Oh Harold darling why did he die? Why, why, why did he? Oh Harold I wish you were here.

Here she ran out of paper – and continued on the back of a map of the journeys of St Paul torn from her Bible. 'I try and stave it off, not to think about it, and when I am alone it rushes out at me. . . . Harold I want you so badly, I wish I could go to sleep.'

She got better and at the beginning of December went up to London. 'Lunch alone with Harold and it is as if we were newly married.' She took little Detto – whom they now began to call Ben – to Marshall & Snelgrove to buy him a dressing-gown. 'Very good, no tears, rather overawed altogether.'

They were making improvements at Long Barn. Harold had made a formal plan for the garden, and they were having the ancient barn in the field dismantled and its timbers reassembled as the basis of a new wing at right angles to the house, giving them a fifty-foot drawing-room – the 'Big Room' – and two extra bedrooms. As their son Nigel has written, Long Barn 'was not simple', even though it was the merest cottage in comparison with Knole. By the time they had finished there were seven main bedrooms and four bathrooms.

Vita's accommodation was better than Harold's. She had as her writing and sitting room the best downstairs room apart from the Big Room; it had windows on two sides, a fine fireplace, and she set her writing-table across the middle. Her bedroom too was large, with a wildly sloping floor, down which her children used to race tennis balls. Harold's bedroom was a sort of slip-room off hers. A small study was built on to the Big Room for him later. Once there were two of them, the children did not live in the main house at all; they and their nanny occupied the small 'gardener's cottage' that came with the house.

After Christmas Vita stayed on at Knole for a while as she had the previous year. She and Harold had been incessantly intimate in their recent joys and troubles. Now she wrote to him: 'Darling, how elaborate one is; at least you are not, you are a dear simple straightforward merry guide; so perhaps you won't understand it when I say it is almost a relief to be parted.' It was bewildering and tiring, she wrote, to be so much in love. 'For once I have got time to look round and realize, which otherwise I never have. I can get outside it, and outside you, and outside us.' She was expressing, for the first time since her marriage, a quite natural need for her own space and a separate identity. Rosamund was at Knole and Violet was expected.

Harold and Vita decided to buy the London house they were renting, 182 Ebury Street. B.M. lent them the money. Vita worried about their finances. 'But I am going to make £300 a year by writing. I've got three or four stories written, which could begin a book, and Harold who has a sense of humour could do a sort of "Xmas Garland"* book quite easily, – so the mars will be quite rich after all.' It was understood between them that Vita did *not* have a sense of humour. But like many people of whom that is said, she greatly enjoyed the jokes and puns she made herself – and had a pretty laugh.

'Poor little mars, they do love each other. ... I love you and belong to you', she wrote, 'and my name is written all over your little soft white self.' At about the same time she told him, 'Darling I do like arranging about your shirts.' She was being very wifely. Every role that Vita played, she played thoroughly. She was conventional in her marriage and they were both conventional in the social life they built up at Ebury Street. Decades later, when they were reminiscing, Vita told Harold that they made a mistake in 'remaining Edwardian too long'; she said, as Harold recorded in his diary in 1940, 'that if in 1916 we had got in touch with Bloomsbury, we should have profited more than we did by carrying on with Mrs George Keppel, Mrs Ronald Greville and the Edwardian relics. We are amused to confess that we had never even heard of Bloomsbury in 1916.' But they agreed, in retrospect, that they had had 'the best of both the plutocratic and the Bohemian worlds.'

Because of the building operations at Long Barn they could not live there in early 1916, but divided their time between Ebury Street and Knole. Vita's war effort was part-time work at the Red Cross enquiry office for the wounded and missing. They also went out a good deal and entertained. For her birthday in March, Harold gave her a field to add to the Long Barn property, and by late spring, with Kent threatened by Zeppelin raids, they took possession of the house again. Ben was beginning to talk.

Money continued to seem a problem, and the Rolls-Royce B.M. had given them proved more trouble than it was worth, as Vita explained to her: 'Petrol has gone up again, and is now 2/6 a gallon instead of 1/- so I think I shall have to talk to Bond and send him to make munish [munitions] and store the momo [motor].'

Money was being raised for war charities by tableaux and 'charity matinées' in which young society women disported themselves on stage and the public paid to see them. In April 1916 Vita had attended 'an absurd charity matinée with play by Yeats [*The Hawk's Well*], preceded by interminable peroration by the author, which is ignominiously checked.' After, she and Harold had dined alone, both with colds and 'rather bored by after-dinner advent of George Moore' – the

*A Christmas Garland:* literary parodies by Max Beerbohm, 1912.

Irish novelist was a neighbour of theirs in Ebury Street and a regular visitor, who tended to outstay his welcome.

Vita herself took part in tableaux organized by Mrs Leeds in June, and she was in an Italian masque set up by the Countess of Huntingdon at His Majesty's Theatre and one put on by Lady Alington at the Palace Theatre; in addition, Vita and Violet Keppel ran a 'shawl-stall'. In all this amateur theatricality Vita was in a double sense acting; her real life, more and more, was down at Long Barn, where already her best days were spent alone, simply described in her diary as 'garden and lessons' – that is, gardening and writing. In June an article of hers about Prinkipo – the prison island off Constantinople where the Turks were then holding General Townshend – appeared in *Country Life*, and she was still working on her history, never to be published, of the Italian states.

She was less enthusiastic about Harold's 'lessons' – the time he had to spend at the Foreign Office. 'Oh my sweet,' he wrote to her in August, 'you are not jealous about my lessons are you – as you wouldn't like me if I wasn't keen – just as I love you for your keenness about your beastly dead Italians.' She was very keen on them, and scribbled to her mother (who had just made a great new friend, the architect Edwin Lutyens):

> I am writing in the reading-room of the London Library, where I am studying an Italian volume so ponderous that it cannot be taken away. It is a lovely room looking on St James's Square, and I feel very dusty and scholarly, and all the bespectacled old men glare at me as much as to say What are you doing with that big book, you mar?

Harold and Vita – who was now twenty-four – both played up to still being 'mars' and celebrated their youngness continually. When Harold turned thirty that autumn, he declared he still felt seventeen. The more 'mar' they behaved, the better were their relations with B.M., as her sovereignty was less threatened. That summer she bought them Brook Farm, adjacent to Long Barn, for £700.

The 'mars' sometimes went to grand weekend parties, such as the one at Cold Overton Hall in Rutland that August, from where Vita wrote to B.M.: 'The food is marvellous: caviare, quails stuffed with pâté de foie gras, peaches; tuberoses and malmaisons; bath salts; Rolls-Royces at the station. (I seem to have heard something in London about a war?)'

She appreciated the good food: she was pregnant again, perhaps not on purpose – she referred to the expected baby as 'Ben's little "mistake"-brother-or-sister'. Ben had his hair cut for the first time in September and Vita put a lock away in an envelope – fine, golden brown, and still full of lights nearly 60 years later when Ben himself was no longer alive. On the anniversary of the still birth of their second child, Harold filled her room with lilies and tuberoses. They worked hard on autumn tasks in the garden at Long Barn: 'Design new plan for east garden. So happy.' Lilies and roses were going in there, and she begged a lot of perennials from Knole.

Early in October 1916, Harold's younger sister Gwen was married to Francis Cecil ('Sam') St Aubyn, who was to go to the front a week later. Ben went to the wedding too: 'very good in church, but conversational, and conducts the organ'. Vita was very moved by this wedding: 'Poor little Gwen so white and quiet.'

Harold and Vita were at Knole in December when the Winston Churchills were staying. After dinner Churchill told them 'the whole story of the Dardanelles, and we nearly cry with emotion.' Churchill was on the telephone half the day 'cabinet-making'; the rest of the time he painted in the Great Hall. Vita was charmed by him. She was less charmed by the Christmas party at Knole: George Moore, who repeated himself all the time, was there, and Harold was kept at the Foreign Office over a great deal of the holiday. Being with B.M. so much was what Vita called 't.i. [thin ice]'. Harold was all right, because Archie Clark-Kerr had turned up in London to keep him company. He wrote to Vita two days after Christmas: 'Poor Gob – it isn't much fun being at Knole is it for either of us? But I feel it is our duty, or rather your little black duty, and that it is the least we can do to make it all easier for poor old B.M., who would be incapable of coping with the situation alone.' The 'situation' of course was Olive Rubens in the converted laundry.

Vita was contradictory in the demands she was making on her own marriage. On the one hand she resented Harold's absence, at work or for seeing his friends. His letters to her are full of excuses and apologies and of indulgent references to her sadnesses and sulks. He stressed the importance to him of his career and of the contacts he was making: Vita was his 'little gentle helper', 'my little lonely one', who must put up with woman's lot. Mostly she accepted this; as she wrote, 'all the gentleness and all the femininity in me was called out by Harold alone' – with him her fierce, devious, deviant self was suppressed. Nevertheless, she had a premonition that their bubble of loving domesticity might burst. Adventure and romance, indistinctly visualized, were as ever her fantasies:

Darlingest I wish I could love you quietly but I can't; it is all tickly and upsets me, and I've never been so much in love with you as I am now. I'm afraid if we pull too hard on the string it will snap one day. I want to go away for a bit by myself presently, I won't go for more than a fortnight. . . .

After the war we will go away to Italy, and I will go first and we will meet there ; this is always my dream, but we will be parted for quite a long time first, and have very little luggage.

Whatever the roots of her unease, her fantasies still centred on Harold.

Their baby was born early and without complications on 19 January, after a labour of only four and a half hours, at 182 Ebury Street.

Son born at 2.30 a.m., just got an emergency nurse in time and the doctor. Great surprise, – after which we all went to sleep again. ... He weighs 6lb 10oz and has an average amount of hair, – fair, and quite straight ; an enormous nose, but a pretty mouth and eyes set wide apart, so although he is ugly he promises well.

B.M. came next day ; there were no rows, and the name 'Nigel' was agreed on without controversy. Violet – of whom Vita had been seeing a great deal in London – and Rosamund were early visitors, on different days. (Violet was having a public flirtation with Osbert Sitwell, who confided in B.M. that he was 'very unhappy about the way Violet Keppel treats him'.) Before Vita had fully recovered, Rosamund's mother fell ill and died ; Vita supported her old friend in her unhappiness, and Mrs Grosvenor left a letter for Vita, bequeathing Rosamund to her loving care. 'I have not fulfilled this trust,' Vita wrote in 1920.

It was not until late April that the Nicolsons let 182 Ebury Street to Gwen and Sam St Aubyn and moved down to Long Barn for the spring and summer. Lord Sackville was back from the war with gallstone trouble. From Long Barn Vita was able to support her mother. 'Vita is such a dear and calls every day for a very long visit. I hardly see Lionel. He is always in a hurry or comes into the room, looks out of the window, taps with his finger and says nothing, looks bored and says goodbye. Poor, poor Lionel and poor me.' In the warm library, he read aloud to Olive as he had once read to her.

Violet came to Long Barn for the odd weekend, though she did not admire cottages or Tudor architecture – low ceilings, small leaded panes, exposed beams, dark oak, sloping floors – and regretted Vita's domesticity. After one such visit, she wrote to Vita that on the way back to London she had looked at Knole, 'which seemed to me more beautiful than ever. How I adore that place ! Had you been a man, I should most certainly have married you, as I think I am the only person who loves Knole as much as you do !'

Vita was not a man, and Knole was to be Eddy's. In May she and Harold planted nut trees at Long Barn, box hedges and more roses, and they discussed Harold's career : he would go into politics.

Her father and Olive spent a night together at Long Barn, which offended B.M. Vita was beginning to think her parents would both be happier if they separated formally. Meanwhile B.M. was buying three large adjoining houses in Sussex Square, Brighton, as her own very ample private refuge. Lutyens, whom she nicknamed 'McNed' and who was now her pet, was making designs for knocking the three into one and redesigning the garden, to be reached by a tunnel under the road. (The Cenotaph that he designed was unveiled in Whitehall that summer: he was a man of the utmost distinction, but B.M. had him under her thumb.)

The first serious row that Harold and Vita had had with B.M. for months was about her marriage problems and occurred during dinner at Hill Street. They had let her see that they now found the Seery inheritance a distasteful subject, an embarrassment rather than a triumph. Vita hastened to put things right next day: 'but really we did not exactly mean that, certainly not from *our* point of view, who have benefited vastly by it; we were thinking of Dada's point of view, if you remember. ... How could we mean to hurt you, who owe you every-thing we have, from our happy marriage down to the breadcrumbs for our chickens. ... '

It took the sun out of the sky, Vita wrote, to feel that there was a black cloud between Long Barn and Hill Street. So the marital impasse con-tinued, and with it Vita's emotional and financial dependence on her mother. B.M. brought McNed over to Long Barn and he advised them about alterations to the staircase – which they were decorating with the sky-blue fretted wooden panels they had bought in Constantinople – and drew pictures for Ben.

The Russian Exhibition in London was all the rage and Vita went to it with Violet; B.M. made a 'Bakst' room at Hill Street. Violet confided her tangled love affairs to Vita; she had also made a great friend of Margaret (Pat) Dansey, who lived with her uncle Lord Fitzhardinge at Berkeley Castle in Gloucestershire. To Pat, too, Violet talked endlessly – about Vita.

# CHAPTER 8

PUBLICATION of the volume of Vita's poems that had been accepted by John Lane of the Bodley Head had been postponed on the outbreak of war. She had had *Constantinople: Eight Poems* privately printed in 1915, and in the summer of 1917 Lane rescheduled her book, which was to contain early poems, the Constantinople poems and some new ones. When she showed them to Harold in July, his response was, 'Oh my darling clever little mar, I can't make your poetries out. They seem to proceed from something I don't know in you. It is rather a shut-out really, but they *are* so much better, so much more fluent and forceful.'

In August *Country Life* printed her poem 'Mariana in the North' ('All her youth is gone, her beautiful youth is gone') and also 'A Frugal Life', which was written for Ben and Nigel. The whole volume, *Poems of West and East*, did not come out until October. Before that, Vita went with her mother and Lutyens to Munstead to see Gertrude Jekyll's house (re-modelled by Lutyens twenty-five years before) and her famous garden, the style and spirit of which had so great an influence on English garden-ing, including Vita's. Vita did not on this occasion express much excite-ment: 'Miss Jekyll rather fat, and rather grumbly; garden not at its best, but can see it must be lovely.' She already knew Miss Jekyll's practice of making 'one-colour' gardens by subdividing the larger garden, and was planning a yellow and white enclosure with Harold at Long Barn.

Violet was the last summer visitor in early September, before the Nicolsons returned to London. She left after a stay of a week, only to return the next day because the air raids in London frightened her; she stayed another few nights. B.M., coming over from Knole, was struck by the free way Violet chattered about her *louche* private life: 'She cer-tainly has very immoral ideas or a supreme desire to amuse herself.'

On 2 October Vita went up to London to find Ebury Street cordoned off, two bombs having exploded only fifty yards from No 182. (She and

Harold had to abandon Pimlico for that autumn and moved in with B.M. at Hill Street.) It was the day her book came out. Harold prepared her for disappointment: 'Ducky don't be discouraged if you don't get any reviews as they only review War poems.' But she too had written a war poem, 'A Fallen Soldier', and the *Observer* printed it next Sunday along with a favourable notice of her book. Four days later *Poems of West and East* also had a very good review in the *Morning Post*.

B.M. bought 100 copies of that issue of the paper and sent them to her friends and relations; she enquired at Bumpus of Oxford Street about sales; she wrote to Selfridges' book department; she bullied every bookshop in London, 'especially Times Book Club where they are very slack about it. I am whipping up the shop now that the book is an undoubted success.'

Harold took the opposite tack. 'I went into Hatchards and bought your book because I was feeling so lonely. They gave it without a murmur, but I was not brave enough to ask whether they had sold a lot as they might have said "no".' He poured cold water on another of her aspirations: 'Darling I don't think you will get a job in any Govt office. Official employment means pay and pay means long hours and they simply don't want people who come for the afternoon or morning only.' In this, he was probably right.

At the end of October 1917 Vita and Harold were invited to Knebworth House in Hertfordshire for the weekend. B.M. bought her daughter a violet and blue dress from Worth and a new evening coat for this grand occasion; 'Her dressing has not been good enough recently.' The other guests were the Laverys, Eddie Marsh, Lady Herbert Harvey, Sir Louis Mallet (Harold's former chief), Osbert Sitwell and Hugo Rumbold. On her return Vita found a long letter from Violet.

> Darling . . . I simply can't get on without a periodical glimpse of your radiant domesticity, and you will become smug to an intolerable degree if the vagabond – what Dorothy [Heneage] calls 'rackety' element, as supplied by me, is indefinitely withheld from you. We mustn't let it happen. We are absolutely essential to one another, at least in *my* eyes !

Violet little knew how aptly timed her appeal was. Vita's 'radiant domesticity' was about to become a little dimmed.

At Knebworth, Harold suspected, he had contracted a venereal infection. His doctor said he must tell Vita about it, as if the tests were positive she too would have to have a check-up. This meant telling Vita a lot of other things. It is unlikely that, before this crisis, he had ever talked candidly to her about his homosexual pleasures and infatuations, though he often referred in a teasing way to the men he was specially fond of ('Hadji's* dining with ARCHIE tonight – which is a spike [i.e., of jealousy] for Mar – only Muriel will be there').

Up to this time, Vita's passionate nature – she was as highly sexed as both her parents and more deeply passionate – had centred, since her marriage, entirely on Harold, maybe more than he really wanted: a few months later, she was to tell her mother that Harold was 'cold'. Certainly she was still physically wanting him after the birth of Nigel:

> Darling, come up and peep in at my door, and if I am asleep kiss me and creep away like a little mouse; and if I am not asleep kiss me all the same, and then stay with me.
>
> I shall not be asleep, and anyway you are more precious than sleep.
>
> I love you. Darling how undull love can be, even though it is married and has a little boy, two little boys, of its own. I lie and wait for you with as much thrill as though you had never told me you loved me till yesterday.

She had been willing against all odds and in the face, perhaps, of her own nature as well as Harold's to make her marriage her romance and her adventure.

The crucial talk between a horribly upset Harold and Vita took place on 6 November. Vita, in this crisis, did not turn to Violet; she went away alone to Oxford, where she stayed one night with Irene Pirie, the only one of her close women friends who was married. Harold dined alone at Hill Street with B.M., who wrote in her diary that he 'told me he would kill himself if Vita died, he certainly loves her as much as ever.' B.M. knew nothing of the infection, though she did note a few days after that 'I am worried about Harold who looks very ill.'

The day Vita took refuge in Oxford, Harold wrote to her three times. First:

> My sweet one I feel so unhappy about it all. It is such a ghastly thing to hang over one – you don't realize how it haunts me. Even if things go right, – and there is nothing in our fears, I have exposed you to things you hate and loathe and of course you cannot help rather hating me for it.
>
> Darling you have been so sweet this dreadful week. . . . Darling if the worst comes to the worst I fear we will have a bloody time ahead. You will have to have treatment – and it may last a fortnight. Anyhow thank God it can't be bad as we have taken the thing in time. . . . Don't leave this lying about.

Then, later the same day:

> It will be such an awful business if the report is not satisfactory. I simply *dread* it. Darling if you hated me today, how much will you hate me if it really does

* 'Hadji', meaning pilgrim, was Harold's father's pet-name for him, now adopted by Vita.

come ? I haven't the courage to face it all. . . . Darling I can't believe that our
love and happiness would not survive even such a disaster. Dear one – let's
face it together and bravely.

They did. Vita's response to Harold in this embarrassment, and subsequent explanations and revelations, go a very long way to explain his
almost superhuman tolerance of her behaviour to him in the following
three years. For her, the immediate aftermath was complex: she had to
rethink her whole marriage and her picture of her husband, of his sexual
nature – and her own. She had to recognize a parallel duality in her own
nature that was sexual and not just temperamental. The unthinkable,
after the first shock, becomes the thing most thought about. It was a
turning-point.

From Oxford, she responded to the distracted Harold quickly and
kindly. His third letter :

> You sent me a nice telegram – which was dear and sweet of you. . . . Darling
> you are so sweet and dominating and I can think of nothing but you. I am so
> flight [frightened] darling I'm sorry . . . I have had a nightmare week . . . I fear
> it will make you loathe me. And all that bright sunlight world will be cut off
> like a search-light going out. . . . Goodnight my saint : my true angel.

She took up her life again, going with B.M. to Augustus John's studio to
see his portraits of Lutyens : 'John is just like Christ. Shop with B.M. in
the afternoon. Go to a party after dinner at the Colefaxes, where
Robert Nichols and Siegfried Sassoon read their poems. I refuse to read
mine! Nichols a horrid little bounder. Sassoon very shy but quite
attractive.'

She went with the Sitwell brothers to see an exhibition ('horrible') of
Roger Fry's furniture at the Omega Workshop, and spent a quiet
weekend at Knole with her father, Olive Rubens and Harold. He and
she were close again (in all but the sexual sense, which was not yet
permitted), full of plans and tendernesses. Vita read aloud to him the first
draft of what was to be her first published novel, *Heritage*. 'So happy.'

People comfort themselves and each other in different ways.
Unhappy B.M. lunched at this time with Lady Tredegar in Grosvenor
Square. 'She did not mince matters about her husband living openly
with a woman at the Ritz. I showed her my collection of Opals.' B.M.
had also started a collection of *risqué* stories of the coarsest kind, which
she wrote out in the back of her diary, a practice she continued for many
years. Protractedly and painfully menopausal, she still had not bridged
the menopause, a fact in which she took pride. She also had a new rich
friend, Lord Leverhulme the soap tycoon, who kept her supplied with
Vinolia soap.

The last year of the Great War was the bleakest for civilians in England. Many of Vita's friends – Patrick Shaw-Stewart, Edward Horner, the Grenfell boys – had been killed. Food shortages were beginning to bite. B.M., housekeeping at Knole, noted on 9 February 1918 that there had been no meat in the shops for over two weeks (the Sackvilles ate venison from the park); there was no butter to be had or margarine or coal. Visitors brought their sugar ration with them, 'and the whole conversation is on food.' Vita cheered herself up by buying at Reville 'a most lovely coat made of black velvet with a broad stripe of orange, and a fur collar'.

She was working hard expanding *Heritage*: 'altering the end, killing the grandmother, sending Ruth and Westmacott out into the night, reviving Malory, jumbling everybody up again when they flattered themselves they had got to the end of their troubles, – and incidentally hoping to make it of publishable length.'

She showed the manuscript to her literary neighbour, George Moore:

He was charming about it . . . he even suggested a means by which I might extend it to the necessary length. The means he suggested were due to what he described as a 'real-life story' he had read in some American newspaper. Practically every reviewer who subsequently condescended to notice my book observed that nothing of the sort could ever have happened in real life. Thus I am wholly indebted to George Moore for the eventual publication of my novel.[1]

In this extensive rewrite, she codified the confusions and conclusions arising out of the crisis with Harold. In the characters of Malory and Rawdon Westmacott she created two models of the V. Sackville-West hero, who was to reappear in almost all her fiction. Malory was the traveller with no dependents, no address; he was the man she would have liked to have been, and her ideal man, from her woman's point of view. Malory is one of those people who 'should not marry, or, if they do, should at least choose a partner as inconstant as themselves . . . it is a new kind of eugenics, a sort of moral eugenics.'

Rawdon Westmacott in the novel, though a man of Kent, was 'a Bedouin in corduroy, with a thin, fierce face, the grace of an antelope, and the wildness of a hawk'. Both Rawdon and the woman he loves, Ruth, have a mixed Spanish-Kentish ancestry: for the first time Vita explored the double heritage in herself, exploiting the family stories about Pepita and expressing her own duality in terms of conflicting inheritance. Malory asks himself whether Ruth is not 'cursed with a dual nature' – 'the one coarse and unbridled, the other delicate, conventional, practical, motherly, refined. . . . And is it, can it be, the result of the separate, antagonistic strains in her blood, the southern and the northern legacy ?'

Parallel with the southern-northern duality goes another. Malory tells Ruth that 'love was passion and friendship – passion in the secret night, but comradeship in the open places under the sun, and that whereas passion was the drunkenness of love, friendship was its food and clear water and warmth.' The split between love as 'passion in the secret night' and as loyal comradeship was to become very marked with Vita; it was the way she accommodated the discrepancy between her temperament and Harold's, and his and her own sexual complexity.

She sent the manuscript of *Heritage* to Hugh Walpole, who approved of it, saying its style derived from Conrad and from *Wuthering Heights*. He put it into the hands of the literary agent A.P.Watt ; Collins, the first publisher approached, accepted it.

But the early months of 1918 were not propitious. Mikki, her loved old dog, died and was buried in the wood at Long Barn. Harold was taken up with his work and his new friendship with Oswald (Tom) Mosley. Violet seemed equally taken up with what B.M. called 'a fine flirtation' with Commander Arthur Marsden, a hero of the Battle of Jutland.

In mid-March Harold was to take a holiday and spend it with Vita down at Long Barn. B.M. wrote in her diary that Vita had told her Harold was 'as much of a lover as ever – lucky mortals !' But the idyll was not as complete as B.M. presumed. Harold had been officially clear of infection since the end of January, but two days before his holiday was due to begin, he wrote to Vita from the Ritz in London that he had just been to see his doctor

and he was a devil – not about his bill but about their having themselves to each other – and it is just going to be a holiday too. Anyhow I will tell you about it. . . . Only he says 6 months from Knebworth – oh dear oh dear. That will take us to April 20. . . . Oh my sweet – isn't it a sell ? I asked him if we couldn't take precautions, but he was a devil.

He wrote a second time the same day from the Foreign Office. 'He says that after April 20 there will be no risk at all and that I am quite cured. . . . Darling do you mind awfully having a diseased husband ? He was frightfully opty [optimistic] about it not happening again.' Harold was worried that Vita would 'hate me and loathe me and turn from me in abhorrence. Darling if you were here you would just laugh and say "Silly Hadji" and it would be all right.'

It was lovely weather day after day during the fortnight they were together at the cottage. They planted sweet peas and divided the phlox. The jonquils and the daffodils were still in bloom. From time to time they heard the menacing sound of the guns booming from across the Channel. At the end of March, Harold went back to his work at the Foreign Office, returning as usual most evenings and all weekends. Violet invited herself to stay with Vita on 13 April, for a fortnight.

On 18 April the floodgates of Vita's reserve broke, and at ten o'clock in the evening she and Violet began to talk as they had never talked before. 'Violet had struck the secret of my duality; she attacked me about it, and I made no attempt to conceal it from her or from myself.'[2] Though Vita must have had disturbing new thoughts since her talks with Harold, she had never put them into words. Violet had always consciously directed her appeal towards what she called the 'rackety' side of Vita's personality: maybe Vita had been talking to her about the themes of *Heritage* and the fuse, once lit, could not be extinguished. 'I talked myself out, until I could hear my own voice getting hoarse, and the fire went out, and all the servants had long since gone to bed, and there was not a soul in the house except Violet and me, and I talked out the whole of myself with absolute sincerity and pain.'[3]

Violet listened; this was what she had been waiting for. She told Vita then how she loved her and why, and in what ways. Thus began the romantic love affair that, as Vita was to write over two years later, changed her life. The 20th of April – an important day for Harold and Vita's marriage – came and went unmarked: Vita and Violet had scampered off for the first of their trips to Polperro in Cornwall, where they stayed in a cottage lent to them by Hugh Walpole. Harold wrote to Vita three or four times a day in a crescendo of disappointment and depression. But Vita felt, as she was to write later, that she was 'beginning life again in a different capacity'. The adventure had begun.

# CHAPTER 9

DURING that hectic summer of 1918, the first months of her affair with Violet, Vita thought of the whole thing as an escapade, never imagining it would last: Violet's fickleness was proverbial. Excitement over Violet, however, made resuming sexual relations with Harold even less of a success than it might have been. It is possible that Harold's Knebworth misfortune had, as he feared, turned Vita against him sexually in spite of her sympathy and understanding. This distaste set free her other self – and opened the way for Violet, who spelt romance and adventure and everything that domesticity with Harold was not.

He, understandably, was tentative in his approaches; he wrote to her on 9 May: 'I wish I were more violent, and less affectionate ... only I suppose I am too cultured and *fin de siècle* to impose my virility.' She answered him at length by letter, even though, as she said, she would be seeing him almost at once, 'because somehow it's easier'. (It was always easier in letters for Vita and Harold.) She told him she preferred his gentleness and patience to 'the violence you seem to covet'. She had wanderlust, she told him – she longed for 'new places, for movement, for places where no one will want me to order lunch, or pay housebooks'. She acknowledged the selfishness of this and said she knew he would trace it all back to Violet. He would be wrong, 'But ... I feel that Violet and people like that save me from a sort of intellectual stagnation, a bovine complacency.' After the war, she told him, he and she would go off somewhere together. This was her old fantasy: 'I want to go away (with you) where no one knows where we are.'

But for the moment it was Violet she wanted to escape with. She was not honest with Harold in that she played down the intensity of her relationship with Violet, but she no doubt felt she was being sincere; at the beginning, before everything ran out of control, the flight from ordering lunch and everything that went with it was as important as Violet herself.

She began writing *Challenge*, a romantic novel about the conflict between love and duty, set on a Greek island. In the story, Violet is
portrayed as 'Eve' and Vita herself as the troubled 'Julian'. The two of
them were quickly building up a fantasy world, with its own language –
based on Romany, picked up from the works of George Borrow – and its
own mythology. Violet made suggestions and emendations throughout
the writing of the novel, especially in the characterization of Eve and
Julian: 'The description of Julian I thought most adequate. You say it's
not like you! It *is* you, word for word, trait for trait.... I must say I
should like a more *detailed* description of Julian's appearance,' and she
made suggestions. In the manuscript Vita dedicated the book 'with
gratitude for much excellent copy, to the original of Eve.'

More and more frequently Vita was wearing the farm-girl's uniform of
breeches and gaiters she had acquired just before Violet's fateful visit.
For drawing-room wear in 1918 they were outrageous, but they suited
Vita's height and long legs. Even B.M. approved. 'I do want to get her
painted like that; she looks so charming in her corduroy trousers. She
ought to have been a boy!' But the next day Vita turned up looking
equally, differently beautiful 'in a vivid deep rose dress and ditto hat'.
Immediately B.M. arranged for her portrait to be painted by William
Strang – not in her breeches, but the Vita in that picture is nevertheless
the defiant, swashbuckling Vita elicited by Violet.

Harold liked the picture and found in it his own Vita as well. 'It is so
*absolutely* my little Mar. She's all there – her little straight body, her
boyhood of Raleigh manner and above all those sweet gentle eyes.'
Olive Rubens had told him she thought it a little coarse: 'I could see no
coarseness – only a certain blatancy, which is contradicted by the beauty
of the eyes.' One of his strengths in dealing with Vita was his steadfast
refusal to lose sight of the gentle, protective woman in her that he
needed so desperately and whom she never wished to deprive him of.
To preserve the balance in her personality, she needed Harold's vision
of her.

He was dazzled by her new vitality. He told her hopefully that he was
'going to be a Devil – a great blue and red devil with claws – and then his
sweet one will love him again as once she did – and not feel that her own
glowing youth is being wasted on a curate.' (He often wrote of Vita and
himself in that way as 'she' and 'he', as if writing their story.) On 1 July
he told her 'Darling you are such a dominant person. You colour everything like the sun.' All summer, striving to reclaim her, he wrote and
telephoned home several times a day, even though he came home
nearly every evening. Violet, whom she saw continuously and went
away with as often as she dared, wrote nearly as often to her 'Mitya', as
she called Vita: 'I love belonging to you – I glory in it, that you alone out

of so many have bent me to your will, shattered my self-possession, robbed me of my mystery, made me yours, yours, *yours*.' Meanwhile, that summer little Nigel learned to walk and to say 'Ben'.

Any party she went to with Harold at which Violet was not present was rated by Vita as 'beastly', 'deadly' or 'a bore', however illustrious the company. In London she often stayed the night with Violet at 16 Grosvenor Street, the Keppels' house, and she met Violet's close confidante, Pat Dansey. It was altogether a 'mad irresponsible summer of moonlight nights, and infinite escapades, and passionate letters, and music, and poetry. Things were not tragic for us then.'[1] On 14 August Violet wrote to Vita: 'Mitya, Mitya, I have never told you the whole truth. You shall have it now; I have loved you all my life, a long time without knowing, 5 years knowing it as irrevocably as I do now, loved you as my ideal, my inspiration, my perfection.... You are the *grande passion* of my life.' And, with the self-consciousness of love: 'I wonder if our mutual biographers will know how much of my career to attribute to your unconscious influence?'

Oswald ('Ozzie') Dickinson, the brother of Virginia Woolf's friend Violet Dickinson, was a confirmed bachelor, an inspired gossip, and an old friend of Harold's; he held the odd post of Secretary to the Home Office Board of Control in Lunacy. He was a court favourite of Lady Sackville's and, through him, whispers of the change in Harold and Vita's marriage reached her. As 1918 progressed, Harold was observed to be undermining Vita's confidence in public, contradicting her and putting her down – understandably, since she was undermining him in private. Ozzie told B.M. he regretted 'that H. scolds V. a little too much before people. How I hope [she wrote in her diary] with all my heart that H. and V. will never see their love on the wane.'

Vita's summer of ecstasy had made Harold deeply sad; he knew now that his anxiety was not just due to imagination. He wrote it all out to her in long letters. On 9 September:

> Little one – I wish Violet was dead. She has poisoned one of the most sunny things that ever happened. She is like some fierce orchid – glimmering and stinking in the recesses of life – and throwing cadaverous sweetness on the morning breeze. Darling she is evil and I am not evil. Oh my darling – what is it that makes you put her above me?
>
> Oh darling yesterday I wanted to kiss you as if I loved you, and you turned aside. Such a slight deflection ... and yet it hurt me so, it sent me away so hurt, darling.

Vita's problems were compounded by those of her parents. B.M. had recently taken over her new holiday home in Brighton, sending down seven vans of furniture from Knole. Lionel saw this as an opportunity to bring Olive Rubens even deeper into the life of Knole. He planned to move her and her complaisant husband into rooms on the Green Court, giving fussy, tubercular Mr Rubens a sinecure as secretary. Lionel sounded Vita out: 'I should love to know what your impression of Mother's feelings *really* is.... She seems absolutely delighted with Brighton and very happy there.' B.M. was not so amenable: Knole was still her home. Lionel abandoned the plan, and the only advantage of this new trouble from Vita's point of view was that it deflected B.M.'s mind from close attention to her daughter's own activities.

Harold sensibly took an autumn holiday in Rome with Lord Berners and Lord Gerald Wellesley. Vita, at Long Barn with Violet, was affected by his independence and wrote to him: 'But Hadji, listen, I KNOW, as I know the sun will rise tomorrow, that I love you unalterably. I know it would survive any passing liking I had for anyone else.' She was tacitly asking him, as she always would, to be infinitely tolerant of any such 'passing liking'.

She and Violet went to see B.M. in her Brighton house; Ben and Nigel and their nurse were already staying down there with their grandmother. 'House ripping,' Vita wrote in her diary. She had her 'own room' in it; B.M.'s description of Vita's room gives some idea of the Bakst-inspired taste of the day, interpreted by that flamboyant woman.

> Her walls are of shiny emerald green paper, floor green; doors and furniture sapphire blue; ceiling apricot colour. Curtains blue and inside-curtains yellowish. The decoration of the furniture is mainly beads of all colours painted on the blue ground; even the door-plates are treated the same. I have 6 bright orange pots on her green marble mantelpiece, and there are salmon and tomato-colour cushions and lampshades. Pictures by Bakst, George Plank, Rodin, and framed in passe-partout ribbons.

Vita 'looked lovely in that room with her 2 little boys on her knees; a picture I shall not forget'.

Six days later Vita was embarking for the first time on what she called 'the *best* adventure'. In her Ebury Street house she put on men's clothes, met Violet at Hyde Park Corner, and tall thin 'Julian', smoking a cigarette, strolled around Mayfair with his much shorter, plumper girl-friend. 'The extraordinary thing was, how natural it all was for me.' They took a train to Orpington – a suburban town on the line to Sevenoaks – and stayed in a boarding-house for the night as man and wife. In the morning they went on to Sevenoaks and slipped unnoticed through the stables into Knole, where 'Julian' was cast off; Vita was back at Long Barn to welcome Harold from Italy that evening.

B.M.'s diary : 'Poor Harold back from Rome is ill, with Spanish flue and high temperature at Long Barn, with his devoted Vita to look after him.' Violet taunted her for this devotion, mourning the resurrection of Vita's other self : 'Mitya ousted by someone gentle, affectionate, considerate, nice. . . . Aïe ! It is so infinitely and tirelessly *belittling*.' Just as Harold could plead for 'his' Vita in letters of many pages, so Violet could sustain her appeal to 'her' Vita in letters of even more pages. 'I can see you splendid, and dauntless, and free, a wanderer in strange lands, conversing with strange people, exulting in the inviolable chastity of inspiration.' With the instinctive shrewdness of the true neurotic and the habitual manipulator, Violet could always play on Vita's fantasies of herself. Violet made much of the unglamorous lifestyle of Harold's parents, mocking the Nicolsons' house in Cadogan Gardens as 'that horrible bedint house'.

Violet herself was in danger of losing her own freedom. She had always had strings of men friends, but Major Denys Trefusis of the Royal Horse Guards was out of the ordinary. All the time that she had been with Vita she had been writing letters – and knowing Violet's letters, they would have hit their mark – to Denys at the war in France. Now he was coming home on leave, prepared to claim her. Vita was jealous. 'Shall I tell you why ?' Violet asked.

> You are jealous of him because *he is like you* and that's what it is that makes *me like him*. . . . In your heart of hearts you know perfectly well that he is 'one of us' – that he belongs to the all too small fraternity of the adventurers, the reckless, the enterprising, and the free . . . there is a terrible and irresistible affinity between the three of us.

Violet had found a new fantasy, a new game, a new goad for Vita. And she had every intention of marrying Denys, but not yet.

Denys Robert Trefusis was indeed what Violet said Vita ought to be, what Vita would have liked to be, 'a wanderer in strange lands'. Vita liked him very much ; Violet's fantasy of the threefold affinity was realized – except in the closing stages of their drama Vita got on well with Denys – and when the three were together, even at times of great emotional confusion, a feeling of pleasure in each other's company prevailed.

Vita described Denys as a racehorse, a crusader, a greyhound, an ascetic in search of the Holy Grail. In his unpublished book about Russia, 'The Stones of Emptiness', Denys described himself as 'fastidious and nervous' ; he was also brave, every inch a soldier, and had fought at Ypres and on the Somme, after which he spent two months in hospital with gas poisoning. He was tall, handsome and amusing with a sardonic wit, an accomplished sportsman and a fine horseman; he was a fluent Russian speaker, and had been spending time in Russia regularly since 1908. He had great charm and many women had been in love with him. All in all Denys Trefusis was a considerable person and not one to be trifled with.

In October 1918, when Violet and Denys were together in London, Harold and Vita joined B.M. and the children in Brighton. Vita, on edge, went up to London nearly every day, and Harold spoke about his troubles to B.M. for the first time. He told her 'how Violet tries to destroy their love and home life by constantly turning it to ridicule' and that he thought 'Violet was really bad and determined to wreck their married life.' Ozzie Dickinson had told B.M. that Violet had told *him* 'that she intended to separate Vita and Harold'. The fat letters from Violet that arrived in Brighton for Vita each morning would have electrified her mother and husband if they had read them.

> Mitya, you could do anything with me, or rather *Julian* could. I love Julian overwhelmingly, devastatingly, possessively, incoherently, insatiably, passionately, despairingly – also coquettishly, flirtatiously and frivolously. Horrible thought! What friends Denys and Julian would be! They would entertain the greatest possible admiration for each other and would 'hunt in couples'. They would have open and generous competition for Pitti Alushka [i.e. herself, the centre of this fairy-tale] instead of an unconsciously illicit and clandestine one!

Violet acted with great recklessness after Denys had gone back to France; she asked herself down to Brighton, where she had irresistible 'long talks' with B.M. She was conspicuously nice to Ben and Nigel and confided to B.M., who noted it all in her diary, how excited she was at the prospect of marrying Denys. She also told B.M. that 'she did not think V. was at all in love with H. now and she was striking her own line, was very ambitious about her literary future.... I am anxious.' Then Violet brought up the point about how Harold 'nags at V. and is fault-finding before people.'

Her work done, Violet went back to London – and wrote Vita an hysterical letter. Something had happened – probably B.M. had indulged in some of the frankly sexual speculations she so much enjoyed, perhaps about Vita and Harold's married life. In any case, Violet felt she had 'come upon a nest of woolly caterpillars, and my whole nature is polluted':

> Thank goodness, I have been spared this horrible knowledge for much longer than most people. ... We will eliminate the words Lust and Passion from our vocabulary, they are dirty and hideous. ... No wonder I have always lived in

a world of my own – or as much as possible ... no wonder I have always preferred fairy-tales to facts.

Is it possible that Violet, up to this point, had not known the facts of life? Or was it a bid to poison further the wells of married life for Vita? The evidence seems to be that Violet was aiming at a position where both she and Vita would be married women – marriage in their society being the passport to independence of movement and freedom from parental authority – that both husbands should be rejected or otherwise neutralized, and that she and Vita should be free to pursue their ideals of freedom, beauty and excitement. It was the romance of life with Vita that she chiefly wanted : Violet was not very keen on sex, ever.

In this she nearly made a mistake with Vita for whom physical passion was important. On the day that the Armistice was signed, and Harold heard he was to be sent to the Peace Conference in Paris, Vita and her mother had a long talk about Harold being 'physically so cold'. B.M. wrote after : 'I am indeed very sorry that H. is made like that, as he can't help himself, but it is so hard on her, poor child, as she misses passionate love not being returned, and he is always so sleepy and has her in a desperate hurry. So many men are like that and lose eventually the love of their wife.' Vita now, in one aspect of her nature, would have been relieved to have been forcibly rescued from her adventure. Conflict made her wooden, emotionally, to both Harold and Violet, who was complaining about the 'almost monstrous frigidity' of her letters. 'Julian! Julian! Why are you so indifferent? We must go away together, and you shall belong to me as much as you did at Orpington.... If we can't go away together within the next fortnight, I will never see you again.'

And so before Harold went to Paris, the children went to Knole with a new nurse and Vita and Violet went to the south of France, allegedly for three weeks. Ebury Street was let to the Wellesleys.

Vita very nearly did not go. She quarrelled three times about it with Violet. B.M. gave Harold a pep-talk about how to deal with his wife. The married pair had a *tête-à-tête* evening and the next day Vita told her mother at luncheon about 'the wonderful change that had come over H. towards her, that he treated her at last like a lover and that she now felt perfectly happy as the one thing that had been missing in him had been altered. ... She admitted V.K. was amoral and she hated that side of her.'

But then Violet took over again, threatening suicide. Vita and Violet stayed in France from late November 1918 until late March 1919.

Vita described being abroad with Violet at length in her autobiographical manuscript of 1920; it is published, now, for all to read. Memory, especially of love, distorts and selects. Looking at the contemporary evidence, it

was not always so 'free and rhapsodic', nor such fun. In Paris, where
they dined sometimes with Denys, and where 'Julian' and 'Lushka',
without Denys, dined and danced and walked the night streets, Vita
was often depressed: 'Hate life – hate Paris – wish I was dead.' On the
train to Avignon Lushka was 'fractious'. Harold's letters followed her,
veering from plaintive, angry, conciliating, despairing to optimistic.
Someone had lent him Van der Velde's *Married Love*, which impressed
him greatly; he rushed to share his insights with Vita:

> It is wonderful: it goes into every detail. There is a whole chapter which
> explains why Hadji goes to sleep and Mar doesn't. I find I am the *rule* and not
> the exception. ... But I am appalled at my own ignorance. ... I know that
> you must have suffered terribly – and that only a splendid character like yours
> could have kept from hating me.

The book and his new feelings for her were 'going to make our future life
glorious and real'.

Meanwhile in Avignon, where they were happy, Violet made Vita
promise to stay away until the end of January. There was a row, but Vita
gave in. Staying at the Hotel Bristol in Monte Carlo, the girls lost a great
deal of money gambling; and after a thé dansant, during which 'Julian'
danced with his companion, they left in a hurry – were, no doubt,
requested to leave. Vita had to pawn her jewels to pay the bill. They
moved to the Hotel Windsor and Vita received the most outspoken
letter yet from Harold: he called Violet a little swine, said she was like a
bad smell or an illness and bewailed her hold over Vita. 'Of course she
flatters you – that is it – every silly ass woman is bowled over by flattery.
*How* I hate women.'

He spent Christmas at Knole with the children. 'Ben said to tell
Mummy that Daddy wanted her today.' From Monte Carlo Vita sent for
more money – not only to Harold but also to one of Harold's best
friends. 'I didn't at all like your telegraphing to Gerry [Wellesley] behind
my back. Whenever you have been long with that little clammy fiend
you get crooked.'

He had moved to Paris for the Peace Conference in the New Year of
1919, found a flat and expected Vita to join him daily. Eddie Knoblock,
the playwright in whose apartment in Paris Vita and Violet had stayed at
the beginning of their fugue, sent over some things they had left. 'There
were some intimately messy things of Violet's,' Harold informed Vita,
'some dead lip-salve tubes – a bit of dirty ribbon – one shoe – the whole
thing so grubby and beastly I felt physically sick at their being muddled
up with your dear clean intimate possessions.'

'Monte Carlo was perfect, Violet was perfect ...' Vita wrote later;

and Violet would not let Vita go. At the last minute, when Harold had transferred all their belongings to the new flat, had hired servants and was expecting her on the date agreed, she cancelled plans by letter. Crushed with disappointment, he forced himself yet again to be tolerant and immersed himself in the Peace Conference.

Both Vita's parents and Olive Rubens, as well as Harold, wrote Vita serious letters about the plight of her children. B.M. had had enough. 'Vita ought to come back and look after them.' There was nurse trouble : it was discovered that the woman had been mistreating Ben, who had become withdrawn. Nigel, being younger, was very 'hazy' about his mother altogether. Harold's mother took them for a while, but Ben had to sleep on a sofa. At the end of February B.M. wrote to Harold that the situation had become impossible for both grandmothers and that Ben 'had become quite callous'. Passed from hand to hand, the four-year-old Ben was now parked with a friend of B.M.'s in Hampstead. The pressure mounted, and the gossip, and Harold's impotent humiliation.

Vita went home to the children. Violet believed, and Vita let her believe, that the separation was only temporary. Vita was scolded by everyone, and Harold, delighted at her return, took on the role of comforter : 'But you know that as regards me you needn't worry about all this Violet business – and that I understand it all and realize your difficulties.' As soon as Violet herself was back in England, she announced her engagement to Denys Trefusis. She continued to write desperate and suicidal letters to Vita – and even to Harold, thus eliciting his unwilling but always ready sympathy.

B.M. needed sympathy too, having come home to Knole one day in April to find Lionel and Olive in one another's arms under the tulip trees. She had enough spirit left to have a 'long talk' with Vita that evening, 'about V.K., whom she agrees must be a sexual Pervert, and she tries hard to break off with that horrible girl.'

Vita was getting to know her children again and reported to Harold : 'There is no doubt that Nigel is the favourite, and quite between you and me I can see why : he is sunny and happy, while Ben is *désoeuvré* and rather discontented, and terribly destructive. Don't think I have got a down on Ben ... for one thing I feel such sympathy and understanding between him and me.' Ben really loved her, she felt, 'whereas Nigel is all things to all men'. Broadly speaking, she wrote, Ben was like her and Nigel was like Harold. 'If Nigel stays as he is, he will be happy and everybody will love him, but there is a distinct Dostoeffsky [sic] touch about Ben ! I feel he is much more *mine* than Nigel.' Ben had got 'an *idée fixe* that he wants to be in his own home with you and me.'

It was not an unreasonable desire. Harold was coming home on leave and wrote to Vita – 'Oh my little wife' – about shirts and shoes and shampoo. The homecoming was happy ; the family was together at last, at Long Barn. Vita and Denys exchanged friendly, courteous letters about the engagement and agreed not to mention the exchange to Violet. When Harold went back to Paris after his leave, Vita went with him.

# CHAPTER 10

IN PARIS Vita met Michael Sadleir, author and publisher, and while Harold worked at the Conference they made plans to start a magazine. Away from Violet, Vita was anxious to pick up both her writing life and her respectability. She wrote to Hugh Walpole seeking support for a literary review that would publish modern poetry; she was to run the English section, and Sadleir the European. 'I do so want to do something to stem the tide of Osbert Sitwellism and all that slovenly, slip-shod beastliness; I hate worms, and Pierrots, and peg-top trousers, and all the rest of that paraphernalia, and this is to be my effort! Financially of course it means certain ruin.' The review was to be called 'The Critic': 'this has an old-established ring about it.' It came to nothing, but her presentation of the idea is significant. For many poets, their work is an exploration or expression of their hidden, experimental selves. For Vita it was generally the reverse. Her poetry was her link with the 'old-established'; it was her traditional and traditionally English 'northern' self that was to go into her poetry, not her fierce, black, deviant 'Spanish' self. In her poetry she was often at her most prosaic.

She described the conception of the review in an unpublished short memoir of Michael Sadleir, giving also a rare glimpse of herself at the heart of Harold's world. She and Sadleir talked in the hall of the Hotel Majestic, where the British delegation to the Peace Conference was housed:

> Under the gilt and stucco, at a little cane-topped table between the palms, amid the extraordinary jostle of politics and personalities, we used to sit discussing the formation of a quarterly ... and on British Delegation notepaper we drew up the articles of its beliefs. Our tiny conference was carried on, at the hub of the greater conference. Red-tabs, typists, King's Messengers; secretaries, soldiers, correspondents; the Indians, conglomerated always, and a little withdrawn; the short fair beard and blue eyes

of Smuts ; Mr Lloyd George smiling ; Mr Balfour surveying ; a sudden hush –
Foch !

She was back in England for the publication of *Heritage*, her first novel – 'a
whole page of the *Athenaeum, Sunday Times, M[anchester] Guardian,
Birmingham Post* (a tremendous gush), *Punch* (a perfect PIG). . . . Sales
1400 already.' It was a success. B.M. wholeheartedly took up her role as
publicist again ; by publication date, 15 May 1919, she had 'written 157
letters mentioning it to shops and friends.' That very night mother and
daughter had what Vita described as 'an extraordinary conversation' that
went on until two o'clock in the morning. 'She has tumbled to the whole
thing, I'm so glad.' (Arising from *Heritage*, what B.M. had tumbled to
must have been Vita's theory of her temperamental duality, one aspect of
which was called out by Violet. But B.M. believed all that was now over.)
Vita was fascinated by her own personality ; as Harold wrote to her three
days after, 'No poet is a hero to himself (except my Vita who is a heroine to
everyone including her own darling self).'
    The new peace was disrupted by the final break between Vita's
parents. An account of the last row that precipitated this is given by Vita in
*Pepita*, tactfully edited. The quarrel was, as usual, about the Rubens
presence at Knole. Vita did not try to stop her mother leaving : 'She said
she was not surprised and she would have done so, long ago, in my
place.' But Vita had a grim twenty-four hours carrying messages between
her parents – her father cold and courteous, her mother heartbroken and
longing to be begged to stay. He did not beg her to stay and she left Knole.
    Within the same week Vita, by chance, was placed next to Denys
Trefusis at a dinner party. She wrote to Harold in Paris : 'I can't tell you
how much I like him. I really do. . . . He is very intelligent and not a bit
banal. I do wish he was just a stray friend, and not engaged to V. !'
Harold, still detecting a note of 'wanderlust' in her letters (was it, he
wondered, rekindled by her mother's flight from Knole ?) felt uneasy.
'How can I,' he wrote to her, 'who only represent peace and serenity,
cope with V. who represents adventure ?' And a few days later : 'You
have never sent me any of the things I asked for. As a wife you are
hopeless. But as a person to love and adore and worship – you are terribly
unique and obsessing.'

Harold was happy about the success of *Heritage*. They would never be
able to sell Long Barn now, he teased her, because it would soon be a
historic monument safeguarded by 'The Sackville-West Society', and 'we
shall have tourists and a shop with ginger beer, and piccies of the Mar
with her goggles on.' He was not so very far wrong – only the Mar never
let herself be photographed in her spectacles.

'You must keep your gravity of style,' he advised. 'It is no use your trying to be funny. You realize that.' (Being funny was to be Harold's forte in books as in life.) Vita's childhood dreams of fame were revived by her success; she imagined her name as an entry in histories of literature – 'Sackville-West, V., poet and novelist'. She was content at Long Barn that spring of 1919, painting the gate green with Ben's erratic help, telling Harold that she doubted whether they would want to send 'the babies' to Eton : 'I think you and I will be too progressive by then !'

But Violet was never out of her mind. The one emotional hurdle left to cross was Violet's marriage. Violet still fantasized about living with Vita all the time and made crazy plans for an elopement the day before the wedding. She touched again that chord in Vita that made her reckless, forgetful, capable of anything. Vita warned Harold on the last day of May, a fortnight before the wedding, that she might suddenly come to him in Paris : 'I *must* be away or I won't be responsible !'

Her disturbance grew daily. The very next day she was telling Harold, with truth, that she should never have married so young. 'Women, like men, ought to have their years so glutted with freedom that they hate the very idea of freedom. Like assistants in a chocolate shop.' Dreams of flight with Violet swung her away from her new-found pleasure in belonging to the 'old-established' world : society was 'so secure, so fatuous, so conventional, so hypocritical, so white-sepulchre, so cynical, so humbugging, so mean, so ungenerous, so self-defensive, so well-policed ... so virtuously vicious, so viciously virtuous.' And she was 'ABSOLUTELY TERRIFIED' that she was going to make a scandal over Violet's wedding.

Violet tempted her and touched her where it hurt most, as always : 'Cast aside the drab garments of respectability and convention, my beautiful Bird of Paradise, they become you not. Lead the life Nature intended you to lead. Otherwise Mitya, you'll be a failure – you, who might be among the greatest, the most scintillating and romantic figures of all time, you'll be "Mrs Nicolson, who has written some charming verse".'

This, in retrospect, is very near the bone. In Vita's potential for ruthlessness, criminal carelessness and self-abandon may have lain her only chance of testing what genius she had. This was something that was never acknowledged by Harold, and in any case she tried to pro-tect him from all but the most superficial manifestations of that side of her. 'I am so frightened of that side sometimes,' she wrote in 1920, 'it's so brutal and hard and savage, and Harold knows nothing of it. He has blundered on it once or twice, but he doesn't understand.' Now, just before Violet's wedding, she wrote to him : 'Oh Hadji, it's so neat, the division in me, more neat than you'll ever know.... Hadji darling, I wonder how much you realize.'

It was in a mood of panic that she went with her mother on 2 June to the marriage of Lady Diana Manners to Duff Cooper ('a wretched-looking little specimen,' sneered B.M.). On 3 June, the day Denys Trefusis's award of the Military Cross for bravery was announced, she had a scorching response from Harold to her anti-society letter. Harold, who may not have 'understood' everything, saw the situation most clearly from his own point of view. He told her brusquely that she had no will-power at all; that she just drifted, and then attributed the muddle she got in to 'to the conventionality of the world'. He told her she was becoming 'hard and common', that she must keep her head, her sense of proportion and her self-respect – and bring him some black socks. He railed against her tendency to polarize: 'Why do you imagine that there is nothing between eloping with Violet and cooking my dinner?'

Vita left for Paris two days before Violet's wedding, on the day that the *Nation* printed a eulogy of *Heritage*: 'We wish that all first novels were like Miss Sackville-West's, for we should have fewer qualms about the future of the novel.' To avoid seeing Violet and Denys married by going to Paris was disingenuous; the newly-weds were to cross the Channel immediately afterwards to begin their honeymoon in that same city. To be in Paris at all was an act of provocation. While the wedding was taking place in London, Vita sat in her French hotel bedroom watching the clock, knowing that Violet was half-hoping for some last-minute gesture of rescue.

As soon as the Trefusises arrived at the Paris Ritz, Vita went to see Violet. She took her away to a small hotel and made love to her. 'I had her, I didn't care, I only wanted to hurt Denys' – whom she saw the next day, 'an awful interview'.[1] She behaved like a madwoman. She had lost all control. She haunted the Ritz, dining tragically alone in full view of Denys and Violet. Harold was irrelevant – Vita was way beyond his reach – until the Trefusises left Paris for the south. Vita arrived back in England so broken and exhausted that her condition touched even B.M.: 'I can't approve of it but I do feel so miserable for her, poor child.'

Harold tried to encourage her to use her writing to defuse her emotions. 'After all if she can pour out her outbursts and excesses between the safe limits of a cardboard binding', Julian could elope over and over again and she could 'get back on Hadji and marriage by describing the horror of it'. Harold had not yet read *Challenge*.

In fact it was the neglected garden at Long Barn that restored her equilibrium. 'There is nothing in the little enclosed garden now, I got the dead lavender taken away and it is just dug ready for planting. What shall we put there? It is very important. Let's have it all one flower, or at least all one colour.' She was negotiating to buy another twenty acres of land, at £26 per acre. Her conventional side was back in the ascendent, with a compensating exaggeration that drove her to launch an attack on a deviant group – non-masculine men. 'Victor [Cunard] is a nice, easy, pleasant, ineffectual little thing. What contempt one has, *au fond*, for the Victors, Eddie Marshes and Ozzies of this world.' Was this also a sidelong way of protesting against Harold's own mildness and sexual ambivalence?

Two things distracted Vita from brooding too much on Violet's return to England in spite of the stream of histrionic letters and telegrams that she was receiving almost daily. (Denys, on the honeymoon, burned every one of Vita's letters to Violet: he read them first.) She had made a friend of her acquaintance Dorothy Wellesley, Gerry's wife and an aspiring poet, who came to stay at Long Barn. 'I like Dottie, she is rather how [childlike, pathetic]; I hope I have helped her over her poems, and anyway I induced her to take out four for which she would have been frightfully abused, about Jesus.'

The second thing was sinister. She mentioned it over-casually to Harold, on 20 July: 'Oh by the way I sacked Nannie and made her leave at once. It's too long and boring and squalid a story to go into, but it included her purloining a suit of your clothes to dress up in, and in which she walked about the village accompanied by the babies. *C'est un peu fort!*' Perhaps to protect Vita's dignity and because he did not like to look at unpleasant truths, Harold did not in his reply acknowledge the possibility that Nannie, knowing too much about 'Julian' and her employer's private life, had played a grotesque joke on her. 'Was it vice, drink or foolishness that made her do it?' he asked. 'Mere animal high spirits,' replied Vita blandly.

Violet and Denys took Possingworth Manor at Blackboys, twenty miles from Long Barn. The liaison between the women continued – Denys was away a lot – and it took on the dreariness of all unresolvable love-affairs. But by the end of August Vita had agreed to go away yet again with Violet. If Harold was stoical about this, it was because he himself had a new infatuation. He wrote to her from Paris on 15 September about his own 'funny new friend', a dressmaker with a large flat on the rue Royale, who was twenty-seven and 'very attractive'. Harold was unspecific about the dressmaker's sex: it was the couturier Edward Molyneux. 'My sweet – are you jealous? Do you mind?' But he kept up his appeal and told her she was 'all the sacred things of life, my beloved, that's what you are, (the cottage, the babies and all that) and besides that you're *all* that I think clean and sweet and good (*really* good not priggy) and fresh and *tout couvert de rosée* and like apple-blossom.' And he wept

*Vita on holiday in Bangor, Wales.*

*LEFT: Knole in Vita's childhood—the garden side.*

*Vita with her mother (OPPOSITE), 1899, and with her father (BELOW) at Knole.*

*Vita and her mother out for a drive.*

*Violet Keppel with her parents, about 1907.*

*Sir John Murray Scott ('Seery').*

*Portrait of Vita in* 1910 *by Philip de Laszlo.*

*Vita in* 1916.

*Vita in fancy dress.*

*Harold Nicolson, Vita, Rosamund Grosvenor and Lord Sackville*
*on their way to court,* 1913.

*Vita on her wedding day, 1 October 1913. Lady Sackville's comment scribbled on the photograph reads: 'Cut down the nose but it can't be published without being* <u>much</u> *altered especially the nose.'*

*Vita as a young married woman.*

*Vita with her parents and Ben and Nigel.*

*Violet Trefusis in the early 1920s.*

OPPOSITE: *At Long Barn — Vita, Nigel and Ben, 1923, and Vita's sitting-room.*

*Harold Nicolson.*

*In the garden at Long Barn—Nigel, Vita and Ben.*

*Vita in* 1925.

when she went away with Violet to the Continent. Ben was upset again and further alienated B. M. by his negative behaviour.

By early December Harold was at his lowest ebb yet. He spoke of divorce, of permanent foreign exile. Before Vita went away, she had told her mother that she meant her marriage with Harold to be on a platonic footing from now on – chastity and the horror of male sexuality being one of Violet's obsessions – and that Harold had taken it 'like a lamb'. He had not. 'But I want a daughter so, my sweet ... I want a little girl who will be like you – and who will love me like you do – but less selfishly.' He was furious when he heard through the grapevine that 'Julian' had been dancing again in public. 'I am still cross about it, but I will forgive you anything.'

Vita, from Monte Carlo, tried to convey how frighteningly deep was her involvement. 'I don't think you realize except in a very tiny degree what has been going on.' As for having another child – 'But that is *impossible*, darling; there can't be anything of *that* now – just now, I mean. Oh Hadji, can't you realize a little?' But she said that when she left Monte Carlo she meant to break with Violet for ever. (She knew she must, in the end.)

She told Violet just the opposite – that she was going to return to her, this time for ever. It was the only way of getting away. They parted at Cannes, each to rejoin a husband.

When the Trefusises came to London in the New Year of 1920, the two women still met every day, but Vita was busy: looking for a new governess for the boys; negotiating with Collins over the publication of *Challenge*; warding off Kenneth Campbell's renewed 'ludicrous proposals', and entertaining the Mosleys for Harold (who had been made a CMG in the New Year honours). Violet had nothing but Vita on *her* mind.

On the day that Vita came to London to interview Miss Cherry, the new governess, she also had what she called in her diary 'an unpleasant interview' with Violet and Denys together. Denys asked Vita how much money she would have to keep Violet and herself with if they went away together, 'so that I felt like a young man wanting to marry Violet and being interviewed by her father'.[2] Denys was forcing the issue; but when he asked Violet, point-blank, if she wanted to renounce everything and live with Vita, Violet was frightened and asked for a week to think it over. Both Vita and Violet embraced the postures of rebels and outcasts, but backed off, consistently, when in danger of actually being cast out.

Violet telephoned Vita four days later to say it was now or never. Vita broke the news of her permanent departure with Violet to Harold at

Cadogan Gardens. He collapsed. His mother, that good conventional woman, pleaded with Vita not to go. Vita agreed to stay just over Harold's fortnight's holiday and they both went down to Knole, emotionally drained, and did not mention the subject at all. 'I don't know what he thought about during all that fortnight – I don't know whether he took the danger of my leaving him at all seriously. There were he and I, Ben, Nigel and Dada.'³

Normality and the texture of everyday life blanketed the crisis. Harold's loathing of confrontations left Vita in the air. If she was crying for help, her cries went unanswered. When he returned to Paris on 1 February 1920 she wrote to him at once that she was feeling 'all floating and insecure': 'If I were you, and you were me, I would battle so hard to keep you – partly, I dare say, because I would not have the courage and the reserve to do like you and say nothing.' She told him she longed for weapons to fortify herself with, 'so I fish, and fish, and fish, and sometimes I catch a lovely little trout, but never the great salmon that lashes and fights and *convinces* me that it is fighting for its life.' She tried, she wrote, to make him fight, but he never would: 'You just say "Darling Mar!" and leave me to invent my own conviction out of your silence.' But what appeal could he make, replied an exhausted Harold, but that of love? Perhaps he was mistaken in thinking of her as a strong person: 'you see your excessiveness and your ruthlessness give an impression of strength.'

Excessiveness and ruthlessness won the day. Yet in the elopement of Violet and Vita to France in February 1920, from which their husbands finally rescued them with an uncharacteristically decisive swoop from the sky in a private plane, Vita all along had kept Harold posted, with letters and telegrams, as to their whereabouts. No wife who has decided to leave her husband for ever sends him daily messages in case he should be worried. She was still asking to be stopped, whether she knew it or not, and at last, at Amiens, he stopped her – with the backing of Denys, the Sackvilles and the Keppels.

The scenes in the hotel in Amiens, as described by Vita in her autobiographical manuscript, were unreal in their nightmare quality. At such times sane people are, temporarily, clinically insane. Denys told Vita in Amiens that Violet was his wife in all senses. (He later retracted, 'perjuring himself' as he told Harold, to quell Vita's hysteria.) Even if, as was probably the case, Violet's submission had only been partial, her apparent betrayal of all the ideals she had been preaching, and that Vita had been imposing on her own damaged marriage, provoked rage and despair in Vita. Disillusion enabled her to leave for Paris with Harold. It was the crisis: but subconsciously a welcome one perhaps, enabling Vita to save her pride, her love for Violet and her marriage, in one fell swoop.

On 20 February, in Paris, an apathetic Vita received the proofs of *Challenge*, 'about the only thing which has stirred me to any interest since Amiens'. The same day her mother had a sad letter from her; Vita was like 'a broken-hearted lover,' her mother realized. 'If V.T. was a man, I could understand. But for a woman, such a love beats me, but I try so hard to understand.'

B.M. was less understanding when, on Vita's return to London, she read the proofs of *Challenge*. She saw at once the portrayal of Violet in the character Eve and was horrified. She thought the book was dull as well – '*brilliantly dull*' – and with Harold's approval let Vita know it would be a terrible mistake to publish it. 'Harold suggested I should make my letter to Vita much stronger....' But when Vita protested, Harold changed horses and backed Vita; 'it was too weak of him'.

The book was due to be published the following month, March 1920. Violet had adapted a saucy drawing she had made of herself and 'Julian', smoking a cigarette, under a lamppost in Paris for the cover. The book was also to be published in America. Vita was not too hard to sway by threats of gossip, which in spite of her defiance she dreaded, and withdrew her book from Collins in mid-March. (She had to pay them £150 to recover the rights.) The book was already printed, but not bound. 'It will be sewn, and put away in lavender,' Nigel de Grey of Collins wrote to her when he had got over his irritation. American publication was also postponed.

Vita, having conceded over *Challenge*, hit back at the conventional world by writing what Harold called a 'foolish hard little letter' to her friend Enid Bagnold, deploring Enid's engagement to Sir Roderick Jones. For once Harold was outspoken. '*Damn* those Amazonian theories of yours! Surely it is less ridiculous to marry and have babies, heaps of babies, than to live on through a truculent virginity.' But Vita had already gone – over the water to France and possibly Italy with the irresistible Violet, yet again. Harold caught up with them in their Paris hotel, talked to them until the small hours, and they went home – Vita to Long Barn, Violet to Possingworth.

They still snatched days and nights together, often with Violet's friend Pat Dansey as ally and alibi. Vita tried to write again – and realized how out of practice she was. She feared her gift and her fluency had left her for ever. On 5 May she complained in her diary:

> I don't know what's the matter with me. I think I've got softening of the brain. I've been sitting all day in front of a barely begun review of some book, reading over and over again the few sentences I had written.... How I envy H. his clear-cut intellect!

I *must* shake myself out of this inertia. I wish I was poor, dirt poor, miserably poor, and obliged to work for my daily bread. I need a spur. I am a rotten creature.

She finished the review; two days later she wrote two poems, and was more cheerful as a result. She went sailing with Harold and her father on *Sumurun* and enjoyed it, even if she did contact Violet the moment she got home and took her away to a hotel in Sonning.

On 4 June she was at an 'alarming' literary party at Mrs Belloc Lowndes's house: 'Clemence Dane, Hugh Walpole, Maurice Hewlett, Virgilia [Enid Bagnold] and Sir Roderick [Jones], and Rebecca West – an attractive ugly young savage.' She worked at her new novel, set in Lincolnshire, *The Dragon in Shallow Waters*. She dined with Sibyl Colefax, sitting between the poet John Drinkwater and J.C. Squire, editor of the *London Mercury*, directly after an ugly scene with B.M. and Harold about her continuing relationship with Violet – 'contrived to talk to Squire more or less sense'. Violet had sent her an all-or-nothing ultimatum that day. Vita replied that she must stay with Harold but nothing really changed.

Hugh Walpole and Djuna Barnes came down to Long Barn one Sunday at the beginning of July. She gave Walpole *Challenge* to read and he was complimentary; she and he talked on the terrace until midnight. Walpole detected no strain in the house, even though Vita had had a 'disturbed morning' with Violet the previous day. He wrote in his diary that it was 'a very happy house-party'. 'We all talked nineteen to the dozen and Vita looked perfectly beautiful in crimson and orange. She is as lovely as she is clever, with just that touch of easiness that gives her complete distinction. Harold too is a very nice fellow.'[4]

Then she and Violet went to stay with Clemence Dane* and poured out their story to her. She tried to persuade them to give each other up – 'an awful morning'. But Vita was increasingly inclined to agree with Clemence Dane. Two days later Violet was complaining, 'You said today that our love had become a debased and corrupt thing.' Then Violet became ill, and Vita, 'not reluctantly' as she admitted in her diary, went to look after her.

It was Violet's last throw. Vita's love became strained. With Violet in Hindhead on 17 July, she wrote in her diary: 'Oh Christ, how I long for peace at Long Barn! But she is in such distress of mind and so seedy that I must give way to her.' When she got home she wrote cheerfully enough to Harold in Paris that she and Violet were 'separating

*Pen name of Winifred Ashton. Her novel *Legend* came out in 1919.

completely'. 'She is going abroad almost at once ; I have refused to go. GOOD MAR.'

It was on 23 July, during that same week, alone with the children at Long Barn, that she began to write the confession or autobiography that was to be discovered in a locked Gladstone bag after her death and which Nigel Nicolson was to publish, with his commentary, in *Portrait of a Marriage*. (The day after she began to write it, Nigel, then aged three, came in for punishment : 'The babies are more unruly than ever. I beat Nigel yesterday, he is an obstinate little thing, for which I respect him.') Writing the confession was a symptom of recovery ; but it is a painful document, written not to deny but to explore her divided self, her relationship with Harold, and her relationship with Violet, who she believed loved her irrevocably.

She saw Violet while she was writing it ; she came over for Ben's birthday on 6 August (Vita gave him a Meccano set) and that evening Vita wrote in her diary that 'there seems nothing but misery of one sort and another for everyone.'

There was a possibility that Violet's marriage would be annulled. In keeping with her own somewhat tarnished ideals, she had made Vita promise that she would not resume marital relations with Harold : it was the price she exacted for their 'separation'. This caused new trouble between Vita and Harold. When they were staying in Brighton, 'H. lost his poor little temper in V.'s Bed R., saying all women are cruel,' as B.M. put it in her diary. 'He came down to my Room to talk to me till 2 o'clock, poor child. . . . Anyhow, they are very nice to each other before people, and no one but me knows of their unhappiness.'

Violet came rushing down to Brighton next day to strengthen Vita's resolve. Ever after, she would remind Vita of the 'promise made at Brighton. . . . Don't let anything distract you ever *temporarily* from me and from the Great Adventure.' Violet was playing several hands at once. She told B.M. on this same visit that

> she felt very sorry for Denys and would almost think seriously of giving in to him. . . . She said it was different for V. refusing herself to H. as they had been married for 6 years and she had had 3 children but Denys had nothing and perhaps she would end by giving in to him. She strikes me as playing a wicked game with V. . . . Vita sees nothing and believes blindly in V.T.

Vita did believe in Violet ; if she did not, the whole great adventure would have been a tragic deception. She let herself be persuaded to go abroad yet again, in January 1921. Harold was in despair ; he confided in more people, which meant there was more gossip. He saw a lot of

Dorothy Wellesley and poured out his troubles to her. In early February he wrote more violently than usual to Vita, who was again prevaricating about her return: 'you are more selfish than Agrippina in her worst moments ... more optimistic than the Virgin Mary at her most light-hearted, and more weak than some polypus floating and undulating in a pond.' Vita replied from Carcassonne that she loved only him, but felt guilty about Violet now that Denys and even Mrs Keppel had turned against her. 'You see I am responsible.' But if anything were to part her from him and the babies 'I would die of it.' Wild oats were all very well, she said now, but not 'when they grow as high as a jungle. ... I want to be rid of the whole wretched business, and to live with you again.'

Denys's new threat, to divorce Violet, threatened Harold and Vita too. As B.M. wrote in her diary, she feared the scandal for Ben and Nigel's sake. 'I don't want them to blush when their mother's name is mentioned later on.' Scandal frightened Vita equally. She never in all her life had the desire to 'come out' openly about her love for women. When she came home on 9 March 1921, her birthday, she found some doors already closed against her. Mrs Hunter politely asked B.M. not to bring Vita to Hill Hall with her as 'the whole thing horrifies me.'

Denys Trefusis came to an arrangement with Mrs Keppel. He would not divorce Violet; Mrs Keppel would subsidize the marriage financially, and they would live abroad. Violet was sent first to Clingendaal, the Keppel property in Holland, in the charge of an old French governess. It was humiliating for a grown woman, but Mrs Keppel held the purse strings, and Violet, who adored her mother, could not live without money, or without her mother's approval. She began writing her first novel, but she was lonely. She wrote despairingly to Vita, 'You have all you want – a lovely place to live in, love, affection. It is *not fair*.' (Later she joined Denys in Paris, where they shared a home, but the marriage was never more than a front and Denys was not faithful.)

It was not fair at all. Vita knew it was not fair. She wrote the last words of her 'confession' on 28 March 1921, 'in the midst of great unhappiness, which I try to conceal from Harold, who is an angel upon earth.' She was afraid that Violet 'would not choose to live', whereas she herself remained 'safe, secure and undamaged save in my heart'.

Like Harold, she made Dorothy Wellesley her confidante. B.M., apprised now of Vita's nature, was immediately suspicious: 'I don't like at all that friendship either.' And two days later: 'Dottie is rather getting on my nerves the way she runs after V.' Vita and Dottie were going together to stay with Lord Berners at Faringdon. Harold encouraged the friendship and the excursion: anything was better than Violet, and he was grateful to Dottie. 'Enjoy yourself. Tell Dottie she is an angel and very good for both of us.'

Dorothy Wellesley was three years older than Vita ; in the *Dictionary of National Biography* she is described thus :

Slight of build, almost fragile, with blazing blue eyes, fair hair, transparently white skin, she was a natural rebel, rejecting all conventions and accepted ideas, living to proclaim herself an agnostic, a fiery spirit with a passionate love for beauty in all its forms. . . . She was a born romantic by temperament, but the bad fairy at her christening had decreed that her intellectual power should never equal her gifts of the imagination.

The *DNB* entry was written by Vita.

The early summer of 1921 was peaceful. The Nicolsons and their friends played tennis on the new court at Long Barn ; Vita's second novel *The Dragon in Shallow Waters*, finished the previous September and dedicated with nostalgic loyalty 'To L[ushka]', came out. It is a bizarre violent story about bizarre violent people, ending with a blind man precipitating a deaf-mute into a vat of boiling soap. (Vita got her soap-factory material from a visit she made with B.M. to Lord Leverhulme's factory at Port Sunlight.) Enid Bagnold, having read the book, told Vita she was 'an Amazon who played with boulders instead of tennis balls'. Violet's letters, sent clandestinely through Pat Dansey, reached Vita from a long way away :

I look ten years older than when you saw me last year. Each day I mercilessly look at myself in the looking-glass – and see my chin beginning to sag and my throat getting all wrinkled. . . . I suppose all the suffering I have been through has helped, and there seems to be nothing to look forward to. You are the only person who cares what becomes of me.

The letters became less frequent. The great adventure was over.

# PART III
# EXPLORATIONS
## 1921-30

# CHAPTER 11

VITA plunged straight into a fertile writing phase. At the end of June 1921 B.M. was reading the first draft of her short story 'The Heir', a love story between a simple man and a great house. B.M. advised her to 'take out the old housekeeper and make her an old butler, and there will be no woman in the Book'. Vita took her advice, and dedicated the story to her mother.

*The Dragon in Shallow Waters* was listed first of the fiction (above D. H. Lawrence's new novel *Women in Love*) in the 'Best-Sellers' column of *John O'London's Weekly*. But poetry was more important to Vita. She wrote to Edward Marsh, the influential editor of *Georgian Poetry*, reminding him that 'in a rash moment you murmured something about showing the enclosed verses to Mr Squire with a view to the *London Mercury*. Do you really feel disposed to do so?' He did, and Vita became a regular contributor to the *Mercury*, and J.C. Squire, 'also (alas) Mrs Squire', a regular visitor to Long Barn. In early August she asked the poet John Drinkwater to dinner, and they read each other's poems aloud afterwards. (Harold was sailing with Lionel on *Sumurun*.) She received the proofs of a new collection of her poems. ('Are they good? Are they futile? I don't know.') Ben had his seventh birthday; he 'comes down to dinner for the first time, has champagne and falls into a drunken slumber'.

The Nicolsons' domestic life seemed miraculously reconstructed, and Vita's poetry-writing life, in the traditional, anti-modernist mode that she chose, was taking off with speed and ease. But the most interesting and personal pieces of writing that she worked on that year have never been published.

One of these is an unfinished play called 'Marriage', which is an Ibsen-like feminist piece (but not a lesbian one). Cyril and Sheila Temperley live in the country; Sheila is a gifted pianist who abandoned her career on marriage. They have two visitors. One of them is quite unexpected, a strange female who comes to call on her 'old friend' Cyril: she is shown the door. Next comes their friend Paul Ives – the V. Sackville-West hero, the traveller, 'lean, brown, untidy, whimsical', back from Turkestan. Sheila confides her restlessness to Paul, who says: 'We can all make our own freedom, if we're prepared to pay out chunks of selfishness as the price of it': freedom within love is the solution. Sheila argues that this is not fair on the children; there are society's conventions, she says, and nature's conventions, 'and of the two it's nature's conventions that you can't go against.'

In the second act Paul puts into words what Sheila dares not. He tells her she is longing 'to be a whole person by yourself, not just half of a composite person'; and that 'you feel that a man, in spite of his marriage, remains himself; he doesn't become "married man" on legal documents as you become "married woman".'

Sheila tells him she only wants her life to herself for a short while; she would always come back. But if she were to say she wanted a year off, her husband and the world would think her unreasonable. Yet the alternative to marriage was spinsterhood, 'and for a woman who wants children that's an empty sort of existence.' If she just takes her freedom, she risks losing her children.

She tries to talk to her husband Cyril about these problems. He offers her golf, a new car, a holiday together – and is horrified when she says she would rather go alone, as she is always with him. Cyril: 'But of course. We're married.' He threatens divorce, then turns sentimental. 'I've never loved any woman but you, Sheila.' But the double standard he is applying is exposed. He admits that he himself would go big game hunting for six months without her if he was invited; and the reappearance of his mysterious lady friend makes his infidelity all too clear. Sheila is not angry but relieved, and announces she will go abroad next day – as Vita, on learning of Harold's casual relationships, went away with Violet.

But Vita could not write the last act, because she did not know how to. Her unfinished play echoes her own situation with Harold, though she omitted to present any Violet-figure; and she could not complete the play because she had not solved the problem. Very few people have, over sixty years later. 'We're not just Cyril and Sheila Temperley; we're every man and woman bound in marriage.'

On 18 August Vita heard from Pat Dansey that Violet was coming to England. She was frightened – of herself and of Violet. The entry in her diary for 26 August is simply 'L', for Lushka, underlined three times. Partly to escape, she left with Gerald and Dottie Wellesley for a holiday abroad. Just before they left, on 4 September, Vita conceived the long poem that was to be her best-known and most lasting work : *The Land.* Harold noted on that day, 'Vita has an idea of writing sort of English Georgics. Inspired by a chance remark of J.C.Squire's to the effect that it was odd how people did not write poems about occupations.'

A week or so later he saw Vita and the Wellesleys off to Italy ; he was to join them later. The holiday presented no threat to him, but he overreacted emotionally to Vita's departure, as he would to all major partings with her, always. The fear and insecurity caused by her repeated disappearances with Violet left this permanent mark on him. 'I was miserable', wrote Vita in her diary, 'because H. had got out of our taxi half-way to the station, and had walked away looking white and unhappy. I wrote to him in the train, to try and console him a little.'

Travelling with a married couple, one discovers the tone of their relationship. 'My word, they do squabble!' Vita wrote about the Wellesleys, when they reached Verona. From there Gerald, who was keen on the Baroque, went alone to Parma ; Dottie and Vita took a boat from Trieste to Split in Dalmatia, and Vita made a conquest: 'An Albanian on board entered into conversation with me and asked me to go and live with him in the mountains of Albania. I was rather tempted by this suggestion, especially as he was young, tall, dark and good-looking!'

In Ragusa they met Ozzie Dickinson, and 'all three sat on the quays, and watched young men like bronze statues bathing ; this thrilled me inordinately.' Dottie and Ozzie bathed, 'amongst crowds of hairy men ... I sat on the beach, and sulked.' (Vita had never learnt to swim.) After Ozzie left 'a timid little man approached us, politely removing his fez, and enquired our terms. He was so meek and diffident ... I said as respectfully as I could that we were already booked. We parted with expressions of mutual esteem.' Vita seemed anxious to prove to the world, and to herself, her heterosexual status.

On the boat back to Italy, anchored off Cattaro, Vita and Dottie sat star-gazing on deck in the bay, under a tall bare mountain. Vita was suddenly excited 'because it was so exactly like the mountain in my book and I thought how magnificent the cathedral would look, crowning it.' The book was 'Reddín', in which in the aftermath of the affair with Violet she tried to work out a personal philosophy to make sense of her life.

Vita tinkered with 'Reddín' for years ; she wrote it both as a novel and as a long poem but, even though Harold admired both versions, only the poem ever saw the light of day.

> Whence came that name, Reddín, I never knew.
> His image long had wandered in my mind
> Persistent, far removed from human-kind,
> Yet in his wisdom, gentle, mild and sure.[1]

Reddín is an old sculptor-architect of infinite tolerance, integrity and detachment, building a monument to his dogma-free ideals – a cathedral on a cliff. In notes for the novel-version headed 'Themes of this book' Vita wrote that Reddín's philosophy was

a) that this life is merely a bridge, a stepping-stone, a transition, and therefore b) that, *étant donné* how bloody it is anyhow, one is justified in getting the best out of it, whether through art, the body or any form of fun BUT c) that the essential is, that one must always bear the entire unimportance of it constantly in mind.

(This is like her 'Nothing matters' in 'The King's Secret', her childhood novel.) The cathedral is finally destroyed in the triumph of stupidity and convention over intelligence, but 'the principle cannot die'.

In the novel (which she had begun to write in mid-August, worked on in hotel bedrooms throughout the autumn holiday with the Wellesleys, and did not finally abandon, in mid-sentence, until the following June) Reddín has a group of disciples living with him in a community. For biographical purposes, Chloë and Mark are the most interesting, since they may be taken to represent some aspects of Vita herself and of Harold. Chloë is more vital and 'masculine' than Mark. She says to him that she 'can't tolerate lyrical lust'; she prefers a 'healthy animal' attitude. Mark is a gentle, comfort-loving, 'demonstrative neurotic'. With him, Chloë feels 'she must abdicate the masculine, the protective role; she must flatter him, to her own delight ... he should play the man, and she the woman' – but she regrets that she is so much better at playing her role than he is at playing his.

Making love with Mark, she has to brace herself to take 'the cloying weight of his temperament', a 'deadly mass'. Although she loves him and wants him, 'her unquenchable honesty still knew that she loved him most as a man loves a woman' – or, elsewhere in the manuscript, as a woman loves her son. Writing to Harold on 28 February 1923, Vita told him that she loved him 'like born mothers love their children'. Vita was not a born mother, and it was Harold who called out her maternal, protective qualities.

Chloë's lust in 'Reddín' is stronger than Mark's; he meets her with his own 'far meaner' desire. But he loves her, and it is not his fault that he has 'so much less to give'. She recognizes in herself 'the temperament that is wholly shattered by love', even though intellectually she rates sexual love as superficial, comparing it to drunkenness. She and Mark are too alike in their minds, too cerebral and self-conscious, to achieve simply love : 'Where was the honest clasp of lovers ?' Love is slavery, 'a sneaking bastard', unreliable ; honest lust is 'a jolly fellow'.

Harold, with his cooler temperament, would have agreed with this judgement. It is possible that some of the ideas of 'Reddín' are his, a result of his desire to temper Vita's emotional intensity. Chloë, in the manuscript, resented love's slavery, but felt lost without it, and lost too when she gave herself over to lust with another of their companions. And Vita could not finish the novel, as she could not finish the play, because she could not resolve the conflicts.

In Rome Dorothy Wellesley and Vita joined up again on 6 October with Lord Gerald and Harold (who had been amusing himself at Frascati in Lord Berners's Rolls-Royce). The women arrived at midnight. There was a rattle at Harold's bedroom door – 'My darling Viti'. In the following days, as a foursome and in pairs, they went shopping and sightseeing, and they saw something of Geoffrey Scott, the architect whom Vita had met in Florence with Rosamund.

They went on to Venice. Tempers were frayed. Harold's diary: 'Vita says she doesn't like the Salute which makes Dottie very angry. In a state of tension we reach the Piazza ... the Doge's palace comes under Gerry's displeasure. Vita says she thinks it is a nice colour. Gerry says it is like a fat German lady with coarse lace underclothing, and he points to the Salute to show how much better other people do things. ... We then go back to the gondola and go back in silence.'

On to Vienna, 'all rather on edge'. Harold went out with Gerry 'on the bust' before retiring to his 'beastly room'. (Vita, with the themes of 'Reddín' on her mind, did not invite him to hers.) Spirits rose when they discovered how cheap everything was for foreigners in Austria. Vita described the inflation-ridden Vienna of 1921 in a letter to her mother : 'One bought silk stockings at 2,500 kronen a pair – nominally £100, actually about 3 shillings ! It was fantastic.' Dottie had bought a cigarette case nominally costing £2,000, actually four pounds. Vita understood the underlying misery :

But when one had got over the first fun of it, and over the bewilderment of being given a sheaf of 10,000 crown notes in exchange for an English fiver, it all became rather terrible. When one looked closer at the people in the streets, one saw how pinched and shabby they were ; and realized that the shops in the smart streets were nothing but a bluff, and that the whole city was like a proud spacious cemetery full of hunger and misery under the ostentation of the streets and palaces built by the Hapsburgs.

In Munich, where Harold bought Vita a fur coat, there was an argument after dinner about women. Harold's diary : 'Vita said that Gerry and I adopted a "sneering attitude". She admitted that women were silly but put that down to years of oppression.... We then all became very cross and went to bed in a huff.' The next day they quarrelled again in the Munich Gallery. Vita and Dottie objected to being told by their husbands not to talk so loudly. Dottie replied that she for one was proud to be English. In fact they met no nationalistic hostility at all, Vita wrote to her mother, even though the war had only been over three years : 'they are all over one, civility itself' :

> It seems to me most extraordinary, and puts me against them [the Germans] far more than the war does ; it is such an incredible lack of any pride or dignity.... The people in the shops here even joke about the low value of the mark, since what they call 'the *last* war' ; they appear to think in wars. We have come here at the psychological moment when the mark is at its lowest, having crashed from 200 to 700 in about a week.... The whole atmosphere of the place is very different from Vienna ; it is clean and gay and prosperous and orderly ... I buy large quantities of stockings at 9d a pair.

They were home in late October, and B.M. found her daughter 'looking so handsome, beautiful, peaceful and healthy and so delicious with the babies.' Dorothy Wellesley went to see B.M. too, and reassured her that Vita's affection for Violet was 'as dead as *Pork* (I am tired of the expression "as dead as Mutton")'. A poem, perhaps written for Dottie, 'Full Moon', was in the *Observer* the next Sunday ('She was wearing the coral taffeta trousers/Someone had brought her from Isfahan').

The poem was from her new collection, *Orchard and Vineyard*, which came out on 11 November. J.L.Garvin, the editor of the *Observer*, was married that December ; Vita sent him a rather over-generous wedding present of an electric stove, which was what B.M., who cultivated him assiduously for Vita's sake, said that he wanted.

*Orchard and Vineyard*, as its title suggests, contained poems of life in Kent – some of which were to be incorporated into *The Land* – and poems of the Mediterranean. There are poems about Knole and love poems to 'Eve'; poems of rebellion, hate, and bitterness against society written at the worst times during the Violet affair; Long Barn poems ; garden poems, and a home-coming poem, 'Night', dedicated to Harold – to whom she gave eight acres of Kent for his birthday that month, to add to the thirty-three they already owned. Knowing the background, a reader can trace the emotional confusions of the pre-ceding years in *Orchard and Vineyard*; but the common reader, in 1921, did not have the key.

It was announced that autumn that Vita's old admirer Lord Lascelles had become engaged to Princess Mary, daughter of King George v. 'I hear that the King and Queen never left him alone till he proposed and was gladly accepted!' B.M. wrote maliciously in her diary. 'Vita writes how glad he must be now that she refused him again and again!' And B.M. remembered him at Knole in her Chinese Room 'begging me to break down Vita's obstinacy'.

Knole was closed to B.M. now; the Nicolsons and their children spent Christmas with her at Brighton. Harold was working on his life of Tennyson, and Vita was embarking on a history of Knole. B.M. was proud that Vita found useful 'all the notes I had made in all my Books when I had found anything about Knole and the Sackvilles'. Knole was the setting for a film called *The Great Adventure* which Vita, Harold and the Wellesleys saw in January 1922; Lady Diana Manners – now Lady Diana Cooper and Vita's most glamorous contemporary – was in it. 'Diana lovely but amateurish,' Harold noted.

They met Aldous Huxley; they heard Edith Sitwell reciting *Façade*. Vita was invited to contribute articles to the *Weekly Despatch* and was writing more stories to add to 'The Heir' and make up a volume. Her mother was particularly impressed with one of these, 'The Tale of Mr Peter Brown: Chelsea Justice'. It was not a new story; she had pub-lished it in *The New Decameron* under a different title. The theme was one that Vita was to return to again – the eternal triangle, with the familiar friend who loves both husband and wife but the wife more. The hus-band strives to suppress his jealousy, fails, and takes his revenge. It was curious, thought B.M., how Vita's imagination 'runs to weird subjects, so unlike the impression she gives people. She is so calm, so aloof – Darling Girl.'

Vita and Harold were busy and sociable, but not sociable enough for B.M. In her manuscript 'Book of Reminiscences' written that year she assessed her daughter as she was at thirty:

> Her complexion is beautiful; so are her eyes, with their double curtain of long eyelashes.... She has such dignity and repose, she is not in the least con-ceited and really does not make the most of her opportunities by leading such a quiet life and hiding herself so much, while she ought to know everyone of note. ... She is a very difficult person to know. To me, who knows her pretty well, she is a beautiful mask!

Vita wore a thicker mask, her mother thought, 'since the distressing V. affair.' She felt Vita would fall overwhelmingly in love with a man some day : 'She is or *seems* absolutely devoted to Harold, but there is nothing whatever sexual between them, which is strange in such a young and good-looking couple. She is not in the least jealous of H. and willingly allows him to relieve himself with anyone if such is his want or his fancy.' (B.M.'s mastery of English idiom was never perfect.) Where, B.M. wondered, did this unusual arrangement leave Vita ? 'And are her descriptions of Love and Passion a description of her own feelings ?' B.M. did not want Vita to suffer again. 'She seems contented now but the Volcano is there, ready to burst into flames, I am sure.' Sixty years later Vita's Italian daughter-in-law remembered Vita in the same way : as 'a force of nature, like Vesuvius'.

Rosamund Grosvenor came to see Vita at Long Barn in May with her old flame Reggie Raikes. Rosamund, who was to marry Captain Jack Lynch two years later, now could not touch the volcano in Vita.

*The Heir* was published and sold 1,400 copies in the first fortnight ; the only adverse review was by Rebecca West. B.M. decided that this was because Rebecca had befriended the still very unhappy Violet. Vita put some of her permanent preoccupations into the 'makeweight' stories in the volume : 'The Christmas Party', dedicated to A[prile] (her pet-name for Dorothy Wellesley), is about the dramatic revenge taken by a non-conforming woman on her stuffy family. The subject of 'Patience' is a man married to a sweet dull wife and dreaming of a carefree wild girl with whom long ago he travelled to the sun.

Sir Edmund Gosse, doyen of men of letters, wrote to congratulate her on the stories, 'which we have read aloud in the evening family circle'. John Galsworthy wrote too. (Vita had recently met him at the PEN Club and dismissed him as a 'wingless prig'.) In her non-writing life she was seeing a lot of Pat Dansey, who had an eccentrically generous streak and presented Vita with a motor car. But Dorothy Wellesley had become her closest friend ; and Dottie's marriage was going badly. Weekends at the Wellesleys' house Sherfield Court, near Basingstoke, were tense. 'Black', wrote Vita in her diary on Saturday 1 July, and 'Blacker' on Sunday. By September Harold had grown impatient. 'I do think Dottie makes a mistake in trying to be at one and the same time the little bit of thistledown *and* the thistle !'

Vita was finishing her book *Knole and the Sackvilles*. Near the end, she wrote to her cousin Eddy Sackville-West : 'They *were* a rotten lot, and nearly all stark staring mad. You and I have got a jolly sort of heredity to fight against.' Her friend Michael Sadleir at Constable turned the book down (it was expensive to produce). She did not offer it to Collins, because of the embarrassment over the stopping of *Challenge*, which they were still holding, as they said, 'in bond'. In the end

Heinemann offered her an advance of £150, and the book was also taken in America.

Vita was anxious to stop B.M.'s misdirected publicity ventures on her behalf. A warning note had been struck by Eddie Marsh, who took six of her poems for *Georgian Poetry 1922–23*, but turned down 'Leopards at Knole' saying it was 'snobbish – as well as very clumsy in expression'. In July Vita wrote to her mother explaining that 'You see, *social* advertisement is, I am sure, disastrous':

> There is so rigid a line between the social and the professional, and the last thing I want to be branded as is an amateur. I have much to live down, – many disadvantageous advantages.... You see it is *not* only a question of diffidence, but of policy. The people who make or destroy reputations are the professional critics ... and they start out *naturally* with a prejudice against the dilettante.

Vita wanted to avoid the wrong sort of exposure – that offered by the social pages of *Vogue* and the *Tatler*. 'Assuming that there is any merit at all, it will percolate in time; and in any case mine is not the sort of talent ever to write "best-sellers".' B.M. thought she was crazy. When *Knole and the Sackvilles* came out in November, Vita had to plead with her again, 'if you run up against any literary people in London . . . *don't* mention my book to them.'

She had started a new book already; she went with Pat Dansey to Avebury in Wiltshire to research the background for the novel that would be *Grey Wethers*. With Dottie, she went to Wales. Pat and Dottie began to resent one another and competed in bringing new plants for Vita's garden. Vita evoked possessiveness and dependence in nearly all her close women friends; she soon learned not to mix them, to compartmentalize her relationships, as was her inclination in any case.

A new friend in 1922 was Clive Bell; he gave Vita a novel by his sister-in-law Virginia Woolf. Vita wrote to 'Dear Mr Bell' on 10 November: 'I started reading *Jacob's Room* and was getting interested and slightly bewildered when somebody swooped down and borrowed it and took it off me.... But do tell Mrs Woolf that I was thrilled by the little that I had read – if, that is to say, you think she would care to have this message.'[2]

Harold was off to the Lausanne Conference about Turkey. Vita settled down at Long Barn with Canute and Freya, her elk-hounds, and their new puppies Sven, Derry and Anactoria. (The children were staying at Brighton with B.M.) She reported on her activities to Harold in her daily letters. On 22 November: 'I dug up the bed under your window. And I ordered the hedge for the new right of way, – I ordered red and pink thorn, do you think that will be pretty?'

On the same day she wrote to B.M. that Clive Bell had asked her to dinner in London to meet Virginia Woolf, but that she was putting it off 'so as not to cut into my last days here' before going to Ebury Street for the winter. There was so much she wanted to get done. To Harold, 25 November:

> there are new Guirlande roses by the entrance; masses of new orange lilies in my border; lots of manure and leaf-mould; a new strawberry bed; new roses in the oil-jars; no more Dorothy Perkins; Irish yews ordered for the top of the the steps, both flights; so there really remain only the poplars to move now. Don't you long for the spring?

'I shall never love but you,' she told Harold that autumn, 'and you are the love of my life, – which I have never said to a soul but you.' She also told him that Dottie, staying at Long Barn, 'appeared in my room at two in the morning' during a storm, 'but was sternly sent back to her room again incontinently. She is much better ...' – but always wanting Vita to go to her at Sherfield. 'If I show signs of disinclination there are floods of tears and cynicism. Oh dear.' And Pat Dansey, who had been invited to Brighton for Christmas, informed Vita that she was terminally ill and had left her everything she possessed. Vita was embarrassed and at a loss. 'I really think she is the queerest fish I ever came across.' Just how queer, she would discover. Pat's next announcement, her forthcoming demise forgotten, was that she was going to run an orange farm in South Africa and so was giving Vita the contents of the Berkeley Castle cellars – 'all the champagne, and some delicious Sauternes'.

Pat, always in close touch with Violet, let Vita know that that damaged and damaging young woman was again in London at the beginning of December. Harold, in Lausanne, was terrified. Vita sent him a telegram of reassurance, and then this letter:

> Darling, my own darling, *not for a million pounds* would I have anything to do with V. again; I hate her for all the misery she has brought upon us, so there. She did ring me up, (only I *beg* you not to say so to anyone) and I made Dots stay in the room as a witness, while I told her that nothing would tempt me to see her.... I would *never* have anything more to do with her; the boredom of it, and the lies, and the rows – oh no, no, NO.

Three days later she was reviving other hopes; she had found Pilar, the small daughter of the Spanish couple who worked at Ebury Street, 'standing stark naked in the dark passage with the red light of the stove on her little fat body, and her arms round Canute's neck. She looked such a darling. . . . My darling, I wish she was ours. I do love you so.'

Although he had to be away for Christmas, Harold called 1922 the 'best year since 1914'. He had the proofs of his *Tennyson*; when it was published he inscribed a copy for Vita as 'Presented to V.Sackille-West from her lover Harold Nicolson.' 'We might paper a bathroom with the galleys of our respective books!' wrote Vita. 'B.M. would. Oh please God may B.M. never think of doing this. Amen.' (B.M. had once papered a room at Knole entirely with used postage stamps.)

Vita had nearly finished her novel *Grey Wethers* by the end of the year, when *The Heir* was coupled by S.P.B.Mais in the *Daily Express* with Katherine Mansfield's *The Garden Party*. The latter book ran more cleverly 'over the short distance', Mais wrote, but V.Sackville-West's 'possessed a more robust health'. He was more right than he might have wished; Katherine Mansfield was dying of tuberculosis in France.

Vita had also written as much as she could of 'Reddín' ('Nobody will understand it but me'); *Knole and the Sackvilles* was reprinting, and though she called it a pot-boiler it brought her a spate of letters from genealogical scholars, bores and cranks, dreamers, friends and strangers. *The Diary of the Lady Anne Clifford*, a spin-off of the Knole book, was in preparation; *Orchard and Vineyard* had appeared. She had figured in *Georgian Poetry* and many periodicals; she had been elected to the committee of the PEN Club. V.Sackville-West was an established author.

Nigel, aged five, also made an approach to the world of letters in 1922. On Christmas Eve he wrote to the editor of the children's comic *Rainbow*: 'Dear Editor, I am come-ing to see you on January, and the Bruin Boys too. I shald like to come on my Birth-day so look out, for me.' Vita particularly appreciated the 'slight air of menace' he managed to impart. Nigel amused her and Ben moved her. On the last day of the year she wrote to Harold:

> Today I told Ben I was tired and was going to rest. I came into my room 5 minutes later to find him standing beside my bed with tears pouring silently down his face. I said good gracious Ben what's the matter? There was an outburst. He hid a wet face in my neck and sobbed out that he couldn't bear to think I was tired . . . and he had come to see if he could get me a hot water bottle. I hugged him, and he turned rough and cross, and said he must go to his tea.
>
> And when I got into bed I found a very tepid hot water bottle pushed well down to the foot.

The postponed dinner with Clive Bell to meet Virginia Woolf ('Did she look very mad?' enquired Harold) had taken place on 14 December. Vita made no comment on the evening in her diary. Mrs Woolf was more intrigued by Vita than Vita was by her, and wrote on 15 December :

> I am too muzzy-headed to make out anything. This is partly the result of dining to meet the lovely gifted aristocratic Sackville West last night at Clive's. Not much to my severer taste – florid, moustached, parakeet coloured, with all the supple ease of the aristocracy, but not the wit of the artist. She writes 15 pages a day – has finished another book – publishes with Heinemanns – knows everyone – But could I ever know her ? I am to dine there [Ebury Street] on Tuesday.[3]

It was the patrician in Vita that first fascinated Mrs Woolf. The aristocratic manner, she noted, was like an actress's : 'no false shyness or modesty : a bead dropped into her plate at dinner – given to Clive – asks for liqueur – has her hand on all the ropes – makes me feel virgin, shy, schoolgirlish. Yet after dinner I rapped out opinions. She is a grenadier ; hard, handsome, manly; inclined to double chin.'[4]

By 7 January 1923 the grenadier had become 'that new apparition Vita, who gives me a book every other day'. This was disingenuous ; Mrs Woolf had written asking for both the Knole book and *Orchard and Vineyard*. An initial flurry of exchanged dinners was set up.

On 9 January Katherine Mansfield died. She had been uncomfortably significant to Virginia Woolf both as a fellow writer and as a personality. Mrs Woolf told Vita long after that Katherine Mansfield had had 'a quality I adored, and needed ; I think her sharpness and reality'.[5] Her death, in 1923, left a vacuum that Vita was to fill more than adequately.

# CHAPTER 12

VITA began to fall under Virginia Woolf's spell, beguiled by Mrs Woolf's interest in her and by the fascination of her personality. Soon after they met, Mrs Woolf learned that Vita was 'a pronounced Sapphist – and may, thinks Ethel Sands have an eye on me, old though I am.' (She was ten years older than Vita.) 'Snob as I am, I trace her passions 500 years back, and they become romantic to me, like old yellow wine.'[1]

Vita spent ten days in February 1923 with Harold in Lausanne, as he had been begging her to: 'don't bring Dottie unless inevitable ... oh god please come darling.' Dottie had become very dependent. It is impossible to know what part Vita's influence and attraction played in the break-up of the Wellesleys' marriage. It is clear that the worse matters became between the couple, the more Dottie clung to Vita, who wrote to Harold on 12 February:

'I have got to go Sherfield tomorrow, oh damn, damn, *damn*. But the enclosed letter [from Dottie] will show you the sort of state that wretched little thing is in. . . . But it is a great bore, especially as I do *not* want people to say I have anything to do with her marriage having gone wrong, which probably they would be only too pleased to say. . . . I do *not* want to be dragged into this, either for your sake or my own. We have had quite enough of that sort of thing, haven't we?

Vita's affair with Violet had entered the repertoire of the higher gossip. That year, Ronald Firbank's *The Flower Beneath the Foot* came out, in which Vita, whom he had never met, appears as the Hon. Mrs Chilleywater, the literary wife of a young diplomat:

*Née* Victoria Gellybore Frinton, and the sole heir of Lord Seafairer of Sevenelms, Kent, Mrs Harold Chilleywater, since her marriage 'for Love', had developed a disconcerting taste for fiction – a taste that was regarded at the Foreign Office with disapproving forbearance. . . . So far her efforts (written under her maiden name in full with her husband's as well appended) had been confined to lurid studies of low life (of which she knew nothing at all) ; but the Hon. Harold Chilleywater had been gently warned that if he was not to remain at Kairoulla until the close of his career the style of his wife must really grow less *virile*.

Harold had met Ronald Firbank ; and was later to portray him, in turn, as 'Lambert Orme' in *Some People*.

While Vita was worrying about Dorothy Wellesley, *Challenge* – her suppressed love story of Julian and Eve – was coming out in the United States, published by Doran, who had also taken *Knole and the Sackvilles*. It was known in America that *Challenge* had been withdrawn in Britain, but not the reason why. Know-alls trotted out plausible wrong explanations. The New York *Bookman* in June 1923 said portentously that V. Sackville-West's *Challenge* 'was about an actual family, portraying that family in general and possibly in particular. This family was part of her own ; and it was not without influence.' (Julian's surname in the novel is Davenant ; he is caught up in revolutionary politics, and his family portrayed as having long-standing mercantile connections with Greece and the Middle East.) It was the English laws of libel, the *Bookman* said, that forced the withdrawal of the book. The reviewer compared the novel to Conrad's *Nostromo*, and was respectful.

Vita instructed George H. Doran to send a copy of the book to Violet Trefusis, to whom, in the Romany language, it was dedicated.

Harold's *Tennyson* was published in March ; he was back in England, and on publication day he and Vita were at a very Bloomsbury dinner party in Gordon Square with the Woolfs, Duncan Grant, Clive Bell and Lytton Strachey. It was not a success. The Nicolsons as a couple did not mesh with Bloomsbury as a group. 'I mean,' wrote Mrs Woolf, 'we judged them both incurably stupid. He is bluff, but oh so obvious ; she, Duncan thought, took the cue from him and had nothing free to say. There was Lytton, supple and subtle as an old leather glove, to emphasize their stiffness. It was a rocky steep evening.'[2]

Vita, who had accepted the public service and committee side of literary life, misread Virginia Woolf sufficiently to invite her formally to join the PEN Club ; Mrs Woolf declined gracefully (and, declining, suggested that they might call one another by their first names). Vita herself was a guest at the English Association's annual dinner at the Trocadero in May. Lord Grey of Falloden was in the chair, and Vita and the Spanish Ambassador responded to the toast for the guests.

Her mother, impressed by her public success, was less impressed by her performance as a housewife. She was irritated by the state in which

182 Ebury Street was left when the Nicolsons went to Long Barn for the summer: '2 sofas with the Springs on the floor, embroideries on couches quite spoiled and thick dirt everywhere.... I make excuses for her, as she is a genius and is busy writing. Long Barn is so badly kept too!'

B.M. herself was selling her large house in Brighton and moving to White Lodge, at nearby Roedean. She held a seven-day sale at the Brighton house, divesting herself of a great deal of Seery's furniture and valuables – a forty-two-stone diamond necklace that had belonged to Queen Catherine Parr among them – and sculptures by Rodin and Epstein. She gave Vita twelve more perfect pearls to add to those that Seery had left her, so that Vita's pearls were now a long, impressive rope: she wore them in the daytime with tailored silk shirts.

Vita's third novel *Grey Wethers* came out in England, to mixed reviews. It is the archetypal early V. Sackville-West novel, about Clare, married to an over-civilized, articulate, non-masculine man, and in love with lean, dark, red-shirted, gypsy-like Lovel. 'She was frightened that a day might come when she would be forced to be true to herself again; when the decent, ordinary, conventional false self should be suddenly abolished.' Vita's story is narcissistic: she is both Clare and Lovel, in love with both halves of herself, who are in love, in the novel, with one another. (In life, she could not relate easily to strong silent masculine men. She loved Harold; she was to be attracted, in a couple of months, to a weak, over-cultured, civilized man who was drawn to her hard vitality.)

Raymond Mortimer, reviewing *Grey Wethers* in the *Nation*, praised it before saying that 'everything she writes is spoilt by the devastating ease with which she falls into a certain sort of empty rhetoric'. This was ironic, since one of Clare's criticisms of her husband in the novel was that, although his distress was genuine, he was theatrical and 'could not refrain from rhetoric'. Vita in *Grey Wethers* had followed Harold's advice about letting her fantasies of escape play themselves out in her fiction: Clare and Lovel take flight for ever, as Vita and Violet failed to do. But in later years Vita hated to be reminded of *Grey Wethers*.

In July 1923 Vita and Harold took the kind of holiday she liked – alone together and away from it all: a walking tour. The reality was perhaps less romantic. B.M.'s diary:

Harold and Vita arrived [at White Lodge] early and were starving and wanted an early lunch, as they were going to walk all the way from Steyning to Basingstoke. Today they will get to Amberley – 12 miles.... The poor child had left her spectacles in the car, so I started in pursuit of the 2 walkers and found them after ½ an hour already so hot. My heart melted for my poor Vita carrying her own pack and the leather of the straps of the pack were cutting her shoulders.

She understood how Harold, who was putting on weight, needed the exercise; 'but she was panting terribly when I met them, poor things. *Enfin.* I came back to my garden.'

On the last day of July Geoffrey Scott, whom they had seen in Rome the previous autumn, turned up in England. It was Vita he had chiefly come to see.

Geoffrey Scott was eight years older than Vita – tall, thin, short-sighted, witty, a good talker. In 1909, when Vita and Rosamund had met him with Cecil Pinsent in Florence, the two young architects had been working on alterations to the Berensons' Villa I Tatti. Mary Berenson, twenty years older than Geoffrey, had fallen in love with him and been very upset when in 1918 he had married Lady Sybil Cutting, the rich and beautiful daughter of Lord Desart and widow of the American diplomat Bayard Cutting. Lady Sybil lived with her daughter Iris at the nearby Villa Medici.

The small artistic community on the southern slopes of the Fiesole hills was rather incestuous. Lady Sybil had had a liaison with Bernard Berenson. Geoffrey himself, after his marriage to Lady Sybil, had fallen in love with Nicky Mariano, Berenson's librarian and last attachment. When the Nicolsons had seen Geoffrey in Rome during their holiday with the Wellesleys, he and Lady Sybil were having a trial separation: she remained in Florence at the Villa Medici, while he took the post of press secretary at the British Embassy in Rome.

Ben and Nigel were in Brittany with 'Goggy', their French governess, in that summer of 1923, when Vita accompanied Geoffrey Scott to the Lake District for a week. Harold was to spend part of the autumn in Greece researching his new book about Byron, and it was arranged that he and Vita should meet in Italy and go together to stay with the Scotts in Florence.

Ben, aged nine, went away to preparatory school in September – Summer Fields, in Oxford. Vita did not like leaving him there. But he wrote to her, 'My Darlingest Mummy, for goodness sake, do not worry, I am as happy as I am at home. In fact, I am happyer, because I have boys ... at first I felt very unhappy at first when you whent, and from the next morning till now, I loved it.' Vita sent Ben's letter on to Harold – 'please keep it safely for me' – on the tenth anniversary of their wedding: 'My darling precious, I thought about us being married today, and was half sad (because you were away) and half happy (because we still love each other better than anybody else in the world).'

She went to Florence before him, arriving on 15 October. She lunched with B.M. before she left, and B.M. noted shrewdly: 'I do hope she won't fall in love with G.S. there.' She was relieved by Vita's first letter. 'She has written from Florence that she sat in the moonlight with Geoffrey S. and felt quite immune. May it last! Pucci has returned in all haste! to see her.'

But a week later B.M. heard again from Vita 'to whom the inevitable has happened. Oh! my God! may she not be too unhappy! I shall be her great friend and confidante. But I do dread it all for her and poor Harold.'

However much she dreaded it, this 'normal' affair was something B.M. could understand, and something that Vita had no qualms about confiding. 'She says she does not want to ... create a new scandal. But she says she will miss him atrociously and wants to hide it from Harold. I am the only one she has told. And of course my poor child can open her heart to me; I am absolutely safe and so understanding.'

After the Nicolsons left Florence, Vita and Geoffrey wrote daily to one another. He told her that he thought his wife had realized what had happened, but asked no questions. 'I have tried to be very nice to her, reading aloud to her and so on.... My dear nothing can touch you without becoming fine, and I think that is going to be felt and understood.'

B.M. worried because Vita told her that Geoffrey was 'very passionate'. 'She is sure Harold does not mind and Lady Sybil prefers it should be her. He [Geoffrey] has had many affairs but naturally she and G. think this one *is* the one. She is not his mistress, she assured me of it.'

Geoffrey knew all about Violet 'and says his love will redeem [Vita's] reputation which really already has been redeemed.' (B.M. herself was involved in a relationship with Edwin Lutyens that for the next three years was 'certainly close enough to be a love affair,'[3] Lutyens's daughter Mary has written. Vita thought they were probably lovers; she destroyed some of Lutyens's letters to her mother after B.M.'s death.)

Vita and Geoffrey in their letters discussed the 'tidying up of life' necessary to accommodate one another. Pat Dansey was resentful at being put on one side; poor Dorothy Wellesley was even more dependent. 'Do whatever you think best about Dottie,' Geoffrey wrote. 'I'm terribly sorry you should have had such painful things to go through. I'm a bad surgeon myself and understand how wretched it all is.' He begged her not to 'talk', for Sybil's sake. 'I hope B.M. won't tell people. If Ozzie [Dickinson] knows we might as well put it in the papers.'

Lady Sybil, who was older than Geoffrey and thirteen years older than Vita, was not so understanding as the lovers had assumed. She became frantic with misery: 'for twenty-four hours it seemed the smash had come ... she was completely broken.' Geoffrey did not want his marriage broken up: 'If my marriage smashes over this, I shall be persecuted by remorse, for I shall know it's really the wreck of her life. It isn't like Harold who, deeply as his life is rooted in you, *has* his youth, his ambitions, his work and – well other things.' Vita was upset and wrote what she herself called an hysterical letter, offering to give Geoffrey up. Geoffrey showed it to his wife, who wrote very sweetly to Vita just before Christmas, begging her only to be discreet and admitting 'I *am* in love with Geoffrey, just as much as when I married him.' Her attempts at resignation and tolerance did not last. Only ten days later Geoffrey was despairing to Vita of ever achieving what he chose to call 'a working relationship' with someone of Sybil's 'blind, torturing tenacity'.

When they were not agonizing over the Sybil situation, theirs was a very literary love affair. Geoffrey Scott had published *The Architecture of Humanism* in 1914, and was working on *The Portrait of Zélide*. They discussed his work and her poetry in their letters. Vita had begun reviewing books for the *Nation*, and she tied first in a competition for a sea sonnet run by the American *Poetry Review*. Her edition of *The Diary of the Lady Anne Clifford* came out (Lady Anne was the wife of the third Earl of Dorset and daughter of the Earl of Cumberland). And she was seriously compiling material for her long poem *The Land*. She had written to Eddie Marsh that she liked a phrase of his about the 'short lyric cries' of modern poets, 'which exactly expresses the irritation that is driving me into trying the experiment of a volume of *connected* verse'. Staying at Knole on 6 January 1924, she lay down in the afternoon 'and between sleeping and waking started a poem about woods'.

> Here is no colour, here but form and structure,
> The bones of trees, the magpie bark of birches.[4]

Geoffrey Scott arrived in London on 10 January 1924. Vita met him that evening and dined with him at the Berkeley Hotel. They were both shy, their actual relationship having been outstripped by the intimacy of their letters. In her diary Vita called it 'a bewildering and not very real evening'. Next day Geoffrey came down to Knole for the first of several weekends; Vita's father, Harold and the children were there too. B.M., isolated in her house outside Brighton, was worried. Vita had told her 'not to dread a little mar [i.e., a pregnancy by Geoffrey] as she feels cold and does not want "to live" with G.S.', but 'will she be able to resist his passion?'

Very soon Vita took Geoffrey to lunch with B.M. Like all Vita's admirers (Pat Dansey saw B.M. continually), he realized the primacy of B.M. in Vita's life, and wrote her conciliating letters. 'I know that the first thing Vita did, when we realized how much our friendship meant, was to write and tell you ... so I had a great desire that you might know how I feel to her, for if you did I don't think you could disapprove of me altogether.'

It was not easy for Vita to fit the demanding Geoffrey into her everyday life and she began to feel ill at ease. A luncheon with Bogey Harris was uncomfortable 'by reason of the tension between Aprile [Dorothy Wellesley] and Geoffrey, and our knowledge of Bogey's curiosity etc.' Ozzie Dickinson's curiosity was even more acute and was inevitably satisfied by B.M. who was incapable of discretion.

Harold was depressed, ostensibly because a change in government had temporarily made him uneasy at the Foreign Office; he did not speak at all at a lunch party given by B.M. on 1 February. 'I put it down to G.S.,' wrote his mother-in-law in her diary. 'At the best, he can't like it and his pride must suffer.' He began falling asleep after dinner at home and worrying about his health. B.M. was probably right in her surmise that 'I am sure that Harold sits all of a heap and looks unhappy all through this "flirtation" ... and one never knows what she may do suddenly.' Vita took Geoffrey as her guest to the PEN Club dinner – 'laughed a great deal' – and went back with him afterwards to his borrowed flat at 8 Hanover Terrace. On 7 February he bought her a ring.

Her excitement made her attractive – to other men. After a party given by Mary Hutchinson at Chiswick she gave Duff Cooper a lift home in her car, and 'to my astonishment he made love to me ... altogether a queer evening.' The next day he sent her sheaves of flowers and wrote to her that they were sent 'as a sort of ratification – and to show that vows made at midnight are not always false. They were all white and I hoped you would accept their stainless testimony.'

In mid-February Geoffrey went back to Italy, after staying a night with Vita at Knole. She had flu and felt less than romantic. Gossip, fuelled by Ozzie Dickinson and the artist George Plank, B.M.'s neighbour and confidant, disregarded such niceties. It was like the Violet days all over again, wailed B.M.: 'everyone deplores she has taken up with such a bounder. Everybody calls him a *bounder*.'

Vita survived his departure remarkably well. On 22 February she went down to Richmond to dine with the Woolfs 'in the kitchen as usual':

Virginia delicious as ever; how right she is when she says love makes everyone a bore, but that the excitement of life lies in the *béguins* [fancies, infatuations], and the 'little moves' nearer to people – but perhaps she feels this because she's an experimentalist in humanity and has no *grande passion* in her life. Raymond Mortimer came home with me and stayed talking till 1.30.

Duff Cooper's 'little moves' towards her continued and, amused and flattered, she dined with him several times at the Ivy. She told B.M. about it, and Geoffrey, who was not amused at all. Dottie was reinstated as her constant companion; in her letters to Harold Vita always stressed the one-way nature of this relationship, underplaying her own emotional involvement.

Just after Geoffrey left Vita had lunched with Lord Berners to meet Lady Ottoline Morrell, 'whose hair was coming down as usual and whose clothes were dabbed over with splashes of leopard.... Liked Lady Ottoline.' She and Dottie went to lunch with Lady Ottoline at Garsington: 'Pugs, peacocks and Pekinese; photograph albums; talk – mostly about Virginia.' At another luncheon she sat next to George Bernard Shaw and did not like him; 'he sucks his teeth.' At Ethel Sands's house she met Arnold Bennett: 'After dinner discussed modern literature with him, and modern criticism, – his wider view is refreshing after the limitations of Bloomsbury.' Suddenly she was being social. 'Dined at home thank goodness with my little H.' is a diary entry remarkable for its rarity.

Pat Dansey, in spite of regular meetings with Vita, was crazily jealous of everyone. On 8 March 'she suggested blowing out her brains and leaving a letter to be read at the inquest saying it was my fault for being so unkind to her, – but melted finally, – and we parted friends, me wiping the sweat of surprise off my brow.'

Virginia had said that love made everyone a bore. Geoffrey Scott loved Vita. Far away in Italy, both he and his wife were ill with tension and uncertainty. Geoffrey had thought that Vita would come out to him almost at once. But her letters, he complained, were 'preternaturally remote (half-sheets that promise a letter tomorrow which then you don't write)'.

Vita's cooling towards Geoffrey gave Harold the confidence to approach her again sexually. On 10 March he wrote in his diary: 'Vita nuova.' She wrote in hers: 'Hadji. My God!' The experiment may not have been repeated often, but Vita told a relieved B.M. that 'she really thought she could not be really madly in love with anyone, as she was so fond of Harold. She said she got *des béguins* which lasted two or three days and she got over them easily.'

What disappointed Vita in Harold was his absorption in his work and in books at the expense of what she called 'life'. Her absorption in both her own work and her own life could often exclude him for a while; it was understandable if he did not always spring to attention on the occasions when she would have liked him to – but it widened the gap between them. Long Barn, 18 April 1924: 'H. had the day off but didn't take much notice of Ronnie [Balfour] and me as he is deep in [reading about] Jane Carlyle. The dead mean more to him than the living, I think. Ronnie and I went for a moonlight walk after dinner, but he wouldn't come. It is warm, and the nightingales have begun.' B.M. made a terrible fuss when Vita, Harold and Dottie went off to Wales just when she wanted Vita to help her pack up her London house in Hill Street, which she was selling. Her fury over this trivial inconvenience was sustained for weeks. Perhaps the long and painful experience of her mother affected Vita's treatment of other people. The neglected Geoffrey, at least, thought so:

> You see you are very conciliatory by nature and very much affected by 'scenes' when people make them. ... And if I abstain from scenes it wouldn't be fair, would it, to let that count? ... Remember that the pressure to divide us will be steady and persistent. ... I sometimes think you react to people by the amount of passion or suffering they *display* [he cited Violet, B.M., Dottie, Pat]. I'm not going to compete with them.

Harold had long ago come to the same conclusion.

The Woolfs moved from Richmond to Tavistock Square in Bloomsbury, and Vita went to see them there in the middle of the upheaval. (Vita thought the panels painted for the new drawing-room by Duncan Grant and Vanessa Bell were of 'inconceivable hideousness'.) She stayed on for the afternoon, talking with Virginia – 'books and life, as usual. The first time, I think, that I have been alone with her for long.' Another 'little move' had been made.

Meanwhile Geoffrey Scott did not lose hope, though he was frightened and bewildered by her cool letters. He gave up his job at the embassy in Rome – 'it was just one more barrier separating me from you' – and planned to spend six months of the year with his wife in Florence and six with Vita in England. There were a few weeks' grace left for Vita; she worked and gardened throughout the spring at Long Barn, and wrote her first gardening article, a lyrical piece of no practical application called 'Notes on a Late Spring', for the *Evening Standard*. She was also writing for *Vogue* and still working on *The Land*. In May Virginia Woolf asked her to write something for the Hogarth Press – another little move closer.

In June Geoffrey was back. He should have read the signs at once; Vita met him at the station and then 'had to' rush off at once to see Dottie at Sherfield. She had already sent him her 'Principles with regard to

Long Barn', making it clear that no improprieties were to take place under Harold's roof. When B.M. saw Geoffrey at Long Barn she noticed he was 'trembling all over' and looking ill. (B.M. herself was upset again. Lionel had asked her for a divorce so that he could marry Olive Rubens. '*NO* to that terrible and quite unnecessary humiliation of that *snake in the grass* in my place at Knole.')

That same weekend Virginia Woolf, who had met Geoffrey in Florence years before, came to Long Barn for the first time, driving down with Vita and Dottie, 'observing their endearments rather awkwardly' and feeling 'not provincial, but ill-dressed, ill-equipped'. 'That night we sat in the long room, and after Harold had grown sleepy sitting on the fender knocking his head against the fringe of the Italian cover on the mantelpiece, Geoffrey sat with us, and was drawn by Dotty into telling stories for my amusement. He did this very well.'[5] Geoffrey, Virginia thought, had 'the distinguished face of a failure'; she felt that he, Vita, Harold and Dottie were a 'set', intimate and familiar. When on the Sunday they all went over to Knole Geoffrey seemed quite at ease and, wrote Virginia, 'called Lord Sackville Lionel as if he had known him and Vita familiarly for many years'.

She had no idea that Vita and Geoffrey were having an affair that was at flash-point. Geoffrey, believing that Vita might still commit herself entirely to him, had just been told that she and Harold were going off on a holiday together to the Dolomites. In his bedroom at night he wrote notes to her. 'My darling – I am writing this by my window waiting for you to open yours and wave goodnight across the garden.' She had been, he said, her 'old self' with him briefly that evening; she must enjoy her holiday, then 'come back and arrange things better for both of us. It's all in *your* hands really. . . . My gypsy, keep my love, don't kill it and me.' He was bitterly aware of 'the *mockery* of all the effort to obtain some liberty'; having managed to come from Italy to England to be with her, he found her 'absolutely immersed and starting off – to Italy'.

Vita's dereliction of Geoffrey was a relief to her mother. The day before she and Harold left, B.M. told them the Ebury Street house was to be theirs outright – she did not want her loan paid back. She would also pay them £500 a year towards its upkeep, £200 a year towards Ben's school fees and all Harold's supertax (incurred because Vita's income was assessed with his). 'They are *delighted*, bless them.'

# CHAPTER 13

DURING the holiday in the Dolomites in July 1924 Vita wrote almost all her short novel *Seducers in Ecuador*. She wrote to Virginia from Tre Croci, Cadore :

I hope that no one has ever yet, or ever will, throw down a glove I was not ready to pick up. You asked me to write a story for you. On the peaks of mountains, and beside green lakes, I am writing it for you. I shut my eyes to the blue of gentians, to the coral of androsace; I shut my ears to the brawling of rivers ; I shut my nose to the scent of pines ; I concentrate on my story.

But the real challenge, Vita said, was not the story but a letter from Virginia reproaching her for not writing 'intimate letters' but letters of 'impersonal frigidity'. It was difficult to do otherwise in the mountains :

I feel as though all intellect had been swallowed up into sheer physical energy and well-being. This is how one ought to feel, I am convinced. ... Will you ever play truant to Bloomsbury and culture, I wonder, and come travelling with me ? No, of course you won't. I told you once I would rather go to Spain with you than with anyone, and you looked confused, and I felt I had made a gaffe, – been too personal, in fact, – but still the statement remains a true one and I shan't be really satisfied till I have enticed you away.

And she developed her fantasy of going with Virginia to a gathering of Spanish gypsies ; Virginia could look on it, if she liked, 'as copy' – 'as I believe you look upon everything, human relationships included. Oh yes, you like people through the brain better than through the heart, – forgive me if I am wrong. Of course there must be exceptions ; there always are. But generally speaking.'[1] Virginia replied that she had enjoyed the 'intimate letter from the Dolomites. It gave me a great deal of pain – which is I've no doubt the first stage of intimacy.'[2] Vita did not know what to make of the 'pain' she had given. 'Or was it just one of your phrases, poked at me? Do you ever mean what you say, or say what you mean? or do you just enjoy baffling the people who try to creep a little nearer?'[3]

Vita was also giving Geoffrey a good deal of pain; the question of intimacy came up here too, since Vita was, Geoffrey had said, 'less intimate by nature' than he was. He was talking about sex. 'Don't deny too much the poor foolish outlet that Nature has provided.' He was heartened that she liked his book *The Portrait of Zélide*, which she and Harold read on their return to Long Barn. As he said in a very long letter to her written on 2 September, he was unable to reconcile the two Vitas – one loving and supportive, the other hostile and apathetic. If he had behaved badly to her, it was not his fault. (Vita told Virginia, later, that one night in the Hanover Terrace flat he had nearly strangled her.) 'If we lived together none of this would have happened.... My darling, I can't pretend I love you in a mystical platonic way that can make terms with apathy. ... You wanted me entirely, as I wanted you; and you've got it. And Vita you *can't treat love the way you've treated mine*, truly you can't.' He didn't even expect her, now, to leave Harold, but he begged her to tell him the truth about her feelings. He had luncheon, frequently, with a wary but always inquisitive B.M.; he grew iller and more depressed.

On 15 September Vita drove down for her first visit to Monk's House, Rodmell, the Woolfs' spartan country house (no bathroom, no inside lavatory, no telephone). She brought the manuscript of *Seducers in Ecuador* with her. Virginia said she liked it: 'I'm certain that you have done something much more interesting (to me at least) than you've yet done ... I am very glad we are going to publish it, and extremely proud and indeed touched, with my childlike dazzled affection for you, that you should dedicate it to me.'[4]

The book went to the printers and Geoffrey went back to Italy, less demanding but still unable to give up hope. He grieved as her letters once more grew inadequate and infrequent. 'Your future biographer,' he told her, 'scrutinizing the postmarks of your letters – and their contents – during the summer of 1924 ... will conclude that you didn't love the alleged Tinker [Vita's pet name for him] the least bit. Would your ghost resent that? Mine would.' But only his letters to her have survived.

*Seducers in Ecuador* is short and ironic: its subject, as well as its genre, is fantasy. The hero Arthur Lomax puts on coloured spectacles and 'the world is changed for him' thereby, shielding him from the 'too-realistic glare' of the sun. Abandoning common sense, he becomes credulously involved in other people's fantasies. Each fellow passenger on the cruise he takes to Egypt is caught up in some irrational personal myth that keeps him or her going and gives purpose to life. There is no recipient, for example, for the long letters Miss Whitaker writes to an address in Ecuador. At his trial for murder Lomax discovers 'how pitiable a weapon was truth' – individual fantasy was the only potent defence.

Vita was particularly attractive to, and attracted by, mythomanes: Violet, Dottie and Pat (who had recently told Vita she was giving her a block of shares in the *Morning Post* that would make her a director; the shares were non-existent). She herself lived with fantasy versions of herself – Julian, and her 'Spanish gypsy' self, and the self that was for ever master of Knole. She handled her story lightly and with sophistication.

Bloomsbury approved of Vita's new manner. 'They imagine that they have "discovered" you,' Harold told her – he had seen Raymond Mortimer and Clive Bell – 'and can talk of nothing else.' The *Spectator* gave the book knowing praise as 'a slim, fantastic *conte* in the Bloomsbury manner'. Eddy Sackville-West feared that his cousin was being taken over, and hoped that Vita was not being converted to the Bloomsbury mentality. 'I like them all (especially Mrs Woolf),' he wrote to Vita, 'but I mistrust their minds fundamentally.... They are *terrified* of committing themselves to a statement.... I resented the way Mrs Woolf announced the book to me, as much as to say: "Now at last your cousin has entered the path of virtue!"'

In some quarters Vita proved to have out-Bloomsburied Bloomsbury. *Seducers in Ecuador* came out in the United States the following year, and was reviewed in the same issue of the *New York Evening Post*'s Literary Review as Virginia Woolf's *Mrs Dalloway*. In considering the personal and professional relationship between the two women, it is important to realize that although Virginia Woolf never thought of Vita as a great writer, and although Vita always conceded intellectual and artistic supremacy to Virginia, the common reader in their lifetimes took another view. Vita was, simply, more successful. *Seducers* was reviewed at the top of the page, along with a languorous drawing of its author. The notice by Joseph Collins ends: 'It is an amusing story well told, which can do more in an hour's reading to make the reader think and meditate on the values of what he considers realities than a great many novels do.' *Mrs Dalloway*, reviewed below, got a cooler reception from Walter Yust; as a novel 'it lacks that quality of illusion which can turn the day ... into a life richer than any single figure groping through it ... the day is sometimes dull and drear under a fog of words and (sensitively realized) redundancies.'

People who admired Vita's sober 'Georgian' poetry were puzzled.

'*Seducers in Ecuador* was a joke,' Vita wrote to Eddie Marsh. 'Why were you mystified?' Geoffrey Scott was disapproving. He felt it was a self-conscious book, and artificial for Vita: 'Virginia forged her method for her own very personal perception of phenomena. Your intimate instinctive apprehension is I think at the opposite pole to hers (hence its fascination for you, I expect) and is I should say *au fond* nearer to [D.H.] Lawrence's.' He told her that she was capable of writing something 'which will have more lasting-power than the cleverness of Bloomsbury. There's an unwieldy *something* in almost all your books which has more reality in it than any amount of modish psychology and modish technique.'

Vita agreed with this really. The 'unwieldy *something*' that she felt sometimes as her strength and sometimes as her failing was going into *The Land*. Geoffrey wrote her detailed criticism and advice about what she enclosed of it in her letters. He felt it was 'our poem, just as *Zélide* is our book. . . . I'm going to see to it that you don't publish it as a whole [she was publishing extracts in periodicals] till it's reached its full stature and its last polish, for it's by that poem as likely as not that you'll ultimately stand: you will have shot your bolt.'

He knew that the Bloomsbury mentality was a threat to his hold on her, such as it was. A greater threat loomed up briefly in December. Vita went to Paris for a couple of days to see to a sale of remaining objects from Seery's flat in the rue Laffitte: she was to stay with the American lawyer Walter Berry in the rue de Varenne. On arrival, she wrote in panic to Harold that Berry had arranged a dinner party for her that included Violet Trefusis. 'Oh my God. What am I to do? I can't tell Walter B. I feel sick at the idea.' Harold was terrified: 'Oh my darling *do* be careful. You are always so opty about things and *so* weak. And she is such a fiend of destruction. What an old ninny Walter is!' He wrote a second time the same day: 'Her very name brings back all the aching unhappiness of those months: the doubt, the mortification, and the loneliness. I think she is the only person of whom I am frightened.'

But Vita came home unscathed: back to Harold and cold Bloomsbury, which retained doubts about Vita in spite of *Seducers*. She dined with the Woolfs on 19 December, and, according to Virginia, offended Roger Fry's Quakerishness; '& she has the habit of praising & talking indiscriminately about art, which goes down in her set, but not in ours.' It was another 'thorny' evening, until Clive Bell came in and 'addressed himself to conciliate dear old obtuse, aristocratic, passionate, Grenadier-like Vita.'[5]

Virginia shared her circle's scepticism about Vita's writing and her intellect, but she was fascinated by her as a woman, reinventing her through the coloured spectacles of her own fantasy. In a gossipy letter to

Jacques Raverat in France, she described Vita as both an aristocrat and a
novelist, 'but her real claim to consideration is, if I may be so coarse, her
legs':

> Oh they are exquisite – running like slender pillars up into her trunk, which is
> that of a breastless cuirassier (yet she has 2 children) but all about her is
> virginal, savage, patrician; and why she writes, which she does with
> complete competency and a pen of brass, is a puzzle to me. If I were she, I
> should merely stride, with 11 Elk hounds behind me, through my ancestral
> woods.[6]

And stride she did. Leonard Woolf later wrote that he thought that
'striding' was something people only did in novels. That was before he
had seen Vita. He described her at this time as being 'literally – and so
few people ever are literally – in the prime of life, an animal at the height
of its powers, a beautiful flower in full bloom':

> To be driven by Vita on a summer's afternoon at the height of the season
> through the London traffic – she was a very good, but rather flamboyant
> driver – and to hear her put an aggressive taxi driver in his place, even when
> she was in the wrong, made one recognize a note in her voice that Sackvilles
> and Buckhursts were using to serfs in Kent 600 years ago, or even in Nor-
> mandy 300 years before that. She belonged indeed to a world which was
> completely different from ours.[7]

Vita was confiding in her mother. She told B.M. about Eddy Sackville-
West's homosexuality; she told her how she had dressed up as 'Julian' –
'to get copy' – during the Violet period; she told how patient Geoffrey
was, and how cold she felt towards him. Geoffrey was baffled by her.
'But to ask for a possessive lover,' he complained, 'and do everything to
show him he "possesses" nothing, is not only damnable, it's idiotic.' It
was a damnable, idiotic pattern that Vita was to repeat, with different
people, for several years.

In early April 1925 she, Harold and the eleven-year-old Ben went to
Italy. Geoffrey joined them in Venice and he and Vita went around
together. Vita liked him better out of England. Harold and Ben spent
quiet mornings together (one writing a book about Swinburne, the other
writing his diary); then they would meet the two others in the Piazza
San Marco at lunchtime.

Vita told B.M. how devoted Geoffrey had been, 'but she would never
marry him, or anyone, except Harold.' This may have been another of
the times when Vita longed for Harold to take some positive action on
his own behalf. She told her mother that he 'shut himself up within his

shell too much', that he 'cared for too few people'. That was soon to be
remedied ; he was to be lifted out of his emotional flatness by an important new friendship with Raymond Mortimer.

Vita spent as rustic and secluded a spring and summer as she could at
Long Barn. As she wrote in *The Land* :

> I have not understood humanity.
> But those plain things, that gospel of each year,
> Made me the scholar of simplicity.

Lutyens came to stay and designed the Dutch garden on the lower
terrace for her. She told Virginia that 'I cannot write, so am keeping
chickens instead.' But on the last weekend in May she and Harold were
invited to Blenheim to stay with the Duke and Duchess of Marlborough.
There was a house-party of twenty people, and at dinner Vita sat between Winston Churchill – 'I love Winston' – and 'a scientist called
Lindemann [later Lord Cherwell] who is absolutely thrilling'.

This was the sort of society B.M. thought her daughter ought to be
moving in. She decided to pay for a 'proper gardener' at Long Barn so
that Vita would not be 'worn out with gardening in this great heat' ; she
had just brought Vita a load of plants of a kind she would have happily
done without – bright annuals – and watched her planting them out in a
hurry 'as she had to go to London to dine with Virginia Wolff [*sic*] and
meet Foster [*sic*] who wrote that charming book *Passage to India*.' (Another unsuccessful Bloomsbury dinner : Forster praised Edith Sitwell
and said nothing to Vita, 'who sat hurt, modest, silent, like a snubbed
schoolboy'.[8])

Vita heard from Geoffrey at the end of May that his wife Sybil wanted
a divorce. While he had been hanging about in London she had found
solace with Percy Lubbock, and wanted to marry him. This was a most
unexpected twist. 'She says "You've got Vita, so *you'll* be all right." (The
irony of that "got".)' There was a slight danger of Vita being cited in the
divorce, but Harold was not to be told yet, Geoffrey said. 'I feel I belong
nowhere' – he had to leave the Villa Medici. Could he count on Vita ?
'Oh my dear you'll not go back on the tinker will you ?' He was going to
come to England, and he was going to be poor since he had lived on Sybil's
money.

Vita told Harold about this new crisis and made him write to Geoffrey
asking him to keep away. Harold repaid her confidence in him by confiding in her in return. His friendship with Raymond Mortimer had
become a love affair. He wrote gratefully to her on 2 July 1925 :

> My darling – you were so sweet to me last night. Please realize that it is *not*
> important – but only important enough to emerge from an emotion to an

attitude – and as such implying deception on my part if concealed. I feel a great load off my chest, darling – I simply loathe to get into a false position with you. And now *that* is all right – my angel.

Geoffrey, in despair and threatening suicide, went to stay with B.M. (she paid for his rail ticket). When Vita came to discuss the situation with her mother, B.M. equated Geoffrey with Lutyens, 'who clings to me so tenaciously, however fond I am of him'. Added to this, Lionel was asking again for a divorce, and talking of bringing Baron Bildt and Lutyens into the case. Mother and daughter grew even closer in their similar troubles. Vita, that summer, wrote her mother a letter of solidarity that amounted to a love letter:

> I feel that I have never before had you so satisfactorily to myself . . . but when I saw you today in your dining-room, so lovely, so gracious, so graceful, so rich of nature, so warm-hearted, so generous, I suddenly felt as though I knew you a thousand times better, and yet as though I saw you for the first time, – I can't write about it, – but I just adored you and felt I would die for you, – that's all there is about it.

Many people felt like that about Vita, too, over the years; it was an adoration that she subconsciously exacted. Her mother's personality was, she wrote, 'like a great warm sun irradiating all my days – an inspiration and an ideal. I do understand McNed's [Lutyens's] feeling so well.'

Virginia Woolf was unwell in the late summer of 1925, suffering from headaches and exhaustion. Her fascination with Vita grew in letters – 'I try to invent you for myself,' as she wrote on 7 September. Two weeks earlier, she had had 'a perfectly romantic and no doubt untrue vision of you in my mind – stamping out the hops in a great vat in Kent – stark naked, brown as a satyr, and very beautiful. Don't tell me this is an illusion.'[9] Vita, understanding something of Virginia's dangerous depressions, wrote to her encouragingly: 'You are a very, very remarkable person. . . . You are one perpetual Achievement.'[10]

Towards the end of September Harold was asked by the Foreign Office if he was prepared to go to the embassy at either Teheran or Peking as counsellor. He refused: 'Ben requires constant looking after by either V. or me if he is not to go off the rails', and it would cost too much for Vita to keep coming and going. But he changed his mind. His career was at stake: 'it really is the turning-point and if I miss this I shall be done in the eye.' He told Vita he would accept Teheran. 'She is rather dismayed.' At Sherfield, the *partie carrée* of Dottie, the Nicolsons and Raymond Mortimer looked at maps of Persia. 'How poignant everything is,' wrote Vita in her diary.

There was no question of her going out with Harold straight away. Yet she was excited – because she would soon go to Persia? Because she was going to be alone? 30 September 1925:

> Alone. A *good* day. Went round the garden with Barnes [the new gardener]. Wrote 71 lines – Georgics [*The Land*]. A record I think? Very warm; misty. Marvellous to be alone. Discussed his unemotionalism with Hadji after dinner. Wish I had kept a permanent diary. Will do so in future. (*I don't think.*) Life is too exciting altogether, suddenly.

The next day was their wedding anniversary – 'Both so pleased about it.'

In *The Portrait of Zélide* Geoffrey Scott had written:

> It may confidently be asserted that the habit of letter-writing has estranged far more lovers than it has united.... The personality disengaged by the pen is something apart and often ironically diverse from that other personality of act and speech. Thus in the correspondence of lovers there will be four elements at play – four egoisms to be placated instead of two. And by this grim and mathematical law the permutations of possible offence will be calculably multiplied.

He was writing about Benjamin Constant and Zélide: he was thinking about himself and Vita. But what he wrote was only partly true of Vita and Harold. While 'the personality disengaged by the pen' for both Harold and Vita was, as Geoffrey wrote, quite different from 'that other personality of act and speech', it functioned in an entirely positive way. Harold in the flesh, as Vita had said, was unemotional, undemonstrative, with a strong distaste for emotional display. Vita had her moods of withdrawal. But in their letters, they were each other's beloved.

In their letters, each addressed the essential other, and lived their marriage at its closest. They verbalized their affection and need. People with a sexual bond do not have to say so much. The marriage of their correspondence was its platonic ideal, in which both believed. If this was an instinctual psychological device to contain the looseness of their union, it was a successful one – so successful that it took on a life of its own. The more effectively they could meet on the page, the more separate they could be in the everyday. What began as a unifying process legitimized their separateness.

Vita sent letters to Harold ahead, to wait for him in the cities he passed through on the long journey to Persia; and she gave him a St Christopher medal. Nigel, aged eight, sent a letter ahead too: 'It must be funny to leave Long Barn for two years, you will forget what it looks like. But it will be lovely to come home to find the new garden blooming with lovely flowers, and your room will be a 'féte de fluers' [*sic*] arranged by Mummy who will have roses in her hair.'

Harold left on 4 November, and that night Vita wrote to him that he had 'no idea, no conception, of how much I love you. . . . I wish I had gone with you, and let the rest go hang. I feel so much that I am yours.' And the next day :

It just shows one, Hadji, how very superficial all one's *béguins* are, tested by the touchstone of one's real love, – one's life's love, – even though one's *béguins* may be more upsetting and urgent (apparently at least) while they last. . . . Darling, it is very odd, isn't it ? because it is not physical, which is what usually gives this violent quality to love. And I have no jealousy of you, – I who am horribly, murderously jealous.

And the day after that : 'I don't mind who you sleep with, so long as I may keep your heart !' Four days after his departure she copied neatly into her manuscript book a new poem about the frail security of their domestic happiness :

> Sometimes when night has thickened on the woods,
> And we in the house's square security
> Read, speak a little, read again,
> Read life at second-hand, speak of small things,
> Being content and withdrawn for a little hour
> From the dangers and fears that are either wholly absent
> Or wholly invading, – sometimes a shot rings out,
> Sudden and sharp ; complete. It has no sequel,
> No sequel for us, only the sudden crack
> Breaking a silence followed by a silence,
> Too slight a thing for comment ; slight, and usual,
> A shot in the dark, fired by a hand unseen
> At a life unknown ; finding, or missing, the mark ?
> Bringing death ? bringing hurt ? teaching, perhaps, escape,
> Escape from a present threat, a threat recurrent,
> Or ending, once and for all ? But we read on,
> Since the shot was not at our hearts, since the mark was not
> Your heart or mine, not this time, my companion.[11]

All autumn she kept Harold up to date with Nigel's sayings and doings and with the major improvements in the garden that they had planned together. She planted box edgings and had the herring-bone brick path relaid. (Barnes, whose salary was paid by B.M., made these projects possible.) She ordered yew trees 'which will look silly at first, but which when the mars are a little grey handful of ashes will draw charabancs full of tourists from London.' By the last week in November she had planted 'great drifts of Japanese irises' around the pond, and martagon lilies and red anemone in the grass; she had ordered pink spiraea to back the irises. 'You know I really think I could live quite alone for an indefinite period of time, quite content – if I might not live with you, which I prefer. It is very eccentric at my age, I suppose [she was thirty-three], but perfectly genuine.'

She told him about some of the intrusions on her solitude – Geoffrey, for example, who telephoned to her saying he was out of his mind, he was going to Mexico, he was going to kill himself. Occasionally she let him come down to Long Barn. He had begun to seek comfort with Dorothy Warren, a niece of Lady Ottoline's husband Philip, who ran a picture gallery in Brook Street; and Dorothy Warren, much to Vita's irritation, began cultivating Vita both on Geoffrey's behalf and her own. Dorothy wrote Vita a long ambiguous letter on 12 November, saying how worried she was about Geoffrey:

> He has been indescribably wretched and shattered. I have seen him a great deal.... I have never had an opportunity for showing you how I feel about you. To me you seem very wonderful and in every way beautiful. I know that you can do immeasurably more for Geoffrey than any other human being.... Poor Geoffrey, he has no back-stiffening masculine reserves or hypocrisies.

Geoffrey, wanting to keep Vita out of the case, had to produce false evidence of adultery for Sybil to divorce him. Vita told Harold that 'He was provided with a flaxen-haired lady whom he didn't like at all, and whom he thought a wicked waste of money. I said he ought to send in his account to Sybil, but he said no, that wasn't done.' Harold surmised that Vita must be more frightened by this mess than she admitted. 'Darling I'm so sorry for you about Geoffrey. I should feel the same about Tray [Raymond Mortimer] if I felt that he was off his rocker on my account. But I think that Geoffrey is one of the world's muddlers – who takes the same sort of ghoulish pleasure in unhappiness as the hypochondriac does in ill-health.'

Virginia Woolf's health was still precarious; Vita visited her for only half an hour at a time. Virginia wrote in her diary on 27 November: 'Vita has been twice. She is doomed to go to Persia; & I minded the thought so much ... that I conclude I am genuinely fond of her.' The best thing about her recurring illnesses, she thought, was that 'they loosen the earth among the roots. They make changes. People express their affection.'

She was drawing closer to Vita, and Vita to her. In early December Virginia wrote saying her doctor would now allow her to go away;

diffidently, she suggested she might come to Long Barn for a day or two. Two days before, she had written in her diary that if she did not see Vita now, before she left for Persia, it would be too late – 'for the moment of intimacy will be gone, next summer.'[12]

Virginia came to Long Barn, without Leonard, on 17 December. Vita had had Geoffrey there for the previous two days – 'very much against my will' – and took him back to London by car and collected Virginia, in one round trip. They spent 'a peaceful evening', as she wrote in her diary. Late that night she wrote to Harold:

> Virginia is an exquisite companion, and I love her dearly. She has to stay in bed till luncheon, as she is still far from well, and she has lots of lessons to do. . . . Please don't think that
> a)  I shall fall in love with Virginia
> b)  Virginia will fall in love with me
> c)  Leonard will fall in love with me
> d)  I shall fall in love with Leonard
> because it is not so. Only I know my silly Hadji will say to himself 'Allons, bon!' when he hears V. is staying here, and 'Ça y est,' and so on. . . . I am missing you dreadfully. I am missing you specially because Virginia was so very sweet about you, and so understanding.

The next day, a Friday, they walked and shopped in Sevenoaks and talked; and in the evening came the 'moment of intimacy' that Virginia had envisaged, in Vita's sitting-room, with Virginia lying on the sofa by the fire. Vita wrote: 'Talked to her till 3 a.m. – Not a peaceful evening.'

Virginia's experience of close physical contact was limited. She had no sexual life with Leonard. She was clever, critical, ironic, mischievous even – and yet so nervous, fantastical, childlike, that even a kiss or a caressing hand might seem sensational to her. 'I was always sexually cowardly,' she was to write. 'My terror of real life has always kept me in a nunnery.' Clive Bell and Vita, she told Ethel Smyth later, both called her 'a fish': 'And I reply (I think often while holding their hands, and getting exquisite pleasure from contact with either male or female body) "But what I want of you is illusion – to make the world dance."'

Leonard came to collect his wife next day and Vita went up to London with them. 'We have made friends by leaps and bounds, in these two days. I love her, but couldn't fall in love with her, so don't be nervous!' Vita wrote to Harold. Characteristically Virginia distanced herself from what was happening by analysing it in her diary. On 21 December:

These Sapphists *love* women, friendship is never untinged with amorosity....
I liked her & being with her, & the splendour – she shines in the grocer's shop in
Sevenoaks with a candle lit radiance, stalking on legs like beech trees, pink
glowing, grape clustered, pearl hung. That is the secret of her glamour, I
suppose. Anyhow she found me incredibly dowdy.

What effect had 'all this' had on her, Virginia asked herself ; 'Very mixed'
was the answer.

There is her maturity and full breastedness : her being so much in full sail on the
high tides, where I am coasting down backwaters ; her capacity I mean to take
the floor in any company, to represent her country, to visit Chatsworth, to control silver, servants, chow dogs ; her motherhood (but she is a little cold & off-
hand with her boys) her being in short (what I have never been) a real woman.

In 'brain and insight' Virginia felt herself superior. 'But then she is aware
of this, & so lavishes on me the maternal protection which, for some
reason, is what I have always most wished from everyone. What
L[eonard] gives me, & Nessa [her sister Vanessa Bell] gives me, & Vita, in
her more clumsy external way, gives me.'

Vita was invited to luncheon at Charleston with the Woolfs and the
Bells on Boxing Day ; she had met Virginia's sister Vanessa only once
before and was nervous. She described the lunch to Harold as 'very plain
living and high thinking. I like Virginia's sister awfully. ... Virginia *loves*
your mar. She really does. It is a soul-friendship. Very good for me, and
good for her too.'

Dottie Wellesley, predictably, was unenthusiastic. (Virginia later
believed that Vita had 'left Dottie originally, I think, mostly on my
account.'[13]) Harold was philosophical but sounded the obvious warning.
'I am not really bothered about Virginia and think you are probably very
good for each other. I only feel you have not got *la main heureuse* with married couples.' Which was an understatement : even leaving the Wellesleys out of it, Vita had allowed Geoffrey to ruin his life and break his
marriage to no purpose.

Vita and the children spent the New Year as usual at Sherfield with
Dottie and her children. Raymond Mortimer, Clive Bell and Leigh
Ashton (who worked at the Victoria and Albert Museum) were also
staying. The New Year's Eve party got out of hand. A great deal was
drunk, 'Tray being quite frankly *blind*, and Clive with his tongue well-
loosened', as Vita described it to Harold :

Imagine my horror when he [Clive] suddenly said 'I wonder if I *dare* ask Vita a
very indiscreet question ?' and I, being innocent and off my guard, said yes he
might, and he came out with '*Have* you ever gone to bed with Virginia ?' but I

think my 'NEVER!' convinced him and everybody else of its truth. This will show you what the conversation was like!

'I hope Clive's version didn't differ materially from mine,' Vita wrote to Virginia. 'And did your version differ from mine? alas no.'[14]

Dorothy Warren, in love with Geoffrey, now wanted to see Vita all the time to talk about it. Geoffrey saw it would be sensible to marry her, but still loved Vita and wanted to see her all the time to talk about it. Dorothy Warren also loved Vita and wanted.... It was all very time-consuming. Vita went home to close up Long Barn and collect what she wanted to take to Persia. Harold had instructed her to bring lampshades, ashtrays, a tea-set and other English comforts for the rather bleak house in the British Legation compound at Teheran, where there was only an earth closet ('Mar will hate this') and a tiny bath 'heated from a stove *ad hoc*'. From Long Barn she wrote to Virginia: 'Please, in all this muddle of life, continue to be a bright and constant star. Just a few things remain as beacons: poetry, and you, and solitude. You see that I am extremely sentimental. Had you suspected that?'[15] She said goodbye to her sitting-room, and her writing table on which stood her Rodin figure, her marble inkstand, and a bowl of pot pourri made to the Knole recipe. Goodbye to her wintry garden, glimpsed through the terrace door beside which were the dogs' leads hanging on pegs and her mud-stiffened gardening gloves. Goodbye too to provincial England: on 9 January she gave away the prizes at a fancy-dress dance at the Club Hall in Sevenoaks. Goodbye to B.M. at White Lodge, 'in her old flannel nightgown and a miscellany of woollen scarves'; goodbye to Virginia, who dreaded her departure and wrote excited, infatuated letters to 'Dearest Creature'. Virginia was ill again and her iron bed was once more in the drawing-room; they talked in the dark. Vita was excited too: 'I find life altogether intoxicating,' she wrote to Virginia, 'its pain no less than its pleasure, – in which Virginia plays no mean part.'

Her half-packed luggage lay at Knole, where Eddy, as probable heir, had just been given an apartment by Vita's father.

Things scattered all over the room. And Eddy chattering while I try to remember what I have to pack. 'Do you know Tom Eliot?' 'No, I don't. – Kodak films, aspirin, fur gloves, toothpowder.' 'Aren't the woodcuts in *The Anatomy of Melancholy* too lovely!' 'No, Eddy, I think they're quite awful. – Don't put my riding boots in my suitcase, one doesn't ride on board ship.' 'Shall I have my sitting-room pink or yellow?' And so on....

Where is Virginia's quiet room? ... Some day I'll write and tell you all the things you mean to me in my mind. Shall I?[16]

She left Virginia her nearly completed manuscript of *The Land* to read ; Heinemann were going to publish it, not the Hogarth Press. Then Vita and Raymond took Ben and Nigel – 'poor little Niggs', who was going to join his brother at school – to the circus for a goodbye treat ; there was a last party at Clive's, and the morning after, 20 January, her train pulled out of Victoria Station.

# CHAPTER 14

VITA was off, but not on her own : Dorothy Wellesley accompanied her. Vita wrote to Virginia in the train from London, and again the next day on the way from Paris to Milan :

I am reduced to a thing that wants Virginia. I composed a beautiful letter to you in the sleepless nightmare hours of the night, and it has all gone : I just miss you, in a quite simple desperate human way.... It is incredible how essential to me you have become. I suppose you are accustomed to people saying these things. Damn you, spoilt creature ; I shan't make you love me any the more by giving myself away like this. But oh my dear, I *can't* be clever and stand-offish with you : I love you too much for that. Too truly. You have no idea how stand-offish I can be with people I don't love. I have brought it to a fine art. But you have broken down my defences. And I don't really resent it.[1]

She wrote again from Trieste, and from the boat she and Dottie took from there to Cairo, where they met Ronald Balfour. (Virginia's long, loving, exploratory replies can be read in her published *Letters*.) In Cairo Vita decided she had to buy a hat ; she would need one in Teheran for the coronation of the Shah. Dorothy Wellesley described the purchase in *Far Have I Travelled* :

She was furious at having to get a hat. Ronnie and I stood outside ; a whole hour passed. At last she emerged, wearing some sort of black hat into which she had stuck one of the largest emeralds I ever saw. The effect was miraculous. Someone said : 'She looks like the Empress Zenobia.' Her dignity was imperturbable ; at least it appeared so. Only the others laughed.

On 29 January Vita wrote to Virginia from Luxor that 'The only way I can deal with Egypt is as Molly MacCarthy did with Christmas : alphabetically.' And she reeled off a list, starting with 'Amon, Americans, alabaster . . .' all the way down to 'Xerxes, Xenophon ; yaourt ; zest (my own). . . . Do thin silk clothes and sunburn make you envious ? No, you wretch, you prefer your old misty Gloomsbury and your London squares. The wish to steal Virginia overcomes me, – steal her, take her away, and put her in the sun among the objects mentioned alphabetically above.' She described to Virginia their visit to the Valley of the Kings :

> If human beings are one half as exciting to you as natural objects are to me, then indeed I can see why you like living in London. I cannot explain why they should have this intoxicating quality. I can quite see why human beings should have. . . . And, mark you, – I do care so satisfactorily for the few people that matter to me. (For Virginia ? oh dear me YES, for Virginia.)²

Her sunstroke had prevented her and Harold from seeing the Valley of the Kings on their honeymoon ; she regretted this now, telling him it was 'one of the most impressive things I have ever seen ; it is just The Waste Land geographically materialized.' And they had seen Karnak by moonlight. Dottie, she told him, was 'the most satisfactory person to travel with, as she is so thrilled ; she says "Oh look !" every time she sees a donkey. Which is the right attitude.' She reassured him that she was equipped for the last lap of her journey to Persia, which was going to be bitterly cold : she had got a fur coat, a fur cap, 'a Jaeger blanket, and a Jaeger fluffy flea-bag . . . I have 2 Ever-hot bottles. And a Thermos . . . I have also an immense flask filled with Dotz' best brandy.' Vita had also brought with her St Barbara, the wooden figure that was Harold's first present to her.

But before Persia, she and Dottie were making a detour – to India. They sailed down the Suez Canal, 'surely the most loathsome place on earth', across the Indian Ocean to Bombay, where they were met by McNed – Edwin Lutyens – who was working on his New Delhi project. 'Bombay horrid place,' Vita wrote in her diary. India held no magic for either of the women. In Agra, Dottie felt their hotel was full of snakes ; in the night she crept in terror to Vita's room, from which she was, as usual, summarily despatched back to her own – or so Vita told Harold. Dottie sailed home from India ; Vita went on alone, taking a ship from Karachi across the Persian Gulf. Travelling was made relatively easy for her ; as a diplomat's wife, she was looked after at every main stopping-place by British Legation staff.

On the ship, she wrote a disenchanted letter to her father : 'India is a beastly squalid bedint country, and I don't care if I never see it again. The Hindus are a dirty, cringing lot ; give me the Egyptians any day.' She had a sprained ankle, a septic throat, an upset stomach and 'I am feeling rather lonely.' She read Proust and studied her Persian grammar and started writing a new book. She had already decided to write a traveller's tale about this journey; but she was envious of Virginia's excitement about her own new novel, and acknowledged that only the writing of fiction gave that peculiar excitement, 'as good as conducting an orchestra, or modelling in clay. A sense of really giving shape.'

She wrote to Virginia a little self-consciously, in Virginia's own manner, continuing their mutual exploration of one another. Of India she wrote that she had liked the Taj Mahal, 'a pure and sudden lyric. And everywhere squalor, squalor, squalor.' She knew that intellectually and artistically Virginia could run rings round her: 'I don't know whether to be dejected or encouraged when I read the works of Virginia Woolf. Dejected because I shall never be able to write like that, or encouraged because somebody can.'³ From the boat, she wrote:

> Now you (oh yes, I know I said I would write about Virginia going up the Persian Gulf) have the *mot juste* more than any modern writer I know. The only rival I would advance in that particular would be Max [Beerbohm]. I wonder whether it costs you a lot of thought or trouble, or springs ready-armed like Athene from the brow of Zeus? I don't believe it does cost you trouble, confound you! Because you have it in your letters too, where you certainly haven't made a draft. . . .
>
> The funny thing is, that you are the only person I have ever known properly who was aloof from the more vulgarly jolly sides of life. And I wonder whether you lose or gain? I fancy that you gain, – *you*, Virginia, – because you are so constituted and have a sufficient fund of excitement within yourself. . . . You'll think I'm perpetually trying to pull you down from your pedestal, but really I like you best up there. Only it would be fun to transplant you, pedestal and all, just once. . . . Goodnight, darling and remote Virginia.⁴

At the end of February Vita reached Iraq. In Baghdad she stayed with Gertrude Bell, the remarkable woman who was arabist, historian, alpinist, archaeologist and political adviser to the Iraqi Government; at this time she was completing the establishment of a national museum in Baghdad. Miss Bell gave a dinner for Vita, and showed her round the bazaars, and took her to tea with the King of Iraq – 'a charming handsome romantic looking man, who speaks bad French and looks infinitely lonely,' Vita wrote in her diary. She had met Gertrude Bell before, but was far more impressed with her here, 'in her right place, in her own house, with her office in the city, and her white pony in a corner of the garden, and her Arab servants, and her English books, and her Babylonian shards on the mantelpiece, and her long thin nose, and her irrepressible vitality.' (She died only four months after Vita's visit, aged fifty-eight.)

In Baghdad Vita found letters waiting from Virginia, and wrote in reply : 'Like a little warm coal in my heart burns your saying that you miss me. I miss you oh so much.... It is painful but also rather pleasant, if you know what I mean ... it is so good to have so keen and persistent a feeling about somebody. It is a sign of vitality. (No pun intended.)'⁵

Vita told Miss Bell that she wanted a saluki hound to take as a present to Harold. After making a telephone call, Miss Bell then went off to her office. Then, as Vita told her father, 'strings of Arabs began to arrive, holding sloughis [salukis] in leash. And when Gertrude came back to lunch, there was a regular pack, tied up to various posts of the verandah. And all my fault. And they are all still here, on approval.' Vita wanted them all ; on Miss Bell's advice, she picked a young yellow bitch called Zurcha. (She turned out to be irredeemably stupid, and the only really unsatisfactory dog the Nicolsons ever had.)

Vita travelled into Persia through Kurdestan with the Trans-Desert Mail (a convoy of motor cars). During the night bandits on horseback shadowed the convoy ; it was as real an adventure as Vita had ever dreamed of. 'I was almost sorry when we saw ahead of us the lights of Kermanshah.' There on 1 March Harold was waiting for her, in 'a terrible state of impatience, anxiety and excitement'. He saw the headlights, and then the car and 'my Viti sitting there in a little fur cap', with the saluki on her knee. 'Wild excitement.'

They drove the 500 miles from Kermanshah to Teheran together ; she described her pleasure to her father:

> One crosses endless plains, surrounded by amphitheatres of snow mountains, lovely brown plains, with flocks feeding on the slopes ; and then one goes over the barrier of mountains, by most dramatic passes, and from the top (10,000 feet) one surveys Central Asia, in one direction looking towards the Himalayas and in the other towards China. Of course the great charm of the place is the absolute wildness and absence of civilization ; you feel that as it is today, so it has been for the last thousand years, all exactly as it must have been when Marco Polo travelled this way.

They reached Teheran and 'Hadji's little house' on 5 March in brilliant sunshine.

Vita wrote that Teheran in 1926 was 'a squalid city of bad roads, rubbish heaps, and pariah dogs ; crazy little victorias with wretched horses ; a few pretentious buildings, and mean houses on the edge of collapse.'⁶ The city was still contained within its old mud ramparts ; once through the blue and yellow tiled gateway, the wild country began at once. 'We live on partridges, melons, pomegranate jam, and Shiraz wine.'

Vita's prejudices against the diplomatic life were confirmed, though she paid calls, attended and gave luncheons and dinners, as she had in Constantinople; she even gave away the hockey prizes. 'I don't like diplomacy, though I like Persia,' she told her father. 'On Sundays we get away into the country on expeditions.' It was spring in Persia; in the hills and valleys outside the city she and Harold found asphodel, mullein, red and purple poppies, scarlet ranunculus, iris persica in bloom, and wild almond, wisteria, lilac and roses in deserted shrines. In the desert beyond Doschau Tapeh on 26 March they found little purple anemones, and two days later they saw white and yellow tulips and young gazelles.

She described the Shah's birthday party to Virginia: 'So, at 8.15, an immense yellow motor draws up at the door; Harold in uniform and gold lace, little sword getting between his legs; Vita derisive, but decked in emeralds' – and looking 'quite beautiful', Harold thought. He wrote to Clive Bell on 19 March: 'Oh, Vita in Persia! Clive, I assure you, it is a lovely sight. Slow and impertubable she moves with her long slim legs; slowly and imperturbably she receives the unveiled admiration of Persian notables – and after dinner, with little greyhound grunts, she goes to sleep.'⁷ Some evenings Vita worked late, correcting the proofs of *The Land* and making additions. It was in Teheran on 23 March that she wrote the closing passage, the poet evoking her native Kent from the other side of the world:

> That moon, that star, above my English Weald,
> Hung at that hour, and I not there to see.

Vita helped Lady Loraine, wife of the British Minister in Teheran, to arrange and decorate the Gulestan Palace for the coronation of Shah Reza Khan. The palace was in a pitiful state, 'a mixture of splendour and squalor, like an immense jumble sale'. She put on an apron and mixed paints in the great hall, and 'wondered what the Persian is for "stipple"', as she wrote in one of her long letters to Virginia. In the same letter she said she was getting more and more reclusive by nature, and was afraid of this tendency; she did not have Virginia's skill in relating to humanity: 'And that perhaps is one of the reasons why I like women better than men, (even platonically), that they take more trouble and are more skilled in the art of making friendships into a shape; it is their business; men are too spoilt and lazy.'

She and Harold were treated to a sight of the treasures of imperial Persia. This too she described to Virginia:

I am blind. Blinded by diamonds. I have been in Aladdin's cave. Sacks of emeralds were emptied out before our eyes. Sacks of pearls. *Literally.*
We came away shaking the pearls out of our shoes.
Ropes of uncut emeralds. Scabbards encrusted with precious stones. Great hieratic crowns.
All this in a squalid room, with grubby Persians drinking little cups of tea.
... It was simply the Arabian nights, with decor by the Sitwells. Pure fantasy. Oh, *why* weren't you there?[8]

The coronation itself was 'amateur theatricals' in comparison.

Raymond Mortimer, who had been missing Harold badly, came out to join them at the end of March; and in April the three went for a few days to Isfahan – 'lilac, irises and blue tiles', Vita wrote in her diary – joining up there with Gladwyn Jebb, then a young third secretary at the Teheran Legation. Vita liked watching the carpet-makers at work. 'I had thought to gain emancipation by tearing myself up by my roots, and here I was already netted in the love of Persia.'[9]

Raymond told them he was writing a novel about sodomy. (If he was, he never published it.) Vita, Harold reported to Clive on 1 May, said that 'she had already written such a novel, and that the manuscript thereof was now deposited in the vaults of the London, County and Westminster Bank in Sevenoaks. I was to publish it, as her literary executor, after her death.'

This is almost the only documented reference that Vita made to her 1920 manuscript, if indeed that was what she was referring to, and the only documented evidence, however facetious, that she wanted it to be published after her death. It is impossible to be sure of her intentions. But the fact that she never destroyed it is significant; she wrote in the manuscript that she believed her experiences would be of help to other people, and she provided background details that she herself did not need, suggesting that she envisaged future readers. The only other and less definite reference to the manuscript occurs in a letter she wrote to Virginia on 17 September 1926, apologizing for using an old envelope since 'the small stout key which I have lost unlocks not only my reputation but my stationery.' (The manuscript was found in a small carved cupboard which had no lock.) The bit about the bank deposit was probably a red herring or a joke, and Harold took the whole episode lightly: 'Surely a very feminine touch all that – me an elderly widower, an Ambassador doubtless, surely a K.C.M.G., bearing the vicarious brunt of all the criticism.' He did outlive Vita, but he was never to be an ambassador, and what criticism there was for publishing the manuscript fell on their son Nigel.

On 5 May they were in Resht, near the Caspian Sea. Vita's stay was over. She was to depart for Russia, and a long route home. Harold was shattered by this parting. After leaving her, he broke down and wept. Raymond was powerless to help him, shattered himself by such evidence of love and grief. Writing long letters to Vita in the days that followed, Harold described to her every nuance of his sorrow, his prostration, his gradual recovery and the precise quality of his feelings for her.

The expression of love can be self-conscious and self-regarding even when it is heartfelt. In his letters to Vita, as she in hers, Harold made a closed circle of emotion and 'literature'. The words made bearable the emotion; the emotion fuelled the words. Harold was an obsessional and gifted recorder. Sometimes, for such people, an act or an emotion is being put into words even as it is being experienced. This accounts for the impression of theatricality and deliberateness that a sustained reading of his letters may produce:

My own own darling Viti,

When I had closed the bedroom door at Resht, I stood for a moment on the landing with a giddy agony making the whole house swing and wobble. With a great effort I stopped myself bursting in again – to where I should find that dear dear head bowed in tears. . . . Very slowly I went down the stairs and into the garden.

It is fairly clear that Harold envisaged both his diaries and his letters being read some day by other eyes, in print. On 17 June of this same year, 1926, with cheerful irony he apostrophized in his diary: 'Oh my future biographer! On reading this my diary do not say "What an empty life!" Look rather for my letters to Viti which give a fuller picture of my noble and incessant activities in the cause of life and literature.'

Vita did not make such assumptions until rather later. She too was upset by the parting, but more for his grief's sake than for her own. She vowed to him that after this

we will not leave each other any more. Everyone else must be sacrificed, there is *no one* in the world who counts for me but you. . . . It is the tenderness I have for you which hurts so; love is a much fiercer thing; but tenderness is so protective. I cannot bear to think that perhaps you will cry. Darling, the mars must be mad to think they could ever get along without each other. . . . Lucky Tray to be with you.

'That was a curious journey home,' Vita wrote later, 'its beginning in personal heart-sickness, its middle in intense, impersonal interest, its end in sheer farce.'

She travelled as far as Moscow with the Persian General Hassan Arfa and his English wife Hilda; their train tore through the Caucasus, and from the window Vita saw poppies and flax and borage 'in sheets of blue'. In Moscow – Stalin's Moscow – she was met by two huge motor cars decked with Union Jacks and whisked off to the British Mission for the night. Her impressions were limited but depressing; she wrote to Harold:

> Everyone seems to go in fear of being overheard; everyone looks furtive and afraid. All the people at the dinner party at the Mission said to me, one after the other, and not in reply to any prompting on my part, 'You see, it is so dreadful living here. One never knows who will disappear next.' ... One sees people sitting or standing at the street corners in attitudes of despair; not beggars.... And yet they say it is incomparably better than it was a year or two years ago!

Her plan was to stop off in Warsaw to see the Potockis, now living in much reduced circumstances; their castle where she had stayed in 1909 was razed to the ground. On the night train to Poland she had to share a sleeper with four Russian men – 'If this is what comes of democracy, give me tyranny every time.' As they neared the frontier news arrived that there was revolution in Warsaw: the train stopped at Bialystok, just in Poland, and all the passengers were put out. Vita, a group of Germans, a Russian and two Austrians managed to get a local train to Graceivo on the German frontier, where there was a wait of four hours for another train to Berlin. The little group found a café:

> It was all very Slav. We sat, the ten of us, at a long narrow table, like the Last Supper. We were all tired and gloomy. Then a bottle of vodka appeared as though by magic. Tongues were loosed. ... One of the Germans leant across the table and suddenly said to me, 'I have travelled Singer's sewing machines one hundred thousand kilometres over Manchuria.'

Then a woman drank six glasses of vodka and began to dance; a Polish officer played czardas on the piano; conversation flowed in Russian, Polish, German, English, Chinese. Vita showed off her scraps of Persian. Everyone was drunk. 'Somebody played the Blue Danube on the cottage piano, and the two Austrians made love openly.' At last the train came.

Vita wrote all this from the Hotel Kaiserhof in Berlin, on the backs of proof-sheets of *The Land*. 'I think I must have a constitution of iron, as I am not really very tired.'

There was one more small adventure to come for the V. Sackville-West hero-heroine. When the train for Holland and the boat home stopped at Bertheim, a blond young German officer got on; Vita was half-asleep in her 'Jaeger flea-bag'. The officer said 'it was the hand of fate and I must marry him' :

> So I explained I was already married, and he must go away at once. But he wouldn't go, and went down on his knees, and pushed his fingers through his hair, and called me 'Mein Schatz, meine Seele' . . . if I had been that sort of person I should certainly have gone to meet him in Amsterdam, as he suggested ! And all this at 6 o'clock in the morning, with the rain pouring down outside, and me with no powder on, – of which I was painfully aware.

'I know it sounds like a Seducers in Ecuador story,' she told Harold, writing in the train, 'but *padlock* [promise] it isn't.' It was a pity, she said, that it had not been Tray [Raymond] in her place, 'it seemed such a waste.'

The next day, 16 May, she was met at Victoria Station by Dottie and carried away in her Rolls-Royce to Dottie's flat in Mount Street, 'where I drank a bottle of champagne practically straight off, and fell into a swinish sleep.'

# CHAPTER 15

VITA went straight to Oxford to visit the children at Summer Fields – 'I did love them both' – and while in Oxford she called on the Poet Laureate, Robert Bridges; she brought messages from his daughter Elizabeth Daryush who had married a Persian and whom Vita had met in Teheran. 'The Laureate jumped out of a rhododendron bush to open the gate. He is very beautiful and Tennysonian, – slouch hat, a shepherd's muffler, a Norfolk jacket, an evening shirt (starched), grey flannel trousers, pink knitted socks, pumps. Long white hair, white beard; long thighs; beautiful hands. The complete Victorian.' She called at Knole to find that Eddy, 'mincing in black velvet', had been redecorating the tower in which he lived in a very *outré* manner. 'I don't object to homosexuality, but I do hate decadence,' Vita wrote to Harold. 'And it is a nasty fungoid growth on Knole of all places. . . . I don't think Dada likes it much.'

At Long Barn there were seven new elk-hound puppies and four new kittens, and before Vita had been home a week her spaniel Pippin produced five puppies. The garden was full of the spring. Vita to Harold: 'Your new poplar walk is alive. The wood is a blaze of primulas, anemones, tulips, azaleas, irises, polyanthus. . . . The apple garden is a mass of lupins and irises. The turf is perfect. . . . The roses are beautifully pruned; the lilac is smothered in blossom. Your honeysuckle by the big room door also.' Only the tennis court was 'a disaster'. She had 'such a heartache for Hadji, who ought to be here and isn't.' Horne, her old butler, worried about her being lonely. 'If only he knew how infinitely I preferred it to the gossiping, shrieking, parodying popinjays that London has to offer! One evening of Ozzie is as bad as a crowd.' She intended to be 'very eccentric and distinguished, and never see anyone. . . . But the eccentricity is easier to acquire than the distinction. The eccentricity, indeed, is nature.'

The 'shock of meeting after absence', as Virginia put it, and the playful intimacy of their letters, made the reunion of Vita and Virginia a little awkard and constrained. Disillusion was dispelled when Vita spent two days at Rodmell. Virginia, writing to her sister Vanessa, said that Leonard was going to be in London – 'I say no more : as you are bored by Vita, bored by love.... Still, the June nights are long and warm ; the roses flowering ; and the garden full of lust and bees, mingling in the asparagus beds.' Vanessa replied, 'Give my humble respects to Vita, who treats me as an Arab steed looking from the corner of its eye on some long-eared mule.'[1] (In fact, Vita was over-anxious to be friends with Vanessa ; it was Vanessa who was aloof.) Vita wrote to Harold from Rodmell on 13 June :

I am, as you see [from the letter-head] staying with Virginia. She is sitting opposite, embroidering a rose, a black lace fan, a box of matches, and four playing cards, on a mauve canvas background, from a design by her sister, and from time to time she says, 'You have written enough, let us now talk about copulation' ; so if this letter is disjointed it is her fault and not mine.

The Woolfs had just installed a bathroom and lavatory in Monk's House on the proceeds of Virginia's *Mrs Dalloway*, which pleased Vita. It pleased the Woolfs too ; as Vita said 'they both run upstairs every now and then and pull the plug just for the sheer fun of it, and come down and say "It worked very well that time, did you hear ?"' Virginia was saying that Harold ought to give up diplomacy, Vita told him pointedly, and get a job in England.

That weekend deepened her intimacy with Virginia, and Clive Bell's indiscretions were repeated at another gathering at Sherfield : 'Clive bellowing all over the place : have I been to bed with Virginia yet ? If not, am I likely to do so in the near future ? If not, will I give it my attention, as it is high time V. fell in love (poor Clive, if only he knew !).' Vita described going to the ballet with Virginia :

She had got on a new dress. It was very odd indeed, orange and black, with a hat to match, – a sort of top-hat made of straw, with two orange feathers like Mercury's wings, – but although odd it was curiously becoming, and pleased Virginia because there could be absolutely no doubt as to which was the front and which the back.

When they emerged from the theatre into the Haymarket Virginia was shivering, not from cold but from excitement. 'I couldn't get her away from the theatre at all, and we stalked up and down, with the dark blue sky overhead, and groups of well-dressed people talking, and it was all very like *Mrs Dalloway . . .*'; so much so that Virginia became frightened and Vita took her off to the Eiffel Tower for coffee.

Two days later they were at the Eiffel Tower again, dining before going to see the Sitwells' *Façade*. They talked so long that they arrived late. 'But you know, Hadji, I am quite sure that fifty years from now no one will ever have heard of those frauds the Sitwells, any more than they will have heard of George Robey.' (Vita was not in tune with her times.) She proceeded to write a parody of *Façade* – 'Have you read in your *Nation* some bright and witty verses about the Sitwells? Behind the veil of anonymity crouches your mar,' she told Harold.

B.M. came to stay at Long Barn in July. She had quarrelled with nearly all her friends, was in very bad health, and needed constant attention. She had diabetes, colitis, an enlarged heart and the beginnings of cataract. Vita had promised she would go out to Harold again in Persia in October; this prospect filled B.M. with misery, and Vita told Harold that she could not come. Harold accepted this; in a way, not to see Vita was less painful than a brief visit. He could not face 'another wrench like at Resht'.

But he was hurt – as he was hurt when Vita told him that she was dedicating *The Land* to Dorothy Wellesley and not to him. Vita suggested that Raymond should go to Teheran instead of her. 'I don't want that,' Harold replied. 'I really think it might cause too great a scandal.' Nevertheless he consoled himself with an infatuation for young Patrick Buchan Hepburn, who had arrived at the Legation from Constantinople ill and in need of care. He wrote to Vita a great deal about Patrick's charms, partly, perhaps, to tease and provoke. What worried him was that it might not be B.M. who was keeping Vita in England, but her attachment to Virginia. Her 'excuses' reminded him of the Violet time. He was worried too on Virginia's behalf, because of her mental instability. 'It is like smoking over the petrol tank.'

Vita went to Kew Gardens with Virginia on a thundery afternoon, and the Woolfs took on one of Pippin's puppies, and called it Pinker. Half Bloomsbury came to Long Barn for a summer weekend: 'I shall make Clive do host. I have put him and Mary [Hutchinson] next to each other, so they can fuck all night if they want to – which they obviously do. I like her awfully – she has the prettiest manners imaginable, which I like. Real old-world courtesy.' On 17 August she wrote Harold a long, serious letter about his fears of her recreating the Violet situation with Virginia.

But darling you have never understood about V[iolet] a) that it was a madness of which I should never again be capable, – i.e. a thing like that happens once, and burns out the capacity for such a feeling. b) that you could at any moment have reclaimed me, but for some extraordinary reason you wouldn't. I used to beg you to; I *wanted* to be rescued, and you would not hold out a hand.

(This was unfair. Harold had held out his hand to her continually. But she had needed something more than an outstretched hand.)

> You mention Virginia: it is simply laughable. I love Virginia, as who wouldn't? but really, my sweet, one's love for Virginia is a very different thing: a mental thing, a spiritual thing if you like, an intellectual thing, and she inspires a feeling of tenderness which I suppose is because of her funny mixture of hardness and softness, – the hardness of her mind, and her terror of going mad again.

Vita was 'scared to death of arousing physical feelings in her, because of the madness':

> I don't know what effect it would have, you see; and that is a fire with which I have no wish to play. ... I have too much real affection and respect. Also she has never lived with anyone but Leonard, which was a terrible failure, and was abandoned quite soon. So all that remains an unknown quantity.... So you see I am sagacious, – though probably I would be less sagacious if I were more tempted, which is at least frank! ... I *have* gone to bed with her (twice) but that's all; and I told you that before, I think. Now you know all about it, and I hope I haven't shocked you.

She reassured him further by filling her letters with family news. Ben, aged twelve, had become very good at tennis: 'I absolutely adore him.' Nigel cut his head on a tub on the terrace – 'blood was running down on the doorstep, and his poor little white tennis shoes were spattered with red. But my goodness he was brave, that child! for he tried to laugh, and said "Am I dead, Mummy?"' Vita was so pleased with him that she quite forgave him for getting butter on the passports. (She was taking them to Normandy for a week, with Dottie and her two children.) Harold remarked in one of his letters that he was surprised their sons were so 'normal'; 'I should have thought the Mars would have Eddies and Tommies [i.e., homosexuals] and not sort of clever Whites Club men.' Vita was not so sure. 'Darling, I fear the worst for Ben. His instinct for self-adornment is terribly feminine.'

She was not sorry when the boys went back to school. 'Alone. Extraordinary sensation!' She was correcting the proofs of her *Passenger to Teheran*.

*The Land*, with wrappers designed by George Plank, came out on 30 September. It had grown into a work of 2,500 lines, but so extensive a poem was no deterrent to a generation reared on long poems – Hardy's

*The Dynasts* for example, or the long verse narratives of John Mase-field. Robert Bridges's *The Testament of Beauty* came out three years after *The Land*, and enjoyed an even greater success, going through fourteen impressions in its first year; but by 1971 *The Land*, a steady seller, had sold 100,000 copies in Britain alone.

'I sing the cycle of my country's year', it begins, and the poet does precisely that, describing in regular iambics, season by season, the rituals and tasks of farming life. The first-person approach lightens an otherwise impersonal cataloguing of what she calls in the poem the 'classic monotony' of the farming cycle, 'the mild continuous epic of the soil'.

The poem does not set out to be exciting. 'So my pedestrian measure gravely plods,/Telling a loutish life' – and lending itself to parody from cynics, experimentalists and modernists. Harold had seen the parallel with Virgil's *Georgics* all along, but Vita told Richard Church (in 1940):

> I had never read one line of the *Georgics*, either in Latin which I was never taught or in any translation, until I had got halfway through *The Land* and showed a bit of it to a friend of mine who then said 'But you are copying the *Georgics*.' I denied indignantly and truthfully that I was copying any-thing.... He then gave me Lord Burghclere's translation and also the Loeb edition of the *Georgics*, and I was appalled to see that my poem must appear to be a fake or an imitation.
>
> It wasn't a fake. Neither was it an imitation.[2]

What Vita set out to do was to document the age-old Kentish skills and processes and the Kentish landscape, which even in the 1920s were being modified by mechanization. Her sources were not only her own daily observations but encyclopaedias of agriculture and old poems and farming treatises. She incorporated into her deliberately archaic verse-vocabulary country words still in use, and old place-names and field-names of the Weald, as well as words that were already falling into disuse: droil, yeavy, reasty, undern, winsel, kexen, dwale, scrannel, fisking, eild, tedd, spline, yelm, stelch, sneath, yerk, weazen. (Of these 'undern', meaning 'in the afternoon', became part of her private lan-guage with Virginia.)

In this poetry of dung and marl and tilth and toil – classical Georgian verse, poetry in gumboots – she charted the Wealden farmer's yearly round: beekeeping, woodcraft, sheepshearing, sowing, haysel and harvest, craftsmanship, threshing, ploughing, cidermaking and hop-picking – all her life she had enjoyed every year the rowdy camps of hoppers who

> From London slums poured yearly into Kent
> Waking the province with their cockney slang.

She wrote with love, 'The country habit has me by the heart', and with passion, 'Who has not seen the spring is blind, is dead.' The dogged descriptions of processes are further broken up by lyrical passages, often independent poems; the best poetry is in these sections, which have an emblematic quality and reveal a personal vision, as in her picture of a field of fritillaries:

> Sullen and foreign-looking, the snaky flower,
> Scarfed in dull purple, like Egyptian girls
> Camping among the furze, staining the waste
> With foreign colour, sulky, dark, and quaint,
> Dangerous too, as a girl might sidle up,
> An Egyptian girl, with an ancient snaring spell,
> Throwing a net, soft round the limbs and heart,
> Captivity soft and abhorrent, a close-meshed net. . . .

> And I shrank from the English field of fritillaries
> Before it should be too late, before I forgot
> The cherry white in the woods, and the curdled clouds,
> And the lapwings crying free above the plough.

There are other more private touches: 'Tinker' being her nickname for Geoffrey Scott, he read the lines about

> The tinker with his little cart
> Hawking his tinny wares

as addressed to himself. The most famous lyric in *The Land*, which at the end of her life seemed to apply so movingly to the poet herself, was in fact written for Dorothy Wellesley:

> She walks among the loveliness she made,
> Between the apple-blossom and the water –
> She walks among the patterned pied brocade,
> Each flower her son, and every tree her daughter.

J.C.Squire gave *The Land* its first and adulatory review, in The *Observer*. 'I know Squire is a silly old ass and all that, but all the same. . . . What shall I write now? My head is bursting with poetry. I *will* write another long poem. I *will* get myself into English literature. Somehow or other.' Immediately she conceived of 'a companion to *The Land* called

*The Garden*', and began it the same day. 'It will have much more in it than mere gardening, – all my beliefs and unbeliefs.'

She dropped the project – to pick it up again nearly ten years later. B.M.'s illnesses and rages took up days and weeks of her time that autumn. 'She cries all the time. She says she wants to die. It is inexpressibly painful.' Dottie thought that B.M. was chiefly suffering from 'soul-sickness', since 'one couldn't go through life with all one's values so utterly false, without paying for it in the end.'

Vita gave herself a crash-course in English nineteenth-century literature. She decided that 'the Brontës must have been impossible in real life, and of the whole lot one would probably have had most sympathy with Branwell.' Charlotte Brontë's letters to Ellen Nussey 'leave very little doubt in one's mind as to what Charlotte's tendencies really were. Whether she knew it herself is another matter. But they are love-letters pure and simple.' Wordsworth's *Prelude* threw her into a rage : 'I HATE Wordsworth, the old prig, bore, preachifying old solemnity – BOO! BAH ! He makes me feel rude, like D. H. Lawrence.'

She knew why : 'The more I read, the more I am convinced that I should have lived in an age when seriousness and noble thoughts found an echo. . . . 'Not that I like it ; and dislike it the more, that I recognize in myself the natural tendency to precisely such earnest bombast ; so, as we dislike in others what we mistrust in ourselves, I annotate my Wordsworth with angry comments and throw my Arnold across the room. I have now taken to Jane Austen.' But Jane Austen's 'mere sly pokes of humour' did not satisfy her. 'In fact I don't know what I want from literature ; I don't hold with the dunghill despair of Eliot.'

She tried to work out what she did think for the lecture she gave at the Royal Society of Literature, with Gosse in the chair, on 27 October ; her title was 'Some Tendencies of Modern English Poetry'. Virginia sat in the back row 'grinning at me, ironical, *émue*', she told Harold. (Both the Nicolsons had been elected Fellows of the RSL that year.) Virginia was more ironical than Vita realized ; she wrote in her diary : 'Her address was read in sad sulky tones like that of a schoolboy ; her pendulous rich society face, glowing out under a black hat at the end of the dismal smoky room, looked very ancestral & like a picture under glass in a gallery.' Virginia found the respectability of the Royal Society stultifying and Vita 'too innocent to see it'.[3]

She went again to Long Barn for a night that Vita marked '!' in her diary, and they met almost daily when Vita was in London. Vita told Harold that Virginia was not used to 'emotional storms', and was dreading her return to Persia, planned now for February 1927. The two women had reached a new phase of closeness. Vita sent private letters to Virginia inside 'public' ones that could be shown to Leonard. She was reading about Aphra Behn, the raffish seventeenth-century playwright and the first woman known to have earned her living by her pen. In one of her private letters she told Virginia that 'a course of Mrs A.B. has turned me into the complete ruffling rake. No more than Mrs A.B. do I relish, or approve of, chastity.'[4]

But Virginia was not well and was self-protective: 'But don't you see, donkey West, that you'll be tired of me one of these days (I'm so much older) and so I have to take my little precautions. That's why I put the emphasis on "recording" rather than feeling. But donkey West knows she has broken down more ramparts than anyone.' And she turned the tables, pinpointing the alienation, the unyielding heart of darkness, in Vita's own personality:

> And isn't there something obscure in you? There's something that doesn't vibrate in you: it may be purposely – you don't let it: but I see it with other people, as well as with me: something reserved, muted – God knows what. ... It's in your writing, too, by the bye. This thing I call central transparency – sometimes fails you there too. I will lecture you on this at Long Barn.[5]

(Virginia, though delighted by – and a little envious of – the success of *The Land*, could never take it very seriously as poetry.) Her letter, even though it ended 'The flowers have come, and are adorable, dusky, tortured, passionate like you', upset Vita very much – because she recognized its truth, as she told Harold:

> Damn the woman, she has put her finger on it. There *is* something muted. What is it, Hadji? Something that doesn't vibrate, something that doesn't come alive.... It makes everything I do (i.e. write) a little unreal; gives the effect of having been done from the outside. It is the thing which spoils me as a writer; destroys me as a poet. But how did V. discover it? I have never owned it to anybody, scarcely even to myself. It is what spoils my human relationships too, but that I mind less.

It was sad for Vita with her big success – *The Land* was already reprinting – to be facing only her failings. The 'unwieldy *something*' that Geoffrey Scott had seen as her strength seemed to Virginia only a block. Vita expressed her self-doubt in a poem 'Year's End' written that autumn, in which the poet is described as a merchant 'adding up my balance sheet':

> If all the barter, all the trafficking,
> Exchange of coin and bargaining of thought
> That fill the folios of my huckstering,
> Total to one unprofitable nought,
> Shall I not clear my goods and quit the ring?[6]

Virginia wanted to talk about death. Writing *To the Lighthouse*, she was thinking of death as 'a great excitement', something active. Yet death was 'the one experience I shall never describe' she told Vita, who sat at her feet in a velvet jacket and red-striped silk shirt, while Virginia knotted the famous pearls into 'heaps of great lustrous eggs'. So Virginia wrote in her diary. Vita described the afternoon to Harold :

> Darling, I know Virginia will die, and it will be too awful. (I don't mean *here*, over the weekend ; but die young.) I went to Tavistock Square yesterday, and she sat in the dusk in the light of the fire, and I sat on the floor as I always do, and she rumpled my hair as she always does ... and said you would resent her next summer. But I said, no, you wouldn't. .... I really adore her. Not 'in love' but just love – devotion.

During the next Long Barn weekend, Virginia told Vita, 'Now that you have mastered the question of technique, throw your technique into the air and let it smash on the pavement.' Vita could not do this ; but she started rewriting 'Reddín' as a poem.

1926 had been a crowded year. There was the Persian experience ; her intense friendship with Virginia ; the publication of *The Land* and *Passenger to Teheran*, coupled with a shaking of faith in her literary and human quality ; and, throughout the year, a dialogue with Harold about the nature of their relations with each other and with outsiders. Raymond Mortimer, impressed by the strength of the Nicolsons' 'open' marriage, had told Harold after Vita left Persia that he thought theirs was an ideal that should be put forward for all married couples. Vita knew it was not so simple :

> Tray's theory is all very well as far as it goes. But he leaves out the stipulation that the two people who are to achieve this odd spirito-mystico-practical unity must start with very special temperaments, i.e., it is all very well to say the ideal is 'marriage with liaisons'. But if you were in love with another woman, or I with another man, we should both or either of us be finding a natural sexual fulfilment which would inevitably rob our own relationship of something. As it is, the liaisons which you and I contract are something perfectly apart from the more natural attitude we have towards each other, and don't interfere.

It would be dangerous, she thought, for 'ordinary people', and in any case one could not make laws about emotional relationships : 'either you love, or you don't love, and that's that.'

The day after Christmas 1926, lying in bed with flu, she went even further in her distaste for regulating relationships. Apart from the fact that 'the servants would leave', she asked him, what was the point of marriage at all? (She and the children were at Knole; perhaps the compromise life her father led with Olive Rubens affected her mood.)

> You see if the mars had just lived together, they would be living together still, just as happily, and it would make no difference to their passion for the garden, or to their interest in their mars. The whole system of marriage is wrong.... It ought, at least, to be optional; and no stigma if you prefer a less claustrophobic form of contract. For it *is* claustrophobic.

It was only very intelligent people (like themselves) who could make marriage work – and intelligence alone would not have sufficed 'if our temperamental weaknesses didn't happen to dovetail as well as they do' – and their shared need for personal liberty. She came back always to the same point. 'But of course the real secret is that we love each other. One always comes back to these simple human things in the end, and "intelligence" goes on the scrapheap.'

She wrote to Virginia at Christmas too. 'I am in bed, and watch the fire on the ceiling, and hear the clock strike, and think how delicious it will be when you come to stay here.' She was setting huge importance on Virginia's coming to Knole before she made her deferred visit to Persia. 'My bed's at least nine foot wide, and I feel like the Princess and the Pea, – only there is no Pea. It is a four-poster, all of which I like. Come and see for yourself.'⁷

Virginia came to Knole in mid-January 1927. 'We wandered all over the house yesterday,' Vita told Harold on the nineteenth, 'pulling up the blinds, she was thrilled. She and Dada got on splendidly.' Virginia's imagination caught fire at Knole, though she felt critical of the heaviness, excessive 'conscious beauty' and the 'general lack of distinction' of the arrangements. What pleased her was 'Vita stalking in her Turkish dress, attended by small boys, down the gallery, wafting them on like some tall sailingship – a sort of covey of noble English life.' She watched the horse-drawn cart bringing in wood from the park to be sawn up for the great fireplaces. 'How do you see that?' she asked Vita. 'She said she saw it as something that had gone on for hundreds of years.' All the centuries were lined up together at Knole, 'and so we reach the days of Elizabeth quite easily.'⁸

By the end of January *The Land* was in its third printing. Eddie Marsh had told Vita he thought she was 'the best living poet under 80' – thus excluding her from comparison with almost everyone but Hardy and Bridges. Vita, encouraged, let her hopes and ambitions revive. She began to hope that *The Land* might win the Hawthornden Prize; three members of the panel of judges had already voiced their enthusiasm to her.

*

She travelled out to Persia the second time with Leigh Ashton, Gladwyn Jebb's sister Marjorie – and, at the last minute, Dorothy Wellesley, who wrote in her memoirs how Vita 'suddenly came into my sitting-room at Mount Street. This was a Thursday. "Will you come to Persia on Monday?" "Of course."'

Vita spent her last morning with Virginia, and wrote to her from Ebury Street before she left: 'Beloved Virginia, one last goodbye before I go. I feel torn in a thousand pieces – it is *bloody* – *I can't tell you* how I hate leaving you – in fact I don't feel I can – you have become so essential to me. Bless you for all the happiness you give me.' As a postscript she scribbled 'Put "honey" when you write. Darling, please go on loving me. I am so miserable. Don't forget me.'⁹ And in the train she wrote that she would remember Virginia 'standing in your blue apron and waving – oh damn it Virginia, I wish I didn't love you so much. No I don't.'

She said she was going to work hard while she was away. 'It is quite true that you have had more influence on me intellectually than anyone, and for this alone I love you. . . . You do like me to write well don't you? And I hate writing badly – and having written so badly in the past.'¹⁰ Virginia herself was plunged into a crisis between the lovers Clive Bell and Mary Hutchinson, which left her so drained that she could only think of Vita 'as being very distant and beautiful and calm. A lighthouse in clean waters.' (Her *To the Lighthouse* came out the day after Vita's return from Persia.)

In answer to Vita's letter about trying to write well, she pursued her thought of Vita as 'a real woman' and herself as 'a eunuch': 'Here in my cave I see lots of things you blazing beauties make invisible by the light of your own glory.' Yes, she liked Vita to write well:

> The danger for you with your sense of tradition and all those words – a gift of the Gods though – is that you help this too easily into existence. . . . I mean I think there are odder, deeper, more angular thoughts in your mind than you have yet let come out. Still, you'll get the Hawthornden, Oh yes, and I shall be vaguely jealous, proud, and disgusted.¹¹

Vita had been in Teheran less than a week when she heard that *The Land* had indeed won the Hawthornden Prize.

Before that she and her party had passed through Moscow, where she found herself a fellow guest with Denys Trefusis at dinner at the British Embassy; and she described Moscow to Virginia – 'all the traffic passing to and fro across the frozen river as though it were a road; and sleighs everywhere, and coachmen stuffed out with straw' – thus filling Virginia's imagination, as during the visit to Knole, with scenes and images that were later to explode in *Orlando*. While Vita was away,

Virginia did not conceive precisely *Orlando* but a project she called 'The Jessamy Brides': 'Sapphism is to be suggested. Satire is to be the main note – satire and wildness. The Ladies are to have Constantinople in view.... My own lyric vein is to be satirized.' She wanted, she said, an 'escapade' in writing. And she wrote to Vita, her 'Darling Honey', 'I lie in bed making up stories about you.'

'I have come over those familiar mountains, and crossed that familiar plain,' Vita wrote to her on arrival in Teheran, 'and it seemed from the first as though I had never been away.'[12] But by the end of February Vita was writing in her diary that she had been depressed for the whole month 'owing to 1) inability to write 2) fear of Hadji continuing in diplomacy. The F.O. says he will have to come back in Sept. for another year. God help us! I had expected to find him disgusted with exile and social duties, but it is quite the contrary.' Her long letters to Virginia were filled with discontent about her own sterility and about Harold's attitude to the diplomatic life. 'I can't bear there to be a third year of this business. But Harold is in a very Empire-building frame of mind. Enormous skill will be necessary to get him out of it.'[13]

She told Virginia that she remained 'wisely silent' to Harold on this matter. But her silences were thunderous. He knew exactly what she thought. He wrote in his diary on 12 March: 'Woke up in the morning with a conviction that I shall chuck the diplomatic life.' He applied at once for a job with the Anglo-Persian Oil Company.

Vita was ecstatic, and a week later they left on what was the highlight of her trip: a tough twelve-day excursion with Harold, Gladwyn Jebb Copley Amory from the American Legation and Lionel Smith from Baghdad, across the Bakhtiari Mountains from Shalamzar to the oilfields on the far side. Dorothy Wellesley, who did not enjoy the rigours of camp life, went home. Barbara, the wooden saint, came along, and was unpacked each night and set up in Vita's tent. From Shalamzar Vita wrote to Virginia: 'Darling, I wrote you a letter from Isfahan; rather excited I was, and over-tired, and wanting you. There was a new moon over the poplars in the Isfahan garden ... curtseying away like the one we saw when we went for a walk at Long Barn, (the evening you behaved so monstrously).' Vita was feeling sad, 'thinking of people who had gone out of my life. ... Oh if only you were here. I'm alone with four men.'[14] Seeing Denys had made her think about Violet, who had appreciated adventures.

There were moments of serious disillusion with the trip. On 8 April, in a muddy wood at Shalil, Vita wrote in her diary that they had 'confessed to each other that we hated it all'. Harold was the most depressed: 'A terrible feeling of despair descends on me. I say that I loathe the Bakhtiari Mountains and wish I hadn't come. V. is an angel of comfort.' That evening in the damp camp, he had 'a nerve-storm caused by a sudden loathing for V.'s hold-all'. And then Vita was upset because Lionel Smith told her that he believed Gertrude Bell, knowing herself to be ill, had committed suicide.

Their spirits improved with the weather. They were a little early for the best flowers, but the ink-blue grape hyacinths were in bloom, and Vita collected rhyzomes of small dark irises. She was planning a second Persian travel book about this expedition, and taking her own photographs for it. The book, which contains some of her best writing and expresses her passion for wild places, was called *Twelve Days* and dedicated to Harold. In it she has interesting things to say about the then emergent oil industry, especially when read in the light of Persia's (Iran's) later development as an oil state. She wrote about the question of future social progress – 'and over this task our imaginary Shah would be lucky if he escaped with his life. Tradition, national character, and, in Persia, the priests, are stubborn foes to contend with.' Half a century later she was to be proved right.

But in 1927 she saw the country as 'a potential paradise', and the approach to the oilfields on the other side of the mountains as a transition from paradise into 'a hell of civilization'. When she was there, there were about 100 oil wells working over an area of fifty square miles. This great resource had only been exploited for ten years, although Vita wrote that the native Bakhtiari, familiar with the substance that floated on top of their puddles, had always known some of its uses.

From Persepolis, Vita wrote to Virginia :

> I've driven a motor over nearly a thousand miles of Persia within the last week. I am dirty, sunburnt, well ... the notion that one escapes from civilization is a mistaken notion: on the contrary, one's preoccupation from morning to night is : Have we cooked the eggs long enough ? have we enough Bromo left ? who washed the plates this morning, because *I* didn't ? who put away the tin-opener, because if nobody did, it's lost ?[15]

As for Virginia complaining that she used no endearments in her letters – when Vita woke in the Persian dawn, she said Virginia's name.

In Abadan Harold went to see the officials of APOC about a possible job ; he did not get one, and so did not resign from the Foreign Office. But he was coming home on leave, and he and Vita travelled home together via Damascus, Beirut, Alexandria and Marseilles, reaching London on 5 May. Raymond Mortimer and Dottie Wellesley met them at Folkestone.

# CHAPTER 16

HAROLD'S homecoming to a blossoming Long Barn was so emotional
that he was sick. Vita plunged back into her gardening and saw Virginia,
who found her 'unchanged, though I daresay one's relation changes
from day to day'. The two went to Oxford for the night on 18 May,
staying at the Clarendon Hotel. Virginia had to read a paper to the
women undergraduates at St Hugh's. She described Vita at St Hugh's to
her sister Vanessa:

> very striking; like a willow tree; so dashing, on her long white legs with a
> crimson bow; but rather awkward, forced indeed to take her stockings down
> and rub her legs with ointment at dinner, owing to midges – I like this in the
> aristocracy. I like the legs; I like the bites; I like the complete arrogance and
> unreality of their minds . . .

and she cited Vita's casually buying a silk dressing-gown for five
pounds, and at luncheon picking the filling out of a custard tart and
dropping the pastry back into the dish; and over-tipping porters, all
'very splendid and voluptuous and absurd':

> Also she has a heart of gold, and a mind which, if slow, works doggedly; and
> has its moments of lucidity – But enough – You will never succumb to the
> charms of any of your sex – What an arid garden the world must be for you!
> What avenues of stone pavements and iron railings!!¹

The day Virginia wrote that, the Nicolsons had met Roy Campbell, the
South African poet, and his wife Mary for the first time in the post office
in Weald village, where the Campbells had rented a house. Vita had
read Campbell's long poem *The Flaming Terrapin* the previous year, and
had sent it to Virginia, calling it 'a wild uneven thing, almost ridiculous
in parts, almost magnificent in others.'² She was disposed to be

interested in their new neighbours. Roy Campbell was twenty-six, and his attractive, rebellious wife Mary, one of the several beautiful daughters of Dr Garman of Birmingham, a couple of years older. They had recently arrived from South Africa, where Roy had been editing the journal *Voorslag,* which he had set up with William Plomer but which had folded through lack of readers. He was now trying to establish himself as a writer in England, following the success of *Terrapin.* The Campbells had two small daughters and no money apart from twenty pounds a month from Roy's family.

On 23 May Vita started writing her Bakhtiari book, *Twelve Days,* and the Campbells came to dinner for the first time. Virginia was unwell, and Vita visited her to find her 'incredibly lovely and fragile on two chairs under a gold cloak'. It was hard to tell how ill she really was. 'Virginia brilliant, one is used to; but Virginia defeated is newly and surprisingly endearing. Dear Clive, I would go to the ends of the earth for your sister-in-law,' Vita wrote to Clive Bell.[3]

Vita was in a mood to 'go to the ends of the earth' for something or somebody. Friends took Ben and Nigel's cottage at Long Barn for part of the summer, and bulldog Ethel Smyth came to Long Barn for a night to listen to the nightingales. Mary Campbell called; so did Roy Campbell, and told Harold the story of his erratic life to date – 'another Rimbaud', thought Harold. Vita began writing the life of the literary adventuress Aphra Behn; and at Sherfield one Sunday in mid-June, she wrote provocatively, irresponsibly, to Virginia.

Do you know what I should do if you were not a person to be rather strict with? I should steal my own motor out of the garage at 10 p.m. tomorrow night, be at Rodmell by 11.5 ... throw gravel at your window, then you'd come down and let me in; I'd stay with you till 5, and be home by half past six. But, you being you, I can't; more's the pity.

She had just lent Virginia *Challenge*, her novel about Julian and Eve/ Violet. 'Perhaps I sowed all my wild oats then. Yet I don't feel that the impulse has left me; no, by God; and for a different Virginia I'd fly to Sussex in the night.'[4] In another note that summer Vita wrote, 'My poor darling, I do hate these damned headaches you get. I wish you were ROBUST.'

But Virginia was not robust. She had been reading *Challenge* when Vita's letter from Sherfield came, and saw that the letter itself was a challenge – '"if only you weren't so elderly and valetudinarian" was what you said in effect, "we would be spending the day together".' This was, in effect, what Vita was saying. But Virginia was not available for the sort of escapade that Vita longed for, even though she had wired 'Come then' when she got the letter.[5]

Virginia was well enough to go with Leonard and Harold to see Vita presented with the Hawthornden Prize on 16 June. Vita wore a black Mexican hat and a knotted red tie; she made no speech of thanks. After, the Nicolsons and the Woolfs went to eat ices at Gunters. Virginia was scornful of the whole occasion. She thought it 'a horrid show-up' of 'all us chattering writers. . . . The whole business of writing became infinitely distasteful.' It was, she wrote in her diary, 'the thick dull middle class of letters' that met, not the aristocracy. 'Vita cried at night'⁶, no doubt because of Virginia's ambivalence about her triumph.

Edith Sitwell was rude about *The Land* and its prize in the news-papers. Vita minded, and complained to Virginia that Edith said it was the worst poem in the English language: 'now I'm *not* vain, as you know, but I'm hanged if it's as bad as that!'⁷ Virginia replied that *The Land* 'must be selling like melting snow'; and as for Edith Sitwell, whom Virginia knew and liked, 'I don't think you probably realize how hard it is for the natural innovator as she is, to be fair to the natural traditionalist as you are.' Vita was 'tarred' by the Haw-thornden, that most establishment of prizes, also 'you sell, and she don't – all good reasons why a Sitwell should vomit in public.'⁸ Vita preferred to think it was all revenge for the skit on *Façade* she had written. Or so she told Wilfred Meynell, adding: 'Please, *please* don't read any of my novels . . . they are the vile indiscretions of youth, and I can't bear to think of them.'⁹ She was pinning her reputation now on *The Land*.

In late June Harold spent a week in Paris with Raymond Mortimer, where he engaged a quiet young man, Couve de Murville (later Prime Minister of France), as a summer tutor for the boys. Vita meanwhile took Virginia again to Kew, and then to a restaurant 'and had lots of Chianti and went back to Tavistock [Square] and sat in the basement and talked more.' The Campbells came to dinner again at Long Barn, with Eddy Sackville-West and David Garnett as fellow guests. On 29 June there was a total eclipse of the sun – the first visible in Britain for 200 years. Vita especially was interested in the night skies; she had inherited a taste for astronomy from her father. The Nicolsons, the Woolfs, Quentin Bell and Eddy travelled by a night train from London to Richmond in north Yorkshire, where at 3.30 am coaches were laid on to take spectators to Bardon Fell, the best vantage-point.

In the train the Nicolsons slept, Harold with his head on Vita's knee: she 'looked like Sappho by Leighton, asleep; so we plunged through the Midlands . . . ' wrote Virginia in her diary. It was icy cold on the Yorkshire hillside before dawn, and the eclipse was something of an anti-climax. Vita travelled back with Dottie, who had come up separately, and on the train was overcome with depression. 'Hate the Midlands, think of Persia, and burst into tears. A [prile] appalled.'

During a weekend with Virginia at Long Barn in early July – when Virginia told her the 'story about the moths' and 'talked about going mad' – Vita put the enigmatic note 'Inauguration' in her diary. Virginia wrote a fuller account of this visit:

> Such opulence and freedom, flowers all out, butler, silver, dogs, biscuits, wine, hot water, log fires, Italian cabinets, Persian rugs, books. ... Vita very opulent, in her brown velvet coat with the baggy pockets, pearl necklace, & slightly furred cheeks.... I liked Harold too. He is a spontaneous childlike man, of no great boring power.

Vita seemed very free and easy, she wrote, always a pleasure to watch, '& recalling some image of a ship breasting a sea, nobly, magnificently, with all sails spread, & the gold sunlight on them.'

But Virginia still questioned Vita's poetry, and even her intelligence. 'She never breaks fresh ground. She picks up what the tide rolls to her feet. For example, she follows, with simple instinct, all the inherited tradition of furnishing, so that her house is gracious, glowing, stately, but without novelty or adventure.' (The products of the Omega Workshops were not for Vita. Her taste in interior decoration, absorbed from her childhood at Knole, was sixteenth-century filtered through Edwardian.)

Virginia travelled back to London (leaving her pink mackintosh and scarlet gloves behind her) with Raymond Mortimer, discussing their hosts. 'She the most noble character he said. ... They lack only what we have – some cutting edge, some invaluable idiosyncracy, intensity, for which I would not have all the sons & all the moons in the world.'[10]

Vita, in her present restlessness, had already strayed from Virginia, who did not accommodate her sexual vitality. But that weekend she had told all about her escapade. Perhaps conveying to Virginia her needs and nature constituted the 'inauguration' – of a new phase. Virginia was mockingly jealous of this episode, as she was to be of others. 'You only be a careful dolphin in your gambolling, or you'll find Virginia's soft crevices lined with hooks': gambols at Ebury Street at four in the morning, 'I'm not so sure.'[11] Just before the eclipse expedition, Vita had spent a night at Ebury Street with Mary Hutchinson, Clive Bell's friend. On 28 June Mary had written to Vita: 'I left a pearl earring on the table by your bed. I remember exactly where I put it – at the corner near you. Will you be very nice and post it to me soon? ... Did you sleep among the thorns and petals?' Vita was not rejecting Virginia; but Virginia was not only dangerously vulnerable, she was inaccessible to simple desire, and she was not young. Vita wrote to her after the Long Barn weekend: 'It is all very well, you know, but these snatches of happiness are extremely exasperating, – and why have you such an art of keeping so much of yourself up your sleeve? ... I like making you jealous, my darling, (and shall continue to do so) but it's ridiculous that you should be.'[12]

Their friendship continued; they went to the Zoo together, and Vita gave Virginia driving lessons in Regent's Park. The Woolfs had just bought their first car out of the profits from *To the Lighthouse*. Jealousy made Virginia more in love with Vita, not less; she looked with uncharacteristic blatancy for excuses to come to Long Barn alone; she used nursery sexual imagery in her frequent love-letters; she begged Vita, 'Honey Dearest', not to go abroad. 'Stay in England. Love Virginia. Take her in your arms.' She was even jealous of Dorothy Wellesley now, and self-mockingly wailed to Vanessa that 'poor Billy' – herself – 'isn't one thing or the other, not a man nor a woman, so what's he to do?' Vita, for her part, was icy when Virginia teased her about her own new admirer, Philip Morrell, who had made a declaration of love. 'I won't be trifled with. I really mean this,' Vita told her. While hating and resenting possessiveness in others, she was regally possessive herself.

The boys came home for the summer holidays, and Vita's routine was broken. 'How *can* one write? The door bursts open all the time. "Where is my hammock?" "May we play tennis?" "What can we do now?"' She was, perversely, trying to write a poem, 'Solitude'. She was also seeing to the planning of her 'Hawthornden' (which means hawthorn wood) – a field to be planted with trees (not hawthorn, but hazel and poplar) – in celebration of her prize. Towards the end of August, she finished *Aphra Behn*, put the manuscript in the post, and felt 'free as a lark': 'Free to read, free to garden, free to think and free to be nice to my children. A delirious sensation, – but already new energies stir in me, 24 hours after Aphra is finished. God damn this energy, thank God for it.'

Vita's diary, Friday 2 September 1927: 'Sent for by M.C. in the morning. Take her to the station.' 'Why did you send for me?' Vita asked Mary Campbell, who was going up to London for a night. 'Because I wanted you so. There is nothing else to say,' replied Mary. It was the invitation to a love affair and an answer to Vita's restlessness and excess energy.

From then on they met almost every day, usually in the evening, and walked in the lanes and woods. Mary charted their affair in an eloquent love-journal which confirms the complexity of their relationship and the depth of Mary's dependence and passion. She was having a difficult time with her husband Roy, who was depressed, unwell, out of work and drinking heavily. Mary had found comfort with a woman in the past, as she would after Vita. A famous incident when Roy hung her out of their bedroom window over a London street had been provoked by her luxurious reminiscence of an earlier woman lover's beauty. (Vita wrote an unpublished poem, 'Interior', about this incident, noting beneath that 'This was the story Mary Campbell told me about Roy.')

Mary Campbell loved her poet husband, but life with him was unpredictable, materially impoverished, often frightening. She herself was dark and boyish; she painted and played the guitar, and wore romantic clothes – velvet cloaks and breeches in black and red. Augustus John, Roy's drinking companion, called her 'Little Lord Fondleroy'. Childlike, she found in Vita more than a lover. She called Vita her St Anne, her Demeter, lover, mother, 'everything in women that I most need and love': 'You are sometimes like a mother to me. No one can imagine the tenderness of a lover suddenly descending to being maternal. It is a lovely moment when the mother's voice and hands turn into the lover's.' This fusing of mother and lover touched an eternal chord in Vita also. She wrote to her own difficult mother shortly after she fell in love with Mary, 'You have *absolutely no idea* how much I love and *admire* you – darling darling B.M. – unique and so lovely. I was talking about you to Mary Campbell; she said "What a deep passion you seem to have for your mother." I was taken aback by her perception, and simply said, Yes I have.'

She took Mary to Knole and kissed her in the bedroom that was still hers; in her old sitting-room at Knole they read Shakespeare's sonnets together. She made love to Mary on the sofa in her sitting-room at Long Barn where Virginia had made her definitive 'little move' towards her; and she took Mary up to her own bedroom. When Nigel had flu and needed her attention, she took the considerable risk of sleeping with Mary, with the feverish ten-year-old in bed in a small room off her own. 'Lovely misty moonlight nights.'

When the boys went back to school, the Campbells moved into the 'babies' cottage' at Long Barn. Roy Campbell was pleased because it was rent-free; he quite liked the Nicolsons, and appreciated the use of their library. Mary was pleased because she was nearer to Vita.

There was another new friend too – the young actress Valerie Taylor, a friend of Clive's, who one night stayed until 1 a.m. confiding her love troubles to Vita, and another time until 3.30 a.m., after dressing up earlier in the day as Lord Byron. 'We talked about H[arold] writing a play about Byron in which she would act.' Vita continued to see Dottie and Virginia regularly too: these two had formed an uneasy alliance, Dottie having invested money in the Hogarth Press in order to edit a series of 'Hogarth Living Poets' for the Woolfs. 'Lady G. Wellesley has bought me,' said

Virginia. But 'I won't belong to the two of you, or to the one of you, if the two of us belong to the one. In short, if Dottie's yours, I'm not.'[13]

Virginia was brooding on the book that was to be *Orlando*. On 20 September she had written in her journal : 'One of these days, though, I shall sketch here, like a grand historical picture, the outlines of all my friends.... Vita should be Orlando, a young nobleman ... and it should be truthful, but fantastic.' Vita heard about the project on 10 October :

> But listen : suppose Orlando turns out to be about Vita ; and it's all about you and the lusts of your flesh and the lure of your mind (heart you have none, who go gallivanting down the lanes with [Mary] Campbell) – suppose there's the kind of shimmer of reality which sometimes attaches to my people.... Shall you mind ?

Vita did not mind at all :

> My God, Virginia, if ever I was thrilled and terrified it is at the prospect of being projected into the shape of Orlando. What fun for you ; what fun for me. You see, any vengeance that you want to take will be ready in your hand. Yes, go ahead, toss up your pancake, brown it nicely on both sides, pour brandy over it, and serve hot. You have my full permission.

All she asked was that Virginia should dedicate the book to her 'victim'. She went on – for her relation with Virginia was suddenly flooded with its old magic—

> And what a lovely letter you wrote me, Campbell or no Campbell. (How flattered she'd be if she knew. But she doesn't, and shan't.) ... But how right I was ... to force myself on you at Richmond, and to lay the trail for the explosion which happened on the sofa in my room here when you behaved so disgracefully and acquired me for ever.

The autumn nights were so beautiful, she wrote ; she herself was being 'good, industrious and loving' :

> but how long will it be, though, before I break out ? I would never break out if I had you here, but you leave me unguarded. Now, none of that means anything at all, so don't imagine that it does. I am Virginia's good puppy, beating my tail on the floor, responsive to a kind pat.[14]

Vita had already broken out. Nevertheless the idea of being Orlando in Virginia's book stirred her imagination deeply. Her own fantasies were to be given form, as well as Virginia's. At once, she became 'Orlando' in her secret life with Mary.

A few days later she was disturbed in a less pleasant way. 'The blow falls,' she wrote on 14 October. Harold, after six months' duty at the Foreign Office in London, was to go to Berlin; he was to leave in ten days. Added to this, her passionate involvement with Mary was at its height and an infatuated Valerie Taylor was still coming to see her. Her emotional tension, and her real fear and distress at Harold's going, expressed itself dramatically. Driving with Valerie on 17 October she was suddenly struck by semi-blindness and what she described as crippling neuralgia. Harold, in his diary, wrote out his gloom at being sent to Berlin and his anxiety over Vita's condition. On this page of his diary she has written: 'Darling, how much I love you!' (So they did read each other's diaries sometimes.)

Harold wrote to Vita the day he left: 'Little one, not be angry with me for being so obstinate and selfish. It [diplomacy] *is* Othello's occupation – and however much it may depress and irritate me, I feel that without it I should become *not* a cup of tea but a large jug of tepid milk.' From Berlin he wrote that if he gave up his diplomatic career 'merely for emotional reasons I should feel a worm – unworthy of what is one of the few serious and virile sides of my nature'.

Vita would have done well to understand this, but she did not. After seeing him off she went and wept at Dottie's flat. Virginia was sympathetic too, but Virginia could think of nothing now but *Orlando*. What used she and Violet to quarrel about? she asked Vita, and what used she and Lord Lascelles to talk about? (He was always very tongue-tied, replied Vita, 'so we didn't get very far.' But he had nice hands.) Vita translated the phrases Virginia wanted in French for the book – signing her translations 'Orlando'. The two went to Knole to choose obscure family portraits as possible illustrations, and to a London photographer for 'Orlando', in his female incarnation, to be photographed as a Lely portrait. 'I was miserable,' Vita told Harold, 'draped in an inadequate bit of pink satin with all my clothes slipping off – but V. was delighted and kept diving under the black cloth of the camera to peep at the effect.'

Vita's diary, Saturday 5 November 1927: 'A very lovely sunny day; a brown and blue and purple day. Went for a walk with Mary in the morning.... Roy telephoned to say he would remain in London to-night. I wrote my Oxford paper [to be given at St Hugh's] while she played the gramophone in the evening. She dined with me. A very happy day.' But Mary was, as Vita wrote to Harold that night, 'in rather a fuss about Roy', since he had met Augustus John in London which 'always means that he will get drunk, and then he will be ill for a fortnight.'

The next day Vita and Mary met Roy from the train. At dusk Vita went out 'to shoot a pheasant', and met both the Campbells: Roy told Vita there and then that he knew about her and Mary. All three went back into Vita's sitting-room. Roy announced that he himself was sleeping with Dorothy Warren. 'He went off quite amicable, then Mary came back and said he had changed completely.'

Vita's diary, 7 November:

A dreadful day. Roy had kept Mary up practically all night with threats of murder, suicide etc. Went on doing my Oxford paper miserably with these constant incursions to tell me of R.'s changes of mind etc. We got Mr Burnett to him. In a rainy dusk I walked up to the village with M. to get beer for him. After dinner unable to bear things any longer I went up to the cottage and talked to him. She, poor child, quite numbed and dead tired. Rang up A [prile] in sheer misery.

Vita reported to Harold that Roy 'went for her [Mary] last night with a knife', but not the reason for it. The rows and violence went on for days. 'Hasn't Mar been beautifully alone these days? Not a soul,' she wrote blandly to Harold in Berlin. Her diary, 9 October: 'Our boxes arrived from Teheran. Started unpacking them in the big room, when Clive and his brother, Valerie and Virginia arrived after lunch. Took them up to Knole after. Very cold, freezing. Roy came down just before lunch to say they were going to be divorced. I told him not to be so silly.' After her visitors had gone she went up to the cottage and found Roy calmer. 'He came down after dinner to talk to me till Mary joined us. Made certain arrangements; feeling much happier.' Roy had sent down a generous letter to Vita on a torn-out leaf from an exercise book:

I am tired of trying to hate you and I realize that there is no way in which I could harm you (as I would have liked to) without equally harming us all. I do not dislike any of your personal characteristics and I liked you very much before I knew anything. All this acrimony on my part is due rather to our respective positions in the tangle. I am much more angry with M.

He and Vita, wrote Roy, 'may both reach a state of mind when we realize that we have not done each other any *lasting* harm: and I want to reach that state of mind as quickly as possible because this is absolute Hell.'

Vita agreed with him, as her poems written in the following weeks prove. She felt a strong fellow-feeling for him, just as she had for

Denys Trefusis, as the sixth of her first sequence of sonnets written to Mary in the following weeks shows :

> We both have known your beauty, both enjoyed
> Your passion, as a shared and secret thing ;
> On that account, each other we avoid
> Who both have tapped your passion at its spring.
> Is this a reason ? should we not more truly
> Meet in our common love that is your due ?
> Across your body not discover newly
> A bond the deeper for its source in you ?[15]

But the hell continued, not only because of jealousy but because Mary rebelled against the restricting 'arrangements' that Roy and Vita had agreed on. She showered Vita with desperate notes of love on pages torn from account books and copy-books : 'Is the night never coming again when I can spend hours in your arms, when I can realize your big sort of protectiveness all round me, and be quite naked except for a covering of your rose-leaf kisses ?' She reproached Vita for saying that the price of their love was too high. 'Darling is it very often that we get weeks of such amazing happiness ... and I *don't regret it at any time*, even when I suffer most it becomes more worthwhile.' Roy's unhappiness was the only thing that Mary regretted. If Vita's commitment was not equal to her own then Vita was 'guilty', and Mary 'a weak fool to be led away by you'.

Vita was 'guilty' of responding to Mary's desire and of falling in love with her without thinking of the dangerous emotional tempest she might unloose. She felt a growing unease at the self-conscious and rather literary drama that was unfolding :

> Between two poets, you, a scurrying mouse,
> Hurry with news of harsh satiric verse
> Written in virulence, from house to house,
> Yet I believe your interest is perverse.[16]

An added complication was Dorothy Warren, always lurking on the edge of Vita's affairs : first Geoffrey Scott's mistress and now Roy's, she begged Vita to go and see her. Vita did not go ; instead she went to Virginia, and poured out the whole horrid saga and its subplots. Virginia was astringent ('I hate being bored'), critical, slightly disgusted and – as she later admitted – jealous. She told Vita she was making a mess of her life and muddling all her relationships. Vita was reduced to tears. She told Harold a bit about it : 'I felt I was a failure all round. I wanted to come to you.'

Harold answered reassuringly that the real test was '*continuous* relationships', not incidental ones that were based on passion. 'Now I think you have a positive genius for *durable* relationships' – and he cited her relations with her parents, Dottie, Raymond, himself and the children. Vita was not comforted. She knew he was making it too easy for her, and she knew her own patterns :

> You see, what I always feel is, that I've never made one person completely and perfectly happy. You'll say that *you* are. But I have done some damned horrid things even to you, *dans le temps*, – *not* consistent with any ideal of loyalty or love, my darling. You see I've never really got over this, it has scarred me. And yet I know I love you as few people love.

As for Dottie, 'you've no idea of how miserable I have made Dotz. No, darling, your Mar is a born muddler. Neither one thing nor the other, not enough character to be either austere or dissipated. The result is just a mess, and nobody is pleased.'

Harold said she had the impression of 'muddles' because 'your secondary affairs are apt to end in a cry.... You are improvident, and without caution. You drift into a situation and can't get backwards, like a rat in one of those traps with the spikes pointing inwards.' He was always 'a *little* nervous about such secondary things – about Mary Campbell and that sort of thing. Oh please Mar do not get into a mess there.' His advice was sound and his understanding of her correct. But she had already got herself into the mess.

There was another picture session for *Orlando*, this time with Vanessa Bell and Duncan Grant as the photographers ; Virginia read aloud *The Times* obituary notices 'and interlarded them with her own comments, which made us laugh and spoilt the photograph.' Vita went with her mother-in-law and Harold's bachelor brother Freddy to see *The Merchant of Venice* done at the boys' school in Oxford (Nigel was 'a wild success' as Nerissa). Three days later she was in Oxford again, for Ben had to have his tonsils out. She stayed with him for two days.

One of her 'secondary things' temporarily resolved itself : Valerie Taylor and Raymond Mortimer fell in love and seriously thought of getting married. 'She let him sleep with her,' Vita reported to Harold, 'but I haven't told him that she wanted to sleep with me the next night – at Oxford – I *didn't*, but that was no fault of hers. On the whole, I have encouraged a collage rather than matrimony.' (Even the 'collage' was short-lived.)

On the evening of 1 December, alone at Long Barn, Vita in a burst of creative emotional energy wrote no less than eleven sonnets about herself and Mary Campbell. She wrote two more the next morning before going up to London to see Valerie acting in a play. On 5 December, a day that Mary had spent with her, three more were written. Writing to Harold after finishing the first eleven, she said, 'Unfortunately they are so b.s. [the Nicolsons' code-word for 'homosexual'; from 'back-stairs'] that they are quite unprintable. But I feel they acted as a sort of catharsis to a great many pent-up feelings. Perhaps I'll show them to you some day. Not sure though.'

Vita was shortly going to see Harold in Berlin, and he told her to bring the sonnets with her. 'But oh how I hope she isn't in a muddle – oh dear! oh dear! One doesn't write ten [*sic*] sonnets in one night unless one *is* in a muddle.' In fact the outburst of all sixteen sonnets constituted for Vita a return to control; they were a summing-up. She was able, now, to be slightly more frank with Harold about what had happened. 'No more poems. No more sonnets. Yes, of course she gets into muddles when he goes away. Even before he goes. But it's all right. Nothing to worry about.'

The texture of ordinary life sustains people through emotional up-heavals. The 'Hawthornden' wood was duly planted, and central heating installed at Long Barn. Vita fretted at the chaos this had caused – 'And my God how workmen smell. The whole house stinks of them. How I hate the proletariat,' she wrote with the flippant rich woman's arrogance that falls so cruelly on a modern ear. The Ebury Street house was being sold; its furniture, which all belonged to B.M., was to come to Vita and Harold.

Vita was a very sound businesswoman; she managed her money and her land and her tenants well and methodically. It was a facet of her that fascinated Virginia, and it was an area in which she exercised some approximation to moral superiority over Harold, who was not only poorer, but chronically improvident. Why was he so broke? she was asking him at the end of the year. 'I am blowed if I know how you manage it – because after all if you knock off £400 a year for the babies' school, I have no more than you have, and a great deal more to do with it.' (She maintained Long Barn; Harold's salary was his own.) 'This is not a scold, just a puzzle. I love you.'

She left for her week in Berlin on 14 December after a wild request from Mary Hutchinson to spend her last evening with her: 'I will meet you at midnight anywhere – tell me.' In Berlin she was pursued by letters from Mary Campbell to 'my rose, my darling mother'; Mary had had a row driving through London with Roy and Dorothy Warren, 'you should have seen me sitting in your motor in Piccadilly Circus crying quite helplessly.'

The Berlin visit only confirmed Vita's loathing of diplomatic life. 'Very depressed at leaving him in that beastly place,' she wrote in her diary the day she left to spend Christmas with the children at Knole. Harold, after she had gone, confided his impressions to loyal Dorothy Wellesley :

> Vita seemed fairly all right when she was here. Of course it has been a muddle – but not, I think, a very serious one. But what a bore these things are – they make one so uneasy. You see I did warn her and she just scoffed at me. She is without the gift of prevision. I don't like caution much as a quality.... But there is little to be said for such Ophelia-like recklessness as my darling indulges in. You see it is optimism, Dottz, – a sort of refusal to believe that things won't turn out right after all – a sort of drifting attitude.

One might add that it was also a result of her 'Nothing matters' philosophy, and of the idea that physical love was irresistible but ephemeral, a fever from which one soon recovers. An 'honest sensualist', as she called herself, she failed to take into account the fact that the people who fell in love with her invested the affair with a far greater significance, and sometimes were ready to risk the stability of their lives for what they believed to be a great love. At the beginning of an affair, she exacted this total commitment; she attracted and was attracted by personalities who were temperamentally disposed to abandon themselves to love in this way – 'loonies', as Harold and she afterwards called them. Independent women, or those who like herself were chiefly interested in an escapade (such as Mary Hutchinson), had little charm for her. Harold ended his letter to Dottie : 'But she is like that. We can't alter it. All we can do is to be very sweet to our Ophelia – and try and steer her away from danger. But they are an odd family the Sackville-Wests.'

# CHAPTER 17

VITA's father, like her grandfather before him, had grown increasingly isolated and withdrawn over the years. In early January 1928 he fell ill. Influenza brought on pericarditis. Thomas Horder, the royal physician, was called in ; Harold was sent for from Berlin. Olive Rubens, Vita and Harold camped in Lionel's sitting-room so as to be near him at night. He died just after midnight on 28 January. He was sixty-one. His body was placed in a lead case in Knole chapel. Harold wrote an appreciation for *The Times*.

While he was ill, Vita had read a dry assessment of *The Land* by Rebecca West in *T.P.'s Weekly*; the article said the poem expressed conventional emotions with literary grace, and was 'the work of some-one who is used to reading beautiful lines.... There is no line of it which is feeble, but there is no line of it which has any individual beauty.' So that when Virginia, who was aware of how much Vita minded losing her father, wrote two days before his death that 'I've been reading The Land – so good, I think, some lines', what sounds like mean praise was the most comforting comment she could have made.

Virginia understood that losing Dada meant that Vita lost Knole. It passed now to Lionel's younger brother, Vita's Uncle Charlie, and then to Charlie's son Eddy. For three days, until the funeral, Knole for the first and last time belonged wholly to Vita. She made arrangements, she administered the household, she gave orders. She described what those three days meant to her in a letter to Ben, later, when he was at Eton and feeling unable to fit in. She and Ben, she told him, both shared the 'Sackville weakness' of indecisiveness and withdrawal, and of being – as she once wrote to Eddy – 'at a wrong angle to life'. But she learned that it could be overcome : 'it has to do with Grandpapa's death, and the three or four days in which I had to rule Knole and make every decision. ... But I had to do it, and it really marked a turning-point in my life. In fact, my mental muscles grew surprisingly, and I have never been quite the same since.' She felt, she told Ben, 'that you and I are very much in sympathy, and that my own difficulties were the same as your difficulties, and that therefore you and I understand (or *could* understand) each other in a curiously intimate sort of way, as perhaps Niggs and Daddy could never understand, being people who could naturally come to terms with life.' Vita divided the family into 'camps': herself and Ben, Harold and Nigel.

Olive Rubens, on account of her ambiguous position, did not come to the funeral. Neither did Lady Sackville. Among the many letters of condolence, Vita received a gentle note from Violet: 'I know what a flawless companionship yours was, and often as a child was awed by your twin silences which I didn't then realize arose from a perfect understanding of one another.'

At Long Barn, when it was all over, 'Reticulata out, and anemone blanda', Vita noted in her diary on 11 February. Roy Campbell was recovering from an operation for appendicitis; Mary spent days and nights again with Vita, who wrote her four more sonnets, this time of an elegiac nature. Vita was going to Berlin again, and Roy was anxious to leave the cottage as soon as possible. She also wrote farewell poems to her father, and poems about her kinship with him. 'Heredity', which is about him, is in her *Collected Poems*; in the manuscript version she added a final verse, about Ben. What was this family temperament,

> Our weakness and our strength
> Making us into one?
> – God, I have seen it again
> In the features of my son.

It was painful going back to Knole to collect Canute, the elk-hound she had given her father; it was worse going through his personal possessions:

Knole was looking particularly lovely, outside, in the sunshine; but gloomy inside, as all the blinds were down and dust-sheets like shrouds over everything, which I really prefer, as I didn't like everything looking just the same. Anyhow I feel as if I have now broken the ice of going there, though I shan't go there without some inevitable reason ever in future.

She had written generously to her cousin: 'Dear Eddy, Knole is now to you what it used to be to me; but I know you love it as much as I do.' She knew for a fact that he did not, and day-dreamed to Harold that if neither Charlie nor Eddy wanted Knole 'I would be quite ready to take it off their hands.' And, in desperate half-joke: 'I want Knole.... I've got an idea about it : shall we take it some day ? . . . I've taken Dada's revolver. And the bullets.' She loathed her Uncle Charlie's American second wife Anne, and hated to think of her as châtelaine. Anne was the main reason why Vita kept away from Knole.

By the end of February she was in Berlin with Harold at the flat he had taken at 24 Brücken Allee. She arrived, as Harold reported to Virginia, with her spectacles held together by an old pipe-cleaner, hiccoughs, and 200 cigarettes that she had smuggled through the customs on the strength of a diplomatic visa. She herself told Virginia :

> This *is* a bloody place, to be sure ; and my feelings which if I gave way to them would be all rebellion and despair – just temper and tears – are complicated by a feeling that I mustn't hate Berlin because of Harold, i.e. it is an implied criticism of him, and a resentment, and I can't bear to harbour any thought which reflects on him – besides, he can't help it, I suppose – so what with one emotion and another it is very difficult.

Harold still wanted to be an ambassador – 'but can you see your poor Vita as an ambassadress ? I can't – and the prospect fills me with dismay. Really fate does play queer tricks on one – when all one wants is to garden and write and talk to Potto [Virginia]. . . . Poor Orlando.'[1]
    Harold described to Clive Bell a freezing walk round the Tiergarten with Vita hissing 'What a bloody place !' through chattering teeth :

> And what am I to say ? 'A wife', am I to say, 'should not only support but encourage her husband in his career' ? I do not say that, but I say : 'Darling, you know I should be wretched without my work.' 'Rubbish,' she answers. And then comes a letter from Virginia saying she feels almost ashamed of having a friend who is married to a man who will (not 'may' mark you) be an Ambassador.[2]

Virginia was unremitting in her support of Vita in the campaign to persuade Harold to give up diplomacy. In her relation to her own husband she was quite different ; she could play the conventional wife with conviction, accompanying Leonard to political meetings in distant and unglamorous towns and never undermining his career or his image of himself. But then she thought more highly of Leonard, whom she loved, than of Harold, whom she learned to like chiefly for Vita's sake.
    Vita's selfishness in the matter of Harold's career was not so much that she stayed at home apart from brief visits, though this was unusual behaviour for a diplomat's wife. (But there were not, in 1928, many diplomats' wives with careers of their own as Vita had.) It was her disparagement of his chosen profession – in which he had shown skill

and aptitude and had been successful – making little of his ability and success and devaluing one aspect of his personality. In spite of her disclaimers, criticism of his chosen work was inevitably an implied criticism of him for choosing it.

In Berlin, Harold had recently met Frederick and Margaret Voigt : he was a journalist and historian, she an American who wrote under her own name of Margaret Goldsmith and acted as an agent representing English-speaking authors in Germany. Vita met the Voigts in the first few days of her visit, and began lunching, dining, and going to the cinema with Margaret regularly. On 8 March Margaret came to 24 Brücken Allee to read part of her novel in progress to Vita ; on 9 March, Vita's birthday, she and her husband, with Sinclair Lewis, were the dinner guests ; on 10 March 'Margaret Voyt [sic] came in the morning with results I had foreseen.'

Bored, unhappy, homesick, Vita may have 'foreseen', but she did not take precautions. As usual she involved herself far too deeply. She said things that she would forget, but which Margaret would not. ' "I love you in every way that it is possible to love anyone, remember that" you said (you were standing back of the divan in the Brücken Allee), and my dear, I cherish this, remember this every day and every night' – so Margaret wrote after Vita's return to England.

Vita wrote to Virginia asking if Margaret could handle the translations of her books into German : 'She is extremely nice, and energetic and intelligent ; and incidentally a bosom friend of mine, though I would not recommend her if I were not sure that you would do well by her.'[3] Virginia smelt a rat at once ; in any case, her books were published in Germany already by Insel Verlag. Vita and Margaret went together to Leipzig to see this same firm about Vita's new project for translating Rilke into English. (Harold was very taken up at this time with a young American, Bobby Sharpe.) Harold and Vita travelled together to Copenhagen where they both lectured – Harold 'most brilliantly and amusingly' according to Vita – and then back to Berlin to make preparations for Vita's departure.

She spent her last evening with Margaret Voigt, and Margaret saw her off. (Harold had a duty dinner, and they both hated station farewells.) Plans were made for Margaret to come to England soon ; and the night Vita left, Margaret wrote to her : 'There is nothing to say – in words – of what today has meant. . . . I never knew that there *was* such one-ness and closeness. . . . Goodnight, my darling, when, o when, will I sleep in your arms until the dawn creeps in ? *May.*'

Vita crossed the Channel from one woman's arms to another. Mary Campbell had written to Vita every day, and Vita to her (but Mary had been firmly frozen out of Long Barn by Vita's French maid Louise Genoux when, in order to feel closer, she had wanted to spend a morning in Vita's sitting-room). She and Roy were on the brink of a trial separation, and she made elaborate plans to spend the first night of Vita's return on 29 March with her in London. The rendezvous she picked was the foyer of the Capitol Picture House in the Haymarket. Vita did as Mary asked. 'My own I still feel warm from your arms. I still burn with last night's love,' Mary wrote on 2 April.

At Long Barn, the bulbs Vita had brought back from Persia were in flower; and Dorothy Wellesley was buying a wonderful new house, Penns-in-the Rocks, at Withyham in Sussex. Vita's boys came home for the Easter holidays, and she bewailed to Harold that Ben, now fourteen, complained he had nothing to do. It must be modern life, Vita told Ben, that gave everyone the idea that 'one must always be being entertained by something'. Nigel set out to show her he could entertain himself:

Niggs, who remained to listen to half this conversation, slipped away in the middle by himself. He went to play golf. I watched him out of the window. His trousers were coming down. He made a tee very carefully and balanced the ball on top of it. Then he addressed the ball, very elaborately; but it rolled off the tee and he had to set it up again. This happened four times. Then he took a tremendous swipe, missed the ball completely, and fell over.

Since Lord Sackville's death, trouble had been brewing with B.M. who was wintering at the Hotel Metropole in Brighton. She was afraid of not getting her wifely due and was working herself into a state of paranoia. (It had only been with great reluctance that she had renounced the executorship of her estranged husband's will.) On the morning of 18 April, Vita was in London at Pembertons, the family lawyers, discussing her father's estate. Her mother turned up unexpectedly at the office and made an unprecedentedly terrible scene. 'Give me your pearls,' she screamed at Vita, 'twelve of them belong to me, and I wish to see how many you have changed, you thief.' Floods of fluent abuse poured from her. 'She was like a mad woman, screaming Thief and Liar, and shaking her fist at me till I thought she was going to hit me.' The presence of two solicitors in the room did nothing to quell the storm of insults. When she started abusing her dead husband, Vita left the room. Finally Lady Sackville retreated to her Rolls, but sent her secretary in again to say Vita must go with her to a jeweller to have twelve pearls cut from her necklace.

Vita went out to the car and there and then, in the street, cut up her pearl necklace. This did not satisfy her mother – who demanded the return of all the jewels she had ever given Vita, who was to bring them to

her at the Savoy Hotel, send them up by a waiter, 'and wait outside her
door like a servant while she looked over them to see how much I had
stolen from her while she was ill.' She screamed at Vita through her car
window that she hated her and wished she would die, until Vita hailed a
passing taxi and escaped.

Devastated, she went to keep a luncheon appointment with
Raymond Mortimer, who comforted her with half a bottle of cham-
pagne. She went on to Virginia, who was soothing and sensibly said,
'Let's go to the Zoo.' Later Virginia went with her to the BBC studios at
Savoy Hill, where Vita was to make the first broadcast of her life – the
day's events had hardly been a good preparation. Afterwards, the two
walked down the Strand and had coffee at the Charing Cross Hotel;
'then I got into my train and came home – shattered, but agreeing with
Virginia's reflection that life was not uneventful.' At home, Mary
Campbell waited.

Lady Sackville had given Vita the jewels on her marriage, fifteen years
before. The family money was in trust, and B.M. was not able to
deprive Vita of her annuity. But Vita determined to accept no further gifts
or allowances of money from her mother, ever. Virginia described her
that afternoon at the Zoo as 'very gallant & wild & tossing her head ...
& saying she was wild and free & would make her money herself by
writing.'[4]

When Vita had got over the shock of her mother's behaviour, she
described to Harold the routine of those early live broadcasts – she did
another the following week:

> You are taken into a studio, which is a large and luxuriously appointed room,
> and there is a desk, heavily padded, and over it hangs a little white box,
> suspended from two wires from the ceiling. There are lots of menacing
> notices about 'DON'T COUGH – you will deafen millions of people', 'DON'T
> RUSTLE YOUR PAPERS', and 'Don't turn to the announcer and say was that all
> right? when you have finished.' ... One has never talked to so few people,
> or so many; it's very queer. And then you cease, and there is an awful grim
> silence as though you had been a complete failure ... and then you hear the
> announcer saying, 'London calling. Weather and News bulletin', and you
> creep away.

The boys heard perfectly, she told him: 'They put the machine on the
kitchen table and sat round it with all the bedints' (that is, servants –
these now consisted of Mrs Staples the cook, George Horne the butler,
Elsie the maid, and French Louise).

Harold reacted furiously to the story of Lady Sackville's crazy outburst; he was even angrier when he heard that B.M. had gone so far as
to telephone to the Foreign Office asking how much his salary was. Vita

was touched by the vehemence of his protectiveness towards her – 'All the femineity [*sic*] in me responded. (It may be very latent, but it is there none the less.)' But she could not bear the idea of anybody taking her part against her mother. She knew B.M. 'must be feeling very lonely, somewhere in her strange heart. I wish I could go and take her part against us.' Whatever her mother did, Vita would always love her.

The crisis over, or in abeyance, Harold stopped telephoning Vita from Berlin as he had been doing. It upset him too much: 'You said "Goodnight darling Hadji" and dropped from me five hundred miles. And then Niggs' giggle! You see it was not only a giggle I heard but the unmistakable giggle of my own darling Niggs. It wrung my heart – and when I put back the receiver and was back in Berlin I felt the tears come to my eyes.' They agreed to use the telephone only in emergencies. They still, as always when apart, wrote to one another every day.

Vita and Margaret Voigt wrote to one another every day too. A week after the B.M. row, Margaret arrived in London. (Her husband was working for the *Manchester Guardian*.) She had thought she would stay with Vita at Long Barn, but instead Vita arranged for her to borrow Vanessa Bell's flat at 37 Gordon Square. This was arranged through Virginia (Vanessa was in Cassis), who heartily disliked Margaret's 'vulgar, pushing, crude, coarse' American voice on the telephone. 'This is one of the effects of jealousy,'[5] she conceded; and she came to Long Barn to take a photograph of Vita in country clothes for *Orlando* (the last one in the illustrated edition) and took Vita to Lenare in London to have 'Orlando' photographed in Victorian dress.

Margaret Voigt went down to Long Barn for a weekend and, like all Vita's lovers, was taken to see Knole – from the outside, now. Then Vita went with Dottie Wellesley to see her new house, instead of back to London with Margaret – who was hurt, but interpreted Vita's decision significantly: 'You are so loyal, your loyalty is like a flame in my mind ... perhaps because out of it you pay alimony – in energy, in devotion, in giving part of yourself – for ever to the loves, or passions, or friendships or ties, which, in themselves, may have lost some of their meaning.' She was right. Partly because she felt some responsibility for the fires she had lit, partly because she did not like anyone who loved her to stop loving her and partly, as Margaret surmised, out of simple loyalty, Vita did not drop people (Geoffrey Scott excepted). With the years, Vita's list of emotional pensioners grew, and with it her correspondence and the demands on her time. Nearly all the women whom she had loved said, 'I was not like the others'; and they were right in that Vita, in her intense erotic, sympathetic concentration on the loved person, temporarily gave herself wholeheartedly in a different way to each one. Or rather, she wholeheartedly gave a part of herself – and never the part that belonged to Harold and home, not after Violet.

Margaret Voigt was rather soon to become an emotional pensioner herself. Only a week after Margaret's arrival, Vita was telling Harold that 'she gets on my nerves.' What had worked in Germany did not work now. Vita had her *béguins* and 'real affections,' she told Harold, 'but they are nothing like my feelings for you. . . . I forget about people very quickly when I am away from them. I part from them with violent *abschiedstimmung*' – which she knew from experience would quickly fade. (But she did not modify her behaviour as a result of experience.)

The only hope, Vita said, was 'to carry one's life inside oneself, so as to be essentially free and essentially independent' (she was working on her 'Reddín' poem again) ; 'but then the irrational passions come in, and Reason is made to look silly.'

Someone who was about to leave her behind was Mary Campbell. Roy had already left for Martigues in the South of France and Mary, though still passionately in love with Vita, had decided in favour of her marriage and was going to join him. Vita took Mary to the train, then met Margaret off another train and brought her back to Long Barn. Mary went on writing to Vita : she needed continual reassurance that Vita cared for her, she found it hard to resume marital relations with Roy ; sometimes she asked Vita to send money (which she did) as they were dirt-poor. The two Campbell girls were left behind in the charge of a woman in Weald village, and Mary and Vita's parting was softened by the knowledge that Mary would soon return for them. She came in June, but her brief visit changed nothing and Vita did not beg her to stay.

Vita made a new literary friend that summer – the young Cyril Connolly. He wrote her an eight-page letter 'all about poetry, and begging not to be considered a neo-Bloomsbury young man'. Eddy Sackville-West warned her against him : 'He is very clever, but a SPONGE, and a terrible mischief-maker ; and the more dangerous because he knows how to make himself very charming.' (Harold met Connolly in Berlin that same summer – 'like the young Beethoven with spots'.) In June Connolly spent two nights at Long Barn, and afterwards wrote Vita an immensely long letter about 'the value of exile, homesickness and obscurity as literary stimuli'; and about her own 'loping, impersonal poem' *The Land*, its qualities and defects ; about what was wrong with romanticism, religion and the writing of Virginia Woolf. 'Let's have a famous literary controversy.' He liked Vita.

The day after he left she gave herself what she called a torture-treat. She went up to Knole after dark and wandered about the garden. (Uncle

Charlie had given her a master-key, her most treasured possession.) She had the place so entirely to herself 'that I might have been the only person alive in the world, – and not the world of today, mark you, but the world of at least 300 years ago. . . . Darling Hadji, it may be looney, but there is some sort of umbilical cord that ties me to Knole.' Harold replied sympathetically, but said he was glad Knole wasn't hers 'as it would be a bore for Hadji, who doesn't like being a prince consort.' His own family could not compete in her eyes in grandeur and glamour, as he knew.

Vita went alone to the dark garden, she did not take Margaret. The two had established their fantasy love-world at Long Barn (in which Margaret played the 'peasant' to Vita's aristocrat, and Vita was 'David' to Margaret as she would be to later lovers). Margaret wanted to be childishly dependent on Vita, as Mary Campbell had been. 'Never have I been more your child than I am this evening,' she wrote; and 'Darling, my dearest, I wish I were three years old and that I could crawl into your arms and just stay there while you take on the *régie* of my life.'

For four days at the end of June Vita was quite alone at Long Barn, and spoke to no one outside the house, and 'felt quite different in consequence'. She was trying to finish *Twelve Days*. Margaret saw the writing on the wall, and wrote on 3 July: 'Our relationship – outwardly – has taken on a shape so different from what I thought it would. I did not realize that we should be together so little, that our outward lives would be so unmelted together, or I should never in the world have let myself get into the habit of leaning on you so much, needing you so much.' Margaret was very good, proud and dignified. She continued to help Vita with her translations of Rilke, and Vita persuaded Harold to write a preface to Margaret's biography of Frederick the Great. By early September Vita was telling Harold that Margaret was 'a real brick as to character', and that there were 'no misunderstandings or false positions'.

No longer immersed in passion, Vita helped Dottie with her new garden, renewed her protests to Harold about his job and Berlin, 'that filthy, filthy place', and revitalized her changed intimacy with Virginia, who made what she called a 'good, rather happy visit' to Long Barn on 7 July:

I'm interested by the gnawing down of strata in friendship; how one passes unconsciously to different terms; takes things easier; don't mind hardly at all about dress or anything; scarcely feel it as an exciting atmosphere, which, too, has its drawback from the 'fizzing' point of view; yet is saner, perhaps deeper. Lay by the blackcurrant bushes lecturing Vita on her floundering habits with the Campbells for instance.[6]

This time Vita did not cry; Virginia was 'absolutely enchanting', she told Harold. Vita had just finished a story that she called in manuscript 'A History' (she was to publish it in *Harper's Bazaar* in 1930 under the title 'Liberty'), which constitutes a footnote to the Mary Campbell affair. It is about two lovers who are so humbled and shamed by the nobility of the wronged husband that they decide to part. In the story, the bond between the husband and the lover – whose name is 'David' – is nearly as strong as between lover and lover, or as between the husband and wife. The husband shoots himself because he is unable to transcend his jealousy and live up to his own ideals of personal liberty.

The early part of the story follows, step by step, the story of Vita and the Campbells. Roy Campbell, though he threatened suicide in the worst times, did not shoot himself; but Vita always said she understood his point of view and that in his position she would have reacted as strongly as he did. Emotional troilism always attracted her.

# CHAPTER 18

B.M. grew increasingly insane. She was spreading a crazy rumour, via Ozzie Dickinson, that Vita planned to divorce Harold and marry Eddy, in order to regain Knole. 'The day will come when we may have to put her under some kind of control,' thought Harold. B.M. descended on Knole in mid-August 1928 to collect what she considered to be hers, and coldly instructed Vita to take all her jewels and other valuables over to Knole to be inspected. 'Remember that I have never signed any deed of gift, to the best of my recollection.'

Vita was already harassed with the boys home again for the summer. She, who was always busy, could not comprehend the natural aimlessness of boys – 'they simply hang about and flop, and groan. They rush after me whenever they see me, simply because they have nothing else to do.... They *never* read. They never do anything, in fact !'

She solved the problem by engaging the services of a young woman called Audrey Le Bosquet, soon known to them all as Boski ; she was to live in the 'babies' cottage', look after the boys in the holidays and act as Vita's secretary in term-time, for a salary of £225 a year. Harold did not like the idea of Boski. He wrote to Vita sharply reminding her of B.M. who 'thought that by cutting out everything that barred her egoism she would attain complete independence : and found herself alone in a desert.' His Mar should not say to herself, 'I should be at peace if only people wouldn't interrupt,' but, 'If I don't manage to absorb my Acid X better, I shall end by becoming a neuropath.' (Acid X was 'things-we-don't-want-to-do'.)

O my love my love – it would be such a good thing if you could throw a little more eccentricity into your writing and a little less eccentricity into your life. How I wish I could get at the fool (was it Violet ??) who gave you the idea that responsibilities, instead of being the stepping-stones through a marsh, were something to evade and to regard with shame.

Vita agreed with him in principle about Acid X. But *he* wouldn't like it, she countered, if he was told to have entire charge of two children for four months of the year: 'I should like to see you try it; you would be screaming at the end of a week.'

> Supposing that someone, – say Eddy, – told you that he had to look after two boys and that it was too much of a good thing, you would instantly agree. You know you would. It would never cross your mind to say he was being unreasonable. Why then is it different for me? Sex, I suppose. Well, I don't see that it makes any difference, so there.

Just before she left with the boys for a holiday with Harold in Germany, a literary controversy began. In July Vita had read *Lady Chatterley's Lover*, published in Italy: 'It is not a good book as a whole, though there are some good passages in it; but never have I read in any language such descriptions of sensuality. ... Not a book to be left lying about.' Two weeks later she read Leonard Woolf's review in the *Nation* of Radclyffe Hall's lesbian novel *The Well of Loneliness* and reported to Harold: 'It is a perfectly serious attempt to write a quite frank and completely unpornographic book about b.s.ness [homosexuality]. The pity is, that although serious and not sentimental, it is not a work of art. He [Leonard] says this.' Vita was going to bring the novel to Germany with her; Cyril Connolly and Raymond were with Harold already, and she was longing to discuss it with them. 'Of course I simply *itch* to try the same thing myself.... You see, if one may write about b.s.ness, the field of fiction is immediately doubled.'

But it appeared that one might not, after all, 'write about b.s.ness'. While Vita was in Germany, *The Well of Loneliness* was banned. Leonard Woolf and E.M. Forster set about collecting signatures to protest against the ban – 'not yours,' wrote Virginia to Vita, 'for *your* proclivities are too well known.' Vita answered this from Potsdam, while Ben and Nigel were swimming in the lake: 'I feel very violently about *The Well of Loneliness*. Not on account of what you call my proclivities; not because I think it is a good book; but really on principle. ... Personally, I should like to renounce my nationality, as a gesture; but I don't want to become a German, even though I did go to a revue last night in which two ravishing young women sang a frankly lesbian song.'[1]

Later in the year, on 1 November, Vita attended a meeting in the studio of architect Clough Williams-Ellis to discuss the defence of the novel. George Bernard Shaw spoke amusingly, according to Virginia; otherwise the company was 'a dowdy lot', in which her Vita shone out 'like a lamp or a torch in all this petty bourgeoisdom; a tribute to the breeding of the Sackvilles, for without care of her clothes she appears among them . . . like a lamppost, straight, glowing.'²

At the trial in November, Sir Chartres Biron found the book to be obscene. 'I hope they appeal,' wrote Vita. 'I hope there is a row.' Radclyffe Hall did appeal; Vita went along to the hearing, 'but it was very dull, so I came away and went shopping', and to tea with Mary Hutchinson. The appeal failed. Afterwards, Radclyffe Hall, who had recognized her in court, wrote to Vita (care of Mrs Leonard Woolf, at 52 Tavistock Square) complaining about the way her case had been conducted – and, more pointedly, about the huge expenses she had incurred.

Earlier, Vita and Virginia had taken their much discussed and long-planned holiday together. Vita had returned from Germany in mid-September – 'auratum lilies still out' – and taken Ben to start his new public-school life at Eton, 'poor little boy'. On 24 September she and Virginia set out for six days in France.

Virginia, who had so longed for this expedition, was apprehensive. Unlike Vita, she was almost never separated from her husband for more than one night. She confessed in her diary that she was 'alarmed' by the thought of a week alone with Vita: they might 'find each other out'.

Vita wrote five pages of an unpublished 'Diary of a Journey to France with Virginia Woolf in 1928'. It is unfinished and rather flat. The main impression it gives is of Virginia fretting because she had not heard from Leonard, and of Vita worrying in case Virginia was overtired. It was, on the face of it, a modest and unadventurous little holiday – they even went home a day earlier than they had planned. It was as much as Virginia, temperamentally, could manage. They spent their first evening in Paris, drinking coffee at the Brasserie Lutétia in the rue de Sèvres, writing to their respective husbands on the torn-out fly-leaves of their respective books. Virginia admitted to Vita that 'she and Leonard had had a small and sudden row that morning about her going abroad with me.'

They went on next day to Saulieu, where there was a fair, and Virginia bought a green corduroy coat for Leonard. Then they sat in a field and wrote again to their husbands. Vita was enjoying it more than Virginia. Vita to Harold: 'Darling, it is very nice: I feel amused and irresponsible. I can talk about life and literature to my heart's content, – and it amuses me to be suddenly in the middle of Burgundy with Virginia.' Virginia to Leonard: 'I don't think I could stand more than a week away from you, as there are so many things to say to you, which I can't say to Vita – though she is more sympathetic and more intelligent than you think.'

Next day, breakfasting in Vita's room, they entered on 'a heated argument about men and women'. Virginia was 'curiously feminist', wrote Vita, who always herself denied being a feminist – though her every attitude – to domestic life, to her work, to the bureaucracy that insisted on labelling her 'Mrs Harold Nicolson' – belied her. Virginia, wrote Vita, 'dislikes the possessiveness and love of domination in men. In fact she dislikes the quality of masculinity. Says that women stimulate her imagination, by their grace and their art of life.'

Virginia nevertheless hated the word 'feminist', which she called in *Three Guineas* 'a vicious and corrupt word that has done much harm in its day'. Its day she hoped was over, and men and women would fight together against tyranny. The 'patriarchal state', however, remained her chief enemy. Vita rejected the 'feminist' label for the same reason, but she certainly never rejected the masculine 'quality', which was too much and too valuable a part of her own make-up for her to wish to do so. In *All Passion Spent* Vita was to define feminism in a totally negative way – to describe the fussy, claustrophobic, knowing female ritual that surrounds a bride before her wedding, ministering to her so that she in turn may 'minister to a man'.

At Avallon Vita found letters from Harold; Virginia was upset because there was nothing from Leonard, and in the end she sent him a telegram. Virginia's attitude to the masculine domination she condemned so eloquently could hardly, in practice, have been more equivocal.

That night there was a violent thunderstorm. Vita went to Virginia's room thinking she might be frightened: 'We talked about science and religion for an hour – and the ultimate principle, – and then as the storm had gone over I left her to go to sleep again.' Five years later she was to ask Virginia whether she remembered that important night – 'when I came along the dark passage to your room in a thunderstorm and we lay talking about whether we were frightened of death or not? That is the sort of occasion on which the things I want to say to you, – and to you only, – get said.'[3] After Virginia's death, Vita wrote that physical fear had that night released in Virginia 'the founts of spiritual horror'.[4] It was still remaining next day when they reached Vézelay, and both of them wrote home again. Vita told Harold how protective Virginia made her feel: 'The combination of that brilliant brain and that fragile body is very loveable – so independent in all mental ways, so dependent in all practical ways.'

They spent their last night at Offranville in Normandy at the house of Ethel Sands and Nan Hudson; Virginia read aloud to them her improper memoir of 'Old Bloomsbury', and 'the two old virgins bridled with horrified delight.' Vita felt she now understood Virginia for the first time : 'She has a sweet and childlike nature ; from which her intellect is completely separate. But of course no one would believe this, except Leonard and Vanessa.'

In retrospect, the holiday seemed to Virginia an achievement, and a great success, as it did to Vita, who wrote to her : 'I was very happy. Were you? . . . Anyhow, I've returned home a changed being. All this summer I was as nervous as a cat, – starting, dreaming, brooding, – now I'm all vigorous and sturdy again, and ravenous for life once more. And all thanks to you, I believe. . . . I do bless you for all you've been to me.'[5] Vita was newly conscious of the significance of her friendship with Virginia ; soon after their return, she was going back through Virginia's letters to her and dictating all but the most personal passages to Boski, to be typed. This awareness was largely tied up with the publication of *Orlando*.

They had had a private joke that their friendship might be broken for ever when Vita actually read *Orlando*. She did not read it in manuscript ; a week after they returned from Burgundy, on 11 October, an early copy arrived at Long Barn with the morning post. Vita spent all day reading it in growing excitement and incredulity, taking time off to write to Harold

> in such a turmoil of excitement and confusion that I scarcely know where (or who !) I am. . . . Parts of it make me cry, parts of it make me laugh ; the whole of it dazzles and bewilders me. . . . Nicholas Greene you will recognize as Gosse, the Archduchess Harriet as Lord Lascelles !
>
> Well, I don't know, – it seems to me a book unique in English literature. . . . I feel infinitely honoured at having been the peg on which it was hung and very humble. Oh I do want to know what Hadji thinks.

That evening, having finished the book, she wrote a long, euphoric, reverent letter to Virginia. In it she said that Virginia had invented a new form of narcissism – for Vita found herself 'in love with Orlando. This is a complication I had not foreseen.'[6]

In truth, Vita's indirect narcissism – her fascination with projections of her masculine aspect – was not new. But Virginia had not only 're-invented' Vita ; she had created her own work of art, while immortalizing Vita's myths and fantasies of herself and of Knole with more wit and magic than Vita could have done for herself. Virginia Woolf's triumph in *Orlando* was that she succeeded on the 'public' level, while writing the most private of books – 'the longest and most charming love-letter in literature', as Nigel Nicolson has said.[7] There on the page is Knole, unnamed, but with its heraldic leopards, great stone walls, the dolphins and mermaids of its ballroom frieze, the deer park, tapestries, silver furniture and the cart bringing wood for the house in from the park. There are references that anyone who knew Vita well would recognize, and others – like the 'porpoise in a fishmonger's shop' – that were private between Vita and Virginia.

*Orlando* is a phantasmagoria of images and incidents and fantasies from Vita's life and personality, spread over three centuries. Orlando is a young man in a great house in the first Elizabeth's reign, writing dramas with juvenile fluency, as had Vita. The delicious Russian princess Sasha with whom Orlando falls in love as they skate on the frozen Thames, and who betrays him, is Virginia's Violet Trefusis. 'Jour de ma vie', their coded signal for elopement, is the Sackville motto. *The Land* becomes 'The Oak Tree', Orlando's *magnum opus*. Lord Lascelles, as the transvestite Archduchess, cuts a ludicrous figure. Orlando – the centuries flowing by – becomes Ambassador to Constantinople in the reign of King Charles; he marries Rosina Pepita ('dancer, father unknown') and falls into a coma – awakening not as the young man he was but as a beautiful young woman, returning with her saluki hound to England in the eighteenth century, and to Canute her elk-hound, Pippin the spaniel, and her great house.

'Different though the sexes are,' wrote Virginia here, 'they intermix. In every human being a vacillation from one sex to another takes place, and often it is only the clothes that keep the male or female likeness.' Orlando has enjoyed the love of both sexes equally. But now she is a woman, she loves in the reign of Queen Victoria the explorer-sailor Marmaduke Bonthrop Shelmerdine, who stands for Harold; and in their delighted love for one another,

> 'You're a woman, Shel!' she cried.
> 'You're a man, Orlando!' he cried.

And yet, loving him, '"I am a woman", she thought, "a real woman, at last." She thanked Bonthrop from the bottom of her heart for having given her this rare and unexpected delight.' And Orlando gives birth to a son. That short fanciful passage may be as true an ikon of the way in which Vita's and Harold's natures meshed as anyone has achieved.

> 'Are you positive you aren't a man?' he would ask anxiously, and she would echo.
> 'Can it be possible you're not a woman?' and then they must put it to the proof without more ado. For each was so surprised at the quickness of the other's sympathy, and it was to each such a revelation that a woman could be as tolerant and free-spoken as a man, and a man as strange and subtle as a woman.

*Orlando* voices too the doubts of Vita (and of others) about the right way to define a union like theirs. 'She was married, true; but if one's husband was always sailing round Cape Horn, was it marriage? If one liked him, was it marriage? If one liked other people, was it marriage? And finally, if one still wished more than anything in the whole world to write poetry, was it marriage?'

The book ends in 'the present day' – on 11 October 1928, publication day, the very day on which Vita read it, with Orlando welcoming a Queen to the great house, as Queen Elizabeth was once welcomed to Knole. Orlando says to her, 'The dead Lord, my father, shall lead you in.'

Vita even felt comforted by *Orlando* for the death of her father. For in *Orlando* Virginia gave Vita back to Knole and Knole back to Vita, for ever. 'I feel, somehow, that Knole knows about Orlando, and is pleased,' Vita wrote to Harold, signing herself 'Orlando'.

Harold, in the guise of Marmaduke Bonthrop Shelmerdine, descends from an aeroplane in the last paragraph, a wild bird over his head. '"It's the goose!" Orlando cried. "The wild goose."' This puzzled Vita: 'The more I think about it, the weaker I think the end is,' She confided to Harold. 'I simply cannot make out what was in her mind. What does the wild goose stand for? Fame? Love? Death? Marriage? Obviously a person of V.'s intellect has had *some* object in view, but what was it? The symbolism doesn't come off.'

Vita had a literal mind. Virginia Woolf, according to her own account, by no means always had 'some object in view' when she used what seemed to other people to be 'symbols'. But the wild goose came into the book earlier, wheeling overhead while Orlando is driving home to her great house. If it must be interpreted, it may perhaps be read as the other nameless thing, after Knole, that Vita most desired. Not fame, nor love, but genius or greatness – the true art of expression and feeling that was always just out of her reach – the element that Virginia felt was absent from her writing. Virginia, wholly affectionately, mockingly, wanted in *Orlando* to give Vita everything.

Vita's other criticism of *Orlando*, made privately to Harold ('and you must keep this *entirely* to yourself, not tell Eddy or anyone') was that 'the general inference is too inconclusive.' Virginia had confused the issue, Vita felt, by making Orlando marry and have a child. 'Marriage and motherhood would either modify or destroy Orlando, as a character; they do neither.' Vita, 'as a character', was herself modified by marriage and motherhood; she was disappointed that Orlando, the incarnation of her inviolate self, was not left to stand alone. But this was Virginia's book; and Vita as a 'real woman', in spite of her Orlando qualities, was important to the virginal, childless Virginia.

*

There was no attempt made to conceal the original of Orlando : rather
the reverse. Three of the eight photographs that illustrate the first edition are of Vita herself. The one of her supposedly as a Lely portrait,
'draped in pink satin', that had so delighted Virginia, is called 'Orlando
on her return to England'. The one taken by Lenare is entitled 'Orlando
about the year 1840' – with Vita posing in a checked wool skirt, an
eastern shawl and a garden hat, and not looking 1840 in the least ; and
'Orlando at the present time' is Vita standing in long grass by a five-
barred gate with her two dogs, conventionally dressed in skirt, blouse
and cardigan, again looking very much herself.

Raymond Mortimer, reviewing *Orlando* in the *Bookman*, wrote that 'it
is no secret that Orlando is a portrait of Mrs Harold Nicolson,
who writes under her unmarried name V.Sackville-West.' American
journals picked this up at once. The London *Daily Mail* headed its
review 'A Fantastic Biography : Mrs H.Nicolson and Orlando. 300 Years
as Man and Woman.' At the end of November, the *Daily Chronicle*
summed up *Orlando*'s impact : 'The book in Bloomsbury is a joke, in
Mayfair a necessity, and in America a classic.'

Vita compiled a scrapbook of the notices, as if *Orlando* were her own
book. For Virginia's career, it was a turning-point. Leonard Woolf has
written that 'in the first six months the Hogarth Press sold 8,104 copies,
over twice as many as *To the Lighthouse*, and Harcourt, Brace sold 13,031
copies in the first six months.... The effect upon Virginia's earnings as
a novelist was immediate.'[8]

Harold saw the point of *Orlando* and what it meant to Vita ; it was as he
wrote to her 'a book in which you and Knole are identified for ever, a
book which will perpetuate that identity into years when both you and I
are dead. This is an intimate secret which the book holds probably for
you and me alone ; Virginia may not have understood it.' Virginia did
understand it. But it was hard for Harold to believe that anyone else
knew his private Vita. Mary Campbell, who also had her own private
Vita, read *Orlando* and wrote from France :

> I hate the idea that you who are so hidden and secret and proud even with
> people you know best, should be suddenly presented so nakedly for anyone
> to read about.... Vita darling you have been so much Orlando to me that
> how can I help absolutely understanding and *loving* the book. ... Through all
> the slight mockery which is always in the tone of Virginia's voice, and the
> analysis etc, *Orlando* is written by someone who loves you so obviously. ...
> Don't you remember when we imagined you as the young Orlando ?

There was one important aspect of Vita completely omitted from the
book, wrote Mary. 'It is just hinted at by the word "luxurious".' What
Mary meant was that '*Orlando* is too safe too sexless and too easy-going

to be really like you. But then I am thinking of him as he appears to *me*, he is something so different to Virginia. Ah! an entire book about Orlando with no mention of her deep fiery sensuality – that strange mixture of fire and gloom and heat and cold – seems to *me* slightly pale.'

Mary came back to England to see Vita, briefly, that autumn. 'Virginia is right, darling,' she wrote sadly from Paris, on her way back to Roy in Provence. 'I wish she weren't, but you have never lost yourself in love.'

One person who was appalled by *Orlando* was Vita's mother. She defaced her copy of the book, scarring it with comments, underlinings and exclamation marks. She glued a newspaper photograph of Virginia – of whom up until now she had respectfully approved – on the flyleaf, writing alongside: 'The awful face of a mad woman whose successful mad desire is to separate people who care for each other. I loathe this woman for having changed my Vita and taken her away from me.' (Vita and B.M. had not met since the scene over the pearls.) She drummed up support from Harold's sister Gwen: 'Gwen fears Harold will be dismissed from the service for allowing that book to be published.'

B.M. wrote to everyone: to Mrs Belloc Lowndes, to whom she had appealed when *Challenge* was about to be published; to 'Mr Gossip' (Alan Parsons) of the *Morning Post*, asking him not to mention the book in his column; she wrote to her old friend 'Garve', J.L.Garvin the editor of the *Observer*, begging him to stop the book being reviewed in his paper. In her letter she enumerated to Garvin all the equivocal sexual suggestions in *Orlando*, with page references. She quoted Virginia's phrase 'Love is slipping off one's petticoats', commenting: 'All that is so coarse and will be so shocking to the middle classes, mostly. . . . 'And poor Lord Carnock [Harold's father, who died shortly after] is horrified, ditto his wife and myself; I have turned my face to the wall. . . . I have spent years, *hiding* what Harold and Vita really are, I am sorry to confess it. And it makes it twice as dreadful now and such food for indecent gossip.' Garvin gave the book for review to J.C.Squire, Vita's supporter in her pre-Bloomsbury days. Under the heading 'Prose-de-Société', he called *Orlando* 'a very pleasant trifle. . . . But I think that even of its kind it is not in the first order.' It was, he felt, conceived 'frivolously and chancily'. He did not forbear to mention that Vita had posed for the illustrations, nor that the book was dedicated to her.

B.M. had not finished. She put it about that she suspected Vita herself of having written the book; in bookshops, she busied herself hiding copies of *Orlando* under piles of other books. She did everything, in short, to ensure that *Orlando*'s legitimate success was more of a *succès de scandale* than it need have been. She also wrote to Mr Chute, Ben's housemaster at Eton, saying that Ben's parents did not get on and that Ben had an unhappy home life.

Virginia gave Vita the manuscript of *Orlando*, beautifully bound; it took 'an immediate place among my most treasured possessions'. Vita went with Virginia to Cambridge to hear her read her paper on 'Women and Fiction' to undergraduates of Girton – one of two lectures that were later to be published as *A Room of One's Own*, a short and marvellous book that carries the full weight of Virginia's feminist-humanist feeling. It plays variations on some of the themes of *Orlando*: the artist, Virginia said, must be in some sense androgynous in order to be great. She developed too the subject of women's friendships, and their uncharted revolutionary potential: when women cease to be rivals for men's approval, and begin to like each other, a whole new world opens.

Vita too was finding new wings. On 6 December she made a speech to the National Trust: 'I like speaking in public ... it excites me.' The larger public afforded by the new medium of radio was increasingly made open to her. It had begun that year with a series of talks on modern poetry, at fifteen guineas a time – high rates for 1928. She showed a talent for broadcasting; but her path to success was smoothed by an important new friendship.

# CHAPTER 19

V ITA still saw Margaret Goldsmith Voigt regularly, and they corresponded daily ; Margaret, still in love, made no demands. '*You owe me nothing, except that which gives itself,*' she wrote to Vita on 20 November 1928. 'My darling, do you understand ? There can be no question of emotional alimony from you to me.'

Vita's great new friend was to be Hilda Matheson, Director of Talks at the BBC. Four years older than Vita, fair and blue-eyed, Hilda was Scottish, the daughter of a Presbyterian minister. She had studied history at Oxford as a 'home student', and in World War I had worked for British Intelligence in Rome. Before joining the BBC, she had been Nancy Astor's political secretary. Hilda was a person of great capacities and of personal distinction, but devotion was her primary characteristic : she was in the background doing the work where others took the credit. To younger broadcasters at the first BBC studios in Savoy Hill she seemed a battle-axe. Vita wrote after her death, 'I always thought of her as a sturdy pony';[1] her pet-name for Hilda was 'Stoker'.

She and Vita had met earlier in the year to discuss the series of poetry talks. In October Hilda wrote again to 'Dear Mrs Nicolson', tactfully saying how much she had enjoyed *Twelve Days* – which had come out rather in the shadow of *Orlando*. She came to Long Barn in early December with Hugh Walpole, to discuss a broadcast discussion Hugh and Vita were going to do on 'The Modern Woman'. Vita wrote about Hilda to Harold after that visit, 'I should think she was an angel of unselfishness, – or, rather, unegoism, – and she loves all country things which always wins my heart. She has become a real friend.' Harold, adept at reading the signs, wrote on 13 December, 'Hadji is rather worried about Miss Mathison [*sic*].'

Vita and Hugh Walpole did their discussion on the modern woman on 10 December. Vita got stage-fright in the middle : 'there was Hilda's nice reassuring smile; but there, also, was the microphone.' Hugh covered for her, and no one seemed to notice. She poured out to Harold afterwards all that she would have liked to have said over the air, and more: 'Woman *cannot* combine careers with normal life.... They love too much; they allow love to override everything else. Men don't. Or, rather, men see to it that the people who love should submit themselves.' She herself, she said, loved him too much. He was more important to her than anything else.

> But, darling, I am not a good person for you to be married to, – said she, avoiding the word wife. When people like you and me marry, – *positive* people, when men and women ought to be positive and negative respectively, complementary elements, – life revolves itself into a compromise which is truly satisfactory to neither. But I love you, I can never cure myself of loving you; so what is to be done?

These thoughts found public utterance only when she came to write *All Passion Spent* a couple of years later. In this novel, writing about someone who was living according to his own creed, she wrote that 'Most people fall into the error of making their whole lives a fuzz, pleasing nobody, least of all themselves. Compromise is the very breath of negation.' Yet compromise made the Nicolsons' life together possible. 'I can never cure myself of loving you,' Vita wrote to him; in *All Passion Spent* she described her heroine's love for her husband as 'a straight black line drawn right through her life. It had hurt her, it had damaged her, it had diminished her, but she had been unable to curve away from it.'

Men, she had said to Harold, 'see to it that the people who love should submit themselves'; in *All Passion Spent* she described how the husband

> would continue to enjoy his free, varied and masculine life with no ring upon his finger or difference in his name to indicate the change in his estate; but whenever he felt inclined to come home she must be there, ready to lay down her book, her papers or her letters.... It would not do, in such a world of assumptions, to assume that she had equal rights.

Vita finished the letter to Harold – in which lay in embryo so much of *All Passion Spent* – by saying again that Harold ought never to have married her. 'I feel my inadequacy most bitterly. What good am I to you? None. What with one thing and another.'

One thing and another now included Hilda Matheson. Harold's note of warning came too late. After the frustrating radio discussion Vita had stayed the night at Hilda's house, 31 Sumner Place in South Kensington. In the morning Hilda was unwell and did not go in to the BBC, and their love affair began.

To professional women like Hilda Matheson, who came from educated but unworldly backgrounds and supported themselves on their modest salaries, a rich, famous, gifted woman like Vita Sackville-West was an exciting and glamorous figure. To be intimate with her was not only intoxicating but flattering, like a fairy story. Vita in turn drew reassurance from knowing the impact that she made, and responded with passion.

'If anything can save me from becoming the kind of dried-up person I dread to think of, you will, and this will,' Hilda wrote to Vita on the day that Vita was writing the long letter to Harold quoted above. She did not feel altogether at ease in Vita's circle – especially 'when the air is heavily charged as it is when Dottie is about – it makes me afraid to look at you.' (Virginia too, that December, commented on Dottie and her 'pecking exacting ways'; Vita seemed to her 'pathetically gentle and kind' with Dottie. Margaret Voigt would have called it paying emotional alimony.)

Vita was passionately in love with Hilda – in her sudden, uncontrolled, needy way. By Christmas she had already written fifty letters to Hilda, who brought to love the integrity that she brought to friendship and to her work; she wrote to Vita in Berlin (where she had gone, with the boys, to spend Christmas with Harold):

> Love – all you've given to me – all the physical side of it too – seems to me to be life in its very highest expression – it's mixed up for me with any decent thinking or feeling I've got or ever had – with everything in fact that is true and beautiful and of good report. And yet I suppose some people would regard it as shameful and vicious.

Hilda had never committed herself so deeply. She had had no affairs with men – women like her, in 1928, were often too clever, serious or ambitious for the middle-class professional men who might otherwise have married them – many good friendships with women, and one physical flare-up, as she put it, with another woman; but that had been over for three years.

Hilda wrote to Vita so frequently that Vita, embarrassed, had to intercept the postal deliveries to 24 Brücken Allee. But Hilda often sent her letters 'express', so that they were delivered at noticeable times, such as in the middle of dinner. Vita had to remind Hilda of the need for discretion; Hilda was so proud and happy that she wanted to tell all the world. She shared the house in Sumner Place with two other single women, the historian Marjorie Graves, and Dorothy Spencer, who 'has a ribald tongue, enriched by a classical education and a past (I should guess) of her own.' They both knew what had happened. Vita begged Hilda to be careful – because of Harold, and the boys, and because of public opinion. Hilda unwillingly saw her point.

> But I see you're right – that homosexual love is more difficult in itself and takes a lot more intelligence and sensitivity. Perhaps that's why it usually seems to work badly with men – perhaps they're less sensitive on those things.... It feels very natural and inevitable to love you as I do – in every way – but as if it would be wrong if I didn't.

One of Hilda's old friends was Janet Vaughan. (The scientist daughter of Virginia Woolf's first love Madge Symons – who is the original of 'Sally' in *Mrs Dalloway* – she was later Dame Janet Vaughan, Principal of Somerville College, Oxford.) Hilda talked about Vita for hours to Janet, who was 'nice and intelligent both in her mind and in her imagination.... I gather from her that not only is Bloomsbury talking about you and me – which they *would* do bless them – but also the B.B.C.' This was the last thing that Vita wanted to hear. She was never in the least tempted to become publicly known as a lesbian. Not only did she have a traditional care for her 'reputation' – and for Harold's – but the secrecy of her affairs added, for her, the element of adventure that she needed.

For her part Hilda was discovering that 'some kinds of men regard with horror and distrust all friendships between women and infer that they are all what they regard as vicious – because obviously thousands of relationships – like the ones I have had in the past – may be homosexual in origin or in foundation, without ever taking the form these queer gentlemen suspect and finding a complete expression.' She wrote shrewdly too about Vita's own personality and problems : 'I suspect it is ... an experimenting interest, and interest in the game of exercising wiles and seeing what happens, that gets you into what you call scrapes – specially when rather bored – I don't deplore any propensity in you, my angel. I take you as I find you.' People of Vita's complexity and power of feeling, thought Hilda, had to find outlets, 'and if they haven't got one they want and like, they have to make believe with shadows or substitutes or ersatz articles of some sort or other. Isn't that what happens ?' It was indeed what happened. Not always satisfactorily, as Hilda surmised, 'but better than a vacuum'.

And back again to the problem of concealment : 'One is so torn between a hatred of pretence, a resentment that there should be any occasion for pretence, and an instinct to hide one's lovely secret from the lewd gaze of people who think evil. I should adore to marry Orlando – don't be silly – don't you know I have all the domestic instincts ?' She satisfied these by using Long Barn for weekends while Vita was in Berlin. From there she wrote on 18 January 1929, presumably in response to one of Vita's less romantic remarks, 'I don't think I agree that the physical side is the only magic part of love – I don't feel it is with us.'

The day before she wrote that, Virginia and Leonard Woolf arrived in Berlin to visit the Nicolsons, joined a day later by Duncan Grant, Vanessa Bell and her son Quentin. The party stayed at the Prinz Albrecht Hotel. Vita had been longing for Virginia to come – 'Because, really, you have no idea how miserable I am here.' She had, though, been amused by going to what she called 'the sodomites' ball': 'A lot of them were dressed as women, but I fancy I was the only genuine article in the room. . . . There are certainly very queer things to be seen in Berlin, and I think Potto [Virginia] will enjoy himself.'[2]

But no one enjoyed the visit very much. Harold was very busy both with his work and his own circle of friends, and was irritated when the Woolfs balked at attending two luncheon parties he had arranged for them. The group was too large and diverse for there to be many things that all could enjoy doing together (Eddy was also in Berlin); Vanessa did not see why they all had to spend so much time with the Nicolsons at all.

The visit was further shadowed by its aftermath. Virginia overreacted to a sleeping drug given her by Vanessa on the Channel crossing and was ill for several weeks. Vita wrote to her that 'your little shaky pencil letters wring my heart. . . . Berlin did that to you – the fiend.' She herself meanwhile had met the playwright Pirandello, who introduced her to a red-haired woman photographer, Frau Riess; she showed Vita 'photographs of Josephine Baker stripped to the waist, – very beautiful, – and other photographs of an indecency which I won't describe. . . . She fair gave me the creeps.'

Fretting about Virginia's continuing illness, she wrote: 'Do you know what I believe it was, apart from the flu? SUPPRESSED RANDINESS. So there. You remember your admissions as the searchlight went round and round?' (Vita and Virginia, during the visit, had been to the top of the Funkturm together: 'V. most indiscreet,' Vita had written in her diary.) And she asked Virginia not to let Leonard send to Berlin a new novel called *Belated Adventure* in the next batch to be reviewed by her for the *Nation* 'as it is partly about me and I couldn't possibly do it.'[3] (*Belated Adventure*, Margaret Goldsmith's second novel, took a few digs at the 'parlour-adventurers' of Bloomsbury, and included a character-study of Vita as 'Hester Drummond'.)

Before Vita returned to England, she and Harold escaped together for a few days to Italy. It was freezing cold in Rapallo, but 'the truants were exuberantly happy,' Vita told Virginia. Hilda Matheson was instructed to type the envelopes of her letters to Rapallo: Harold did not know the depth and extent of this involvement, and Vita did not want him to. They were perfectly content together, walking and writing.

Vita had had an idea for a novel – 'and I'm going to write it this summer and make my fortune. Such a joke it will be, and I hope everybody will be seriously annoyed.'⁴ This was to be *The Edwardians*, her own romance of Knole, begun frivolously, perhaps as a complement to *Orlando*. It was to be her most commercially successful book. Meanwhile she was happy with Harold : 'Every morning while I still lie in delicious sleep in an enormous *letto matrimoniale* (but alone), I am aroused by a clash of opening shutters next door, and then a figure dressed in canary-yellow pyjamas bursts into my room' to open her shutters to the sunrise over the sea.

After Rapallo, she was more than ever appalled at the prospect of Harold staying in Berlin. 'You wouldn't like to leave Leonard in similar circumstances ? no, of course you wouldn't,' she wrote to Virginia. 'Long Barn, Virginia, my own room, Pippin, England – and my Harold left behind in Berlin, hating it. . . . I should be so happy to come back, wholeheartedly, if only he were coming too.'⁵

Left behind in England, Vita's friends had been combining in their desolation. Dottie Wellesley had been in touch with Hilda : 'I would so much like to see you. To talk. But is it a good plan ? I don't want either of us to hurt one another inadvertently. I know we shouldn't do so intentionally. I have been a great deal alone since Vita left.'

'Darling,' wrote Hilda to Vita after she had seen Dottie, 'why is there this legend that you are so detached about people ? I noticed Margaret Goldsmith elaborated it, and Dottie seemed to assume it.' Hilda, in her position of lover of the moment, assumed no such thing. She acknowledged Vita's fundamental feeling for Harold ('He seems to me so entirely the right sort of person for you to be married to – in some ways') and she learned more about Vita's 'scrapes' when Vita sent her a letter she had received from Mary Campbell. For the first time, Hilda began to wonder whether she was any more than another of Vita's 'scrapes' herself.

Dottie also saw Virginia and complained to her of Vita's coldness. Then Dottie made a scene when it was Hilda who was deputed to meet Vita off the boat at Folkestone this time. Hilda, Dottie and Virginia – but mostly Hilda – took up most of Vita's spare time that spring.

She was working on a short book about the poet Andrew Marvell as well as on her novel. When the Poet Laureate, Robert Bridges, died that summer, Vita was one of the poets seriously proposed as his successor. (Edith Sitwell's proposal was less than serious. Miss Sackville-West, she said, 'had it not been for a flaw in fate, would have been one of Nature's

Gentlemen.') It was *The Land*, of course, that had brought Vita this prestige; it had become a famous poem at all levels. Vita read it aloud from the pulpit at the Savoy Chapel, and the General Bus Company used seven lines from it as their caption on a poster advertising the country in spring.

The only source of trouble was still B.M., who had so influenced Vita's old admirer Kenneth Campbell against her that he resigned as a trustee of the family Trust. Vita fulminated that civilization was in a poor way 'when 85% of people would consider Tray [Raymond] doomed to eternal damnation, and Kenneth a reputable citizen.' Lady Sackville was buying yet another house – a large villa on five acres in Crown End Lane near Streatham Common, on the fringes of south London. She was calling in the furniture she had given Harold for his flat in Berlin.

Harold was not in good health and was ready to think again about leaving diplomatic life. Virginia had suggested that he should stand for Parliament as a Labour candidate. 'Ha! Ha! Hee! Hee!' he wrote to Vita. 'But I have no money, and am not Labour – and don't know. But I should think and talk it over.' Meanwhile Hilda Matheson was ready to give Harold, as well as Vita, regular work at the BBC. At Long Barn, Hilda herself, the 'sturdy pony', was put to work – cutting down brushwood, weeding, and helping Vita make an aviary for the budgerigars, Vita's new craze. Dorothy Wellesley continued to court Hilda, asking her to the Mount Street flat, receiving her in her bedroom, inviting intimate conversations.

Vita's friendship with Virginia was sustained by what Vita called their 'funny little expeditions' – to Hampstead to see Keats's house, or to see the old Roman baths off the Strand. Vita kept Virginia up to date with her novel in progress; the Hogarth Press was going to publish *The Edwardians*. 'It is absolutely packed with the aristocracy. Shall you like that? I feel that for snobbish reasons alone it ought to be highly popular. I hope so, because Leonard's offer was very handsome, – and I should hate to ruin the Press.'[6] And some weeks later: 'I try to remember exactly the smell of the bus that used to meet one at the station in 1908. ... The impression of waste and extravagance which assailed one the moment one entered the doors of the house. The crowds of servants; people's names in little slits on their bedroom doors; sleepy maids waiting about after dinner in the passages.' Vita was only thirty-seven, but the world of her childhood was already a lost world – 'a great deal more vivid,' she told Virginia, 'than many things which have occurred since, but will they convey anything whatever to anybody else? Still I peg on.'[7]

Harold was home briefly in mid-June 1929 for a BBC discussion between him and Vita on 'Marriage'. 'We won't be able to mention sex, I presume,' he wrote to her. 'We can do a long bit about men's and women's professions clashing. It will be rather fun.' They rehearsed their script after a dinner party at Dottie's house which included the talk's producer, Hilda – feeling as always 'a kind of upstart and intruder' in that company of easy intimates, and unable to get close to Vita.

The radio discussion was reckoned to be a success. Harold stressed that marriage was a living organism, 'a plant and not a piece of furniture. It grows; it changes; it develops.' Vita objected to the tendency of most men 'to regard *themselves* as the plant and the woman as the soil'; men imagined that marriage should contribute to their growth, at the expense of the women's vitality. In her longest uninterrupted statement, she said that this state of affairs was bad for both sexes, since 'it taught men to be domineering and inconsiderate, and it taught women to be sly. What *you* call feminine.' Harold set up all the arguments and trod the more danger-ous ground. Speaking of the temperamental difference between men and women – so 'sharp and wide' that it is 'only superficially affected by forms of sexual aberration' – he said he thought 'the most virile woman is infinitely more feminine than the most effeminate man'. Vita argued with him when he claimed that a man's work was a necessity, and a woman's career a luxury. And when he asked her whether she did not agree that 'the joys of motherhood' were sufficient compensation, she replied, 'No, most emphatically I don't.' She also disagreed 'profoundly' that it should always be the woman 'who surrenders her opportunity to her duty'. They agreed that a woman should cultivate the male qualities of reason, tolerance and impersonality, and a man 'the feminine qualities of gentleness, sensitiveness and intuition'.[8]

After he had gone back to Berlin, she wrote to him about what their own marriage meant to her:

> You are dearer to me than anybody has been or ever could be. If you died I should kill myself as soon as I had made provision for the boys. I really mean this. I could not live if I lost you. Every time I get you to myself you become dearer to me. I do not think one could conceive of a love more exclusive, more tender, or more pure than I have for you. It is absolutely divorced from physical love, – sex, – *now*. I feel it is immortal.

Physical desire, she wrote, 'is the most misleading of all human emotions. I simply feel that you are me and I am you, – what you meant by saying that "you became the lonely me" when we parted.'

In mid-July Vita and Hilda Matheson went away for a holiday together to the Val d'Isère in French Savoy. The choice of place was Hilda's; she had stayed at the *curé*'s house in the Val d'Isère before, with other friends. One of these, Janet Vaughan, let slip to Virginia that this trip had been long-planned. Vita had been at pains to spare Virginia's feelings by keeping her departure secret until the last minute, and then announcing it as a sudden decision. Virginia was cross, confused and jealous. 'Why do I mind? what do I mind? how much do I mind?' Hilda Matheson seemed to her an unworthy rival :

> One of the facts is that these Hildas are a chronic case ; & as this one won't disappear & is unattached, she may be permanent. And, like the damned intellectual snob that I am, I hate to be linked, even by an arm, with Hilda. Her earnest aspiring competent wooden face appears before me, seeking guidance to the grave question of who's to broadcast. A queer trait in Vita – her passion for the earnest middle-class intellectual, however drab & dreary. And why do I write this down ? I have not even told Leonard.⁹

Over three years later Virginia, remembering, was 'in a rage of jealousy' all over again, 'thinking you had been in love with Hilda that summer you went to the Alps together! Because you said you weren't. Now were you? ... Do you remember coming to confession, or rather justification, in my lodge [her garden-hut at Rodmell]? And you weren't guilty then were you ? You swore you weren't.'¹⁰ Vita had to lie to Virginia.

In the Val d'Isère, she and Hilda walked in the mountains for eleven hours a day with packs on their backs, starting from their base in the *curé*'s house – which was shared by his cow Marquise 'whom one is liable to meet in the passage'. Vita collected plants and posted them off to her gardener Barnes at Long Barn : androsace, saxifrage *oppositifolia*, draba, white viola, gentians, sedum. Hilda was practical and could 'make a pudding out of apricot jam and snow' and read maps.

There were few roads there in 1929 ; the Col d'Isère could be reached only on foot, as could the Col de la Vanoise, where they stayed in a refuge 8,000 feet up. From there Vita wrote excitedly to Harold about more flowers, 'much better than the Dolomites' – they had seen rock roses, Alpenrose, five different kinds of gentian, soldanella, lychnis, cenisia, anemone, geums, silene, potentilla, achillea and 'our own little vanilla orchis'.

In Berlin, Harold had received an offer from the Beaverbrook Press of a job on the London *Evening Standard* at £3,000 a year. He wrote to Vita and to Leonard Woolf for their reactions. Vita, still in the mountains, was delighted by the idea ; she arranged to meet him at Karlsruhe on 1 August to discuss it, parting from Hilda at Geneva. She and Harold motored together down the Mosel Valley and agreed that he should leave the diplomatic service and take the job : Vita carried back with her to London a letter from Harold to Lord Beaverbrook.

She was overjoyed; Harold had qualms, not only about leaving the diplomatic service but about joining Beaverbrook. Back in Berlin he confessed in his diary his dread that 'impending moves in the service may offer me a good chance when it is too late.... I should rather be Minister at Athens than toil under Lord Beaverbrook.' He was not excited at all; he was depressed and apprehensive.

As soon as Vita got home she set about looking for a flat in London – preferably in Bloomsbury – for Harold. But events that August conspired to extinguish her excitement. Eddy Sackville-West – 'heavily made-up, with a great gold bracelet on one wrist, and *two* enormous rings' – came to dinner at Long Barn and told her that the tapestry from the chapel at Knole had been sold to the Boston Museum. 'I don't know what they got for it; I wouldn't ask. It was announced on the wireless, in the News, funny.... Anyway, *I* am never going to Knole again; or perhaps just once before I die.'

Then she got a sharp attack of lumbago and was in pain for days. (Hilda came to look after her.) While she was still laid low, she heard that Geoffrey Scott had died suddenly in New York from pneumonia. She had met him in the street, in London, just before she went to France, looking 'very much aged, and unshaved'. She was upset to hear of his death. 'How awful to die like that in a foreign hospital, far away from all one's friends.... I wish I could have become friends with him again, I always thought that I should some day.' Then a few days later she heard from Pat Dansey that Denys Trefusis was dead too. His marriage to Violet was non-existent; they would have soon been divorced had his terminal tuberculosis not made divorce unnecessary. Violet did not look after him in his illness and rarely visited him during the last weeks.

The boys were becoming more of a pleasure to Vita at last. She wrote to Harold romantically of being 'in love' with her graceful fifteen-year-old Ben; Nigel was still cast by her for comedy. She described his efforts to catch butterflies with 'a torn net, a cracked pot which leaks, and a handbook': 'He sets out, dropping first one thing and then another. Then he tears wildly after some insect, and falls flat on his nose. When he does catch anything, it immediately escapes. He must certainly go into the films.'

The boys' holidays were disturbed by Vita's mother. At the end of August she invited her grandsons to her new house at Streatham (she still would not see Vita) and proceeded to fill their adolescent ears with scandal. She told them that Vita had stolen her silver; that Virginia – whom both boys loved – was a wicked woman and the cause of the rift between herself and Vita; that she was saving up painfully so that Nigel could go to Eton like Ben; that Vita ought to be in Berlin with their father. She asked Ben if he had yet been in love, and told them about their grandfather's betrayal of her with Olive Rubens.

The boys came home rather shocked, and told their mother all about it. Vita was angry, but knew that it might have been even worse: 'I began to get really nervous as to what she might have said!' But when she asked the boys what was the worst thing that 'Grannyma' had said, it was, in their opinion, that Vita ought to have been 'laid in the grave' with her father.

Vita had a 'long talk' with her sons that night about B. M.'s personality problems, and spent 'a happy day alone with the boys' next day. When Harold heard about this incident, he wrote that 'It is all very well to say she is mad. She is not mad, she is just evil.'

# CHAPTER 20

SOON after she came back from meeting Harold to discuss the Beaverbrook offer, Vita had sent a collection of poems that she called *King's Daughter* to Leonard Woolf at the Hogarth Press. The nature of the poems was such that she felt she had to clear them with Harold :

> I shall have to show them to you before they are published. It is not on the score of their goodness or badness that I am worried . . . but you see they are love poems, and purely artificial at that, – I mean, *very* artificial, rather 17th century most of them, and although I should have thought this would be sufficiently obvious (that they were just 'literary' I mean) it has since occurred to me that people will think them Lesbian. I should not like this, either for my own sake or yours. . . . I would like an honest opinion please.

He replied that on no account should she publish the poems until he had seen them. When he had read them, he wrote again : 'I cannot pretend, my sweet, that I like your little book.' He pinned his objection on the poems themselves, not on their lesbian implication. 'I don't mind one hang really about what people say about its Bilitis side, but I do care very much about your reputation and I frankly don't think any of these poems good enough for publication. Or rather for publication at your stage of reputation.' He asked her to withdraw the book.

Vita was taken aback. She had been quite prepared for an objection to the poems' lesbian content, 'but I wasn't prepared for you to say they were downright bad.' (Neither was being quite candid : Vita's love poems were never written just as literary exercises, and Harold may have masked, even to himself, a distaste for the content beneath a literary judgement.) The poems had already been printed, confessed Vita ; and Virginia 'thinks they're good.'

Virginia had actually said, 'Damn Harold. And why should you attach any importance to the criticism of a diplomat ?' On a blazing hot

4th of September, the Woolfs and Vita had a picnic in Ashdown Forest, 'and lay out on the grass and discussed *King's Daughter*.' Virginia thought Vita had been remarkably calm and modest, 'a less touchy poet never was. But then can a real poet be an un-touchy poet ?' She found Vita that day 'much as usual; striding; silk stockings; shirt & skirt; opulent; easy; absent', and, back at Long Barn, 'talking spaciously & serenely' to the boys' holiday tutor, and arguing equably with Ben about whether Nigel ('riding round in between the flowerbeds on his bicycle') ought not to go in and wash his feet.[1]

Harold was home again within a few days of this in order to finalize the arrangements about his new job. On the first Sunday he was back, Vita wrote in her diary : 'Did nothing all day but talk with Hadji and the boys. Blazing hot. The boys bathed nearly all the afternoon.' (The Nicolsons had just made a swimming-pool at Long Barn.) And Vita talked Harold round about the publication of *King's Daughter*, which was imminent. The poems in it were written during her affair with Mary Campbell, but she included only three from her long sequence of sonnets. Most of the verses that make up the book are lighter, slighter lyrics with a mannered, pastoral, or nursery-rhyme air; and she included one much earlier poem, 'Full Moon'. The only new poem of any solidity in the volume is 'The Greater Cats', a Yeatsian piece that Yeats himself admired:

> The greater cats with golden eyes
> Stare out between the bars.

When Harold was at Long Barn, there was necessarily a loss of intimacy between Vita and Virginia. 'It is always complicated when he comes home', as Vita told her; she put his arrangements first, and muddled her arrangements with Virginia. There was an elegiac note in their friendship that autumn of 1929. Vita broadcast a review of *A Room of One's Own*, and Virginia wrote afterwards : 'I thought your voice, saying Virginia Woolf, was a trumpet call, moving me to tears; but I daresay you were suppressing laughter. It's an odd feeling, hearing oneself praised to 50 million old ladies in Surbiton by one with whom one has watched the dawn and heard the nightingale.'[2] And Vita had had a sad dream about Virginia; she had dreamt that Leonard and Virginia had never really been married, and decided it was high time to hold the ceremony. 'So you had a fashionable wedding. You were dressed in a robe of mediaeval cut, made of cloth-of-gold, and you wore a long veil. ... You did not invite me to the wedding. So I stood in the crowd, and saw you pass on Leonard's arm.' For some reason not hard to deduce, wrote Vita, this dream made her miserable and she woke in tears.

She knew great changes were coming now that Harold was to be home for good. 'At any rate, all sorts of different landscapes seem to open, whichever way I look.' She signed this letter to Virginia 'Orlando', and added a postscript: 'The fact that I don't see *you* prevents these from being (some of) the happiest days of my life.'³ But the intensity of their friendship did not survive these breaks and changes.

Hilda Matheson too had to take second place, surmising correctly that once Vita and Harold had a flat in London 'you won't ever come and stay in Sumner Place with me.' She was never pushed away very far, for she and Vita met regularly when Vita came to the BBC to broadcast her weekly fiction review. Hilda gradually became a devoted friend to all the Nicolsons, and was included in family plans and discussions. It was with Hilda that Vita found the flat – 4 King's Bench Walk – in the Temple. While Harold was in Berlin packing up and saying his goodbyes to the diplomatic service, Vita called in plumbers, electricians and decorators, and with her secretary Boski discovered the joys of Woolworths: 'It is the most intoxicating shop. We bought mousetraps, dusters, saucepans, a tin plate for Henry [Harold's dog], cork mats to put under plates, glass towel rails, tumblers, a hammer, nails, – oh endless things, – it was great fun.' She also bought a Duncan Grant painting for the flat.

Hilda Matheson asked Virginia to broadcast as well, and Virginia gave a talk on Beau Brummell. But Virginia – sensing that Hilda, as she had suspected, was going to be 'permanent' – continued to despise her and resented Hilda's suggestions for editing the talk. Afterwards she 'poured her rage hot as lava over Vita':

And then I discussed her friends, Vita's friends, & said that here, in their secondrateness, was the beginning of my alienation. I can't have it said 'Vita's great friends – Dottie, Hilda and Virginia.' I detest the 2ndrate schoolgirl atmosphere. She sat silent for the most part, & only said I was right. Harold had said the same. The thing to do is to check it. She can't stop what she's begun.⁴

Virginia still had the power to upset Vita when she attacked her on this subject. Virginia made her feel, as she had before, that her life was a failure and that she was incapable of sustaining any one unspoilt relationship. 'What shall I do about it, Virginia?' Her 'mistakes', she claimed, were 'silly surface things', and her love for Virginia 'absolutely true, vivid and unalterable'.

Her own nature too seemed unalterable. She accepted Virginia's criticisms with humility, as she usually accepted Harold's. But in a manuscript book she wrote three stark lines –

> You defeat me with words, yet I know
> That my life is lived out in a cave where the birds
> Of your soul never go.

– echoing, unconsciously or not, words that Virginia had written to her
two years before: 'Here in my cave I see lots of things you blazing
beauties make invisible by the light of your own glory.'

The end of 1929 brought Vita a fragile reconciliation with her mother.
They had communicated only through B.M.'s secretary, who had been
to Long Barn and reported to his mistress (as she wrote in her diary) that
Harold 'was dressed in an extraordinary bright yellow swetter [*sic*] without any collar. One of his B[ugger] costumes !!!' B.M. had also had a
bulletin from George Plank, who had seen Vita at Dottie's house. 'He
thinks she takes herself very seriously now – considers herself of
national importance, as she is so successful on the wireless. He thinks,
as I do, that she is afraid of Harold, mentally, and she wants his moral
support with her writings. She certainly does not get good reviews over
*King's Daughter* as she did about *The Land*, that wonderful *Land*.'

There had been no scandal over the subject matter of *King's Daughter*;
but Harold had been right in that devotees of *The Land* found little of
significance in this new volume. Vita's *Andrew Marvell* came out that
autumn too: a short monograph, the first in a prestigious Faber
series 'The Poets on the Poets'. (The second in the series was by
T. S. Eliot on Dante.)

The reunion with B.M. came about after Vita had gone to Knole,
painfully and unwillingly, for the wedding of Eddy's sister Diana to
Lord Romilly. She spent 'a bloody afternoon', only comforted by the
sweetness of the older servants, who realized what she was feeling. On
7 December B.M. wrote in her diary: 'Vita wrote to me about the wedding of Diana and Ld Romilly and her own feelings in Knole chapel; I do
understand it. She wrote very dearly.'

On Christmas Eve Vita took the children up to Streatham; she also
took some of the family silver that B.M. considered had been stolen
from her. It was the first time that they had met in almost two years.
Both were wary, and intending to keep their distance. B.M. described
their meeting – describing at the same time a woman, her daughter, now
past the first bloom of youth and stripped of the romance and glamour
with which her lovers saw her:

She hugged me and said: oh Mama! and I kissed her and said like in the old
days: Mauvaise little Mar. She looked very handsome, in spite of the regrettable moustache. But she had a lovely colour and her hair was beautifully

waved. She has become stout round the hips, and looks exactly as if she was *enceinte* ; she did not even look so big when Nigel was coming.

By the end of February 1930, what B.M. called 'the Awful Nightmare' of her estrangement from Vita was over. She gave Vita back the controversial pearls and Vita accepted them, as she accepted B.M. herself.

B.M. was not impressed by the modern miracle of wireless, nor even by her daughter's new fame as a broadcaster. Wireless, she thought, made the voices sound 'so *fat*'. Vita's prominence, which she owed to Hilda Matheson, won her new friends and fans, and bred some resentment. The *Manchester Guardian*, in an article on 'the dangers of microphone monopoly', suggested politely that Vita was given too much airtime : 'It is hardly fair to anyone, it is certainly most unfair to Miss Sackville-West, to be entrusted with the task of reviewing the whole range of fiction from January to December for an audience of such magnitude and diversity.' Virginia, for all her distaste for Hilda, remained a supporter. After Vita and Harold broadcast a discussion on 'Happiness' that spring, she wrote to her : 'How on earth have you mastered the art of being subtle, profound, humorous, arch, coy, satirical, affectionate, intimate, profane, colloquial, solemn, sensible, poetical and a dear old shabby sheep dog – on the wireless ?'[5]

On 4 March, the day that Vita finished writing *The Edwardians*, they heard that Westwood, the farm adjacent to Long Barn, was being bought by poultry farmers. The Nicolsons disliked the ideas of an extensive prospect of chicken-houses, and thought of overbidding in order to secure the four fields in question for themselves. Or was this the moment to sell Long Barn and move on ? Harold thought so. They had exhausted the potential of both house and garden. Vita was indecisive : 'Long Barn is very nice and pretty.'

On 3 April, when she was with Dorothy Wellesley at Penns-in-the-Rocks, Dottie's land agent told her about a property for sale just outside the village of Sissinghurst, some twenty miles east of Long Barn and deeper into Kent. Vita, Dottie and Nigel drove over to see it next day. 'Fell flat in love with it,' Vita wrote in her diary. Her love affair with Sissinghurst was to last until the end of life.

She took Harold and Ben to see it the following day. 'Hadji pleased but cautious.' They went again, without the children, on Sunday. 'We come suddenly upon the nut-walk and that settles it,' wrote Harold in his diary. 'From that moment we decide to buy.' The weather was overcast and they could not see the view. When they took Harold's mother to Sissinghurst, it was pouring with rain ; she was as unimpressed as were Ben and Nigel. Sissinghurst Castle was a ruin, or a complex of ruins, in seven acres of muddy wilderness. There was no water or electricity laid on ; there was no single habitable room. Twenty-three years later, Vita wrote :

> The amount of old bedsteads, ploughshares, old cabbage-stalks, old broken-down earth closets, old matted wire, and mountains of sardine tins, all muddled up in a tangle of bindweed, nettles and ground elder, should have sufficed to daunt anybody.
>
> Yet the place, when I first saw it on a spring day in 1930, caught instantly at my heart and my imagination. I saw what might be made of it. It was Sleeping Beauty's castle.[6]

Harold found an old print of the castle in a book in the London Library and they began to research its history. They discovered that in the reign of Henry VIII it had been the home of Sir John Baker, whose daughter had married Thomas Sackville in 1554 – thus Sissinghurst could be considered a 'family house', which meant much to Vita. By the mid-eighteenth century the castle was already abandoned and falling down. During the Seven Years War, part of it had been used to house French prisoners. Some of the building had been demolished around 1800, and what remained used as the parish workhouse. For more than 100 years before Vita and Harold acquired it, disconnected fragments of ancient rose-red brick castle had been used as stables, stores and labourers' dwellings by the adjoining Castle Farm.

To restore Sissinghurst, to make even a part of it habitable, was a formidable undertaking. There was no house as such : the most impressive single fragment was a high square tower with two flanking octagonal turrets. Harold summed it all up for Vita on 24 April. It was going to cost over £12,000 to buy the property, and at least another £15,000 to put it in order. 'For £30,000 we could buy a beautiful place replete with park, garage, h & c, central heating, historical associations, and two lodges r. and l.' Yet Sissinghurst had romantic family associations – 'it is, for you, an ancestral mansion. . . . It is in Kent. It is in a part of Kent we like. It is self-contained. I could make a lake.' Most important of all, 'We like it.'

So Vita made an offer of £12,375, and her offer was accepted, by telephone, on the evening of 6 May. They hugged each other. Harold started drawing up plans. B.M. agreed to allow the family trustees to raise £13,000 for the purchase money. Vita, in a flood of energy and excitement, finished correcting the proofs of *The Edwardians* and plunged straight into writing a new novel, which was to be *All Passion Spent*.

The next weekend she and Harold stayed at the George Hotel in Cranbrook, the nearest town to Sissinghurst, and tramped all over the mud and rubble of their new domain in the pouring rain – 'but we were very happy.' Vita could not keep away. She returned within days and optimistically made her first Sissinghurst planting, as an act of faith – a lavender bush. Dottie and Hilda (who were now close friends) met her there and the three ate a picnic lunch on the steps of the tower that was to be Vita's private citadel. It was a perfect day – the first time that Vita had ever seen Sissinghurst in sunshine. What she had written to Virginia a few months earlier, before she had seen or even heard of Sissinghurst, was now literally true: 'all sorts of different landscapes seem to open, whichever way I look.'[7]

PART IV

SISSINGHURST

1930-45

# CHAPTER 21

VITA began at once to write *Sissinghurst*, a poem of commitment and homecoming, of total immersion :

> A tired swimmer in the waves of time
> I throw my hands up : let the surface close :
> Sink down through centuries to another clime,
> And buried find the castle and the rose.

The 'rose' was an old gallica they found established among the rubble and the nettles. 'Established is very much the right word, for no amount of digging will abolish it from the place where it is not wanted : it reappears as certainly as bindweed.'[1] The 'Sissinghurst rose' is a dark velvety red, not unlike another gallica called 'Tuscany'.

Vita dedicated *Sissinghurst* to 'V.W.', which enraged B.M., who complained again to the boys about 'that wicked Virgin Wolf'. (When the poem was published the following year B.M. tried – unsuccessfully – to buy up the whole edition from the Hogarth Press in order to suppress it.) Virginia herself, partly stimulated by Vita's new life, 'so full and flush', was writing *The Waves*. As Sissinghurst absorbed Vita's life and energies, so a new friendship, with Ethel Smyth – over seventy, deaf, demanding, vital, garrulous, adoring – began to take over Virginia's. By the time Vita took Virginia to see Sissinghurst for the first time on 23 May 1930, Ethel Smyth was already in the ascendant.

*The Edwardians* came out on 29 May ; on that day Vita worked in the woods on her 'Reddín' poem, always a refuge in time of uncertainty. But by early June it was apparent that the Hogarth Press had a success on its hands. 'Vita's book is such a best seller that Leonard and I are hauling in money like pilchards from a net,' Virginia wrote to her nephew Quentin. 'We sell about 800 every day.' By 30 July sales had topped

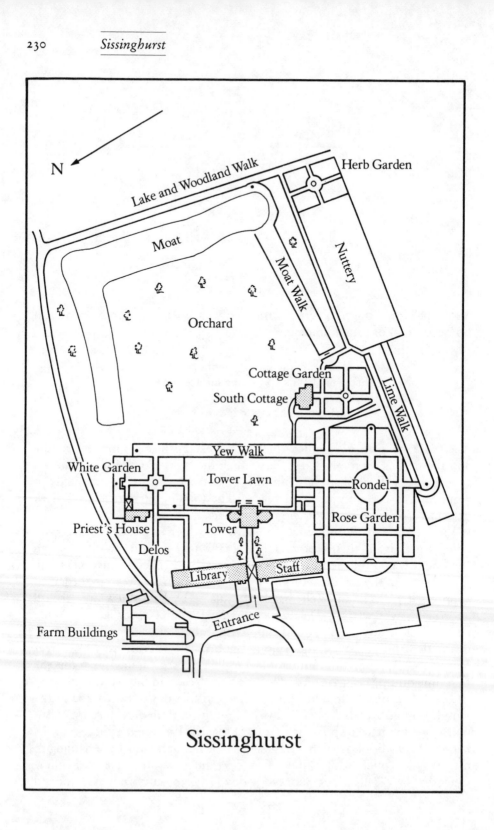

N

Lake and Woodland Walk

Herb Garden

Moat

Nuttery

Moat Walk

Orchard

Lime Walk

Cottage Garden

South Cottage

Yew Walk

White Garden

Tower Lawn

Rondel

Priest's House

Rose Garden

Tower

Delos

Library

Staff

Entrance

Farm Buildings

**Sissinghurst**

20,000 already. In America the book was chosen by the Literary Guild, and Hugh Walpole wrote a 'London Literary Letter' for the *New York Herald Tribune* entirely about that gifted couple V. Sackville-West and Harold Nicolson. The success of *The Edwardians* was long-lasting; cheap editions followed, and in 1936 Leonard Woolf told Vita that over 64,000 copies of the sixpenny Penguin edition had been sold.

Vita had done what she set out to do: write a popular success; and she had done it by recreating the lavish, feudal, immoral *ancien régime* of her childhood. She starts her story in 1905; Chevron, the great house in the book, is Knole in every detail, from the leopards on the battlements to the hierarchy of indoor and outdoor servants, the 'endless, extravagant meals', the gorgeous, sombre state bedrooms and the Christmas-tree ceremony in the Great Hall. She promotes the lady of the house to the rank of Duchess, and divides her own personality between the two children of the house – Sebastian the young heir, dark, moody and glamorous, and Viola his withdrawn, straight-haired, sceptical sister. 'No character in this book is wholly fictitious,' she wrote provocatively in her Author's Note. She even gave to Sebastian her own dogs, Henry and Sarah. (The latter had replaced the much-lamented Pippin.)

Romola Cheyne, 'a woman who erred with a certain magnificence', is modelled on Mrs Keppel; and Lady Roehampton, a contemporary of Sebastian's mother, a generous 'overblown rose' with whom Sebastian has a disastrous love affair, stands for the Countess of Westmorland, as Vita told Virginia:

a lovely sumptuous creature who came to Knole when I was eight, and who first set my feet along the wrong path, I fancy, but who died herself, relatively young, of drugs and a plethora of lovers. (No, it wasn't Lady Westmorland who set my feet along the wrong path now I come to think of it, but the Queen of Roumania who appeared in my schoolroom one day.)[2]

Sebastian's love life provides the tenuous plot. After Lady Roehampton, he tries to seduce Teresa, a pretty, bourgeois doctor's wife who is dazzled by both Chevron and Sebastian. He tempts her in the silver-filled state bedroom by moonlight, 'speaking of the great shadowy bed', but she flees – a virtuous wife from another world than his. He is consoled by a bohemian model with a 'red generous mouth' and a 'thick white throat', lax and amusing and amoral. Finally he engages himself to a worldly marriage with a nice, dull, plain girl from a suitable family.

Or will he run away from Chevron and all it entails? The subversive element is provided by Leonard Anquetil, a saturnine outsider – modelled on Bill Bickerton, an explorer whom Vita knew slightly – who is sceptical of all Chevron stands for and of all Sebastian's family's values. Befriending the two young people, he sows doubts in their minds also. Viola needs little persuading. Sebastian, because of his passionate love for tradition and for his house and land, is torn. Is Chevron 'a dead thing' or something 'intrinsically real' and valuable? He sees the shallowness of his mother's friends and the stupidity under the surface glitter of their lives. Their values are social, not moral. Even his love for Chevron is not pure: it depends on an assumption of his superiority, on feudal relationships with servants and estate workers, to keep it going. It requires a conformity with the vacuous social round and the hypocritical social conventions of his class.

This ambivalence is not resolved; the author herself had not, would never, really resolve it. It provides the necessary tension in a novel that is precisely as vulgar, vivid, problematic, false and fascinating as its subject matter, the wealthy upper classes of Edwardian England.

The novel ends with the end of that era, and the coronation in 1910 of George v. This is Vita's final major set-piece; she had witnessed the ceremony herself as a girl of eighteen, with her father. Coming away from the Abbey, his coach stopped in the traffic, Sebastian looks out of the window straight into the challenging eyes of Leonard Anquetil, who tells him he is going off to foreign parts again. 'Come with me,' says Anquetil. So perhaps Sebastian will leave Chevron – just for a few years. Then he will come back.

*The Edwardians* is a novel of compromise. Vita felt compromised, in a slightly different sense, by having written it: 'Oh, that bloody book! I blush to think you read it,' she said to Virginia. And to the American writer Frederick Prokosch: 'You ask which of my novels I prefer. I dislike them all, – *Seducers in Ecuador* is the only one I might save from the rubbish-heap.'[3]

Leonard Woolf was right when he wrote that inside Vita was 'an honest, simple, sentimental, romantic, naïve, and competent writer':

> When she let all this go off together in a novel about high life, she produced in *The Edwardians* a kind of period piece and a best-seller. .... Novels by serious writers of genius often eventually become best-sellers, but most contemporary best-sellers are written by second-class writers whose psychological brew contains a touch of naïvety, a touch of sentimentality, the story telling gift, and a mysterious sympathy with the day-dreams of ordinary people. Vita was very nearly a best-seller of this kind. She only just missed being one because she did not have quite enough of the third and fourth element in the best-selling brew.[4]

*The Edwardians* brought her many fan-letters, including one from her old nursemaid Giovanna, now Mrs Tubman and living in New Zealand. She would love, she said, to see 'the lady whose neck I washed when she was a little girl!! Do you remember?' Giovanna also remembered 'the Duchess who moved about continually whilst she was being dressed, who wore a ruby and diamond dog-collar with the large tulle bow...!!!' Vita's description of Sebastian's mother at her elaborate toilette was a picture of her own mother going through that same sensual ritual. The quality of her writing must reflect some of the impact that sensuality made on Vita as a child: for one of her fan-letters, unsigned, was a piece of pornographic writing from a woman inflamed to auto-eroticism by Vita's brief description of the Duchess's elaborate Edwardian undergarments.

Long Barn was particularly beautiful that summer. 1 July: 'Hadji came down in the evening. We dine on the terrace these days. One of the most lovely evenings I ever remember, – quite still. We went and lay in the half-finished stack in Paige's field. Young green moon, and a lovely sunset light.'

They went for a weekend to Wilton, the home of Lord Pembroke; the Churchills were there. Winston Churchill 'goes for a long walk with Vita and tells her all his troubles and hopes,' noted Harold. Churchill was the one person 'with whom I would gladly elope if asked,' said Vita, who was a success with statesmen: at Chequers, later in the year, the Prime Minister Ramsay MacDonald 'pours out to Vita the miseries of his soul'.

The money earned by *The Edwardians* gave Vita a freer hand with Sissinghurst. Virginia introduced her to Hugo, an antique dealer in Warren Street, where she bought an oak table, a Spanish walnut table, an oak cupboard and two chairs – all for under fifty pounds. She bought quantities of linen – both for her household and for Boski, who was leaving to get married. She bought from the Woolfs their old Minerva platen printing press, to be displayed at Sissinghurst.

The tower was the first part of Sissinghurst to be made habitable. They broke through to the turret adjoining the room on the first floor that Vita decided, on 12 July, must be her writing room and library. 'We decided', she wrote in her diary on return to Long Barn, 'to have the fireplace built across the corner of the tower room, and keep the arch at the entrance to the turret.' This they did. The furniture from Hugo arrived, 'and we carried it up, and had our tea at a table, for the first time in our history at Sissinghurst.... We came home to find Stephen Spender already arrived.' (Then a young man of twenty-two, he was a new friend of both Nicolsons that summer.) Even though Vita was bothered by the back pain that always plagued her on and off, she managed, on her next visit, to paint the corner cupboard in her tower room green (as it still is).

*The Edwardians* also paid for the Italian holiday that Vita, Harold and the boys took in August. They stayed in Portofino, where Vita worked on her new novel, *All Passion Spent*, and then went on to Florence, where they joined Dorothy Wellesley and Hilda Matheson, who were taking a holiday together. Harold went home first, by train, to his work on the *Evening Standard*, and Vita and the boys motored home in leisurely fashion. From Milan they wrote a joint letter to Harold. They had lost the car keys in Piacenza after stopping for a drink; Ben wrote that 'Mummy was frightfully good about it, and, unlike the Italians, kept her head, and searched calmly. I mention this, because Niggs and I were so impressed.' Nigel enclosed his 'log' of their times and mileages, hoping his father would be impressed not only by this but by 'Mummy's superb driving and average'. 'The babies are so sweet,' Vita wrote; 'they are being so efficient.' The three reached Newhaven on 29 August and had breakfast with the Woolfs at Rodmell on their way home – Virginia marvelling at their travel-stained car, 'sandshoes and Florentine candlepieces, novels and so on tumbling about on the seats.'[5]

At home, Harold was already working with architect friends on the design of the 'boys' cottage' at Sissinghurst. They had abandoned their earlier plans for linking the tower with other extant buildings, and had agreed on a grouping of separate units. The boys' cottage was converted from the ruinous building called the Priest's House, which would also contain a bathroom, and downstairs the kitchen and the family dining-room. Vita and Harold's bedrooms and bathroom, and Harold's sitting-room and small bookroom, were to be in another converted fragment, the South Cottage. They made no arrangements for guest rooms, though there was room for development in the gatehouse block, at present stables. Their plan meant that they would all constantly have to cross the garden for various purposes, ill or well, day or night, fair weather or foul. And although private sitting-rooms for both Vita and Harold were considered priorities, a general family sitting-room was not.

They let the Castle Farm to A.O.R. ('Ozzie') Beale, a prominent local farmer, but the conversions took more money than they had planned. Vita had to borrow from the money left by Seery to B.M., on which B.M. charged interest; she also tried to make Vita sign a deed saying she would never claim her allowance, nor arrears on it. Vita had no intention of ever taking a personal allowance from her mother again, but she refused to sign anything just in case, she said, she was ever in need on the boys' account.

When this squabble had cleared, B.M. proved generous once more – she offered to pay for the furnishing of the boys' cottage, and as the year progressed sent van-loads of valuables over to Sissinghurst: Persian rugs, glass, silver and ebony mirrors from Knole; twelve Nash engravings of Knole; Jacobean chests; a copy of the Kneller portrait of Charles

*Virginia Woolf photographed by Vita at Rodmell, June 1926.*

Geoffrey Scott at the
Villa Medici, Florence.

Dorothy Wellesley in
the pool at Sherfield,
a photograph titled
by Vita: 'Leda and
the Swan.'

*Roy and Mary Campbell.*

*Vita photographed by Virginia Woolf on holiday in France, September 1928.*

*Hilda Matheson on holiday with Vita, 1929.*

*One of the photographs of Vita taken by Virginia Woolf for Orlando.*

*Sissinghurst in the early days.*

*The Nicolson family and Pippin,* 1929.

*Harold and Vita in the Tower.*

*Evelyn Irons with Socks.*

*Vita with Sarah
photographed by
Evelyn Irons.*

*Vita photographed
by Lenare, 1933.*

*Gwen St Aubyn with
Martin, 1934.*

*Vita photographed
by Evelyn Irons.*

*OPPOSITE: Two views of
the Big Room (now called
the Library), Sissinghurst.*

*Vita's bedroom in the
South Cottage.*

*The dining-room in the Priest's House.*

ABOVE: *Vita's writing table in the Tower.*

LEFT: *The Tower seen from the White Garden.*

*Gwen with 'the Trouts': Edy Craig, Christopher St John and Tony Attwood, May 1939.*

*Nigel and Ben, 1939.*

*Vita with Rollo.*          OPPOSITE: *Vita and Harold, in* 1955 *(ABOVE) and in* 1959 *(BELOW).*

Sackville, and a large white bath. Vita might not take her allowance, but B.M.'s largesse, as it always had, held her in thrall.

The Nicolsons did not live full-time at Sissinghurst until April 1932, two years after they bought it; but Vita slept there for the first time on 16 October 1930, alone, in the turret adjoining her future writing room. She had the dogs, Henry and Sarah, with her: 'Not frightened. Listened to Hadji [on the radio] discussing Germany.' She wrote to him that evening, 'Hayter has cleared the moat walk, and a lovely wall has come into view.' Hilda Matheson came to spend the next day and night with her – together, they edged paths with tiles – and after that, Harold. They marked out the garden by the South Cottage, and planted madonna lilies. 'We sleep in the top of the tower on two camp beds. We read by candles.' Coming and going from Long Barn, Vita continued her gardening – she planted a fig – and supervized the building operations, often with Hilda as a companion. In the South Cottage the workmen uncovered '*the* most lovely, huge, stone Tudor fireplace in my bedroom.' (Most of the work was carried out by the local firm of H.C.Punnett, who sent in his bills to 'The Hon. Mrs Arold Nickleson'.)

Vita was happy. Harold was not. That first night at Sissinghurst with Vita he confessed in his diary how unhappy he was. He felt poor, unsuccessful, humiliated, middle-aged. Being a journalist, an author and a broadcaster (he did a regular radio feature 'People and Things') did not satisfy him. All the fears that he had had about abandoning his diplomatic career seemed justified. 'I have never been unhappy like this before.' Vita knew it. Ben was not happy either. He hated Eton; Vita knew this too, and wondered whether they ought to take him away. Her own bubble was pricked in the late autumn, when the deterioration of her relationship with Virginia was brought home to her. On 30 October Virginia had written that the loss of intimacy meant that 'a black crust forms': 'But how am I ever to see you, apart from Hilda? Is an afternoon alone never possible? Not since Rodmell and then only for two minutes have we been alone in a room together – let alone the other place.' Virginia's long self-exploratory letters were now addressed to Ethel Smyth, not to Vita, who, though she had brought this upon herself, resented it. 'The other night, sitting on the floor by my side, Vita suffered considerably from jealousy of Ethel. She praised her, stoutly, but bitterly. She has all the abandonment that I, living in this age of subtlety and reserve, have lost. She claims you; rushes in where I force myself to hold back.'[6]

Virginia was not always so subtle and reserved. 3 December 1930: 'Is there no chance that we could have a happy day one day next week, and go to the Mint or the Tower or The Zoo or eat muffins in a shop?

'Or do you want to drop me ? Answer.
'Do you bequeath me to Ethel ? Answer.'

Ethel Smyth wrote in her diary that Vita 'I think is the only person except Vanessa Bell and Leonard, her husband, whom [Virginia] really loves.'[7] Ethel also said of Virginia that 'One can't have relations with her as with others. The fact is that you have to take what you can of Virginia.'[8]

Maybe Vita, for all her present jealousy, had taken and given all that was possible. Her diary entry, two days after Virginia's appeal, shows where her heart was : 'Hilda and I spent the whole day at Sissinghurst arranging H[arold]'s sitting room, bedroom, and my bedroom. Paige came over from Long Barn with a lorry of furniture.' The next night she and Harold slept in the South Cottage for the first time. A lake was being made where there was 'an obviously artificial embankment surrounding two marshy meadows' and a stream coming down from the wood. The stream was dammed, and within three days 'a sheet of water lay placidly where the useless swamp had been.'[9] On Christmas Day 1930, Vita insisted that they take Christmas dinner from Long Barn over to Sissinghurst and eat it there.

In mid-February 1931, after a light fall of snow that did not lie, Vita planted '500 daffodil and narcissus where the cherries are to go, at the end of the moat. Six wild geese flew over. A lovely afternoon. Planted roses, and the Persian peach. Saw a big white owl. . . .' Everything in the garden was becoming lovely ; and in the same month the Nicolsons dined with Albert Einstein, and met Charlie Chaplin at luncheon.

So what was missing ? Something was. On 23 January Vita had told Virginia that she got more pain than pleasure from praise of her books. Furthermore : 'If I, who am the most fortunate of women can ask What is life for ? how can other people live at all ?'[10] Virginia and Vita resumed their expeditions – they went to see Dickens's house in Doughty Street – but Virginia could not relieve Vita's irrational depression. Dorothy Wellesley and Hilda Matheson were away, on holiday together in Sicily. On 3 March Vita finished *All Passion Spent*, dedicating to 'Benedict and Nigel, who are young, this story of people who are old'. Lady Slane, the heroine of *All Passion Spent*, is very old indeed : she is eighty-eight.

This novel is more important than *The Edwardians* for understanding Vita ; she managed through gentle Lady Slane's meditations on the past to express her own ungentle feelings about the distorting effects marriage and the expectations of society have on the individual. Lady Slane has been a gracious, submissive 'appendage' to her Viceroy husband ; 'always a lonely woman, always at variance with the creeds to which she apparently conformed', she decides on his death to live out her remaining years according to her own beliefs, and to be true to herself at last.

It was Vita's widowed mother-in-law, Lady Carnock, who gave her the idea for her heroine. Lady Carnock clung to her family and made her home with Freddy, her eldest son; Lady Slane in the novel does what Vita thought Lady Carnock ought to have done. She chooses to live with her aged French maid Genoux (the name of Vita's own French maid in real life) in a tranquil old house in Hampstead that she fell in love with thirty years previously. Vita made use here of the expeditions she had made to Hampstead Heath and to Keats's house with Virginia; and Lady Slane's house, which is as much a character in the book as any of the human beings, must surely be in Church Row although Vita does not specify this. Lady Slane's memories of diplomatic and viceregal life are fed by Vita's own memories of her brief visit to India, and include a virtuoso passage, rather in Virginia's manner, about a wheeling cloud of yellow and white butterflies encountered on a desert road in Persia.

Lady Slane affronts her conventional, ageing children by taking no further interest in them. She affronts them further by a too-casual renunciation of her valuable jewels, and by giving away an inherited fortune. She drastically simplifies her life, seeing only a group of elderly eccentrics with no social position – 'fond fantastics' who like herself live according to their own lights, 'artists in appreciation' though not in achievement. Achievement was not very important, since it entailed truckling to the values and hierarchies of the market-place. (There is a connection between the ideas of *All Passion Spent* and those of Virginia Woolf's *A Room of One's Own* and *Three Guineas*, which was conceived in 1931 though not published until 1938.)

Leonard Woolf, Vita's publisher, thought that *All Passion Spent* was her best novel. It has moved tens of thousands of readers, who found and still find Vita's fierce simplicities inspirational. 'To thine own self be true' was Vita's creed, and the fact that she herself never achieved Lady Slane's simplification of life – by giving away her jewels, for example, or renouncing her inherited wealth – accentuates the tears of things. In any case, in 1931 Vita was not ready to withdraw. Her old Lady Slane's vitality is on the wane; she has strength, at the end, for only one last 'strange and lovely thing' before she dies. For Lady Slane, 'Those days were gone when feeling burst its bounds and poured hot from the foundry, when the heart seemed likely to split with complex and contradictory desires.' Not so, for Vita. A couple of days after finishing *All Passion Spent* she was falling in love. The volcano was erupting again.

She wrote to her new love that spring, 'Damn love. By its feverish persuasions it wrecks our energies. By its moments of ecstasy it deludes us into thinking that life is worth living.' And again: 'It is a great mistake to fall in love, and yet it seems to be the only thing that lifts life out of a trough.' Vita, nearing forty, recognized the functional necessity to her of passionate love for relieving tension and depression – a simple, partial explanation of her often inexplicable love affairs. With a similar self-knowledge, she had described in *The Edwardians*, through the character of Sebastian, how people like herself tried to square their own sexual and romantic needs with the expectations of others :

> Sebastian was one of those charming but dangerous people who never do harm except by accident ; such discontent as internally ate him away, remained his private knowledge. . . . In some complicated way, this sense of his own detachment persuaded him of their immunity. He was playing a game with a soft ball ; a game in which nobody had any business to get hurt.

But someone always gets hurt.

Vita occasionally wrote what she called 'diary poems' : personal free-form poems never intended for publication, unworked on, spontaneous, unlike the formal prosody of her 'real' poetry. She wrote a diary poem now, which suggests again how only when she was in love did she feel in step with 'irrational humanity', released from her sense of stagnation and alienation.

> This is pain.
> I recognize it.
> I feared I had forgotten how to feel it.
> I feared, that I was so lapped in happiness and security,
> That I had forgotten the sting of pain, of sensation ;
> But here is the familiar turmoil, the stinging.
> I welcome it ; I fear it ; I welcome my own fear of it.
> I am glad to find that I can still be afraid of my own sensations.
> I am glad to find that I can still be swept by a sensation I cannot
>     logically explain to others ;
> That I am still capable of an irrational passion,
> I who had grown so ordered, rational,
> I have stablished my contact with irrational humanity.
> Wars, hatreds, envy, all seemed childish to me.
> But with this sudden springing and stinging of pain in me
> All those things become intelligible again, even inevitable.
> The desert of my heart has flowered again, become alive.
> I suffer, but I am glad to discover in myself that I still have the
>     capacity to suffer.

Evelyn Irons was Scottish, aged thirty, a graduate of Somerville College, Oxford, and in 1931 the Women's Page editor of the *Daily Mail*. Intending to write a feature about V. Sackville-West, she had sent a set of questions that Vita found intriguing; she asked Miss Irons to lunch at King's Bench Walk. Two days later, on 6 March, Miss Irons came down to Sissinghurst for the night; they walked down to the new lake, by moonlight, after dinner. Evelyn Irons later recalled to Vita how that night she had stood 'in front of the fire in your room at Sissinghurst, looking at you and thinking that I had fallen in love with you, not dreaming that you would ever be in love with me, and yet feeling tremendously happy and excited. . . . Strewth, but you looked so sweet in your little dressing-gown.'

Soon after that Vita went to a party at Evelyn's flat at 80 Royal Hospital Road in Chelsea, 'making a grand entrance bearing a cask of olives as a contribution'. Evelyn told Vita at that party that she was 'desperately in love' with her. Within a few days they were lovers and Evelyn was spending as much time at Sissinghurst with Vita as both of them could manage. 'Sleeping Beauty's castle' had come alive for Vita. Evelyn worked in the garden with her, weeding and clearing away rubbish. It was in that first year at Sissinghurst that Vita evolved the comfortable costume that would stand up to nettles, thickets, mud, barbed wire and broken cans, as well as digging and planting. From now on she customarily wore whipcord breeches from Simpsons of Piccadilly, high boots with laced canvas uppers made to her own design (with a pair of secateurs stuck into the top), a rough jacket or jerkin over a blouse – and her pearls and dangling earrings.

Outside troubles increased her absorption in the garden and the private idyll with Evelyn. Roy Campbell's revenge had taken literary form. Vita saw well in advance of its publication *The Georgiad*, a 'satirical fantasy' in verse – a blistering attack on Bloomsbury and the Georgian poets, but also on the Nicolsons, especially Vita – who is 'Georgiana', the hostess at 'Summer Schools of Love' for 'piping nancy boys and crashing bores'. He mocked her love of dogs (mentioning Canute) and *The Land*:

> Write with your spade, and garden with your pen,
> Shovel your couplets to their long repose
> And type your turnips down the field in rows.

And as for her appearance:

> Her gruff moustaches dropping from her mouth,
> One to the North, the other to the South,
> Seemed more the whiskers of some brine-wet seal
> Than of a priestess of the High Ideal –
> Spent passion from her eyes had sprung a leak
> And from her fountain-pen; that very week
> She had been jilted more than seven times
> And couldn't cope with it for all her rhymes.

Her marriage with the 'wittol', Harold, gets similar treatment :

> Who lecture (both the wittol and his wife)
> Upon the Radio, about married life,
> As if their life were one protracted kiss
> And they the models of connubial bliss,
> Though it is true they burn with the same flame –
> Fickle in faith, in failure still the same.

Vita and Harold decided on a policy of non-retaliation. On 23 March Vita answered an enquiry from Herbert E. Palmer with dignity and without untruth :

> *The Georgiad* – well that's a painful and complicated subject. I admire Roy's poetry enormously, and have reviewed it in the most enthusiastic terms whenever I got the chance – and so has my husband. I am afraid there is no doubt that the whole poem is the most violent and muddled attack on us both – our house, our garden, our friends, and even our dogs !

She told Palmer that Roy had lived with them for eight months 'when we lent him and his wife a cottage in our garden' :

> Indeed, he wrote some of *The Georgiad* while he was living here, which was not perhaps in the best of taste. It is only fair to Roy to say that he and I did have a frightful row, and that therefore I suppose he was justified in attacking me, but he had no grievance against Harold, who had never done him anything but good turns. . . .
>
> However, I know he is a very queer character and I don't really bear him any grudge, and I shall continue to think of him as a very fine poet. I detest literary rows and will never be drawn into them.[11]

Better to indulge her already strong reclusive tendencies and withdraw into the garden and her new love. She was spending as much time at Sissinghurst as at Long Barn ; she had a boat on the lake now, and drifted away the long evenings with Evelyn.

When the boys (Nigel was now at Eton with Ben) were home at Long Barn for Easter, the lovers' meetings were less frequent. That only sharpened desire. But one real difficulty was that Evelyn was not free ; she lived with another young woman, Olive Rinder, who had tuberculosis and was inclined to be hysterical. Nevertheless Olive behaved with almost excessive generosity and actively encouraged Evelyn's affair with Vita. Another difficulty from Evelyn's point of view was Harold :

> Not that I disliked him. But I had to go back to London on Saturday mornings, usually, because he was coming by the next train for the weekend. As both he and Vita agreed that she should have her girl-friends while he had his boys, I

didn't see the need for all this concealment. But Vita was determined to keep our relationship under wraps.[12]

Evelyn, like Hilda Matheson in the past, would not have minded people 'talking about us' (as Olive Rinder had heard someone 'talking about' Vita and Mary Campbell): 'I'm in one of my announcing-it-in-the-Times moods,' wrote Evelyn. 'I don't believe it will be disastrous but even if it is it's well worth it.' Vita would never agree with this view, however much in love she was. 'Our correspondence is degenerating into a mere calendar of assignations,' she wrote to Evelyn from Long Barn on 27 April; 'inevitable, I suppose, between clandestine lovers. But what a world of romance is encircled by those two words.' For Vita secrecy was of the essence. She would always want to keep her 'world of romance' away from the outside world and apart from her life with Harold, which made the weekends his and no one else's. Vita was infinitely secretive and devious, though she believed herself to be candid.

In her deviousness she enjoyed the risk of private jokes in public places: as when she wrote one of the 'Country Notes' that she contributed to the *New Statesman* entirely on the subject of 'Scrape'. 'Scrape' was the word that Dottie, Hilda and Harold used to describe her inconvenient affairs; 'Scrape' was the private pet name she gave to Evelyn; 'scrape' is also a disease of sheep. She wrote in her article that scrape (in sheep) was 'nothing less than homesickness; it occurs only in sheep pining for their native land': 'The native land, in this case, happens to be the Highlands of Scotland. ... The only remedy, according to my friend, is to cross the breed with a southern ram, when the North apparently agrees to settle down comfortably with the South.'[13]

Being in love always helped Vita to write. Her translations of Rilke's *Duino Elegies* – begun with Margaret Goldsmith Voigt and completed in the end in collaboration with Eddy Sackville-West – had come out in a limited, signed edition with illustrations by Eric Gill. 'My own production has become simply terrific (in quantity I mean, not quality),' she wrote to Evelyn in mid-May. 'I never stop writing stories and articles. ... I must make the most of it while the fit is on me – but they are cheap stuff.' The stories were published the following year under the title *Thirty Clocks Strike the Hour*, the title story being an evocation of herself as a child in Seery's Paris apartment. She was writing poetry too: the love poems dated '1931' in her *Collected Poems* are poems to Evelyn, but she did not publish the more erotic ones. As another risky joke, she persuaded Evelyn to write a magazine story to be marketed as 'by V. Sackville-West' – Evelyn taking the fee.

As she had with Hilda, Vita discussed the pleasures and problems of homosexual love with Evelyn. Vita loved Evelyn in the fashionable dresses she wore to Ascot, or to cover the Paris collections for her newspaper. She loved to give Evelyn presents – a new suitcase full of men's silk pyjamas, flowers delivered to her office at the *Daily Mail*, a diamond wrist-watch, Alella wine, a ring – 'your shackle'. Evelyn was not accustomed to playing the feminine role; she loved Orlando, but she also loved Vita the woman. They exploited their diversity; as Vita said, 'in me you have two strings of the lyre on which to play.' The fourfold variety provided by what Evelyn called their 'hermaphrodite minds' was agreeable. 'Such is our inter-homosexual homosexuality,' wrote Evelyn, 'that we do not take obvious advantage of this arrangement, but choose to appear in similar roles. On Friday, for instance, it will be gardener and water-boy.'

But already by mid-August Vita's total abandonment to love was becoming modified and Evelyn was being forced to realize what others before and after her had to realize. She began to feel that she was for Vita 'a joke or a diversion. I am not part of your life at all. Not that I feel I am not damned lucky to have any share in you, however small, I love and adore your letters and I think you are a darling to write to me every day and to lunch with me when you might be lunching at Boulestin's.'

Olive Rinder was proving, after all, a complication. Her encouragement of Evelyn's affair with Vita masked desperation; she became ill, and gave up her job. '*Damn* my married life, as well as yours,' wrote Evelyn. More dangerously, Vita was moving into one of her destructive triangular relationships. Olive came down to Sissinghurst one day, and was wholly fascinated by Vita, and told her so. 'Don't fall in love with her for her fragility, as one is so apt to do,' warned Evelyn. But Vita, ever susceptible to fragility and adoration, did not rebuff Olive. Vita loved to be loved.

# CHAPTER 22

ALL *Passion Spent* came out at the end of May 1931, at the height of Vita's passionate involvement with Evelyn Irons. On 11 June Virginia wrote to Vita that sales were '*very* good. . . . Lord! What fun!' Vita had been worried about the novel when she had read it in proof; it seemed to her then 'a feeble book'. 'It is quite, quite meaningless,' she had told Evelyn, 'and the reviewers will cut me to bits.' She felt reconciled to it after publication though, in a way that she never was to *The Edwardians*. *All Passion Spent* brought her a great many letters from readers, 'far more than about *The Edwardians*. This pleases me, as it is a better book.' She began a new novel straight away, *Family History*, giving its heroine the name 'Evelyn'.

The twin triumphs of *The Edwardians* and *All Passion Spent* were shared with the Woolfs, her publishers. But Virginia grieved for the loss of Vita, or for what seemed to her the loss of Vita. Potto (Virginia's name for the self that loved Vita) was 'dead of a broken heart' at the end of July. In October Ethel Smyth – who sometimes came to Long Barn to listen to the nightingales through her ear trumpet – intervened. Virginia had been asking her, '"But do you think V[ita] *really* wants me in her life?" and I was touched and sorry for her great loneliness'; so generous old Ethel wrote to Vita, adding shrewdly enough:

> For of course you and I know [Virginia] is in a way on the rim of everyone's life – probably even of Vanessa's or Leonard's; that the human contact others can achieve is not for such as her – and would not be even if her life had been full of lovemaking of all sorts. . . . And so I wanted you to turn on the human tap somehow – anyhow I felt she wanted to be reassured that you 'wanted her in your life' – in some very human way.

Vita went to see Virginia – they walked 'round and round Tavistock Square discussing *The Waves*' – before going on to broadcast, and then to dine in Chelsea with Evelyn and Olive. She went with Virginia a few nights later to hear a performance of Ethel Smyth's *The Wreckers*, and they gave the composer dinner afterwards.

Vita even introduced Evelyn to Virginia, who had expressed a wish to see a newspaper being printed. Leonard came too, and Evelyn showed the three of them round the *Daily Mail*; they talked to the linotype operators in the composing room, saw the headlines being set, and Virginia, no stranger to printing, asked questions that showed she knew what she was talking about. In the 'morgue', where obituaries are stored until such time as they are necessary, Vita and Virginia read their own and each other's. Vita summarized them both in verse. Of her own, she wrote :

> An ancient house and a stately name
> For me, and a strange romantic vein
> 'Spanish gypsy and Spanish duke
> Mixed with her very English strain,
> With a dash of the goatherd Basque thrown in,
> And a few cheap novels as bad as sin,
> And some honest lines of verse.'[1]

This was all after Vita and Evelyn Irons had been away on holiday together in Provence. Virginia knew that Vita had taken a companion : Harold did not. The idea was that the change and the warmth would benefit Vita's recurring back pain and sciatica. She took some trouble to conceal from Harold the fact that she did not go alone, writing 'I' and not 'we' even in her diary, and scribbling 'Egypt Egypt Egypt' all over references to Les Baux, one of the places they visited and the highlight of the holiday, in letters from Evelyn afterwards.

There were reasons for this deception. Harold was still at a low ebb. At the beginning of the year 1931, in the face of disapproval from Vita (who loathed Oswald Mosley), he had joined Mosley's New Party. He liked Mosley, and he wanted more than anything to get back into public life. In April he gave up his radio spot 'People and Things' to concentrate on politics. In August he resigned from the *Evening Standard* in order to edit *Action*, the journal of the New Party, at a much lower salary. (Vita saw this as an opportunity to help Olive Rinder, and secured her the job of editing *Action*'s women's page.)

It was a terrible gamble and Harold was not confident. On 12 September he joined Vita at Sissinghurst and wrote in his diary, 'Gloom : damp : fear : worry : perplexity : depression.' In his anxiety he leaned heavily on the permanence and understanding of his relationship with Vita. She responded with the feminine reassurance he so urgently needed. She had described what happened between them at these times in *All Passion Spent*: 'She must be swift to detect his need for reassurance when a momentary discouragement overcame him; when, mooning, he strayed up to her and drooped over her chair, saying nothing, but waiting (as she knew) for some soft protection to come from her and fold itself around him like a cloak.'

On the day she left for France with Evelyn he listed in his diary what it was that made them so indispensable to each other, and thought with gratitude of their perfect harmony. 'No one else knows or understands.' To her he wrote: 'I do so share the pleasure of your being among the olives. Even when not with you I am so identified with you that when you find things to be warm and lovely a faint transference of pleasure comes to me.' In Provence, Vita and Evelyn walked the twelve miles from Tarascon to Les Baux; they went on to Arles and Nîmes, Vita possessively passionate and writing poetry: 'Love thou but me; all other realms I'll give thee':

> Am I not generous? I would not stint thee,
> I spread the whole of nature for thy choice.
> Only, with my own cipher would imprint thee,
> That thou should'st answer to my single voice.[2]

This she sent Evelyn on their return from France. While she was away, Ben and Nigel sent a telegram to their parents on their wedding anniversary: 'Congratulations on 18 years conjugal bliss Benedict and Nigel.' Vita would have found no irony in this. Nor, most probably, even if he had been in possession of the facts, would Harold.

Vita came home to nothing but trouble and need. Ben had had 'what appears to be a sort of nervous breakdown' at Eton. Vita went to see him; 'Hadji was too busy to come.' The first issue of *Action* was coming out. 'Hadji is busy, much *too* busy. I wish he wouldn't – but it's no good saying anything,' Vita wrote in her diary on 14 October. The following weekend at Long Barn he was 'in a state of nerves', Vita told Evelyn, because of his paper and because of the forthcoming election in which he was standing as a New Party candidate. Vita did not fail him. 'My saint,' he wrote to her, 'I have seldom felt the effect of your love so deeply as I felt it last night. I was all unfortified and unstrung – and you put me right.'

At the election on 27 October the New Party did very badly, all twenty-four candidates losing their deposits. It was the end of it for Harold. (Mosley turned to Fascism after this and Harold did not follow him.) *Action* folded soon after, putting Olive Rinder out of a job again. Olive's relations with Evelyn were increasingly unhappy too.

This was largely Vita's fault. Olive's expressions of love had intensified and Vita had responded. *Two* daily letters had been arriving in Vita's unmistakeable dark blue envelopes at the flat in Royal Hospital Road, causing domestic unease. Vita was still in love with Evelyn, more so after the success of their Provençal holiday, and the confusion, unhappiness and guilt of the three-way jealousies led to rows, explanations, reconciliations and more rows.

It was a low point in the lives of both the Nicolsons, in spite of Vita's success with her novels. *The Georgiad* was out and talked about. Two days before Christmas 1931 Vita went to Harold's bank – he was without a job or an income – and extracted 'an unwilling loan' from them, presumably by guaranteeing it herself. 'My future financial prospects are so black that I groan to gaze into the abyss. I feel irreparably shallow,' Harold wrote in his diary. Vita, deep in an emotional morass, was reduced to deception, disingenuity, and letters of unworthy diplomatic equivocation to both Evelyn and Olive, whose own 'marriage' was now badly damaged.

In the midst of this, Vita was writing as many articles and reviews as she possibly could, not so much from the excitement of love now as the need to earn money. She called them her 'bones' – on the analogy of a dog bringing back bones to its master. Virginia saw Vita (through reports from Ethel Smyth, via Hilda – who was also without a job, having nobly resigned in protest against Reith's refusal to let Harold praise *Ulysses* on the BBC) as supporting 'the weight of the Nicolsons on her shoulders, working working so she can't sleep o' nights.'[3] Virginia did not see why the Nicolsons did not simplify their life – the butler, the sons at Eton, and both Long Barn and Sissinghurst 'in full swing' seemed unnecessary to Virginia.

But unlike her Lady Slane in *All Passion Spent*, Vita still wanted to have everything, do everything, in love and in life, and she still had the energy to try. Or was she being 'true to herself'? As Olive Rinder wrote to her on 11 January 1932, 'But you do like to have your cake and eat it, – and *so* many cakes, so many, a surfeit of sweet things.... Darling, darling, I adore you.' Olive and Vita were not lovers in the full sense until that January; and then Olive, like others before her, abandoned herself childishly to Vita's will. 'I am absolutely yours, and anything you tell me to do (however unpleasant) I will do.'

Sissinghurst, in spite of unhappiness and upheavals, was taking shape. By the beginning of 1932 they had laid the main paths, put down turf, made 'Sissinghurst Crescent' to the east of Vita and Harold's cottage, with steps down to the Moat Walk. They had made a rose garden by the boys' cottage, and nearly all the old rubbish had been cleared away. Yet at Sissinghurst for the last weekend in January, a depressed Harold wrote in his diary : 'There is a dead and drowned mouse in the lily pool. I feel like that mouse – static, obese and decaying. Viti is calm, comforting and considerate.' She was encouraging him to write again, which he did. She kept from him as much as possible the chaos in her private life, from a wish not to burden him further – and because she knew he would react with despairing disapproval of her 'muddles'. Calculating the extent of his debts in his diary, Harold wrote : 'It is I who have muddled things – not Viti. And she never even lets me imagine a feeling of reproach.' He blamed Vita for nothing. Repressing the fact that it had been she who had begged him over years to leave a profession that suited him, he settled the blame on the difficulties with B.M. over money :

> the whole of our present anxieties and humiliations derives from our renouncing the settlement annuity of £2,400. For this I have left diplomacy and tarred myself with the brush of journalism. People think I have sold my soul for money. They do not understand that I have voluntarily abandoned my rights and my pride. What a muddle.

In his loss of self-esteem, he had moments of uncertainty about the way Sissinghurst itself was developing; over this, he was able to voice his feelings of dislocation, pointing out to Vita that if they slept in the South Cottage and ate in the Priest's House, 'when we are old we shall die if we have to go a long country walk from meal to meal. And at night.' But Vita liked it the way it was. He also complained that he had no room that was truly his own, either at Sissinghurst or at King's Bench Walk; 'I do not want to make any room ugly, but I should like to feel that there were open to me, in some personal habitation, an orgy of bad taste. The bore about it is that I love Viti's taste – and never wish in reality to depart from it. Only I want a room of my own.' But Vita could always talk him round or make him laugh, and ended the argument by proposing that they should take off together for Biarritz or Syracuse, even though they had no money. Meanwhile Vita's maid Louise Genoux was airing the Persian carpets that B.M. had just sent over from Streatham – 'moth-eaten but superb', as he said : 'It is typical of our existence that with no settled income ... we should live in a muddle of museum carpets, ruined castles, and penury. ... That is our life. Work – uncertainty – and huge capitalistic schemes. And are we wrong ? My God ! we are not wrong.' B.M. sent them not only carpets but glass, a blue buddha, and eight bronze garden urns from Bagatelle. A soft Chinese carpet was destined for Harold's sitting-room – which, decoration apart, was utterly a room of his own since Vita never used it, preferring her tower room at all times.

Virginia first climbed Vita's tower on 29 March 1932, when she and Leonard came to a lunch of salmon and raspberries and cream and 'little variegated chocolates given by Lady Sackville' and 'oh lots of drinks'. Vita wore breeches and a pink shirt; Sissinghurst was romantic, but the austere Woolfs were appalled by the amount of work and effort involved.

For two years the Nicolsons had been living half at Long Barn and half at Sissinghurst; in early April Vita forced the issue by letting Long Barn, and Sissinghurst, with the telephone now installed, became their one family home. She was still seeing – and making love to – both Evelyn Irons and Olive Rinder, and fending off crises with both. 'Life is too complicated, – I sometimes feel that I can't manage it all,'[4] she wrote enigmatically to Virginia, who had gone to Greece. She did not confide her 'muddle' to Virginia this time, or respond to her concerned enquiry – 'Why is life so complicated at the moment? Money? Dottie? Writing?'[5]

Vita took Evelyn with her when she went to lecture at Somerville College, Oxford, Evelyn's old college. At the beginning of July, Evelyn and Olive went away together to a cottage at Lamorna in Cornwall. Vita had just sent the manuscript of her new novel *Family History* to the Hogarth Press and was free. She arranged to visit the pair in Cornwall, telling everyone that she was going away by herself as a complete break. Evelyn was sworn to secrecy: 'Look here, I have *not* told H. N. that I shall join you. So please don't tell anyone.' Harold encouraged her to stay away as long as she needed. 'It is far more important for you to get your batteries filled up than to worry about my being lonely. . . . So I shall not expect you till I see you my own darling.'

The visit to Lamorna was a disaster. 'There were frightful rows, sordid, humiliating ones, because of all the entanglements and jealousies. . . . It was hell.' That was Evelyn's opinion. Vita came home and said nothing to Harold. The letters between the three women grew longer and more desperate. Vita wrote to Evelyn on 15 July:

> And oh my God I do hate this mess I've brought you both into, unintentionally. Would you agree to her [Olive] coming down here for a day, or not? You seem to have taken control. I don't blame you, – I should do the same, in your case. I think I shall go to my banana island, alone. At least I should bring trouble on no one there.

Evelyn Irons was taking control of her life in a way that Vita did not envisage. Unlike many of the people who loved Vita, she had nothing infantile or masochistic in her make-up. The previous day at a party she had met another woman, with whom she had fallen in love. Exhausted by the quarrels and betrayals of the past months, but still deeply involved with Vita, she put off telling her. But by 1 August Vita was suspicious. 'Darling, What is this mysterious expedition that has taken you away for the weekend? And why were you so anxious suddenly for Olga [Olive] to come here? I have a feeling that something is afoot.' So Evelyn told Vita the truth. This was a situation to which Vita was unaccustomed. She wrote to Evelyn :

> I feel physically sick from conflicting emotions. I think we had better cry quits over all reproaches and wishings that we had behaved differently. The only thing I can possibly say in my own defence is that things happened so gradually and so insidiously that there was no *definite* moment when I realized what was happening. . . . Another thing is that I never ceased to love you, – and haven't now, – and am more than ever convinced that it is possible to love two people. . . . Let us remember Les Baux, and forget everything else.

Olive Rinder was the real victim of the story, as she had to move out of Evelyn's flat when her new love (who was to be a lifelong one) moved in. Vita found Olive a bungalow, Nightingale Cottage, near Sissinghurst and looked after her financially. Harold, while knowing little of the background, approved of her caring for Olive, for whom, after the end of *Action*, he too felt some responsibility. 'I do hope O.R. is better – poor wounded little chaffinch – so plucky.'

Vita went on writing to Evelyn, principally about Olive's state of health, enclosing in her letters small tokens of nostalgia – a luggage label from their trip to Provence, a sprig of rosemary from a cutting taken at Les Baux. In October, she wrote :

> Darling, I thought I would just let you know that Olive really does seem better. . . .
> Shall you ever come down to see her here? It is an odd reversal, isn't it? Sissinghurst is terribly smart now, with a flagged path from the porch to my tower, and electric light . . . you won't recognize it.

But Evelyn did not come.

On 11 August, six days after she had learnt of her defection, Vita posted a poem she had just written to Miss Evelyn Irons at the *Daily Mail*, marking the envelope 'Personal'. She called the poem 'Valediction'.

> Do not forget, my Dear, that once we loved.
> Remember only, free of stain or smutch,
> That passion once went naked and ungloved,
> And that your flesh was startled by my touch.

And though the processes of mortal change
Delude you now to different belief,
Consider only that the heart's a strange
Quick turn-coat, undeserving of your grief.

Forget, – regret, – should these two words be brothers?
If rhyme to rhyme be kith, so let them be!
Pass from my heart towards the heart of others,
But in your passing, half-remember me.[6]

Harold knew that she was upset, but Vita's self-concealment was practised and effective. When, a few days after this, she and Harold and the boys were at the Woolfs' for Sunday lunch, Virginia noticed nothing amiss; the whole family seemed to her 'very flourishing ... overflowing into every corner of life.'[7]

But to someone else she seemed 'a tragic figure.... All this beauty of environment, and she is not happy.' This was on the day before she posted 'Valediction', and the percipient visitor to Sissinghurst was an older woman, Christopher St John. Vita showed Christopher and her companions her bedroom: 'Contemplating a worn piece of green velvet on her dressing-table, I felt my whole being dissolve in love. *I have never never ceased to love her from that moment*,' wrote Christopher.

The great actress Ellen Terry, the heroine of Vita's youth, had ended her life in a picturesque and primitive cottage at Smallhythe, only a few miles from Sissinghurst, which was now occupied by a curious trio: Ellen Terry's ageing daughter Edith (Edy) Craig, the painter Claire Atwood (known as 'Tony') and Christopher St John.

Christopher St John's real name was Christabel Marshall; she had been living with Edy Craig since 1899, sharing her London flat in Covent Garden as well as, later, the cottage at Smallhythe. She supported herself inadequately by music criticism and by illuminated calligraphy. She was a fervent Catholic convert; her 'St John' stood for St John the Baptist, for whom she had a special devotion. When Vita met her in 1932, she and Edy Craig had just completed their joint editing of Ellen Terry's *Memoirs*.

Edy Craig produced plays in her old barn at Smallhythe, which had been converted into a theatre. Vita was invited to read *The Land* at the Barn Theatre; after a rehearsal, she had described the set-up to Evelyn Irons:

The producer is the most tearing old Lesbian – not unlike your friend Radclyffe Hall – but without any charms for me, I hasten to add.... Seeing me trying to sharpen a pencil, she came up and took it away. 'Here, give me that,' she said, 'no woman knows how to sharpen a pencil.' You may imagine Orlando's indignation.

The Barn Theatre put on one major annual performance as a memorial to Ellen Terry. Vita and Harold had gone over to see John Gielgud and Peggy Ashcroft in *Twelfth Night* on 24 July. It was not the dominant Edy Craig who had been most struck with Vita but her companion Christopher St John, who saw her for the first time that night. The irises of Vita's eyes, Christopher noticed, were 'set in the white like islands. This is rare in the normal and well-balanced.' Vita, she thought, was a frightened woman. The invitation to Sissinghurst, where Christopher fell irrevocably in love over a strip of worn green velvet, was sent as a thank-you for the theatrical event.

Meanwhile Vita, abandoned by Evelyn, was saddled with Olive; Boski had left and Hilda was taking over some of her secretarial duties; and the Croydon Repertory Company was putting on an adaptation of *The Edwardians*. *The Land* was read by Vita at the Barn Theatre on 18 September; the Woolfs, Stephen Spender, William Plomer, Eddy Sackville-West, Raymond Mortimer and their painter friend Eardley Knollys all came, as well as the local gentry. 'It is very enjoyable and Viti is pleased bless her sweet heart,' Harold wrote in his diary.

What Vita did not know was that during her reading Stephen Spender and William Plomer were overcome by giggles. They liked Vita, but the combination of her breeches, *The Land* and the solemn rustic setting were suddenly too much. Loyal Virginia scolded them furiously afterwards. Vita's reading, she railed at them, had brought tears of emotion to her eyes. (She could not bear Vita to be laughed at by anyone but herself.)

Vita's radio reviewing was drying up now that Hilda was no longer Director of Talks; but *Family History*, appearing in mid-October, sold 6,000 copies before publication. This not very distinguished novel, which Vita dedicated to her mother, is chiefly interesting in that the plot turns on the destructiveness of possessive 'feminine' love. In it Vita also attempted a spelling reform that met with no one's approval and that she never repeated. She adopted 'thatt' as an alternative to 'that', to 'differentiate between the conjunction and the demonstrative adjective or relative pronoun' in the interest of clarity: as in, for example, 'I fear that thatt will irritate my readers.'

'Thatt' apart, *Family History* is the story of a forty-year-old widow, Evelyn Jarrold, romantic, feminine and conventional. She has a close relationship with her handsome seventeen-year-old Etonian son Dan, who adores her. This sentimental mother-son relationship is not much like Vita's with Ben, but Dan in the book is an idealized portrait of Ben –

as Vita told him. The year *Family History* was published Ben showed her a poem he had written. Vita was thrilled, and wrote to him : 'Aren't you thankful I didn't get it in time to include it in *Family History* ? Ha ! ha ! But how I wish now I had composed a few poems on Dan's behalf, instead of making him a painter only. I might have known that he would be a poet as well as a painter. How silly of me.' In *Family History* Dan's mother Evelyn falls in love with Miles Vane-Merrick, fifteen years younger than herself – the age-gap perhaps replacing homosexuality as a focus for the world's disapproval. Vane-Merrick is the V. Sackville-West hero with touches of Harold : he is 'an Elizabethan man', a Member of Parliament, scholar and author, tall, handsome, country-loving, politically left-wing, committed to his work and to his home – a castle in the country which is in fact Sissinghurst, described in detail, still at the nettle-clearing stage. Evelyn resents Miles's need to be alone to fulfil his commitments to writing, politics and farming ; she wants him to be with her all the time, in an uninterrupted romantic idyll. Although the two are deeply in love, their relationship is wrecked by her unreasonable expectations.

The novel is a justification of the 'separate development' idea of marriage that Harold and Vita themselves practised, and a condemnation of claustrophobic possessive love. Unable to live without Miles, Evelyn dies – after a tear-jerking thirty-two-page illness worthy of a Victorian romance. The novel also includes a sketch of the Bloomsbury ambiance (deeply distrusted by the conventional heroine) in the household of Miles's intellectual friends Viola and Leonard Anquetil, who first appeared as the socially subversive elements in *The Edwardians*. The novel is saved from being a tract by the fact that although the author disapproves of Evelyn's values, she adequately conveys her charm, her attraction and her good faith.

Harold's *Public Faces* came out around the same time as Vita's *Family History*, and Michael Sadleir, his publisher at Constable, told him proudly that 1,600 copies had been sold pre-publication. Harold told him of Vita's much larger figure. 'He says, "But then she has broken through." I say, "Broken through what ?" He says, "The middle-class belt." Buy a pair of shoes at Fortnum and Mason.' But he did not resent her success. 'She is eternal sun to me,' he wrote on an October Sunday of pouring rain. And Vita was never impressed by the success of her novels.

In the vacuum left by the loss of Evelyn Irons she allowed herself to be consoled by Christopher St John's adoration – a mistake, and unfair on Christopher. She took Christopher to see Long Barn, she let her hold her hand, she gave her a string of blue beads from Persia and she gave her hope.

Christopher's devotion was also a refuge from money worries – her own and B.M.'s. Her mother was gradually going blind; Vita found special paper with raised ridges for her to write on. B.M. was also getting odder – she gave luncheon parties in her bathroom at White Lodge, since it was the warmest room in the house. Lunching with her on 4 November and trying to sort out the bitter entanglement of her money quarrels with Lutyens, Vita burst into tears and shouted 'that she had to do everything and make money for everybody'. B.M. was suddenly sorry for her, and stepped up the hampers of groceries that she still ordered regularly from Selfridges to be delivered to Sissinghurst every week.

Another source of Vita's tension was the news that Violet Trefusis had been to see Virginia about the possibility of Hogarth publishing her novel *Tandem*. 'Lord what fun!' wrote Virginia to Vita,

> I quite see now why you were so enamoured – then: she's a little too full, now, overblown rather; but what seduction! What a voice – lisping, faltering, what warmth, suppleness and in her way – it's not mine . . . how lovely, like a squirrel among buck hares – a red squirrel among brown nuts. We glanced and winked through the leaves.[8]

Vita went to visit Christopher at Edy Craig's flat in Covent Garden in early November, and allowed Christopher to come with her in the car all the way to Tonbridge, where she was put on a train back to London. Vita told her that 'the list of those whom she really loved was a short one, and now I was on it.' Driving out of London, on the Westminster Bridge Road, Vita 'stretched out her left hand to me and said: "I do love you, for all you give me."' (Christopher, like Mary Campbell, kept a love-journal about Vita.) Before putting her on the train home Vita parked the car in a side street in Tonbridge. 'Then she gave me a lover's kiss. In all my dreams of her I never dreamed of that. . . . I never knew unalloyed bliss with V. except on that November day.' She wrote to Vita on 10 November:

> Orlando de-breeched, allow me to tell you that you are as dear to me thus, as breeched. I can never think of your sex, only of your humanity. I could love you in breeches, or in skirts, or in any other garments, or in none. I know you must be a woman – evidence your husband and your sons. But I don't think of you as a woman, or as a man either. Perhaps as someone who is both, the complete human being who transcends both.

On 20 December 1932 Vita gave Christopher – who was very ugly, odd-looking, and in her late fifties – one night of love, never to be repeated. In the short term, Vita was not going to have to take the consequences: within ten days she would be aboard the *Bremen*, with Harold, bound for New York and three months in the United States.

# CHAPTER 23

THE lecture tour in America was undertaken to make money. When Hilda Matheson took over Boski's secretarial duties, she pointed out to Vita and Harold that they were living beyond their means, which they knew only too well, 'and must either reduce our living or increase our means'. They decided on the latter course. Hilda worked out the time-tables and accounts with the Colston Leigh Bureau (Vita, being the better known in America, had the more strenuous schedule) and saw them off on the *Bremen* on 29 December 1932. They left behind them a Sissinghurst that had changed again in the course of the year : the avenues of poplars had been planted, and the yews in the front courtyard, the Yew Walk and the Rondel. Hilda was in charge of every-thing at Sissinghurst while they were away ; her own home was now Rocks Farm, on Dorothy Wellesley's estate at Withyham.

In America, they did one of their 'What I Think About Marriage' radio debates ; and Vita had prepared lectures on novel-writing, 'Novels and Novelists', 'Changes in English Social Life', 'The Modern Spirit in Literature', 'Travels through Persia' and 'D.H.Lawrence and Virginia Woolf'. She chose these last two as writers she could admire whole-heartedly. Her admiration for Lawrence had increased since she read his published letters ; she went so far as to say to Ben that she felt he was 'a sort of Christ, a second Shelley' :

> A really and truly *pure* spirit – all flame, and no dross. It seems so ironical that the bishops and the Sir John Reiths [Director General of the BBC] of this age should regard him as a pornographical writer ... and the people who mis-understand his poems and who misunderstood *Lady Chatterley's Lover* are the really filthy people, not Lawrence himself.

When they arrived in New York in early January 1933 they stayed at the Waldorf Astoria, and at a dinner there on their first evening she and

Harold met the Lindberghs. Colonel Lindbergh, five years before, had made the first transatlantic solo flight; they had been tragically in the news more recently when their only child was kidnapped and murdered. 'One thinks of what they have been through and is shy to meet them,' as Harold wrote. Anne Morrow Lindbergh was now pregnant again; and the Nicolsons and the Lindberghs were to see more of one another in the future.

New York was suffering the effects of the Great Depression; the hotels were half-empty and the atmosphere sombre. The advent of the Nicolsons, especially Vita, was an occasion of public interest. Her appearance on arrival was reported in detail:

> Wearing a brown felt hat of masculine design and unpressed brim, Miss Sackville-West bore out in appearance her theories of independence for women. She wore a woollen ensemble of blue, including a Slavic shirtwaist, cerise earrings and glass beads of similar value or color. Her brogues included thong lacings to the calf of her leg. She nervously removed her masculine hat when greeted, after the fashion of her gallant husband.

Most press comment was free of this note of light irony: both she and Harold got a unanimously good press in America. Reporters called her tall, beautiful, soft-voiced; they praised her naturalness and her fine dark eyes, the amber or red velvet dresses she wore for lecturing, and her jewels. Sadly, they often wrongly referred to her as 'heiress of Knole': 'She has inherited the biggest house in England.' In Buffalo a photographer asked her to wipe off her rouge 'and refuses to believe it is my natural complexion until I offer to let him rub my cheek with a handkerchief.'[1]

Her first lectures, at Springfield and Yale, went well, and she began to relax. They had a heavy programme, which Harold enjoyed less than Vita. On 13 January he wrote to Ben:

> Mummy has lectured four times already and I three times. We are a popular success. Mummy is lionised like nohow. She is given orchids and met by groups of people at stations. You know how modest she is. It will do her good. But really it is extraordinary what a wide public she has in this country and how famous she is.

Harold disliked the stretches of time when they were separated by their different itineraries and engagements. 'I was not made to be a lecturer in the USA unless accompanied by my own neighbour.' ('Neighbour' had a special affectionate significance for Vita and Harold. At Long Barn, where they had slept in adjoining rooms, they had begun each day that Harold was home by calling out to one another, 'Good morning, neighbour !')

In Boston, Vita avoided a visit to the museum, where the tapestry from the chapel at Knole now hung. In Washington, she stayed at the British Embassy, designed by Lutyens : 'McNed's Embassy here is lovely, but the roof leaks and all the fires smoke. How delighted Grannyma would be if I told her that !' she wrote to Ben. She went to tea with President Hoover at the White House before going on alone to lecture in Buffalo, Niagara and Toronto. 'Oh my sweetheart,' Harold wrote to her, 'how young you looked as you came down the stairs last night with your little bags. Such a mar. So alone. So wanted and so alone.' From Niagara Falls she excitedly described to him how she had been shown round by Dr Harry Grant, an old man 'half scholar and half philosopher' who lived alone in a house opposite the Falls : 'And Niagara roars continually at the edge of his lawn.... I think it is very good for you and me to have come to America. I am glad we did. I am getting a lot out of it. There may be moments when we are tired and nauseated and bored, but on the whole it is infinitely valuable.' But when Harold met her again in Chicago he thought she looked tired. 'I fear this is all a dreadful strain for her.' She was off again, in a blizzard, to St Louis – where the college girls put her in a difficult position by asking her to 'explain' *Orlando*, and where she gratifyingly observed that the copies of *All Passion Spent* she was asked to autograph had 'changed from 9th edition to 10th'. She moved on to speak in Kansas City, Des Moines, Bloomington and Minneapolis. From Des Moines on 15 February she wrote to Evelyn Irons:

Everything is just a whirl in my head – a whirl of parties, railway trains, lecture-halls, autograph books, strange houses, strange hotels, reporters, flash-light photographs, and women, women, women. If anything could cure me of a weakness for my own sex it would be a sojourn among the Women's Clubs of America. There just don't seem to be any men here at all, and I am beginning to long for an honest trouser....

Bless you, my bad but darling Scrape. I love you very dearly, – God knows why. Perhaps because you made me so unhappy.

She wrote to Evelyn again from Columbus, Ohio, about an arrangement she had made to bring Olive Rinder some money while she was away. Olive was to write articles, which Hilda Matheson was to send out to magazines as by V. Sackville-West.

If she has done 16 bones [articles] as she says, she ought to get £244 (roughly) for them. For God's sake don't tell anyone she does them, though. It is a rather discreditable arrangement, – I mean, I don't approve of ghosting, – but it was the only way I could think of to keep her supplied with funds and yet let her feel that she was earning them herself.

She rejoined Harold in Cincinnati, and again Harold noticed how good she was at this new enterprise. 'Toying with her orchids she faces thousands with a smile,' as he told Nigel. A note of loving irony creeps into his letter to Ben the same day; her new talent for oratory and the receiving of adulation, he wrote, 'is going to prove highly inconvenient in the future. I see a women's club being started in Hastings for the sole purpose of giving Mummy scope for her new attainment.' And to Vita herself – who was off once more, to Philadelphia: 'My sweet – what a strong old horse you are – touch wood. . . . I confess that I myself find all this slushy adulation very trying – and irritating in the sense that all unrealities are irritating. Of course I know that you and I are very gifted and charming. Only we are not gifted and charming in the way these people suppose.'

While they were away Ben, now eighteen, had left school and was spending some months abroad before going up to Balliol College, Oxford – his father's old college – in the autumn. From France, he had been writing regularly to his parents about, among other matters, his sexual anxieties. Harold wrote reassuringly to him from Lexington, Kentucky, that both he and Vita would be 'sympathetic and unshocked' whatever he told them. From Lake Forest, Illinois, Vita also broached the subject of sex with Ben; she had not seen what Harold had said, 'but I'm sure it was a good letter'. She went on :

Sex is probably the most exciting but not the most important thing in life. Its very excitingness easily makes it appear the most important. I remember someone saying to me once, 'I feel I want to live for nothing but this.' And then, years afterwards, I met that person and they said they were sickened. . . . Promiscuity is *essentially* cheap and sickening. Not on moral grounds, – you know that I am without conventional morality, – but on, almost, aesthetic grounds. It is *cheap*. Easy. Vulgar. Lowering. A real prostitution of oneself. . . .
    God, what priggish letters I do write to you! They aren't really priggish, though. They are only because I love you so much. . . . It all comes back to my old motto, of which you must be sick by this time, 'To thine own self be true'. . . . I wish I had had somebody to give me this advice, when I was 18. I had to work it all out for myself. Luckily, I fell in love with Daddy.

When she arrived back in Washington early in the morning of 25 February Harold, who had heard again from Ben, greeted her at the station with the words, 'I'm afraid you will mind. Ben says he is homosexual.' Later in the day Vita wrote another long letter to Ben even though, as she said, 'I know I can't write wise and amusing letters like Daddy':

> But Daddy was wrong in one respect: I *don't* mind. I should mind very much if I thought it meant that you thought you would necessarily miss what you call, and rightly, 'the whole happiness and joy of marriage'. Put that out of your head at once. It doesn't follow in the least. Two of the happiest married people I know, whose names I must conceal for reasons of discretion, are both homosexual, – for you know, probably, that homosexuality applies to women as well as to men. And then, again, take Duncan and Vanessa. (They aren't actually married, but they have lived together for years, and it amounts to the same thing as being married.) They love each other even as Daddy and I do, though Duncan is almost entirely homosexual. So you see it is not necessarily a bar to happiness of *our* sort. ...
>
> So I don't feel gloomy about your future life, – you see, I do really believe that marriage of the kind that Daddy and I have been able to achieve, enriched by children like you and Niggs, is the happiest thing one can aim for on this earth, – I don't feel gloomy about it, because I see no reason why you shouldn't achieve it too, eventually, after you have sown your wild oats and got bored by their incessant crop. One gets such a lesson in this country [America]: one realizes how much one longs, humanly, for *roots*; and the deepest roots of all are those one finds in one's own home, among one's own belongings. Which is a thing one can achieve only by happy marriage, – or at least, that's my idea of it.
>
> So don't worry, my Benzie, about homosexuality. As a matter of fact, you know so few attractive women that you may be wrong about yourself altogether. ... I know that a lot of unhappiness comes from a muddle as to what matters and what doesn't matter. I do so want you to avoid the latter. I don't want you to worry over things that aren't worth worrying about.

Vita spent some time in New England, staying with a wealthy teacher at Smith College, Mina Curtiss, at her farm in the Berkshire hills. At a dinner in Northampton she met Robert Frost, 'a handsome man who goes in for good conversation'. Hilda Matheson telephoned to her from Dorothy Wellesley's house – Vita spoke to both of them – with the home news: Mrs Staples, the Nicolsons' cook since 1926, was going to marry the gardener, George Hayter. She was forty-one and he was twenty-six; Louise Genoux, Vita's maid, was scandalized. The marriage took place, though Vita and Harold went on calling her Mrs Staples, from long habit.

On 20 March Vita was in Santa Cruz, where she went to tea with Mabel Dodge Luhan – 'plump and dark, dressed in black with a white jabot; her hair cut square like a mediaeval page'. Dorothy Brett was there, 'very untidy and chinless and deaf, her head tied up in an Indian handkerchief'. She had studied painting at the Slade with Carrington and Mark Gertler, and had become a friend of Virginia's; she had not been home for nine years – both she and Mabel Dodge Luhan had been adoring supporters of D.H.Lawrence, who had died in 1930 – and she bombarded Vita with questions. 'How is Duncan? Does he still fall in love with young men? Is it true that Carrington killed herself? How is Ottoline? How is Virginia? How are Gertler and Siegfried Sassoon?'[2] Vita bellowed her indiscreet answers into Brett's ear-trumpet.

The best part of the Nicolsons' American tour came at the end. In late March they were together at Smoke Tree Ranch in Southern California, 'a three-roomed cottage in the middle of the desert, with nothing but a few cowboys and a stray coyote to interrupt,' she wrote to Virginia. 'Magnificent stars overhead, and mountains all around. The desert itself is carpeted with rosy verbena. It is exactly like Persia, and we are as happy as larks.' William Randolph Hearst had asked them to stay, but hearing that George Bernard Shaw was to be there they declined, being in need of peace and quiet.

> Los Angeles is hell. Take Peacehaven [a spoiled resort village on the Sussex coast], multiply it by 400 square miles, sprinkle it all along the French Riviera, and then empty the Chelsea Flower Show all over it, adding a number of Spanish exhibition buildings, and you have the Los Angeles coast. The Americans have an unequalled genius for making everything hideous.[3]

Hollywood, however, had been fun; they had been shown round by Gary Cooper. And in Pasadena, Vita told Virginia, a young lady had rushed up to her 'and said she was writing a book about you and me. Isn't that nice for us? Would I give her an interview to tell her our (yours and mine) views on Imagery? Fortunately I was able to say I had only just time to catch my train.'

When they came home, she said, they would be 'battered but enriched – not only by dollars.' By the time they regretfully left Smoke Tree Ranch Vita was telling Harold about the plot of a new novel she was going to write – another novel of transformation and renewal, like *All Passion Spent*. Harold commented in his diary:

> It is about a middle-aged woman who has had some deep sorrow in her life and becomes benevolent and neutral. It is divided into two halves. One half is in life the other in death. The life part is to take the form of the Grand Canyon. ... The death part is to take the shape of a wind-jammer from which, at stated intervals, people tumble overboard.... It is the sort of thing which only she could carry off and the sort of thing which she could do better than other sorts of things. (Hope she reads that bit.)

Vita conceived the book that was to be *Grand Canyon* before she ever saw the Grand Canyon. The novel was not to be written for some years, and she did not in fact use the theme of death at sea until she came to write her very last book, nearly thirty years later.

They reached Grand Canyon on 1 April. Vita was immeasurably elated. They watched a dance of Hopi Indians (something that she was to use in the novel) at the El Tovar Hotel. 'Viti (who with difficulty has been able to tear herself away from the adjoining junk shop where there are bead-work gloves, and turquoise rings, and chunks of petrified wood – and from which she has purchased among other things a little green stick with a feather at one end and at the other a stone painted to match) is deeply impressed by the Grand Canyon. So am I,' wrote Harold, who was not quite so carried away as she was. From the Indian watch tower at Desert View they saw the Canyon in all its colours, and the Painted Desert beyond. 'Viti says it is like nothing on earth. She adds that she feels "increased". I say that I do too.' Vita's responses to places were violent and monopolistic.

From Charleston in South Carolina – the last stop before they came home – she wrote to Virginia that the Grand Canyon was 'the most astonishing thing in the world.... You can't imagine, Virginia, what the Painted Desert is like. It is every colour of the rainbow, broken by great pink cliffs the colour of the rocks in Devonshire. And the sun blazes every day, and the air makes you want to leap over the moon.'

She and Harold were going to come back 'in order to motor all through Texas, Arizona, California and Mexico taking tents with us in order to camp in the desert. ... Why don't you and Leonard come with us?'⁴ But Vita never went back to the United States.

Between them, Harold calculated, they had visited fifty-three different cities, made seventy-two different journeys, spent sixty-three nights in the train, and covered 33,527 miles. The *Bremen*, in which they returned, reached Cherbourg on 21 April, and Ben and Nigel were waiting to meet them. Then Southampton, and London, where Hilda Matheson was at 4 King's Bench Walk to greet them.

Old Lady Sackville was piqued by the way Hilda appeared to be organizing Vita's life. 'I have received *instructions* from Miss Hilda M. about meeting or seeing Vita,' she wrote crossly in her diary the day before the *Bremen* docked. When, two days after they came home, the Nicolsons went to see her at White Lodge, she and Harold had a violent quarrel. A couple of weeks later, on 9 May, Ben went to see his grand-mother on his own.

Several times already B.M. had spoken to the children against their parents and their parents' friends, but never had she gone so far as she did on this occasion. In her senile resentment she spilled out to Ben the crude facts of his parents' unconventional private lives. She told him that his father had had boys in all the cities where he had been *en poste* ; she told him the Violet Trefusis story, and said that the marriage had nearly been wrecked a second time by his mother's relationship with Virginia Woolf. When Ben came home, alone at dinner with his parents, he told them what B.M. had said. 'It was they who were deeply embarrassed, not I,' Ben wrote. 'I took their embarrassment to mean that they were shocked that Lady Sackville should do anything so monstrous. It never occurred to me that they were also distressed that the central drama of their lives was being played back to them by their own adolescent son.'⁵

Ben later said that he had been bewildered but not seriously disturbed by his grandmother's assertions. He knew his parents were not wicked people, as B.M. had suggested. He was eighteen years old ; he was already aware of his own sexual ambivalence and he may have guessed the identity of the 'two happiest married people I know' who were 'both homosexual' in the letter his mother had written to him from America.

But he may not have guessed. Young people, out of self-protection, put up defences. Both the Nicolson boys, in adolescence, must have known a great deal that they did not realize they knew, or want to know. Ben was an extremely sensitive person : he had already had some kind of emotional crisis at school. This cruel display of facts may have made Ben's layer of defences even thicker, flattening feelings that would have been unmanageable and insulating him permanently from intimate involvement with anyone. In later life he was to have many friends, but seemed unable to sustain a relationship for long with lovers of either sex. If this was the price he paid, it was a high one.

Harold and Vita were appalled by what had happened. They had always been at pains to present their marriage to the children as a model of affection and solidity. Although B.M.'s attempt to set Ben against them failed, Harold wrote in his diary, 'it will have been a shock to him, and might have had very serious consequences. Feel sick with anger.' When Virginia and Leonard came to Sissinghurst at the end of the month, they were told the story over lunch. 'The old woman ought to be shot,' was Virginia's reaction. She wrote to Vita afterwards : 'You see, when one's 18, words, news, revelations about one's parents have an immeasurable force ; and that she should have taken it on herself to say them.... It seemed to me so dastardly, so immoral : so fiendishly inhuman.'⁶ Vita replied :

Virginia, darling, you are an angel, – an angel, I mean, to understand so unfailingly when one really minds about something as I minded my mother telling Ben about my morals and Harold's. Not that I am in any way ashamed of my morals or H's. Only Ben might have had a horrid imprint sealed on his mind. Luckily he didn't – a tribute, I think, to our bringing up of him ? (That's a boast. But you, also, even you, boast sometimes.... mine, merely the way in which I have brought up my sons, so that they should accept without wincing the revelation that their father and mother are both to be numbered among the outcasts of the human race.) Anyway you are a darling to have realized that I minded.[7]

Harold went to Venning, their lawyer, to put him in the picture about B.M.'s state of mind, in case some restraining action should become necessary. But it was Vita, not Harold, who had had the courage to do the humanly right thing for Ben, on the night he had come back from White Lodge and told them what had happened. As Ben later wrote, his father 'with his fastidiousness could never have brought himself to enlighten me ; by letter, perhaps, but not face to face' :

It was my mother who sat on my bed at midnight and into the small hours, and I suppose it was the first intimate talk we had ever had. She told me that everything was true except the part about Virginia endangering their marriage, but none of it mattered a hoot because the love they bore each other was so powerful that it could withstand anything.[8]

She had told him only the truth ; and their relationship was unharmed. Ben, after his months in France, was to spend the summer studying art in Italy. Vita wrote to Virginia : 'Wouldn't you like to be eighteen and going off to Italy alone for two months ? I would. He is very nice, is Ben.'[9]

# CHAPTER 24

VIRGINIA herself had been away in Italy when Vita first came back from the United States. Vita had told her she had better come back soon 'or I shall begin exploring London for a divertissement.... Would it surprise you to learn that I miss you very much indeed? In order to console myself I am thinking of taking up with Marlene Dietrich. So don't linger too long at Montepulciano if you value the rather touching fidelity of your old sheepdog.'[1]

This teasing truculence towards Virginia was becoming a signal of Vita's restlessness, of the dreaded emotional vacuum that Virginia herself could no longer fill. There were no great reunions with anyone when Vita came home; there was only the crisis with Ben and B.M. Hilda's role was administrative and supportive. Olive Rinder was a recipient of emotional and financial alimony. Christopher St John was to hand; she had written many long letters to 'My Lord Orlando' in her beautiful script while Vita was away, but Vita did not love Christopher, who wrote in her love-journal:

> In the letter she wrote me from the *Bremen* as she neared England, she said: 'Don't say you are disappointed in me. I couldn't bear that. There is no one in whose estimation I would rather stand high than in yours.' Well, I wasn't disappointed in *her*, but I was disappointed in the development of our relationship. She did not seek me out swiftly when she came home.

On a hot day in June, Vita took Christopher for a drive. 'I loved her so dearly that day.... "Shall we ever have another night together?" I asked, longing to reach through her body her innermost heart. "Why not?" she said.' There never was another night together, but Christopher never stopped loving Vita. Seeing herself as St Christopher to Vita's Christ, she swore to 'carry her over' for ever. Vita, having allowed this situation to develop, carried it as her own burden for as long as Christopher lived ; she was never disloyal to the Smallhythe trio.

She and Harold gave one of their joint performances, 'Impressions of America', at the Barn Theatre at Smallhythe. George Plank, who was in the audience, described the peculiar success of their technique, now much-practised, to B.M. : 'I think they have invented an excellent form of entertainment. There is a very great art in the *way* they do it : Vita sitting at a table, and Harold walking about, and it is done with as much naturalness as though they were at home, and entirely unrehearsed – simply a few *subjects* jotted down and then they discuss them.'

Vita tried and failed to begin her American novel ; and the Woolfs asked her to gather up material for a *Collected Poems* to be published by them. Vita thought Leonard was right when he said 'it would prepare the ground for any longish poem I might write later.' But she could not rid herself of the suspicion 'that it is all a little pretentious'. Harold, after *Peacemaking*, was writing a life of Lord Curzon, and she admired his application and literary skill – different, and often superior, it seemed to her, to her own. 'I like his lucid mind, and his ease of expression. He is like a person who knows how to use a scythe, – rhythmic, sharp and sure.' They were both reviewing books for the *Daily Telegraph* as well, but Vita felt underemployed and impotent.

They had royalties in a bank in Paris and used this money for an Italian holiday in the car, driven this time by Jack Copper, their new chauffeur. Nearly twenty years later, Harold received a fan-letter from a stranger recalling a characteristic glimpse he had caught of the Nicolsons in a restaurant at Dieppe at the start of that long-ago holiday :

> You were deep in the perusal of a French newspaper, rocking your chair backwards and forwards, until with a crash you disappeared backwards from our view. I half-rose to go to your assistance, but the sight of Miss Sackville-West, aloof, mildly amused, quite unperturbed, and evidently used to this kind of thing, made me return to my seat and watch your return unharmed to your table.

Harold was as clumsy and inept in practical matters as he was neat and incisive in literary ones.

They came home in mid-July, after meeting Ben in Bologna, to find that Nigel had appendicitis. They drove to Eton overnight and brought him back to London for an operation.

Nigel was not the only invalid in the family that summer. While they were in America, Harold's younger sister, Gwen St Aubyn, of whom he was very fond, had been in a bad car accident and damaged her skull. Vita and her sister-in-law had never been close ; Gwen moved in a different social circle. But towards the end of July 1933 Vita began seeing far more of Gwen, whose nerves were in pieces after the accident and who was going to need rest as well as medical care for many months. Sissinghurst was an ideal setting in which to gain strength and to rest.

Gwen had five children of her own (she had contributed articles on child care to Evelyn Irons's page in the *Daily Mail*), but in her present weakness she called out Vita's protective instincts. Against opposition from her family Gwen was under instruction in the Roman Catholic faith, and her growing belief was to affect Vita both in her thinking and in her writing. Yet in superficial ways Gwen was far more worldly than Vita, who was surprisingly affected by this too : Virginia observed that Vita had started slightly painting her lips, but unskilfully – 'Now why ?' Gwen spent more and more time at Sissinghurst ; to Christopher St John, who came regularly that autumn to give Ben lessons in calligraphy, she looked like 'a battered, a dissolute child'. Vita explained her growing friendship with Gwen to Virginia in August, telling her at the same time why she could not come over to Rodmell : 'The point is, that I've got my sister-in-law staying here, and she's been ill, and I am supposed to provide the cure. Country rustication and all that. And Harold is writing a book about Lord Curzon, whereas I am not writing any book at all, so I am free to look after his sister, – which I like doing.'[2]

Gwen was editing a book of advice to parents (*The Family Book*, 1934), which interested Vita. They sat on the steps of the tower discussing family relationships and the inner lives of women. Vita's affection for people of her own sex often led her into dominating, 'maternal' relationships with them ; and her own mother at this time was causing her new anguish. B.M. was going to law against her own butler, who had issued a writ for non-payment of wages. She accused Vita and Harold of being in league with the butler in order to ruin her, and turned them out of her house. Small wonder, with the Ben incident still fresh in her mind, that Vita was ready to share Gwen's preoccupation with mothers and children. And at the core of Vita's interest was her constant self-questioning about her own psychology. She wrote in her manuscript book at this time a poem 'To My Mother' which includes these stanzas :

Was it some vein of loaded ore,
Some difficult darkness of your soul,
That worked in me an alchemy
And held me in a new control ?

Some strangeness in your foreign blood
Some dangerous temper of your steel
That stamped me with the different
Reversed impression of your seal ?

Some mixture of that Latin strain
Commingled with my English race,
That dowered me with double wealth ;
The double substance of your grace ?

Was it some glance of your blue eyes,
Some gesture of your lovely hands,
That twisted me to dreams and rhymes
And led me to the senseless lands ?

Vita had written the poem as a dedication to her mother of her *Collected Poems* (optimistically subtitled 'Volume I' – there was never a Volume II), but B.M. would not accept it. She did not want to 'be in a book with V. Woolf, the author of that awful book *Orlando*, and also I don't want to give to the Public so much of our intimity [*sic*].' She allowed Vita to put simply 'To my Mother'. B.M. was moved and disturbed by the love poems, and liked the others. Vita seized on any opportunity for reconciliation, and wrote to her :

I am glad you liked 'Reddín' [included in *Collected Poems*]. I put quite a lot into that poem, of what I believe and hold to be true. It was a real confession of faith.

But, darling, why do you say that you think you and I have neglected or misunderstood love ? I don't think we have ! I know I love you – and I know you love me – in spite of all our squabbles and quarrels and unkindnesses and differences of opinion.... We are both rather difficult people, perhaps, but perhaps our difficultness makes us understand each other better than anyone else in the world would believe ?

Vita began giving talks on gardening on the BBC every Friday evening ; they were printed in the *Listener*. She advised her listeners according to the system that she and Harold were following at Sissinghurst, arguing in favour of 'straight determined lines' as a basis for garden design, broken by overhanging shrubs and straying plants : 'Too severe a formality is almost as repellant as the complete absence of it.'

The harmony between herself and Harold was not always perfect that year, in the garden. He would have liked to do away with her aviary of budgerigars, and they squabbled. Harold's diary :

*27 September 1933* Measure the central path in the kitchen garden, and Gwen helps me. Finally Vita refuses to abide by our decision to remove the miserable little trees which stand in the way of my design. The romantic temperament as usual obstructing the classic.

*30 September* Try to measure out vista in kitchen garden prolonging the paved paths but come up against artichokes and V's indignation. Thereafter weed lawn sadly. We have a discussion about women's rights afterwards.

But that year they completed some important and permanent projects – principally the pergola resting on column fragments in the Rose Garden (now the White Garden), with beneath it the paved space where they ate in summer; they called it the Erechtheum, after one of the temples of the Acropolis.

Harold still had no regular income. Rupert Hart-Davis, then working for the publisher Cape, tried to woo Vita away from the Hogarth Press with mentions of far greater advances than Leonard Woolf could ever offer, but Vita could not be moved. She wrote to Virginia that Hart-Davis was 'too amiable by half', and that she could tell Leonard that 'no temptation to leave the Hogarth Press is any temptation at all.'[3] The Woolfs were touched by her loyalty and did not forget it. After the success of *The Edwardians* and *All Passion Spent* in particular, Vita could have found a welcome at any of the larger, richer publishing houses. (*All Passion Spent* had already been made into a play, under the title *Indian Summer*.)

Harold thought of swallowing his pride and asking the *Evening Standard* to take him back, but was saved when Vita discovered that she had nearly £3,000 in her French bank. However, the strain was telling on her too. One October afternoon, after working on the proofs of *Collected Poems*, she felt giddy and collapsed by the lake. 'I do not think it is anything more than nerves,' wrote Harold. Gwen's condition too still gave cause for anxiety. Her doctor said it would be another year before she was well. Vita described Gwen's treatment to Virginia: a 'red-hot rabbit-hutch' was put over her head twice a day, which made her faint. 'They seem to think that this will dispel the injury to her brain.'[4] Gwen's doctor approved of her spending most of her time in the tranquillity of Sissinghurst, and explained the benefits of the arrangement to Gwen's husband who was, Harold said, 'quite sensible' about it. 'He quite sees that Gwen must be left to make her own arrangements, and not [be] bothered by obligations, domestic or otherwise.' A room was furnished for Gwen at the top of Vita's tower.

Vita's *Collected Poems*, when they came out in late November, did not cause much of a stir. The reception, or lack of it, seemed to justify her self-deprecating line in 'To Enid Bagnold', included in the book – 'And I, God's truth, a damned out-moded poet.' (W. H. Auden came to Sissinghurst that year, provoking in Harold the reflection that 'were I a communist, the type of person I should most wish to attack would not be the millionaire or the imperialist, but the soft, reasonable, tolerant, secure, self-satisfied intellectual like Vita and myself.' But Vita, as a poet, was not self-satisfied.) Virginia wrote to her, after publication, 'You're an odd mixture as a poet. I like you for being "out-moded" and not caring a damn : that's why you're free to change ; free and lusty.'[5]

Ever since *The Land*, Virginia had been gently urging Vita towards change ; but Vita suspected that she could not change. She, who had always thought of herself as avant-garde, at least in her attitudes and opinions, felt her fragile sense of herself and her values threatened.

Though Vita could not know it, Virginia's way of speaking about her to others had subtly changed too ; she wrote to Lady Ottoline Morrell on the last day of the year : 'And Vita came with her sons, one Eton, one Oxford, which explains why she has to spin those sleepwalking servantgirl novels' (but this did not prevent Virginia from being delighted at the prospect of Vita's next novel for the Hogarth Press) :

> I remain always very fond of her – this I say because on the surface she's rather red and black and gaudy, I know : and very slow ; and very, compared to us, primitive : but she is incapable of insincerity or pose, and digs and digs, and waters, and walks her dogs, and reads her poets, and falls in love with every pretty woman, just like a man, and is to my mind genuinely aristocratic ; but I can't swear that she won't bore you.

On Christmas Eve 1933, there had been an unhappy scene at Sissinghurst. All four Nicolsons – Gwen was with her own family – were in the boys' bedroom listening to the Christmas broadcast. It began, as Harold described in his diary, with someone 'reading out in a sing-song voice the more rhetorical passages of the New Testament'. 'Oh God,' said Nigel, 'Poetry !' This produced in Vita what Harold called 'a nerve storm'. She turned off the wireless, 'and we troop down the stairs again with bowed heads' :

> We try and eat in silence. Then Vita bursts into tears and leaves the room. She wanders sobbing by the lake in the dark. I am very worried. She then returns and says that Niggs is cynical and sneers at all that matters. He has all my worst qualities. Hard and cold. Never *feels* anything. 'Oh yes he is kind and affectionate and all that, but he has no passion – all with him is hard cold intelligence.' Poor Niggs has gone to bed in self-imposed disgrace rather puzzled at what it is all about.

Harold blamed himself for taking Vita and domestic happiness too much for granted. 'She is a dark river moving deeply among shadows' :

> She really does not care for the domestic affections. She would wish life to be conducted on a series of grandes passions. Or she thinks she would. In practice – had I been a passionate man – I should have suffered tortures of

jealousy on her behalf, have made endless scenes, – and we should now have separated, – I living in Montevideo as H.M.Minister, and she breeding Samoyeds in the Gobi desert.

Here, in general if not in detail, Harold as usual was right. Given that Vita was Vita, the survival of the marriage depended on Harold being as he was, however much she sometimes longed for him to be otherwise. Vita's own diary betrayed nothing of her disturbance; Harold, on the last day of the year, summed up his precarious financial situation, and added:

> Another, and sadder, worry is Vita's health. Her nerves have been better than last year, but they are pretty bad. She is apt to have emotional storms, which are beautifully controlled, but which may be symptoms of an approaching climacteric which frightens me. Her edition of collected poems has not received much critical notice, and this has been a deep disappointment to her. I cannot but feel that the next two years will be difficult for her and unhappy.

But Vita, nearly forty-two, was not menopausal, and the next two years were not as bad as he feared. Gwen St Aubyn had an operation on her head in January 1934, and Vita took her away to convalesce in Portofino, where they found that the medieval *castello* was to let, complete with servants. There was a lovely garden with iris and narcissus already in bloom, and olive terraces down to the sea. Better still, the *castello* at Portofino was the setting of a popular novel, *The Enchanted April* by Elizabeth Russell (1928), in which two disillusioned married women escape from their household duties to the romantic castle and an irresponsible way of life; they are joined at the end by their husbands, and find their lives and their marriages renewed. Harold wrote to Vita: 'It all comes from Gwen reading Tauchnitz editions of the works of Lady Russell. I hope you are both very uncomfortable and happy. Bless you sweet babies.' Gwen told her brother that she was 'happier than I ever have been in all my life. You see for once I have no responsibilities, Vita having taken them all.' And Vita to Virginia:

> I am writing to you on the terrace of a tiny old castle perched above the sea. . . . The sea sparkles three hundred feet below . . . a large bottle of golden wine stands at my elbow.
>     I write and write and write, – which reminds me, would you please tell Leonard that I can probably give him my new book by May or June. . . . It is, at present, called *The Dark Island*.[6]

*The Dark Island* it remained; she was writing a story whose setting, not uninfluenced by the position of the *castello*, was mainly her fantasy of St Michael's Mount in Cornwall, which Gwen's husband Sam was due to inherit.

Harold joined them in Portofino and the three went on to Monte Carlo – where they had tea with Somerset Maugham, and Harold went off for a few days on his own devices – and thence to Marseilles, where they took a boat to Tangier. In Casablanca, walking by the sea, Vita and Harold discussed women's lives and whether women 'enjoyed their freedom'. Harold's diary, 23 February :

> I state that women who would have been quite happy and contented as married in 1910 are now feeling restless and nervous. V. says that in every revolution there is a transitional stage. That women have for centuries been suppressed and that one cannot expect them to slide quite naturally into freedom. This saddens me. I know that there is no such thing as equality between the sexes and that women are not fulfilling their proper functions unless subservient to some man. But I do not say so, as it would hurt Vita's feelings.

It would have more than hurt Vita's feelings. It would have filled her with rage and despair. The argument continued :

> Love seems so wide a thing to women that unless their emotions are canalized by some sort of social discipline they get lost. Gwen, for instance, thirty years ago would have felt herself fortunate at having a faithful husband and five adoring children. But now she feels that these obligations limit herself, that there is a more important function for her somewhere beyond the function of wife and mother.

This not unreasonable feeling was presumably part of what Harold meant by saying women 'get lost' for want of 'social discipline'. (It was well for their marriage that he made an exception in the case of his own wife. Harold did not like women very much, though he could be charming to them. Vita, for him, was in a category of her own.) 'V. regards this new feeling as a revolt against the centennial domination of the male. But the male always had a sense of responsibility. Women seem to lack that sense and only to have a feeling of possession or belonging.'

From a tent on the edge of the Sahara Vita wrote to Virginia about feasts of sheep roasted whole eaten under the stars, and dervish dancers who 'stuck daggers and hammered nails into their naked stomachs. ... Oh, it's fun, being abroad ! How smug it makes England seem. It hasn't rained here for three years.'[7] Harold went home alone by train, while Vita and Gwen travelled back through France slowly ; arriving in England on 23 March, they found him in a nursing-home with blood-poisoning, the result of a mosquito bite in Morocco.

Vita found trouble of another kind as well. She had been declining to

see the pathetically amorous Christopher St John; Christopher confided her misery in Ethel Smyth, who challenged Vita with her
hardness. Ethel passed the story on to Virginia, who also approached
Vita on behalf of Christopher, 'that mule-faced harridan of yours'. Vita
was adamant about not seeing Christopher alone, but invited her to
Sissinghurst along with Edy Craig and Tony Atwood.

Also, Ben had failed his prelims at Oxford. He told his mother, 'I am
bad at being made to do anything which, had I my own way, I would not
do.' It was this attitude, rather than his failing the examination, which
disturbed Vita, since it was one that she recognized all too well; she
wrote to Ben rather as Harold had sometimes written to her in the past:
'My dear Ben! really! What *do* you imagine life is made of?'

> I curse you for being lazy, wasteful (time, not money) and *without guts*. I curse
> you for thinking a veneer of culture acquired principally from the conversa-
> tion of people older, better educated, and above all more hard-working than
> yourself, is an adequate substitute for real knowledge, real application, real
> mental muscles.

He had, she said, a 'veneer attitude' to life:

> 'Veneereal disease, that's what's the matter with you.... Don't think I'm
> cross: I'm not: only firm. And determined that you shouldn't go soft and
> squelchy. I have had too many temptations in that direction myself, not to
> know the danger they offer. I haven't overcome them successfully myself....
> Bless your silly black head, my own darling.'

She felt very close to Ben, and he to her. Ben wrote to his father a few
weeks later that he was going to spend a weekend with Robert Birley,
who had taught him at Eton: 'Theirs is a married life which I envy as
much as yours, and Virginia's and Leonard's':

> Mummy has been particularly sweet to me lately, respecting my indepen-
> dence but not for one moment being indifferent. In a way our relations are
> very satisfactory: although we never, or very rarely, and when we do it is
> embarrassing, show affection to each other, we both know (at least I do) that I
> love her so much no vital misunderstanding could ever exist between us. And
> I feel that with you.

When Ben was in Vienna the following summer, and she wrote urging
him to see Schönbrunn, the imperial palace, she said: 'Oh dear, this is
all rather *à la recherche du temps perdu*, – my lost youth, and so on. But I
revive my lost youth in you, so it doesn't matter – "Thou art thy
mother's glass, and she in thee Renews the lovely April of her prime." A

comforting reflection. Bless you, my dark boy, my dark lovely boy.'
Vita also got on well with Gwen's children, especially Philippa, the
eldest. She was less easy with her own Nigel, who wrote to his father
in October, 'I must now write to Mummy. By the way, I am not in
disgrace, am I? She has only written to me once this half.' Harold was
the recipient of Nigel's confidences and replied at length with an equal
intimacy. (Harold wrote remarkable letters to both his sons.) Nigel's
apparently dismissive 'Oh, poetry!' had left its mark on Vita and was
not an isolated incident. In his *Portrait of a Marriage* he cites similar
misunderstandings, including a particularly unhappy one at about this
time:

> She paused one evening at the bottom step of her staircase, turned to me
> shyly and said: 'I have written a new poem, and I would like to dedicate it
> to you.' 'Oh, don't do that,' I replied unthinkingly. 'You know that I don't
> really understand your poetry.' She went up the tower without a word, and
> when she came to dinner I saw that she had been crying. By this in-
> comparably cruel remark I had meant, 'Your poetry is the side of you that I
> have never shared, and cannot claim to share. I don't deserve the
> dedication. It would be a form of intrusion.' But that was not what I said.
> . . . I was then 17.

Nigel did not unjustly use the word 'intrusion' to describe what he had
really meant. Vita kept her working life very private. In all their years
at Sissinghurst, the boys only entered her tower room half a dozen
times. After Nigel had been home for a weekend in November 1934,
she sent a good report of him to Harold, who was in America researching his biography of Anne Lindbergh's father, the statesman
Dwight Morrow. But Nigel wrote to Harold: 'Mummy seemed very
tired to me, or rather not tired, but stale: I think she needs more inter-
course with the outside world. But she does hate it so.'

This was increasingly true. She found it hard to cope with visitors
without Harold there to mediate and talk; she told him she felt
'decreased by talking while others are increased'. Virginia, visiting that
summer, sensed her constraint. Virginia had very little opinion of
Gwen, and this added to the unease. But with Gwen for company
when she needed it, Vita was happy writing, gardening, taking the
boat on the lake, picking up windfall apples to make cider, stripping
bullrushes to stuff cushions: 'You just break them open, and out
comes a great cloud of the most delicious silky floss, golden-white . . .
it is just like putting one's hand into a heap of ducklings without any
bones at all.' Apart from her broadcasts, almost her only outing in the
autumn of 1934 was to lunch with Ivy Compton-Burnett to meet the
scholar-traveller Freya Stark, on whom she reported to Harold: 'She is

neither impressive nor attractive. Small and slight and biscuit-coloured. She is just off to Yemen, alone. . . . She must be a brave woman.'

It was not Gwen St Aubyn who wanted Vita to renounce the world; indeed Gwen conspired with Harold to improve Vita's eccentric wardrobe. Her 'bargain basement' clothes were to go, and 'V. will wear breeches and rags here, plain coats and brilliant shirts for tidier. In London simple dresses and coats with vivid tops – and even in the evenings nice clothes and not bedroom slippers.' Vita unwillingly co-operated, partly because she had to have something to wear for the series of six Northcliffe Lectures she had undertaken to give at the University of London. She wrote to Harold on 9 November: 'I went to try on my new clothes at Jay's; they are all right, I think. But I hate women's shops, and all the clothes talk. Also I hate seeing myself in mirrors, and being asked to look at myself. I do so absolutely loathe my own appearance.' Virginia was unimpressed by the new Vita. 'She has grown opulent & bold & red – tomatoe [*sic*] coloured, and paints her fingers and lips which need no paint – the influence of Gwen; under-neath much the same; only without the porpoise radiance, and the pearls lost lustre.' That was when Vita delivered her manuscript of *The Dark Island*. Leonard Woolf read it first, and told Virginia it was 'perilous fantastic stuff, a woman flagellated in a cave. How much will the public stand?'[8]

On 1 October, the twenty-first anniversary of their marriage, Harold wrote to Vita from America, 'My darling – my own darling – you know when I pause and look back upon that stretch of time I feel such grati-tude for you. I know you loathe marriage and that it is not a natural state for you, but I also know you love me dearly.'

*The Dark Island*, which is dedicated to Gwen St Aubyn, came out ten days later. Four thousand copies were sold in advance of publication, and Doubleday, Doran paid $5,000 for the American rights. It is the most mysterious of Vita's novels, because the most private. As Virginia said, 'you give me the impression of writing too much in the personal zone, as if you couldn't get far enough off to convey the outside aspect,'[9] and so the motivation of the characters remained unclear. Harold did not like the book. 'I hope you do not get disagreeable reviews my dar-ling. I feel rather doubtful about that book somehow. . . . All I mean is that sadism is a subject about which I do not care to read.'

Vita was always humble about her fiction. 'I know you hated my book,' she said to Harold. 'No grievance.' And at Sissinghurst, just before publication, she told Virginia calmly that most people agreed with her in thinking it a bad book. Virginia as always was touched by Vita's 'gentleness, truthfulness, modesty'. Ben, who designed the lettering for the dust-jacket and had read *The Dark Island* in manuscript, got it about right when he wrote to his father : 'She is obviously a poet and not a novelist, and *All Passion* was so good only because it was so poetic. But of course I don't tell her all this. And this novel is interesting as showing her idea of Gwen and an idealized Grannyma in the person of old Lady le Breton.'

The heroine of *The Dark Island* is Shirin, whose gay, 'elemental' character is based on Gwen's. (Shirin was Vita's nickname for Gwen; it means 'sweet' in Persian.) As a young girl, Shirin meets Venn, the young heir to the island of Storn, topped by a Norman castle where he lives with his grandmother Lady le Breton – manipulative, charming, 'beautiful and wicked and good'. Venn's dark nature is revealed at once; he twists the girl's wrists, shows her 'Andromeda's Cave' and tells her 'I should like to chain you up ... naked and beat you and beat you till you screamed.' His 'curious pleasure' in this thought 'reminded him somehow of the curious pleasure he had experienced when, as a prefect, he had first thrashed a lower boy at school'. Venn and Lady le Breton are later described as 'just damned souls, gone wrong': Vita was investigating and elaborating on the blacker, madder aspects of her mother and herself. (Three years after her mother's death, remembering how she had held 'her lovely hands' as she lay unconscious, she said: 'She was *une âme damnée* if ever there was one.')

There was a streak of sadism in Vita's own nature. One remembers her stories of childhood, how she terrorized visiting children and beat them with nettles. There was the side to her that, as she frequently hinted, she had never let Harold see. There are fantasies of erotic violence in some of her unpublished sonnets to Mary Campbell (which she readdressed, in 1931, to Evelyn Irons):

> ... And shall you, gliding in your silken shirt,
> Deny the hidden bruises of your flesh,
> Nor boast the livid honour of your hurt?
> Come; if they fade, I'll brand you deep afresh.

The fantasy of violent revenge for infidelity comes in another Evelyn poem, called in her *Collected Poems* 'Tess':

> Oh then beware! for shouldst thou stray or falter
> From that high mark my arrogance has set,
> Stern as a priest I'll stretch thee on an altar
> And in revenge all tenderness forget.

She expressed her feelings about revenge in the year of *The Dark Island* to Harold, apropos of the kidnapper of the Lindbergh baby:

Personally, I should like to put the man into the electric chair with my own hands, and give him two months agony, to pay him out for the months of mental agony he made them endure. Ben and Gwen both say they can't understand this. But then you know I am very revengeful when I love, and so I can understand other people being revengeful too. It seems to me that people are mostly very tame, – but I daresay I'm wrong. Anyhow I know I would gladly torture anybody who had hurt anybody I really loved.

Like a child, she was capable of giving physical expression to frustration or anger. Yet not only Harold, but Virginia and everyone close to Vita, spoke of her unfailing gentleness as one of the qualities they most loved and valued in her. The violence was the other side of the coin, her 'damned soul', and it was given lurid expression in *The Dark Island*. Shirin, in the book, later marries Venn, not because she loves him but because she loves the castle and the island of Storn. Thus Venn never truly possesses Shirin, though he possesses Storn and treats her as an interloper there.

Rather as Virginia in *Mrs Dalloway* had divided her own personality between Mrs Dalloway and crazed, frightened Septimus, so Vita projected the non-Venn, non-violent side of herself on to Shirin's devoted woman friend Cristina. Cristina is 'tall and tawny', a sculptor and 'something of a gardener'; she thinks Shirin would be 'safer with me'. Cristina, while protecting Shirin, understands how Venn came to be as he is – which is to say, that Vita had some idea of the causation of her own cruel impulses. The domination of his grandmother and the knowledge that he was heir to great possessions had produced in Venn 'a self-belittlement and a corresponding desire for domination'. To the people 'over whom he had been able naturally and legitimately to exercise domination, he had proved a kindly and friendly master; but towards Shirin, who had resisted him, a devil and a sadist, morally and physically.'

Vita's heroes are always in possession of their ancestral homes; she never wrote a fictional version of the loss of Knole. But it was Knole, rather than any single person, that had eluded Vita. This basic grief was a factor in the battle for integration between 'Venn' and 'Cristina' that she sometimes lost. Eddy Sackville-West was one of the few people who wrote to her praising *The Dark Island*, and she replied:

I'm glad you liked the dark island. Was it so very indiscreet? Yes, I suppose it was. But only to the initiated. . . .

Darling Eddy, I do really love you so deeply. . . . Do you remember once at Long Barn we were alone together, and I started telling you how very difficult I had always found it to establish any real contact between us? And then we got interrupted by something or other, and the moment passed, and has never returned.

I think perhaps Knole gets in the way always. Sub-consciously. You won't understand this, and I can't explain.[10]

Cristina, in the novel, witnesses Venn fulfilling his boyhood fantasy and beating the chained, naked Shirin in Andromeda's Cave; and the book ends with Venn killing Cristina in a deliberate sailing accident, and Shirin killing Venn who has spiritually killed her already. The book received cool, puzzled notices in the national press, and rather better ones in provincial newspapers. As Virginia said, 'the grateful provinces adore the aristocracy.' Vita did not publish another novel for eight years.

# CHAPTER 25

GWEN St Aubyn's religious faith found an echo in Vita's search for integration. When Harold was in America she wrote to him, uncharacteristically, 'I pray for you every night and morning and at intervals throughout the day.' Talking to Nigel in January 1935, when he told her he was 'on the borderline' as regards religion, 'I said I was too.' It was in this atmosphere that she decided to write a book about Joan of Arc. 'I envy Gwen, who really believes in the efficacy of prayer. I don't, I can't, but I pray all the same.'

In February 1935 she went to London with Gwen for the latter's confirmation in the Roman Catholic Church, wishing she could 'sympathize more wholeheartedly'. Vita stayed in the car and read a novel while Gwen was at confession, but attended the confirmation, 'feeling a complete outsider'. 'I *wish* I could understand what it all really meant to people who believe,' she wrote to Harold. She channelled her curiosity and ambivalence into her Joan of Arc research: 'She leads one into all kinds of subsidiary reading, such as the psychology of other visionaries.'

In April Vita, Harold, Gwen and Nigel motored across France to Marseilles and joined a cruise ship to Greece; their old friend Hugh Walpole was on board. Harold gave lectures to the cruise passengers on the Greek sites, and on the voyage back Vita gave a talk on modern poetry. Afterwards, they met their driver Copper in Rome, and Nigel and Harold returned by train while Vita and Gwen motored slowly back through France. The point was to see the places most associated with St Joan, Domrémy and Orléans, and to buy the French books about her that Vita needed in Paris. They arrived back at Sissinghurst in early May, in time for the bluebells, and Vita started writing her book at once.

The major Sissinghurst project that year was the completion of the 'big room' (now called the Library), a conversion of part of the gatehouse block with an outside door on to the tower courtyard. In 1930, it had been a stable for cart-horses. They had a large window put in one end and made a fireplace from fragments of an Elizabethan one found buried in the grounds. Harold, surveying the new room before Vita was back from France, felt unhappy about it. He did not like the proportions, and knew they would never love it as they had loved the big room at Long Barn: 'It will always have about it a feeling of a hospital ward in some Turkish barrack.'

In the summer, while Harold was in the United States with Ben, Vita set about furnishing the new room. She put in it the walnut statue of a virgin by the Yugoslav sculptor Rosandic, which was the subject of her poems 'Vestal Virigin' and 'Absence'; the same statue, cast in lead, stood in the garden outside the dining-room window. She got a fine lapis table from her mother, and some pieces from Long Barn. (Long Barn was let furnished to Sidney Bernstein; to ease their financial situation, B.M. had nominally bought it from them for £8,000, but there was no legal transfer. Vita collected the rent, paid the rates and sent B.M. any remainder.) When she had done what she could, she too conceded defeat, writing to Harold on 20 July: 'This is a note of warning: the big room is A FAILURE. Try as I may, I cannot get it to come together.'

They filled the new shelves with some hundreds of their thousands of books, and tried using the room. But it was soon abandoned as a regular family sitting-room. The Nicolsons continued their fragmented family life, the dining-room in the Priest's House being the only room where they were easily able to be together, and that only at meal-times.

The previous summer, Vita had reviewed Dorothy Wellesley's *Poems of Ten Years 1924–34* encouragingly in the *Observer*. Now, suddenly, Dottie had encouragement from an eminent source. Ottoline Morrell brought W. B. Yeats down to Penns-in-the-Rocks; Yeats took to both Dottie and her poetry, and they became fast friends. Yeats, aged seventy, was collecting material for his *Oxford Book of Modern Verse*. Out of touch with current trends, he took Dottie's advice on whom to consider. He included seventeen and a half pages of Dottie's own poetry in his anthology and believed, as he told her, that she would 'grow into a great poet'.

That was just the injection of hope and excitement that Dorothy Wellesley needed. Nor can she have been altogether displeased that Yeats had to be forcibly converted to the work of her famous friend. The poet wrote to her on 6 July: 'I take back what I said of your friend Sackville-West, having found "The Greater Cats" [from *King's Daughter*], that has the irrational element rhetoric never has. It is very moving.'[1] He included it in his anthology.

At the end of October Dottie asked Vita over to Penns to meet him. Vita was not over-excited at the prospect, but 'I should have to go some time, and I should rather like to meet the old man.' She was tired, having sat up late working on St Joan. She described her impressions of Yeats to Harold :

> He is the sort of person who has no small-talk at all, but who either remains silent or else plunges straight into the things that matter to him. So little small-talk has he that he doesn't even say 'How do you do ?' when shaking hands on arrival. He just sits down on the sofa, looks at his nails for two minutes' silence, and then tells one stories about Manley Hopkins or Lady Gregory or Gogarty, or else expounds his views on T. S. Eliot and *les jeunes.*

He also read part of his introduction to his *Oxford Book* aloud. 'A handsome man,' wrote Vita in her diary that night, 'with a fine head but also unfortunately a fine tummy.'

In early 1935 Virginia was writing to Vita with sprightly nostalgia : 'My mind is filled with dreams of romantic meetings. D'you remember once sitting at Kew in a purple storm?' By March Virginia had faced facts and was referring in her diary to 'the defection of Vita'.

> My friendship with Vita is over. Not with a quarrel, not with a bang, but as a ripe fruit falls. . . . But her voice saying 'Virginia?' outside the tower room was as enchanting as ever. Only then nothing happened. And she has grown very fat, very much the indolent country lady, run to seed, incurious now about books ; has written no poetry ; only kindles about dogs, flowers, and new buildings [at Sissinghurst]. . . . And there is no bitterness, only a certain emptiness.[2]

It was Vita's losing her looks that saddened Virginia as much as anything. They met again in London in November, and Virginia wrote to Ethel Smyth that she couldn't really forgive Vita 'for growing so large' :

> with such tomato cheeks and thick black moustache – Surely that wasn't necessary : and the devil is that it shuts up her eyes that were the beaming beauty I first loved her for . . . but she remains, as I say, to me always modesty and gentleness no longer incarnate, but as it were hovering above her, in a nimbus.[3]

Harold did not worry so much about the way she looked. He worried about her refusal to see people. In February he had been reproaching her for her 'love of loneliness' :

You start by minding crowds, you then come to hate parties, after a little even the society of your friends is a strain, no people are encouraged to come, and then finally any living being becomes an interruption to your loneliness and Ben and I and Niggs will be made to feel we are not wanted. Which would be bad luck on us. My sweet – I do so dread it coming to that.

He was still worrying about it when she was in France with Gwen in the spring : 'I wish I knew how far you hated attachment. On the one hand there is your loathing of being an appendage. On the other hand even you must like to feel that it is important to other people what happens to you. . . . *I have a very difficult task.*' Especially since he no longer even knew how to address the envelopes : she preferred now to be 'The Hon. V. Sackville-West' even in her private correspondence, instead of 'The Hon. Mrs Harold Nicolson'. A diary-poem that she had written two years earlier, in the arid period after she came home from America, describes the state of mind that had gradually produced so noticeable an alienation from social life. It is dated in her manuscript book 16 May 1933, but it expresses what she felt most of the time now :

> Days I enjoy are days when nothing happens,
> When I have no engagements written on my block,
> When no one comes to disturb my inward peace,
> When no one comes to take me away from myself
> And turn me into a patchwork, a jig-saw puzzle,
> A broken mirror that once gave a whole reflection,
> Being so contrived that it takes too long a time
> To get myself back to myself when they have gone.
> The years are too strictly measured, and life too short
> For me to afford such bits of myself to my friends.
> And what have I to give my friends in the last resort ?
> An awkwardness, a shyness, and a scrap,
> No thing that's truly me, a bootless waste,
> A waste of myself and them, for my life is mine
> And theirs presumably theirs, and cannot touch.

What hurt Harold most was her apparent lack of interest even in what happened to him. He was still desperate to get back into public life ; in June he heard by telephone that he had failed to be adopted as parliamentary candidate by the Sevenoaks Conservative Association. Vita was in the room at the time but 'paid no attention at all', and went on playing with Martha, her new alsatian puppy. 'It is as if she hadn't been aware in any sense that this may mean a final decision regarding politics versus literature. Strange, very strange.' (Vita did not take politics seriously ; literature was far more important to her.) Harold was bored and frustrated. He longed to be back in his old niche at the Foreign Office. 'I feel terribly out of it all down here and in a backwater.'

He went abroad in the summer, writing *Helen's Tower* and amusing himself in Paris and Venice with Victor Cunard. But 'I would not have her different one single inch', he wrote of Vita on their wedding anniversary; and almost at once, in the autumn, his political future fell into place. Italy invaded Abyssinia, and the news all over Europe was disquieting. Harold was offered the candidacy of a seat at West Leicester; he was adopted as the National Labour candidate.

Vita was in France again in mid-October, taking a further look at the Joan of Arc sites. (Lunching at the Ritz in Paris on the way home, she and Gwen ran into Violet Trefusis; Violet was also on their cross-Channel boat next day. 'Avoid her,' Vita wrote in her diary.) While she was away, Harold wrote to her about his candidacy. He had a problem with money for his election expenses, and asked her to lend him £500. She was quite prepared to do this, but she was not prepared to be involved or to take part in the election as an 'appendage': she regarded it as his business exclusively. This was awkward for Harold, though he had made it clear to the organizers in West Leicester that his wife was not interested in politics. Nevertheless: 'I fear, darling, that you will have to come up twice, as they are very pi here and will think we are divorced. I have spoken vaguely about your not being very strong and having gone to France for a few weeks. But you will have, I fear, to appear at least twice and to sit on the platform.' The first weekend she was home, the gulf between his excitement and her disassociation frightened them both. They had a 'painful dinner' together on the Sunday night. 'Very unhappy about it all,' Vita wrote in her diary. But she still would not agree to go up to Leicester. She wrote to him there the next day:

> I fear you have gone away hurt – and I mind that dreadfully. It is no good going over old ground, so I won't – only to say that apart from what you call 'principle' I do genuinely think that an isolated appearance would be worse than none, because of its inconsistency, and that also it would lead to bazaars and things *after* the election, if you get in, which I do very truly and sincerely hope you will. ... Do you remember also what I said last night, that I had always cared very deeply about your writing and even your broadcasting (don't murder me!) and my admiration for your very rare gift, which I rate *far* higher than you do, is great and has always been accompanied by the very deepest interest, so don't run away with the idea that I 'have never taken any interest' as you said, in the things that mattered to you.

The truth was that Vita took an interest in the things that mattered to Harold where they coincided with the things that mattered to her. Diplomacy and politics were not among these. Harold replied that he was not hurt. 'Only puzzled and disappointed and rather cross.' She was not, he thought, selfish in the ordinary sense, but selfish in the sense that she ignored his 'need and difficulties'. He told his election agent that his wife was 'not up to it' – which he felt was not altogether a lie.

Ben and Nigel (who was now up at Balliol too) went to Leicester to be with their father on polling day. Vita stayed at home, and wrote daily, or twice daily, letters of love and encouragement to Harold. He told her not to bother to wait up to hear the election results: 'My own sweetest Viti – you have been so thoughtful about writing and telegraphing now. It really *does* make a difference to feel you really care what happens to me. Sometimes I feel you don't.' 'Of *course* I shall sit up to listen to the wireless,' retorted Vita; and she heard, in the small hours of 15 November, that he had got in by eighty-seven votes.

Harold was a Member of Parliament. He had achieved what he most wanted and needed. He could happily accommodate himself again to the differences between himself and Vita, differences that in many other couples would by now have become irreconcilable incompatibilities. Rushed and excited, he wrote to her on House of Commons writing paper on 16 December:

> I shall not be able to write much these days which I hate not doing as oh dear I do love you so my old looney my dearest dearest Viti.
>
> I do not think that any person has ever been loved so gaily as you are loved by me. But you do not believe all that since what you like is PASSION and not spent in the least. Really good Triana jealousy and knives. That's what Mar likes. Anything else is just your old armchair.

Vita was already worried in late January 1936 because of Gwen, who had to undergo yet another operation. While this was taking place in London, Vita was telephoned at King's Bench Walk by Miss Macmillan, her new secretary at Sissinghurst. (Hilda Matheson had found a job worthy of her capabilities as Secretary to the African Survey under Sir Malcolm Hailey.) 'Mac', as everyone called Miss Macmillan, told Vita that B.M. was dangerously ill at White Lodge. Vita reached her mother's bedside shortly before she died. Harold arrived just afterwards: 'Take Vita into the other room. . . . She has left a pathetic little typewritten notice saying that she was to be cremated and the ashes flung into the sea. Vita is much harassed and shattered, but inwardly, I think, relieved.'

The boys came from Oxford; Vita very much wanted them to see their grandmother, perhaps because she had been so moved by seeing King George v's ritual lying-in-state at Westminster Hall a few days before. She wrote to Nigel afterwards:

I am glad you came to White Lodge, and realized what death is. I think probably you will never feel any horror about it now. As you say, it is something very quiet and natural. Especially quiet. 'After life's fitful fever he sleeps well.' I do feel that Grannyma's life was a fitful fever, but that now she sleeps well. I feel also that all her faults are forgiven her, and only her virtues are remembered. That is what I prayed for, whenever I knelt at her bedside.

You were both so good to her, and so understanding, and for that I shall always be grateful to you both. Just think how I should have minded, if I had had horrid cynical sons, who hadn't understood my very difficult mother in the least! But you did understand her, and my only regret is that you didn't know her in the days when she was really gay and charming. You would have really loved her then, as I did. I did really love her, Niggs, and I mind awfully her having died, although I know (with my reason) that it is the happiest thing for *her*.

'Stunned', as she wrote in her diary, Vita returned to Gwen's sick-bed. Harold, with B.M.'s secretary, scattered B.M.'s ashes in the sea. 'Miss B.M.' Vita wrote sadly on 9 March, her forty-fourth birthday.

But she had gone out and bought thirty new budgerigars for her aviary, and ordered 200 brown trout for the lake. The Lindberghs were in England and arranged to lease Long Barn. Vita was pleased. 'They are charming, and more muddle-headed than I could have believed possible. I arranged everything for them, even to ordering their coal! They obviously love the place already.' *Saint Joan of Arc* was finished and sent off to Cobden-Sanderson, who were publishing it, with a dedication to her niece, Gwen's daughter Philippa.

B.M.'s death made the Nicolson's financial situation much easier, even though they had to sell £46,000 of her securities to pay death duties. 'You will be well off with £5,000 a year gross plus what you make,' Harold told Vita. The boys would have £1,000 a year each, which gave them independence. But Vita was worrying about her adored Ben's indolence and apparent lack of purpose. She did not like the fact that he took no exercise, shaved only infrequently and forgot to do things he was asked to do. She was relieved when that summer he got a Second in Schools, his final examinations at Oxford, and continued to love in him his 'sort of innocence and idealism and purity . . . I mean he's so utterly uncynical and unblasé.' Cynicism was increasingly becoming the cardinal sin in her value system, and 'character' her preferred virtue. She even gave Harold sober advice about the importance of his making 'considered pronouncements' in the House of Commons: 'I think that in the long run this is what wins respect in public life, more than any amount of brilliance and wit, both of which you have. And in your case, you have so much of both that people might be liable to distrust you, – you know what English people are.' The English, conservative side of her own nature was in the ascendant, and the irresponsible gypsy side fading. She was becoming in small ways more right-wing, and had no patience with Lady Hastings, 'horrible woman', who came to collect contributions for 'the Reds' in the Spanish Civil War. She had little sympathy for the new King Edward VIII's dilemma over Mrs Simpson, which led to the Abdication at the end of the year. 'That all this should have happened for such a 2½d piece of trash! Of course she should never have allowed it, and any decent woman could have prevented it.' Vita hated what she called 'the modern world'. Unlike Harold, she hated *Ulysses*. And her doctor, whom she consulted over a small indisposition, told her she was going through 'the change of life'.

On 27 May 1936 Vita went to London to buy a trout rod, get her first copy of *Saint Joan of Arc* from the publisher, and to lunch with Virginia, who found her 'very solid, physically and mentally. I don't find any corruption or change: but then my relations with her have never altered: always affectionate,' she told Ethel Smyth. Virginia was on the brink of another severe bout of nervous illness, and in actuality Vita's visit upset her so much she had to take chloral afterwards. She begged Ethel not to tell Vita this.

Ethel Smyth disliked *Saint Joan of Arc* very much, and wrote to its author to say so. She was 'upset' and 'staggered' that 'the person who wrote *Passenger to Teheran*' had written what she considered such a bad book. She suspected that Vita had leant too much on the opinions of Gwen St Aubyn. Christopher St John specially asked to review *Saint Joan of Arc* in the *New Statesman*, of which Raymond Mortimer was literary editor. In her love-journal, Christopher condemned Vita's 'insufferably *patronizing* attitude towards a saint of God', and described the book as 'weak and wavering, long-winded' and full of 'feeble jocularity'. Her review was correspondingly severe.

Virginia did not like Vita's book much either; she called it 'a massive and wholesome work' to Vita herself, and 'good hack work' in a letter to Ethel. But it was a Book of the Month in both Britain and the United States, and mostly the notices were respectful. What Vita's friends were really deploring was her absorption in topics for which they felt she was ill-suited and had only tackled because of the religious preoccupations of her sister-in-law.

In fact the subject was well-suited to Vita's temperament and interests, quite apart from the fact that she made responsible use of the available secondary source material. Joan's determined assumption of male clothing was something she could understand, and she attributed to Joan 'as queer a mixture of feminine and masculine attributes as ever relentlessly assaulted the enemy and then wept to see him hurt.' Joan's obstinate, fervent personality she found easy to sympathize with. She wrote from the heart when, discussing Joan's relationship with the Dauphin, she said, 'Tepid people always do regard passionate people as nuisances. Evasive people always do regard dynamic people ... as nuisances.' She approached the problem of Joan's visions and voices in 'a spirit of complete open-mindedness and acknowledgement of our ignorance', as she wrote in her introduction, where she also set out her own religious position :

> I am not, myself, what is called a 'religious' person in the orthodox sense of the phrase, nor yet a member of any organized Church. I do, however, confronted with the ultimate enigma, believe, and believe deeply, in some mysterious central originating force which the natural weakness of human nature finds it necessary to symbolize in a name, an amalgam of fear and comfort.

It was this attitude that the orthodox Catholic Christopher St John would have found 'patronizing'.

Ten days after *Saint Joan of Arc* was published, Vita was going through her mother's belongings at White Lodge and came across some papers 'which absolutely thrilled me'. She took them home. These papers contained the depositions of the Spanish witnesses taken before the Knole succession case of 1910. 'They are exactly like the Jeanne d'Arc witnesses : all labourers and suchlike people, living in a little village in Spain. I have not read them through yet, but have read enough to make my mouth water. They are all people who knew Pepita and her mother.'

She went to the family solicitors and borrowed the reports and files on the Knole succession case. She read everything she could lay her hands on about the romantic life of her gypsy Spanish grandmother. After dinner on 20 August she began to write *Pepita*, which was to be one of the most personal, humane and lively of all her books. By continuing the family story beyond Pepita, she took the opportunity to explore her mother's complex life and personality with humour and insight, and to make some artistic sense of her own childhood and mixed heritage. By committing the Spanish gypsy to paper and to the discipline of history and of art, she completed, for good or ill, the exorcism of the Spanish gypsy in herself – an exorcism that her immersion in Sissinghurst, middle age and, above all, the death of her mother, had begun.

# CHAPTER 26

VITA tried to combat her reclusiveness to please Harold. On the first Sunday in November 1936 they had an invasion: 'Peter Quennell, Cyril Connolly and Mrs C., Mrs Quennell and one of the Paget twins came over from Possingworth in the morning; all very dirty and sozzled.' Then Eddy and Eardley Knollys came to lunch, Sam St Aubyn and two of his daughters for tea, and Ozzie Dickinson. Though Vita liked most of these people individually, she did not enjoy them collectively. 'Quiet day at Sissinghurst' was her preferred diary entry, so much so that the phrase became a family joke. Peter Quennell, after an interval of nearly half a century, published his own recollections of meeting the Nicolsons that Sunday. If his party seemed 'dirty and sozzled' to Vita, she astonished them by her appearance. Her fears that people thought she looked strange were not just paranoia.

> Larger and a little taller than her husband, who, beside her, with his fresh pink face, briar pipe and conventional tweed coat, had a somewhat boyish or under-graduateish air, she resembled a puissant blend of both sexes – Lady Chatterley and her lover rolled into one, I recollect a contemporary humorist observing. From beneath the brim of a hard black Spanish hat sprang locks of wiry black hair. Her eyebrows were heavy; her eyes were very dark; her cheeks had a vivid carmine tinge; and she made no effort to disguise the perceptible moustache that Virginia Woolf affectionately mentions. Though she wore long ear-rings and a small pearl necklace, the end tucked inside a lacy shirt, they were accompanied by a heavy corduroy jacket; while her legs, which reminded Mrs Woolf of stalwart tree trunks, were encased in a gamekeeper's breeches and top-boots laced up to the knee.... She had all the impressiveness that surrounds an archaic cult-statue; and I shook her firm hand with a certain sense of awe.[1]

She was working on *Pepita* until two and three in the morning after gardening all day. In the course of the year the lime walk had been paved and the beds between the limes planted. She was trying to establish a gentian bed, and had started her orchid house. Central heating was being installed in the big room.

In the New Year of 1937 she braved the outside world again and had what she called her 'winter season': three days in London. Harold was away in Africa on a government project, and the party she gave at King's Bench Walk was really for Ben's sake. He had a temporary job at the National Gallery in Trafalgar Square, and Vita thought that if she asked people to meet him they might in return 'ask him to their dinner and luncheon parties'.

When her three days were over, she wrote to Harold: 'I don't understand how people can live in London for choice. Everything seems so unreal and confusing.' But her efforts to make contact with others seemed to be having results – one of the best being that she was getting on more easily with Nigel. 'He told Gwen he had liked being here [at Sissinghurst] with me, which touched me, as I had already felt that we *had* got on much better; less constraint, you know, and so on,' she wrote to Harold.

A regular visitor to Sissinghurst, even in Vita's most anti-social phases, and even though the creature comforts provided were minimal, was Sibyl Colefax. Known chiefly as a lion-hunting hostess, Lady Colefax presented a different face to the Nicolsons, whom she loved and revered. She sent Vita 'a fluffy coat' like one of her own just because Vita had admired it; she felt understood at Sissinghurst, and would write Vita long, illegible screeds of affection and gratitude. Vita preserved some of them, writing on one envelope: 'This is a letter from a supposedly cold and heartless person. I kept it because I minded her always being misjudged.'

While on an early spring holiday with Gwen in North Africa, Vita heard from Mac, her secretary, that she and Harold had been asked to dine at Buckingham Palace on 17 March. In spite of her new policy of moderate social life, she refused to go. She had no evening dress, she told Harold, and no time to have one made. 'I shall just have to lie low, and you will have to lie high if anybody asks where I am.' But she accepted an invitation to watch George VI's coronation procession from Mrs Morrow's room at the Carlton, and she continued to ask a few people down to Sissinghurst.

One of these was Olive Rubens, her father's old love, who in 1932 had made a happy marriage to a General Nation. In May Jack Squire, now a confirmed drunk, came to luncheon. By the time lunch was half over, wrote Vita, 'I had become "darling", and was being told there were only two people in England he loved, one of them being Mr Baldwin, the other me.' In order to part him from the bottle she led him into the garden, 'where he took my arm affectionately because he couldn't walk straight. It was simply awful ... he has a really tragic look in his eyes at times.' More congenial summer visitors were her old friend Enid Bagnold Jones, and the poet Ruth Pitter, whose *A Trophy of Arms* was the winner of that year's Hawthornden Prize, presented by Vita: 'A charming person, a very *real* person; very intelligent, full of ideas. I have seldom got on so readily and easily with anyone. We talked for five hours without stopping, and went for a long walk in the wood.'

A party of Harold's constituents came down to see the garden, and Harold, seeing what he and Vita had made through the visitors' eyes, realized for the first time just how good it was. He took credit for the design himself; but she had made it unique. 'I think the secret of your gardening is simply that you have the courage to abolish ugly or unsuccessful flowers. Except for those beastly red-hot pokers which you have a weakness for there is not an ugly flower in the whole place. ... It is lovely, lovely, lovely – and you must be pleased with your work.' Harold had strong prejudices against certain plants – 'I should be quite happy in life if I knew that I was never going to see a Buddleia again,' he wrote later in the year, and Vita took two buddleias out to please him.

Having finished *Pepita*, she was preparing a small book called *Some Flowers* – short essays, accompanied by photographs. Christopher St John, sending this book out as Christmas presents at the end of the year, told one of her friends that Vita's own garden was 'very beautiful and original'; but then, 'she is helped by a very favourable natural soil, and by the protection of the old walls of her castle ... (Also by pots of money!!)'. The garden plan kept changing; they planted roses where the vegetable garden had been, around the Rondel; and made the old Rose Garden into a herbaceous garden, with a lot of delphiniums.

Vita made herself accept invitations to speak and lecture, and she even went to a royal garden party in July. At the end of the month she was in Oxford, with Gwen, as one of the judges at the Festival of Spoken Poetry. Auden was one of her fellow judges and she wrote of him afterwards to Ben: 'I like him very much, but I do wish he wasn't quite so dirty.... If you wear the openwork sandals of a Spanish muleteer, your feet *must* look as though they had been washed at least once during the past six weeks. His don't.' Her letters to Ben, who was spending the summer abroad, often touched on his casual attitude to life and to work, which continued to worry her. 18 October 1937:

You know that I loathe the modern world quite as much as you do, if not more, and am equally bored by politics and problems. Like you, I should infinitely prefer everything to be secure, settled, humanistic, serene, leisurely, scholarly, and generally charming.... But at the same time one cannot help realizing that art and activity have always gone hand in hand, and that the most vigorous and virile nations have also always been those that produced the greatest art.... The long and the short of it is, I suppose, that since it is no good setting oneself against the modern world and retiring into a little golden centrally-heated cell of one's own, one must adapt it to one's needs, take the best, help where one can, and discard only after due reflection.

These were the lessons she herself was trying to learn after her long retreat in the *huis clos* of Sissinghurst.

She was writing to Ben from Lisieux in France, the home and shrine of St Thérèse, the 'Little Flower of Jesus'. With her was Gwen, to whom, as a Catholic, the cathedral and Thérèse's house meant a great deal; Vita found Lisieux 'a strange place' and was intrigued by the story of Thérèse. They were driven on by Copper through the Dordogne to Rocamadour, 'an astonishing village hooked on to the face of a cliff several hundreds of feet high, and crowned by churches'. At nearby Padirac, Vita and Copper climbed down into the deep *gouffre*. This holi-day made a great impression on Vita. She started a poem about Roca-madour one night back at Sissinghurst; and the next day, 'Think of writing a book on St Teresa of Avila and St ditto of Lisieux.' This was to be *The Eagle and the Dove*, but it was not to be written yet.

*Pepita* came out that same October, a week after her return from France. It was instantly successful, and brought Vita back into close contact with people as nothing else could have. The Hogarth Press sold 10,000 copies in the first two months, and it proved a steady seller. Vita was modest about the book's reception, writing to Harold:

> I don't think I have ever had such nice letters about a book as about *Pepita* ... and lots of very good reviews too. I am pleased on B.M.'s account, but it slightly irritates me ... as really any merit the book may have is chiefly due to the material – and even though one may have put it together skilfully that is just a trick learned from years of experience.

The character study and descriptions of B.M. in *Pepita* were so accurate, affectionate, unsentimental and well-judged that it was this part of the book that elicited the most response. Olive (Rubens) Nation wrote: 'Poor B.M., how much of it would she have understood! Without minimizing her faults, you have made one remember and love her quali-ties. ... I am grateful as I can now again feel for her the same fascination which first attracted me so many years ago. Bravo Mar, as Lionel would have said.' Edwin Lutyens, 'McNed', who had loved B.M. so much and been so foully abused by her, wrote too: 'What a tale to tell and how well told. B.M. comes out as porcelain the glaze of which is crazed. I wish I had had more patience at the end. It failed me! ... The w.c. seats were all screwed down – "she could never ask any man to the house"! ... It was all too much for me and then the troubles began. Oh dear!' George Plank wrote of B.M., after reading *Pepita*, 'I know I shall go on missing her till I die.'

Vita's children appreciated the book too. Nigel, from Oxford, wrote already as the family historian: 'Oh dear, what admirable parents I have got: what a standard, – more what a combination – to have to live up to. Do you think that you or Daddy or Ben or myself or some outsider will ever record a picture of our family, as both you and D. [in *Helen's Tower*] now have of yours?' And Ben, from Bologna, wrote of 'the number of times I got lumps in the throat over Grannyma', and said Vita had 'brought out all the facts however horrible and however wonderful.'

There were two dissenting voices within the family. One was Lord Sackville's, Vita's Uncle Charlie. He wrote from Knole that he was 'cross'. He did not mind what she wrote about Pepita and B.M., but he objected to 'the way in which both my uncle Lionel and your father are portrayed'. (Vita had stressed the passive, withdrawn Sackville qualities of her father and grandfather.) But 'though I may *be* cross, it does not lessen my affection for you.'

The other dissenting voice came from B.M.'s elderly sister Amalia, who was living in Kent, near Canterbury, but not in contact with the family. She was furious that the mud was being stirred up all over again. She wrote to the newspapers and to Vita threatening a libel action, stirring up fresh mud by asserting that B.M.'s father was not Lord Sackville, but a Jew who was murdered in Spain. Then a Lady Norbury, a friend of Amalia's, came to tea at Sissinghurst 'and told me B.M.'s father was really a Basque goatherd.' Vita's lawyer called Amalia's communications 'the vapourings of an ill-balanced mind', and Harold wrote to her soothingly.

Since Harold had become a Member of Parliament he and Vita were less together, although he would be home at weekends – if he were not abroad or invited elsewhere. Their daily letters were without false regrets about this new regime, in which both were leading the life they needed. They told one another of their thoughts and doings, as always; but the yearning, sentimental tone was less evident in Harold's letters. In the past, it had been so often she who was restless, behaving unpredictably, disappearing on some private escapade; now for her it was more often than not 'Quiet day at Sissinghurst', while he was busy, in demand, always off somewhere in a hurry. In the pattern of their lives, they were more like mother and son than husband and wife. In

December 1937 he was invited to stay with the Duke and Duchess of Windsor. 'Are you sure you wouldn't rather spend Xmas with them than here ?' Vita asked him. 'I should quite understand, so don't consider *me*.'

Harold replied that he would not spend Christmas 'with the merry wife of Windsor but only at HOME'. He wrote her a love letter after Christmas ; and to Ben he wrote that though he was 'not in the least "in love" with Mummy', he loved her more than anything else in the world.

> She is not an easy wife in the conventional way. She is a difficult wife. Yet she is everything on earth to me as you know. And why ? ? Because although we have many tastes that are different, many activities that we do not share, essentially she and I are one. And why again ? Because we are each a trifle afraid of the other. We each regard the other with deep respect.

Vita, though shy and diffident except in safe company, was the stronger character : more uncompromising and definite in all her sometimes inconvenient ideas and ideals. Harold was apt to be over-flexible and conciliating ; he needed her certainties.

Writing *Pepita* was a release for Vita and made her able to express herself more freely. She took a sudden emotional jump back towards Virginia, writing to 'My (once) Virginia' on 13 November a long, self-conscious letter. 'You said I was a fool not to write to you when my pen wriggled to do so.' She asked Virginia not to reply; 'I shall know it has arrived and that you will recognize it as a thought of love from your Orlando.'[2] Virginia did reply, reassuringly, saying in effect that she would always be there for Vita ; and life and meaning returned to their letters and meetings.

*Pepita* had brought Knole very close, and Vita tried to defuse her old grief by a rather unreal attempt to fantasize her relationship with her cousin Eddy :

> Knole has been an awful and deep block. I suppose my love for Knole has gone deeper than anything else in my life. If only you had been my brother this block wouldn't have occurred, because I shouldn't have minded in the least if you had succeeded to Dada, in fact, I should have liked it. As it is, I do love you as though you were my brother, and even beyond that, perhaps because I never had a brother – and you are the nearest substitute I can get.[3]

Eddy was well-disposed towards Vita, but he did not welcome or share this fantasy, having himself no need for it. Because Vita always refused to go to Knole, her image of it grew more, rather than less, mythical and magical over the years, even though the creation of Sissinghurst went some way to neutralizing the pain.

\*

Vita was unaccountably attacked by acute gastritis in early 1938. The strange illness continued on and off for two months, until she developed pleurisy as well. Mac, who was a trained nurse, called for an ambulance and took Vita to see a doctor in London. He put her in a nursing-home, and finally lead poisoning was diagnosed. The trouble was traced to the grinders that pulped the apples in the Sissinghurst cider press: 'Gwen says it's poetic justice for writing *The Land.*' Before her illness Vita had been, as Virginia deplored, overweight. By April, when she recovered, she had lost 2½ stone (35 pounds), and she never let herself get so heavy again.

Since she could not work while she had the lead poisoning, she read seedsmen's catalogues and sent off lavish orders. Plants began to arrive from all over England. 'But really I don't suppose it amounts to more than £10, and many people would blow that on a dinner party and 4 theatre stalls and then supper. And *my* investment will go on for years, getting better and better (unless anybody drops gas-bombs on the orchard).'

When, during one of her respites from gastritis in early March, she had lunched with Virginia in London, Kingsley Martin, the editor of the *New Statesman*, dropped in and asked her if she would contribute the 'Country Notes' that she already wrote from time to time on a more regular basis, every two or three weeks. This she did. (The articles were later collected and published in volume form.) For the first time she was forced to put her eight years of Sissinghurst experience into words, and formulate her ideas. There is a 'manifesto' air about her 'Country Notes' of 1938, as the writer and the gardener merged and she spelled out her tenets. 'I believe in exaggeration; I believe in big groups, big masses; I am sure that it is more effective to plant twelve tulips together than to split them into groups of six; more effective to concentrate all the delphiniums into one bed, than to dot them about at intervals of twos and threes.' She kept a 'gardening diary' in 1938, noting down plantings and processes week by week. She was employing three gardeners – Farley, Hayter and Sidney Neve – and a Miss Lee part time. But nothing was done that she did not order and supervise, and she worked as hard as anyone. That year, huge quantities of bulbs, shrubs and flowering trees went in, the results of her sick-bed catalogue reading. Roses were planted in the orchard: '10 more musk, 6 moss, 1 setipoda, 1 oniemensis, 12 rugosa, and some climbers into the trees.' Also two rose macrophylla, a dozen malus and three dozen lilies in the magnolia bed.

That was in February. In March she planted the herb garden, and had some yews removed from one position to another. (This radical ruthlessness was a characteristic: nothing was ever regarded as definitive or inevitable.) Her new pinks that spring were not from cuttings but 'from our own saved seed'; the glasshouses were used not only for raising from seed but for ripening figs, peaches, nectarines and grapes.

After the last late frost in mid-May, which damaged the regale lilies, she sowed 'lots of cornflowers and mixed flower seed' in the orchard. In mid-June she judged the garden to be at its very best, with irises, roses, peonies, cistus, anchusa and delphiniums in bloom. 'Note: Open the garden at this date another year, or even a week earlier.' This was the first year she opened the garden to the public for charity, on a single weekend. But there was a growing number of personal callers, who included professional gardeners, horticulturalists and nurserymen. 'It amuses me how these gardeners are now beginning to tell each other to come here and see the garden,' she wrote to Harold on the last day of what had been a perfect June, 'scented and glowing'. Vita was flattered when the professionals asked her for cuttings or advice. 'If you want real highbrow talk, commend me to three experts talking about auriculas. Bloomsbury is nothing to it. I couldn't understand half they said.'

July was less perfect. 'The herbaceous border threatens to peter out. Note: get something that will flower at this time.' Her snapdragons had to be pulled up and burned on account of rust. 'Weeds awful.' But then the dahlias saved the situation; and Vita filled dull corners all summer with troughs, crocks, sinks and pans filled with alpines and small violas. In the autumn she was planting again: twelve Chinese peonies in the orchard, and red-hot pokers (Harold would not have liked that) in the border along the lime walk. Masses more tulips and fritillaries in the orchard; 200 cyclamen on the moat bank; lilies in the nuttery, and back to the orchard again with more cydonia, and Japanese cherries.

In mid-December, according to her gardening diary, there were arums and nemesia in flower under glass, and she found and picked the first iris stylosa. By Christmas, its fellows were buried under snow so deep 'that in places it comes over the top of Wellington boots'.

At the beginning of August, Vita had been to Rodmell to spend a night at Monk's House with Virginia, like in the old days. There had been a brief break in their new harmony: Vita had had reservations about Virginia's new book *Three Guineas*, and told her so. In *Three Guineas* Virginia combined anti-war arguments with an exposé of the way women were repressed and discouraged in the professions. Her thesis was that the tribal, hierarchical, competitive, aggressive 'male' qualities that made it impossible for women to get to the top in medicine, law, administration or the church were the very same ones that made conflict and confrontation inevitable. In the volatile international situation of Europe in 1938, pacifist sentiments were considered by many people in England to be subversive and undermining. For this reason the book was misunderstood and seriously underestimated. In the past, Vita would have agreed with Virginia's satirical condemnation of uniforms, honours, rituals and exclusive institutions : these were topics on which, ten years before and when Harold had been in diplomacy, they had been at one. But now, everything that was English and traditional was dear to Vita. Nor could she agree with Virginia that women, if left to themselves, free of dominant male conditioning, would be less bellicose than men.

They got over this disagreement, and Vita wrote to Harold, who was on holiday in France, 'Oh my dear, what an enchanting person Virginia is ! How she weaves magic into life ! . . . And Leonard too : I know he is tiresome and wrong-headed and sometimes Jewish [i.e., mean with money] but really with his school-boyish love for pets and toys (gadgets) he is irresistibly young and attractive.'

How wrong people were, Vita said, about Bloomsbury, 'saying that it is devitalized and devitalizing. You couldn't find people less devitalized or devitalizing than the Wolves.' It was Bloomsbury's hangers-on, she thought, that had given it a bad name, 'and of course that drooping Lytton [Strachey] must have done its cause a great deal of harm. I hated Lytton.'

Harold and Vita had just heard that Nigel had got a Third in his finals at Oxford. Their expectations for him had been very high ; while Vita was disappointed and 'incredulous', Harold was upset out of all propor-tion. Vita tried to make him see sense. She had talked to Virginia and Leonard about it, 'and they were not appalled but amused. They said that all their most brilliant friends at Cambridge, who were all expected to get firsts, had only got thirds.'

> I think you exaggerate the importance of academical honours. . . . I know you have a *culte* for Oxford and especially for Balliol, and you are disappointed doubly over Balliol and Niggs, but really it can't alter in the least your, and my, estimate of Niggs as a very intelligent and hard-working person. . . . Niggs is an 100% person whatever Balliol examiners may say. I am sure of that. And you are sure too ; so what does all the rest matter ?

In September, Ben went to America to work at the Fogg Museum in Cambridge, Massachusetts. Earlier in the year in Florence, he had become romantically attached to a girl from California, which both his parents rather gratuitously deplored – Ben was, after all, twenty-four. 'Florence is an awful place for amorous complications,' Vita told him. 'I don't think I have ever been there without some entanglement result-ing, and now you are treading in my footsteps. Funny.' He was still her image of her younger self ; arriving in the States, he sent her a photograph of himself taken on shipboard. 'It was so like you', she wrote, 'that at first I mistook it for a photograph of myself, and was puzzled.'

She was slightly sarcastic about his being in America while Europe was in danger of war. Vita was not belligerent; in April 1937 she had told Harold that she sometimes agreed with the pacifists that 'we ought to retire from the competition, not merely for our own safety but to give a lead away from this insane barbarism.' Harold told her in June 1938 about the Nazi atrocities in Vienna. He was glad to be 'in a position to do something, however slight, to help. I simply could not just remain idle and do nothing.' Vita had no position in public life – 'The only hope for people like myself who can do nothing about it is to shove the thought aside and hope for the best. Otherwise one would go mad, – one would become a lunatic in a world of maniacs.'

When in the autumn war seemed inevitable, the household was issued with gas-masks, and a trench dug in the orchard that had just been so lovingly planted. Thoughts of war could no longer be shoved aside even at Sissinghurst. Vita described the precautionary measures to Ben in America on 9 October :

> Making the big room into a gas-proof shelter meant that sheets of asbestos were screwed over all the windows ... and that the fireplace was similarly blocked, and that piles of blankets were stacked ready to nail over all the doors. It meant that I had to shift all the red amber and the Persian pots, and otherwise make the room ready for sudden occupation by old Mrs Hayter, Mrs Copper, Fay, Mrs Farley, Mrs Adsett, young Adsett and so on. It meant that we bought 6 Thermos bottles, electric torches, tins of Benger's Food, Ovaltine and cocoa ; got a telephone extension put in the big room in case either Mac or I were called out, – Mac as air-warden, me as an ambulance driver ; – and generally upset the whole place.

When all this had been done, Neville Chamberlain returned from Munich bearing 'Peace with honour', and everything had to be restored to normal – for a while.

Neither Harold nor Vita approved of appeasing Hitler – Vita called the appeasement policy 'a wrong, foolish and shortsighted thing' – but reacted with relief to the respite. Harold decided to buy a sailing boat – or rather, Vita was to buy it for him, as B.M. had bought *Sumurun* for Lionel so many years before. Vita's response to tension had been to allow Mac, her Scottish Presbyterian secretary, to fall in love with her. From September, they had been having an affair. Though Mac – whom Vita, in their new relation, called 'Anna' – strove to be 'an oyster of discretion', this new involvement within the walls of Sissinghurst (Mac lived in the gatehouse) brought complications. In the pre-Munich emergency, Mac had written a note thanking Vita 'for giving me such complete happiness'. But soon the notes grew more desperate and despairing, for there was so much in Vita's life – not least the long-standing companionship of Gwen St Aubyn – to come between Mac and her.

In this troubled autumn, on 27 October, Vita's poem *Solitude* was published by the Hogarth Press. Leonard Woolf told her that 'To me it is the best thing you have done.' But Leonard was not a critic of poetry, and Vita knew that her mode of writing was not in the style of the times; indeed Raymond Mortimer, in his careful review in the *New Statesman*, caught in *Solitude* echoes of lines from Landor, Tennyson and Arnold. But the themes of the poem were very much Vita's own, beginning with her 'Rocamadour' verses as part of the dedication to Gwen St Aubyn:

> You said, as we came down the strait ravine,
> 'This is your place, your cliff of solitude,
> A place to match your usual lonely mood . . . '
> How did you know that I was worldly-sick?

In *Solitude*, Vita incorporated ideas and phrases from her diary-poems, from *All Passion Spent* and from *The Dark Island* into a death-concerned, night-concerned, pantheist hymn.

> Night came again to heal my daily scars;
> Shreds of myself returned again to me;
> Shreds of myself, that others took and wove
> Into themselves, till I had ceased to be.
> Poor patchwork of myself was all unripped
> And stitched again into some harmony
> Like the pure purpose of an orchestra.
> I rode my horse across a moonlit cove
> And found therein my chained Andromeda.

'The night I love is Death,' the poet says; as for religion, 'No Church I need; I seek my God direct.' And love?

> Those cheap and easy loves! but what were they,
> Those rash intruders into darkest lairs? . . .
> We take a heart, and leave our own intact.
> Such are the cheap unworthy tricks
> That lure the flesh and leave it slightly smutched
> Yet leave the final, difficult soul untouched,
> As honest as the cornfield and the ricks.

The poem disturbed her intimates, especially the section on love. Mac passed a note to Vita at Sissinghurst: 'You dismiss love very lightly in

*Solitude* or do you mean light love when you are so scornful ? I think you must.' Hilda Matheson wrote a long letter :

> To my great delight I found passages and phrases that had remained in my mind since I read some of it in MS years ago.... Perhaps the real source of my disappointment is that I have found no clue, in this self-communing poem, to the things in you which I have failed to understand in the last few years. I am puzzled by your attitude to love – cheap and easy, a charlatan, the stifling tendrils of ivy – do these epithets apply to your own past attitude to love, or to love itself and all human relationships ? If not, what differentiates love of that quality from love which liberates the heart and opens the eyes ?

Hilda signed her letter 'Your loving Stoker'. What she was tacitly asking, as all Vita's lovers must, was – Is it nothing to you, then, all that we said and did together, that seemed to me to be the most important thing in the world ?

# CHAPTER 27

ESCHEWING solitude, Vita went to a dinner given for Edy Craig at the Savoy Hotel in London – with 'speeches by Sybil Thorndike, Violet Vanbrugh, Knoblock, Dame May Whitty, myself, etc' :

My old Christopher appeared in the most remarkable get-up, – of black brocade with scarlet buttons and puffed sleeves, – a sort of cross between a Victorian housekeeper and an Elizabethan waiting-woman. The first person I ran into was Margaret Goldsmith, who plumped herself down on a sofa beside me and started telling me exactly how and why she had divorced Frederick Voigt.

Vita had her minuscule 'winter season' again just before Christmas 1938. She gave a luncheon for Virginia and Freya Stark at Antoine's, which ended up with Virginia being dropped at Selfridges to buy steak because Freud was coming to dinner, and Vita going with Freya Stark to see a lizard from Southern Arabia. Vita wrote nostalgically to Virginia after the lunch, saying how beautiful she had looked in 'your brown fur cap and your exquisitely ethereal slenderness. ... And to think how the ceilings of Long Barn once swayed above us!... and dolphins sported on the marble slabs.'[1]

Her 'winter season' could also have included dinner at Buckingham Palace in honour of the King of Rumania, but Vita flatly refused to come up in time for this. It was the familiar crisis with Harold, only this time worse. The argument had been going on since the invitation came in November. She had written to him then :

I just couldn't go. I know it will all be lovely and decorative – and gold plate and orchids, and beefeaters – but I just can't bear it when it comes down to all the horrid snobbish details such as long gloves costing two guineas and low backs and half-undressed women and expensive jewels. ...

Oh dear, how difficult life is . . . how deeply I wish life could be simplified. You won't understand what I mean by this – because you like politics and people, and I don't – I am really a very lonely person.

Vita was afraid that she looked peculiar; she finished her letter in shaky, upset handwriting: 'I think perhaps the fact of being an essentially lonely person makes me dread the exposure of a public party more than I should. . . . I hate the idea of being examined under electric lights.'

She got as far as writing to Jay's and finding out what an evening dress and all the necessary accessories would cost. Harold enlisted Gwen on his side. 'She said I would be wrong to funk it – and that I *must* go. But I am too shy – and also I do think it wrong to spend all that money for one evening.' If she went to the party, she said, she would be untrue to herself. She was writing to him with all her jewels littered round her, 'emeralds and diamonds, just taken out of the bank, and they make me feel sick. I simply can't subscribe any longer to the world which these jewels represent. I *can't* buy a dress costing £30 or wear jewels worth £2000 when people are starving.'

Since the money, and the jewels, and the ideology, were all hers, Harold had to throw in his hand. He was not pleased. 'Estrangement,' Vita wrote sadly in her diary. He conceded defeat with a display of reverence that was ironic, or loyal, or a mixture of both. 'My God! I do admire you so my Viti. You are so sound in your values. They ring like a bell.'

When, the following July, Ben's smart new job as Deputy Surveyor of the King's Pictures (under Kenneth Clark) brought him an invitation to a ball at the Palace he, like Vita, refused to go. Harold complained that his attitude showed a lack of intelligence. Vita did not know whether to laugh or cry. She agreed with Ben, but equally she longed for him to shine. 'He really has no sense of responsibility at all,' she said to Harold. 'I wish he had your standards. But he hasn't.'

In January 1939 Vita had a telegram from Hilda Matheson, who was in the south of France with Dorothy Wellesley; Yeats was staying nearby and much in their company. The telegram said that the poet was on his deathbed; Vita was instructed to telephone to the Yeats family in Dublin with the sad news, 'as no privacy could be secured for telegrams to Dublin. I thought it was rather a roundabout way of doing things, from Beaulieu to Dublin via the Weald of Kent, but did what I was asked.'

Alone at Sissinghurst – apart from Mac and the servants – she made a new start on her long-planned poem *The Garden*: 'I get so miserable with no writing on hand.' She told Harold on 13 February, 'I like my life, and don't envy yours, but at the same time I often feel how dull and rustic I must appear to you.' (He was about to fly to Egypt.) 'Anyhow, I have spent the whole morning writing poetry (though no doubt Spender, Auden etc wouldn't call it poetry at all) and that gives me a sense of justification.' She told Virginia she was writing 'a sort of companion to *The Land*'; she was also buying Bettenham Farm with 200 acres. 'Lord how rich life is, when one takes it the right way! Acres of farmland, and a new poem in a big foolscap book, – what more could anyone ask of life!'[2]

This was written in wild, spidery writing. She and Mac had drifted into the habit of taking too much sherry in the evenings. *The Garden* ran out of steam. Vita thought of writing a life of Leonardo, or a life of Jane Carlyle, or of George Sand, or Thomas Sackville: she did none of them. Her writing energies crept into her 'Country Notes' for the *New Statesman*; she called them her 'sticklebacks', and she fed them with whatever was happening around her. After the Bettenham purchase, she wrote on 'Buying a Farm': 'I take an absurd pleasure in owning land ... simply because I love the fields and the orchards so much that I want to feel them safely mine. Safe from any builder-aggressor.'

There were however some seductions in the modern world. Vita and Harold had seen a television set being demonstrated for the Beales at Castle Farm, and Vita fell for it. On 24 February she confessed to Harold that 'I've done something quite idiotic: I've bought a television set.... So we can now watch the Grand National and the Derby and the big football matches being run.' She put it in the big room, as being neutral ground where both family and servants could watch it after supper. There were very few televisions in England in 1939: Vita asked in the neighbours and local farmers to watch the Derby, and ran a Sissinghurst Sweepstake. Harold himself appeared on the screen in May. 'Darling, *how* good you were on the television. It was like having you in the room.' There was another innovation: 'Did I tell you that I had succumbed to pressure and bought a motor mower? I hate it, but it is inevitable. It will save 2 men 2 days time. ... But I shall always loathe it. It hasn't arrived yet, and in order to work off my venom against it I think I had better turn it quickly into a stickleback.' Which she did. In 'Buying a Motor Mower' she described how her old mower had been pulled by a chestnut cob called Gracie Fields 'because she graces the fields (not *my* joke). For her weekly mowing she used to wear leather boots', to protect the lawns. Now, the garden boy pursued the motor, 'looking as though he were pushing some wild sort of pram.'[3]

With war seemingly inevitable, Vita had an instinct to plan long-term for the garden, as an act of faith. She discovered a new pink magnolia, which was slow-growing – 'but I do not think we should be put off by such considerations. A hundred years hence someone will come across it growing among the ruins of the tower ... and will say Someone must have once cared for this place.' For her forty-seventh birthday Harold gave her a Sackville flag to fly from the tower: 'a dream of gaiety and garishness,' said Vita.

Harold had his new boat – the *Mar* – on the river Hamble at Southampton, and was even less at home. Vita was wistful. 'It is horrid to think how many weekends you will be away on the *Mar* – but I suppose the sea air is good for Hadji – so long as he doesn't get drowned.' Gwen was ill, this time with a duodenal ulcer, and was being looked after at the Roman Catholic convent at Staplehurst. (She had spent much of the past months at the convent, preparing her book *Towards a Pattern*, about her conversion.) Nigel was away in the north, working on a social service project with the unemployed; Vita went up to see him at the end of March, and he took her down a coal-mine. At home with Mac and her two alsatians Martha and Martin, she wrote with some desperation to Virginia on 23 April: 'This is Sissinghurst 250 – is that Museum 2621? Is that Virginia? This is Vita speaking. – yes: Vita, – a person you once reckoned as a friend. Oh, had you forgotten? ... I don't like being cut off from you and thus am making an attempt to get in touch.'[4]

When she opened the garden for charity again on the first weekend in May, 800 people came. Vita did not consider this invasion an intrusion at all. 'It is a real experience to open one's garden to the public', she wrote in one of her subsequent 'Country Notes'; 'it is a pleasure; even a form of flattery.... You share your personal delight; the scheme you have built up for ten, twenty years becomes part of the pleasure of inquisitive eager gardeners.'[5] With these interested strangers she was never shy, defensive or stand-offish. She had all the time in the world for them. She, in return, was asked to judge village gardening competitions. The cottage garden at Hurstmonceaux to which she gave a prize in August had, she learnt afterwards, been planned entirely according to her broadcast gardening talks: 'So I felt I had not lived in vain.'

The garden at Sissinghurst reached its first point of perfection, and was already acknowledged as a major personal achievement, in that last summer before the war. As Anne Scott-James has written, 'There are Sissinghurst plants and Sissinghurst ways of combining plants and Sissinghust conceits and fancies. The Sissinghurst style was clear for all to see by 1939.'[6]

In 1913, the year that Vita married, her contemporary and sometimes critic, Rebecca West, had defined genius as 'the abnormal justifying itself'; 'those who know that they are for whatever reason condemned by the laws of life ... make themselves one with life by some magnificent act of creation.' Vita Sackville-West wrote some good books and some good poems, but her 'one magnificent act of creation' was Sissinghurst.

As well as the aviary of budgerigars, there were at Sissinghurst more than 100 white pigeons, sitting decoratively on the roofs and wheeling round the tower, where they nested in one of the turrets. 'I used to feed them at the foot of the tower always, and they were so tame they would settle all over me, – on my head, shoulders, hands. When I saw war was imminent I got very worried about what to do with them, knowing I shouldn't be able to get food for them any longer. And then the most extraordinary thing happened : they all disappeared. It was as if they knew.'

When Germany invaded Poland on 1 September Vita already knew what her war work was to be. She had agreed to be involved in the local administration, recruitment and publicity of the Women's Land Army ; she had already stockpiled straw as bedding for refugees ; she was already designated as an ambulance driver in case of air-raid injury. (On 24 August she was telephoned during lunch to be asked whether her Buick would take an eight-foot stretcher or 'only sitting cases and corpses'.)

On 2 September they went through the routine of gas-proofing the big room all over again. On the 3rd, Britain was at war. 'Unquiet day at Sissinghurst.' Situated between London and the Channel ports, Sissinghurst was in the flight-path of bombers from both sides ; it was bombs, not the greatly feared poisonous gas, that was to be the danger. Vita was in charge of operations at Sissinghurst, and supervised the compulsory black-out, as she described in Country Notes in October :

> Every night I go my rounds like some night-watchman to see that the black-out is complete. It is. Not a chink reveals the life going on beneath these roofs, behind those blinded windows.... I wander round, and towards midnight discover that the only black-out I notice is the black-out of my soul. So deep a grief and sorrow that they are not expressible in words.

Vita had written to Virginia on 16 September : 'Let us write to one another sometimes. .... You ask what I feel, and I can tell you' :

> on the top I mind what you call the incessant bother of small arrangements, – no physical solitude ; people constantly about the place ; five six seven eight people to every meal ; the necessity of having my mother-in-law to stay here for God knows how long. ....
> Then, underneath this, on the second layer, come the anxieties : the young men one cares about whose lives are upset and who are probably going to lose them in a horrible manner, Ben with an anti-aircraft battery, learning to fly low,

at 600 feet, in case of aeroplanes swooping down with machine-guns; Nigel waiting, waiting to be called up into the Guards. . . .

Then on the third layer, deepest of all, comes one's own grief and despair at the wicked folly of it all. . . . I have never felt so tired, – physically and spiritually, – in all my life. . . . I would like to see you.[7]


She did see Virginia, who was 'so sweet and affectionate to me, I was touched'.

It was ironic that Vita had just engaged the best gardener she had yet had. His name was Jack Vass and he had worked in the great gardens at Cliveden. The garden was clearly going to be something of a war casualty, but Vass and Vita could not resist making plans. He drained the pond in the former rose garden, which Vita had longed to do for some time; the space was to be filled in, and Vita's dream of the White Garden was put to Harold on 13 December: 'all white flowers, with some clumps of very pale pink. White clematis, white lavender, white agapanthus, white double-primroses, white anemones, white lilies including giganteum in one corner, and the pale peach-coloured pulverulenta.' Harold's only objection was that the site did not get enough sun. 'Only it is such a good idea that I want it to succeed. . . . Darling how these things take one away from the sorrow of war.' Vita replied that she was being extravagant about the garden on principle – 'Let us plant and be merry, for next autumn we may all be ruined.' In February 1940, she calculated that over the past year she had bought at auction between 11,000 and 12,000 Dutch bulbs. But the White Garden was not realized until after the war.

Nigel went into the Grenadier Guards. Ben was at Rochester with a battery of Gunners commanded by Victor Cazalet, the Nicolsons' near neighbour. Ben's attitude to winning the war was, as Vita put it, 'deplorable'. He was at heart a pacifist; he hated the army and refused for a long time to take a commission. Nigel's attitude was more straightforward and he made a good soldier – 'Nigel is as sound as a bell morally', as Vita put it to Harold. Much as Vita loathed the war, she felt it must now be fought. She tried to instil fortitude into Ben without antagonizing him:

You see, I share much of your weakness and much of your introversion. I share also your late development. . . . You say you suddenly came to maturity at 22; I didn't even begin to until 26 [i.e., when she discovered her own nature, with Violet]. . . . The real difference between us, I think, is that having a more violent nature than yours, I reacted more violently against my own weaknesses and my own introversion.

Churchill took over from Chamberlain as Prime Minister in mid-May 1940, as enemy planes droned over Sissinghurst on their way to drop bombs on the naval dockyards at Chatham. On 17 May Churchill himself telephoned to Harold at Sissinghurst inviting him to join the Government under Duff Cooper at the Ministry of Information. He was delighted and Vita was pleased for him, but thought that his position and Duff's ought to be reversed – 'he's a white mouse compared with you.'

A member of the Home Guard watched each night on the roof of Vita's tower, looking out for parachutists and troop-carrying planes. 'In a steel helmet and rifle he looks most picturesque in the moonlight over the parapet.' A German invasion of England was anticipated and, in that nightmare event, Kent might be compulsorily evacuated by government order. If that happened, Harold warned Vita with brutal urgency,

> You will have to get out the Buick and get it into a fit state to start with a full oil-tank. You should put inside it some food for 24 hours and pack in the back your jewels and my diaries. They are all in book boxes to the right as you enter my bookroom.... You will want clothes and anything else very precious (?Barbara?) but the rest will have to be left behind.

She should take Gwen – who had taken the cottage called Horse-race, over the fields from Sissinghurst – and the Coppers, and make for Harold's brother Eric's house in Devonshire, 'avoiding main roads'. Vita knew that as the local ambulance driver she must not leave her post in any emergency; she sent her choice of important things – Harold's diaries, her will and the manuscript of *Orlando* – to safe-keeping in Devonshire. Harold, accepting that Vita could not leave, wrote to her that even if the Germans occupied Sissinghurst he did not imagine that they would harm her: 'But to be quite sure you are not put to any humiliation I really think you ought to have a bare bodkin [i.e., a means of suicide] handy so that you can take your quietus when necessary. I shall have one also. ... My dearest. I felt so close to you yesterday. We never need to put it into words.' As Vita wrote next day, 'Every time we meet now it must be in both our minds that we may possibly never meet again.' As for the 'bare bodkin', 'I promise you never to do anything rash or impetuous with the latter, but I should like to have it by me. ... There must be *something*, quick and painless and portable.' She hoped it would be cyanide of potassium which, she had read in a newspaper, 'produces unconsciousness in a few seconds and death within two minutes'. But the pills that Harold got from his doctor friend took a quarter of an hour to work. Vita was glad to have them 'though I rather deplore the slow-motion idea of this form of euthanasia. Do you yourself really look forward to that particular fifteen minutes with much pleasure ? I should not mind if we were together.'

Copper spent his spare time manufacturing Molotov cocktails to repel invaders. But then he was called up and the new head gardener Vass as well. William Taylor, an under-gardener who was mildly epileptic, stayed on. Vita attempted to write *Grand Canyon*, without much pleasure, and accepted a commission to contribute a book on English country houses to the patriotic 'Britain in Pictures' series put out by Collins. At the back of her 1940 diary, she made a list of the essential things to be taken if she did in fact have to flee from an invading army :

Boots. Breeches. Jerseys. Shirts. Stockings. Sables. Pyjamas. Underclothes. Handkerchiefs. Parcels [of letters ?]. Aspirin. Dial. Vick. Bicarbonate. Thermos. Dressing-gown. Bedroom slippers. Dressing-table things. Hot water bottles. *Grand Canyon* [manuscript]. Barbara [the wooden saint Harold had given her]. Unpublished poems. Roget [Thesaurus]. Cheque books. Cigarettes and holders and matches. Spectacles. My own copy of *Collected Poems*, with corrections. Bare bodkin. Washing things : toothpowder and brush ; nailbrush ; razor. Sybil's coat. Gloves.

Neither Vita nor Harold, in 1940, believed in their hearts that Britain could win the war. 'I am quite lucidly aware', Harold wrote in his diary on 15 June, 'that in three weeks from now Sissinghurst may be a waste and Vita and I both dead.'

'Life seems difficult to bear,' Vita had written in hers on the same day. George Hayter, the husband of Mrs Staples the cook, collapsed with a nervous breakdown. 'He sobs and shakes and is sick. Nobody can quite get at the reason, not even Mrs Staples. I think it is because of the war.'

A Mrs Rice, engaged to take over some of Copper's duties and to help with the garden, was another case of war-nerves ; she was found dead drunk in her room by Mac and Vita one afternoon. She finally disappeared, leaving no explanation. 'It now transpires that her favourite drink was a mixture of eau-de-cologne and gin, so I don't suppose she is long for this world. There is no more eau-de-cologne to be had in the village: she bought it all up.' Harold's bachelor brother Freddy, Lord Carnock, was drinking heavily too, and becoming more than his old mother Lady Carnock could manage.

Hilda Matheson was running a foreign-language propaganda radio station, to which Vita contributed some talks in French. In October Hilda went into hospital for a thyroid operation and died. She was fifty-two. Dorothy Wellesley, who had become dependent on Hilda, was in a desperate state. Vita went straight over to see her at Penns, and found her 'completely incoherent and inarticulate'. (On the same day Vita heard that Long Barn, now housing refugee children from London, had been damaged by a bomb. 'Not a pleasant day.') Dottie's doctor told Vita that Dottie would need a nurse, but that there was nothing to be done. 'There is no means of coercing or controlling a person who drinks.'

Vita, in spite of her far stronger character, was also increasingly relying on alcohol to get through the long, frightening evenings.

The almost constant air raids had begun in August. London was the focus for the Blitz – and Harold was in London – but there were air battles in the Sissinghurst skies too and bombs fell on Kent night after night. Violet Trefusis had escaped from occupied France, abandoning her beloved house Saint-Loup, which her mother had bought for her. Once in England, she immediately contacted Vita who, tentatively, invited her to Sissinghurst. Violet postponed the visit, and then put it off altogether: she was going down to Somerset. Vita, unnerved by anticipation, apprehension and anti-climax, wrote to her:

> What a dangerous person you are. I think we had better not see too much of each other. We have loved each other too deeply for too many years, and we must not play with fire again. The very sound of your voice on the telephone upsets me. Quite apart from our three years of passionate love-affair, we had years and years of childhood love and friendship behind us. . . .
>
> It makes you dear to me. It makes me dear to you. It represents . . . the little jokes we share – things like the armoury at Duntreath, our childhood things, even the Symphonie Antar gramophone record, which I had put out today to play to you. . . .
>
> I am sorry you are not coming here today; a real disappointment. I hope you will come when you get back from Coker – yet in a way I don't want you to come.[8]

Machine-gun bullets were picked up in the lake field at Sissinghurst; two incendiary bombs fell not far away; unexploded bombs blocked a road from the village; an explosion brought down the plaster from Vita's bedroom ceiling, and Staplehurst station was badly damaged. On 11 September, when the moon was on the wane, Churchill warned the British people over the radio that if invasion came it would be in the next two weeks. In this context Vita wrote to Violet, 'Curious how war has drawn the strands of our lives together again. . . . One travels far, only to come to the same starting-point.'[9]

Violet wrote begging Vita to meet her at some half-way point; Vita said, 'Darling, truly, I think we had better avoid one another, I think the love we have always had for one another is comparable to the time-bomb which may go off at any moment.' She would like Violet to come to Sissinghurst, but if they met 'in some village of Somerset or Dorset, it would lead to all sorts of things I don't want renewed.'[10]

Vita at last agreed to go and meet Violet. She told Harold she was going, 'But don't be alarmed: wild horses wouldn't get me involved with Violet. I feel sorry for her, as she has lost everything in France.' The former vagabonds met – one of them now forty-eight, the other forty-six – for lunch at the Red Lion in Pulborough, in Sussex, on 15 December. Vita stayed that night with her aunt Cecilie at nearby Haslemere, and from there wrote Violet a long, unhappy letter. She dared not take Violet back into her life.

> Yes, it was good to see you – and the absurd happiness of having you beside me in the car, – even the sudden pain of saying goodbye to you was vivifying.
> The past does not worry me. I hold it for ever. The present does not worry me. It formed part of the past today. The future does worry me, *our* future, – and I must clarify my own feelings about it to you. I shall have to do this in a memorandum form. 1) I told you that I was frightened of you. That's true. I don't want to fall in love with you all over again, or to become involved with you in a way that would complicate my life as I have now arranged it.

She did not want all the intrigue that an affair would entail. 'Besides, it wouldn't be just "an affair". It would be a resumption of what you rightly called a Greek tragedy, and I don't want that.' Vita's second point was that she was not free to embark on another adventure, 'and I will not deceive my "collage" any more than I ever deceived you.' Violet had startled her by saying she had never believed in her fidelity. 'I was absolutely faithful to you until the moment I telephoned to you to say I hadn't been faithful.'

Her third point was that they could never revert to their childhood relationship. 'We simply couldn't have this nice, simple, naif, childish connexion without its turning into a passionate love affair again':

> You and I can't be together. I go down country lanes and meet a notice saying 'beware – unexploded bomb'. So I have to go round another way. You are the unexploded bomb to me.
> I don't want you to explode.
> I don't want to disrupt my life.
> My quiet life is dear to me, I hate being dragged away from it.
> This letter will anger you. I don't care if it does, since I know that no anger or irritation will ever destroy the love that exists between us.

And if you really want me, I will come to you, always, – anywhere.

Mitya.[11]

War, and the possibility of death and destruction at any moment, had made Vita vulnerable to Violet as she had not been for decades. Was her letter an expression of victory or of defeat, a move towards life or an acceptance of the dark? The last part of her letter was scrawled in the jerky, spidery way she wrote only when blurred by drink or tears.

# CHAPTER 28

AN unforeseen consequence of Violet's being in England was her casual contact with Harold. They met, inevitably, at parties in London, and had the occasional lunch together. Vita and Violet continued to correspond, every couple of weeks or so, Vita consistently declining Violet's invitations. 'One is called on to bear quite enough these days without adding to it. . . . Now don't say I've been evasive, and don't think that the temptation to be with you isn't strong. It is.'[1] In March 1941 she admitted to Violet 'that I love you perennially, in the odd way we both realize. That doesn't mean that I trust you, or would ever commit myself to you again.' Violet suggested that their story ought to be written, and Vita half-thought so too: 'Could we (you and I) collaborate? – No, I don't think we could. It would be one person's book. I do feel that it is a great and new subject, and I would like to do it. The vivid feelings that I have undergone throughout my life would make a worthwhile story of it.'[2] She did not say anything – here, at any rate – to Violet about her 1920 manuscript, and she never attempted the 'great and new subject' in any other way.

In July 1941 Ben was stationed at Yeovil in Somerset, not far from his parents' old friend Dorothy Heneage at Coker Court. Violet had taken West Coker Manor, and Ben was bound to meet her at Mrs Heneage's. Vita wrote to him all about Violet:

> She will amuse you, but you must beware of her. She is a siren. (Not the air raid sort.) Her appearance will startle you, as she has lost her eye for make-up. She has the loveliest voice in the world; interlards her conversation with French slang so up-to-date that one doesn't understand half of it; is a mythomane as well as being profoundly untruthful; is witty; is an extravagant and fantastic personality; is a bore in the sense that she loves living in a world of intrigues and is determined to involve one in them; is in fact one of the most dangerous people I know. *You have been warned.* At the same time

there is something extremely worthwhile about her, and now that I have given you the lowdown you can be on your guard but also on the look-out for the worthwhile part.

It was funny, Vita wrote to Harold, that Ben, who was probably conceived on their honeymoon at Coker, would now go back to Coker and would meet Violet 'who nearly wrecked our happy marriage but thank goodness failed to do so'. The conjunction of Ben and Violet fascinated her: 'I hope Ben won't fall in love with Violet. He might, you know.'

Nothing could have been more unlikely. But for Vita, Ben was still in some sense a reincarnation of herself; she was still writing him letters reiterating how alike they were ('If ever people were made for the ivory tower, it is you and me') and how for that reason she could understand him and his problems in a special way. But Ben, of necessity, was putting up barriers between himself and his mother. He had been home for a weekend in January, and afterwards had written a letter to his brother that would have shattered Vita had she read it. Ben could not stand the slowness of his mother's mind, or her conservatism. He had told her that his battery was being sent abroad, but that he was not going. This was a relief to him, a fact which she refused to grasp. 'You know Mummy's habit of imagining that what should be so (in her own mind) is so. Thus, if she thinks that one ought to like going, nothing one can say will put it right.'

> I think this lack of reality proceeds from her habit of considering us children aged 12 and 14. At that age what one expressed was not believed in unless it happened to coincide with what she thought, or was picturesque.... Now there is nothing picturesque in not wishing to fight in Kenya.... So my views are ignored, my feebleness is as it were apologized for by tactful silence, I am reinstated as the romantic, wild foolish oh-but-he-is-so-young, dark boy, by having repeated for me the noble sentiment I never expressed – 'Ben is so disappointed at not being sent abroad.'

Ben did not even attempt to explain why he did not want to go. 'That would be as foolish as to explain the Quantum Theory to my gun-team':

> She wishes to disapprove and be jealous, so long as she is given the opportunity to disapprove of wild romantic behaviour rather than tame pedestrian behaviour. You know, all our lives we have disappointed Mummy (though she would not admit it to herself, she is too loyal and too truly loving and unselfish) by not behaving foolishly. We have given her no opportunity to rescue us. She has never been allowed to roast a fatted calf for the prodigal son.

There was worse to come. He had taken a friend home to Sissinghurst for dinner, Ben went on to Nigel. It had been 'a dismal failure':

Mummy was embarrassingly affectionate and incapable of taking anything in. She will never again learn any new fact. It is terrifying to witness this premature senility. Her moral code is based on utterly arbitrary premises, taking no account of the one branch of knowledge in which all must agree the 20th century has advanced in understanding – the science of psychology. To her, an act (such as theft, disloyalty, untruth) is WRONG, irrespective of the forces motivating it. To her, unhappiness depends on environment (hence her confusion when confronted by Eddy 'who has such an easy life, I can't understand it') and not on a state of mind. Drunkenness is vicious pleasure to her, and not as it is to us a hopeless method of forgetting misery. . . .

You see, you and I have had such a protective covering till the age of 22. We have both taken too much for granted, we have been too blind to realize that some of what we were taught is 40 years out of date. . . . Generally, intelligent people's parents belong entirely to another world so that their children are not tempted to copy them, whereas you and I have enlightened parents who provided, up to a late age, a very satisfactory protective covering.

Ben was only now, at twenty-seven, throwing off this 'protective covering', and because his drive for autonomy came so late it came the more brutally. He had to cut himself off emotionally from Vita very thoroughly, misreading her sometimes in order to do so, and he had to keep it up for a very long time. He ended his letter to Nigel by saying that once one has thrown off the protective covering, 'one enters into a new standing with one's parents – the same affection, even heightened, but not the same mutual dependence and understanding. Exactly the same thing happened to Mummy and Daddy in their relationship with their own parents. And if it doesn't happen, terrible unknown forces like Oedipus complexes come into operation. It is a necessary stage in the development of a man.'

Without falling into Ben's copy-book psychological simplifications, it is worth considering whether Vita had ever been maturely objective about her own mother during her mother's lifetime; whether she had ever come out from beneath the perilous, seductive protective covering that B.M. held out, or denied, or imposed, according to whim. Vita often said to Harold that Violet reminded her of B.M. But in some ways in all her love affairs Vita had been enacting B.M. In Violet she had met her match and an equal, in personality, of her mother. Harold was a case apart. So was Virginia.

Vita's relationship with Virginia was strengthened and softened by the anxieties of wartime. Vita kept the Woolfs supplied with butter, which was rationed (at Sissinghurst they made their own) and with knitting-wool spun from the Jacob's sheep bred at Sissinghurst. Vita had managed to get to Rodmell for a few visits; in early October 1940, at Monk's House, Virginia had told her she was 'scribbling her reminiscences', and wrote in her diary that she fell into 'a warm slipper relationship' with Vita at once. Always jealous, she added: 'Sans Gwen its [*sic*] so simple. Gwen, she says, is "as a child" to her.' Virginia thought Gwen was a complete egotist. On their own, Vita and Virginia were lovingly supportive. 'You mean more to me than you will ever know,'[3] wrote Vita in her letter of thanks.

On 17 February 1941 Vita was at Monk's House again, spending a night after giving her well-worn lecture on Persia to the Rodmell Women's Institute. She wrote to Harold:

Virginia has gone to talk to the bedint and I sit alone in her friendly room with its incredible muddle of objects – so crowded that I am afraid of knocking something over. (I've already broken a chair.) Leonard has departed for the market, laden with baskets of apples and carrots. They *are* nice. Leonard has now got a cat, which means that the rooms are further crowded by tin dishes on the floor for the cat to make messes in.

Vanessa Bell came to tea. 'I like her too, and should like her even better if she hadn't a wen on her nose.' All the talk was about Vanessa's twenty-year-old daughter Angelica, who was living with Bunny Garnett – aged fifty – and planning to marry him. 'The situation is slightly complicated by the fact that Duncan [Grant] and Bunny once had an affair.... As Duncan is Angelica's father, it seems to add incest to sodomy. My joke; not theirs, though no doubt they have made it.'

Vita was not making many jokes. All her budgerigars were dying, since she could not get their proper food. She was badly depressed, writing in her diary on 28 February, 'This atrophy of mind has gone on for a week now.' Virginia's mind, had she but known it, was in an even worse state. On 6 March Vita wrote to her, suggesting possible dates for the Woolfs to come to Sissinghurst – by bus, since there was so little petrol to be had. Virginia did not commit herself to a date. It is possible that her first suicide note was written, and her first suicide attempt made, on 18 March. She wrote to Vita on 22 March, enclosing a letter sent to the *New Statesman*, patently for Vita but addressed to 'Miss Virginia Woolf': 'What a queer thought transference! No, I'm not you. No, I don't keep budgerigars. Louie's survive: and she feeds them on scraps.... If we come over, may I bring her a pair if any survive? Do they all die in an instant? When shall we come? Lord knows ... ' On 25 March one of Vita's alsatians, Martin, killed another dog and had to be destroyed. Vita was with him when he was shot. 'All most painful.'

On 28 March, while Leonard was in the house, Virginia drowned herself in the river, leaving letters for him and for Vanessa on the mantelpiece in the sitting-room at Monk's House. Leonard had seen her in her 'lodse' in the garden half an hour before. It was a Friday. On the Monday following, Vita had letters from both Leonard and Vanessa telling her what had happened. She wrote to them at once, and to Harold.

Leonard came home [*sic*] to find a note saying she was going to commit suicide and they think she has drowned herself as he found her stick floating on the river. He says she has not been well for the last few weeks and was terrified of going mad again. He says 'It was, I suppose, the strain of the war and finishing her book [*Between the Acts*]' and she could not rest or eat.

Why, oh why, did he leave her alone, knowing all this? He must be reproaching himself terribly, poor man. They had not yet found the body.

I simply can't take it in, – that lovely mind, that lovely spirit. And she seemed so well when I last saw her, and I had a joky letter from her only a couple of weeks ago.

She must have been quite out of her mind or she would never have brought such sorrow and horror on Leonard and Vanessa.

Vanessa has seen him and says he was amazingly self-controlled and calm, but insisted on being left alone. I cannot help wondering if he will follow her example. I do not see him living without her.

On that same Monday Harold – knowing nothing of what had happened – was writing a very unhappy letter to Vita. Their letters crossed. The Vita he loved was resilient and supportive; as he had written after a previous weekend, 'You are so wise and gentle, darling – I always know that with you I shall find comfort and counsel.' But this last weekend, with Vita depressed by the war, the dead budgerigars, and the shooting of Martin, she had not been wise or gentle. Her reaction to depression had been to drink too much. Harold wrote to her from his desk at the Ministry of Information: 'I do not know what it is, but I never seem to be really able to help you when you are in trouble':

I get anxious when I see you with a bad colour and not listening to anybody and speaking slowly and with difficulty. I always know that those moments mean staggers and it frightens me. I don't think it is nerves but I do think it is something to do with glands or the gland which makes one balance properly. I do worry so when these moods come on you since I want to persuade you to see a doctor and know you will not agree.

Harold was not just being extremely delicate. He and Vita talked freely about the drinking problems of Dorothy Wellesley and his brother Freddy. It was not so much tact that made him refuse to face her with the issue, or to face it himself, but pain and pride – pride in Vita, pride for Vita. He came to use a formula – 'your muzzy moods' – to describe what he noticed. He blurred the truth; even, so far as he could, in his own mind. On this occasion he was so wretched that he added two pages of deeper fears and uncertainties:

> I wonder if you would have been happier if married to a more determined and less sensitive man. On the one hand you would have hated any sense of control or management and other men might not have understood your desire for independence. I have always respected that, and you have often mistaken it for aloofness on my part. What bothers me is whether I have given way too much to your eccentricities, even as Dada gave way too much to B.M.'s eccentricities.
>
> But what has always worried me is your dual personality. The one tender, wise, and with such a sense of responsibility. And the other rather cruel and extravagant. The former has always been what I have clung to as the essential you – but the latter has always alarmed me and I have tried to dismiss it from my mind. . . . I have felt that this side of you was beyond my understanding, and when you have got into a real mess because of it you have been angry with me for not coping with the more violent side of yourself.
>
> I do not think you have ever quite realized how deeply unhappy your eccentric side has often rendered me. When I am unhappy I shut up like an oyster. . . .
>
> I love you so much darling. I hold my head in my hands worrying about you.

Vita's letter to him about Virginia's suicide arrived in London the next day: Harold came straight down to Sissinghurst to be with Vita. Nothing was said; Virginia was not spoken of. 'We are funny people, you and I,' Vita wrote to him, in gratitude for his coming; 'it was Virginia's death that brought you and yet we never mentioned it. . . . I am sorry I went to sleep. I had not slept much the night before and could hardly keep awake, you know how it siezes one at about 4 o'clock the following afternoon.'

His own unhappy letter to her did not arrive until he had gone back to London. It made 'almost unbearable reading,' Vita said in her reply, 'partly because I had expected it to be about Virginia and was genuinely surprised'. She refused to take his anxieties seriously, or to engage with any of the issues he raised. 'I have a very happy nature really and only get into moods of despair occasionally. It is silly and selfish of me to say I mind the war, when so many people are suffering from it so infinitely more':

But truly I do not think I have glands or anything! I feel so well as a rule that it sounds quite funny. Nor do I quite see what you mean by my eccentricity; I can't see that I am eccentric in the least, unless liking to live here is eccentric, but lots of people have been recluses by nature (which I suppose I am)...

So do not worry, my love. I give you my word of honour I am all right... You have always been more sweet to me than I could describe, and I *quite certainly* don't wish I had married anybody else!

It was a letter designed not to deceive but to reassure him, to restore to him 'his' Vita.

On 8 April Vita went to Charleston to see Vanessa. Rather to her dismay Vanessa said Leonard would like to see her too, so she went on to Rodmell.

He was having his tea, – just one tea-cup on the table where they always had tea. The house full of his flowers and all Virginia's things lying about as usual. He said Let us go somewhere more comfortable, and took me up to her sitting-room. There was her needlework on a chair and all her coloured wools hanging over a sort of little towel-horse she had made for them. Her thimble on the table. Her scribbling-block with her writing on it. The window from which one can see the river.

I said Leonard, I do not like you being here alone like this. He turned those piercing blue eyes on me and said it's the only way.

Leonard told Vita that when he could not find Virginia anywhere in the house or garden he had walked to see if she was in a derelict house she was fond of, up on the Downs, called Mad Misery. (Vita remembered Virginia saying she would take her to Mad Misery one day.) 'They have been dragging the river but have given up the search.' Vita knew Virginia could swim, because of a story she had told about swimming in the nude with Rupert Brooke at Cambridge. But Virginia had been wearing her gumboots, which would have filled with water; and, surmised Leonard, she might have weighted her pockets with stones.

He was right. Virginia's body was found by children on 18 April. Leonard gave Vita the manuscript of *Mrs Dalloway* with part of *The Common Reader* 'mixed up with it'; and in July he sent her an early copy of Virginia's last novel, *Between the Acts*.

It has been suggested that *Between the Acts* was in part Virginia's letter of farewell to Vita, in the way that *Orlando* was her letter of love; and that Mrs Manresa in this final book, in her lustful and cornucopian aspects, was a version of Vita. 'It appears that Virginia Woolf was actually writing into her novel a private code to Vita, a code which carried the message of love, hate, lust, infidelity, fear, and death. Only Vita was meant to detect that message, and only she was meant to decipher it.'[4] If this is true, Vita failed to detect and decipher the message, or else repressed the fact that she had done so. She wrote to Ben that for her *Between the Acts* was 'a terrible disappointment'.

There were other disappointments. Gwen had gallstones. The garden was neglected and the lawn sacrificed to make hay for the animals. In July Duff Cooper and Harold were replaced at the Ministry of Information. Vita warned Ben, 'He minds awfully not being in the government any more.... It is not a subject for gay chaff.' She was, in this crisis, the gentle supportive Vita he needed her to be.

Virginia's death had a paradoxically salutary effect on Vita. She had no moral feelings against suicide, except in so far as it hurt other people. She believed Virginia must already have been deranged, to have been capable of so hurting Leonard and Vanessa. (Vita's son Nigel, editing Virginia's letters, came to believe that she died sane, 'courageously on her own terms'.[5]) Vita felt that she herself might have been able to prevent it happening at all. Writing to Harold eight years later, she said that

> the two people I miss most are Virginia and Geoffrey Scott – not that Geoffrey wasn't an awful nuisance to me – he was, and an anxiety.... And Virginia even more so, because she was never a nuisance, but only a delight.... An anxiety of course, and I still think that I might have saved her if only I had been there and had known the state of mind she was getting into. I think she would have told me – as she did tell me on previous occasions.

In the reminiscence of Virginia she wrote for *Horizon* in May 1941, she dwelt upon the Virginia who was 'only a delight', emphasizing her sense of fun and the 'rollicking enjoyment she got out of easy things', in contrast with the public image of Bloomsbury as cold and languid. She wrote of the 'mental excitement' that was the keynote of Virginia's life, and compared her to Coleridge in this; and, in a memorable sentence, said how well her name had suited her: 'Tenuousness and purity were in her baptismal name, and a hint of the fang in the other.'

Virginia's death jolted Vita into a realization of her own priorities and responsibilities, into an acceptance of Harold's dependence on her, and of how much she owed to him. The expressions of affection and solidarity in her letters to him became more explicit and frequent:

> I was thinking to myself, as one does think when one is alone and doing something mechanical like putting dahlias into a trug, I was thinking 'How queer! I suppose Hadji and I have been about as unfaithful to one another

as one well could be from the conventional point of view, even worse than unfaithful if you add in homosexuality, and yet I swear no two people could love one another more than we do after all these years.'

Infidelity was on her mind; Evelyn Irons, who was working in the London Fire Service, was coming down for a night. Vita had not seen her for nine years. There was a moon and the nightingales sang. Vita told Harold about these, but not that Evelyn had been there.

She tried to keep her despairing moods from Harold, but noted them in her diary. 9 September 1941: 'Alone here. A sudden longing for Virginia. Not much good.' 10 September: 'Alone here. The garden is nothing but weeds. Can't cope with them. Depressed. Can't write.' Yet when Christopher St John came for a night and visitors came to tea, she wrote 'Can I never be alone?'

She told Harold she loved him 'sentimentally' now, copying out for him her old diary notes about the day they first saw Sissinghurst, and going even further back in their shared history: 'I'm glad we went to that ball at Hatfield', and 'I see you always as the Hadji who brushed his curls on the way to Constantinople in 1913.' Both she and Harold enjoyed speculating about the marriages their sons would make. Ben's requirements, Vita said, were so exacting that she could think of no way of satisfying them except by an advertisement in the *New Statesman*. 'But he does want to marry, and he *should* marry.' (Ben was becoming very silent during his visits home, she noted sadly.) Harold drew up a list of twenty-one qualities he reckoned necessary for any woman that Nigel married; he thought that Sheila Graham, the girl Nigel brought – unprecedentedly – to Sissinghurst at the end of September, possessed them all. Vita was not at all detached; she was excited, and in suspense. But the weekend passed without an announcement, and later Nigel told them of Miss Graham's engagement to one of his brother officers. 'Poor Niggs! I have a pain in my heart for him,' wrote Vita to Harold.

Vita's diary, 24 February 1942: 'Getting on pretty well with my bloody book.... Staying up late at nights, writing. The only form of happiness I can find – alone with Martha [the dog] and secrecy towards midnight.' She had abandoned her icy tower (coal was hard to come by) when Mac left to nurse the wounded abroad, and established herself in Mac's room in the gatehouse block. She finished *Grand Canyon* on 24 March, and as the evenings lengthened, spent long hours after dinner working in the overgrown garden. She bought a new Japanese cherry – 'It is a lovely thing, with greenish-white flowers like an iceberg.... If only Niggs [to whom she had willed Sissinghurst] doesn't sell this place for building plots, our grandchildren will have really beautiful big flowering trees to look at – but will anybody care about such things in 50 years time ?'

Then came a blow. Leonard Woolf turned down her *Grand Canyon*. (Would it have happened if Virginia had been there ?) 'This is one of the most unpleasant letters I have ever had to write,' he told her, 'primarily because as an author you have always treated us so extraordinarily well that it seems almost unthinkable that the Hogarth Press should reject a book of yours.' John Lehmann, then working with the Press, agreed with him that the book, which was set during the present war, was 'profoundly defeatist' and would make 'a bad impression'.[6]

In her Author's Note, Vita called *Grand Canyon* 'a cautionary tale'. She imagines in it that Germany had won the war in Europe, and that many Europeans fled to the United States. The United States Government makes a treaty with Germany, and is taken over by Germany as a result. Part I takes place in the Grand Canyon Hotel, packed with European refugees. In Part II they have all been killed, but do not know it, as they, or their spirits, wander down the Bright Angel Trail into the Canyon itself. Among the refugees is Mrs Temple, a withdrawn, solitary woman of fifty, not unlike Vita herself. Her tranquil beyond-the-grave relationship with another refugee reflects Vita's with Harold : 'It was like a very prolonged, very quiet orgasm of the understanding instead of the quick and quickly forgotten orgasm of the senses. . . . It might be an unusual form of love, but why should love be so stereotyped, so orthodox always ?'

It was the book's political implications that worried Leonard. First, the supposition of Hitler's total world victory, and secondly the implied criticism of the United States – which was not yet involved in the war when he read the manuscript. A week after she got his letter of rejection Vita sent the manuscript off to Heinemann, who also turned it down. It was taken, after revision, by Michael Joseph, who published it in early November. Her reputation was enough to ensure that 8,000 copies were sold before publication, but she received what she herself called 'some bloody reviews'. *Grand Canyon* was no more of a critical or literary success than *The Dark Island* had been.

# CHAPTER 29

ONCE or twice a week since war broke out, Vita had been visiting a very old lady, Katherine Drummond, who lived with her husband – a retired general – at Sissinghurst Place. Mrs Drummond came to depend on these visits, and she and Vita became like mother and daughter, though Vita sometimes bemoaned the inroads this new friendship made on her time. Vita also made friends with Mrs Drummond's daughter-in-law Bunny, whom she described to Harold as 'a nice decent person. Not exciting, but *so* decent.' It was dull, decent people like Bunny Drummond that Vita got on with better nowadays than her more wordly, socialite neighbours such as Victor Cazalet. Christopher St John's passion for her had become chaste, an almost religious devotion, and they had a 'tryst' to talk on the telephone every Friday evening. Vita had new admirers too – such as Margaret Howard, an aspiring poet who came to see her first in April 1942; thenceforth, according to Christopher's jealous comments and a letter Mrs Howard wrote to Nigel after Vita's death, they 'wrote to each other nearly every day'. Vita also wrote nearly every day to Mac, with the Queen Alexandra Nursing Service overseas.

But her essential loneliness was deepened in 1942 by the departure of her sister-in-law Gwen, who had been living, on and off, at or near Sissinghurst since 1933, and who had become part of the fabric of Vita's life. In 1940 Gwen's husband Sam had inherited from his uncle the title of Lord St Levan and the great family house on St Michael's Mount, off the coast of Cornwall. After three years' war service, Sam was home and intending to live at the Mount, and Gwen – now Lady St Levan – was going too.

Vita was upset. Unreasonably, she felt Gwen's willingness to go and live at St Michael's Mount was a betrayal and a dereliction; she even felt that Harold was a 'quisling' for visiting his sister's new home and admiring it. Both the boys were being sent abroad too. (Ben had been transferred to Intelligence, where he was less unhappy.) Nigel came home on leave before he left: 'We sat talking till 12.30. I was brave and asked him outright about Sheila. ... We talked about life and the war; about being frightened; about not wishing to die. Then he gave me a look I shall never forget, and said: "But I have come to the conclusion that life is not the most valuable of one's possessions."' Vita, in 1942, agreed with him. She had fantasies of suicide that autumn, which she expressed in private unpublished poems. It was not death by means of her always available 'bare bodkin' that she imagined, but death with a real bare bodkin – a knife – in the wood. Harold did not know this, but he knew enough about her to know she needed comfort, and after one of Ben's more successful visits home reassured her that although she had once said she could never establish a complete relationship with anyone, she had, with him and with the boys, established a relation of absolute love and trust.

Vita was, in her isolation, becoming even more conservative and traditionalist. She, who had once argued that women's careers were necessities to them, was amazed when her favourite niece Philippa St Aubyn announced that she was going to train as a children's hospital nurse: 'What a sign of the times, isn't it? Most girls of her age, with a rich father etc, would look forward to "having a good time" after the war. I think B.M. would turn in her grave – and personally it does rather make me shudder to think of our niece being thrown into such bedint company.' Some of the signs of the times – such as Lady Ravensdale arriving at the Drummonds' house 'on Victor Cazalet's housemaid's bicycle' – made her laugh. The Beveridge Report – the blueprint for Britain's post-war welfare state – that came out at the end of the year brought her near to outrage.

I think it sounds dreadful. The proletariat being encouraged to breed like rabbits because each new little rabbit means 8/- a week – as though there weren't too many of them already and not enough work to go round, with 2,000,000 unemployed before the war – and everyone being given everything for nothing, a complete discouragement to thrift or effort. ... Lloyd George gave them old age pensions – and what do they do? grumble about having to contribute to the stamps, and then grumble because they don't get money enough. Oh no, I don't hold with Sir William Beveridge, and it all makes me feel very pre-1792.

(She had made Viola say to Sebastian in *The Edwardians*, 'Darling Sebastian, how well I foresee your old age – shut up inside the walls of Chevron, saying that the country has gone to the dogs, a good Tory to the last. What a pity you didn't live in eighteen-fifty!') Her letter crossed with one from Harold saying 'I really do see in the report many things which I have hoped for for years.' Vita returned to the fray:

I fear Mar is an instinctive Tory. . . . I am all for educating the *peuple* into being less awful, less limited, less silly, and for spending lots of money on 1) extended education 2) better-paid teachers, but *not* for giving them everything for nothing, which they don't appreciate anyhow. Health, yes. Education, yes. Old age pensions, I suppose so, in default of euthanasia which I should prefer, as also for the mental deficients. But not this form of charity which will make people fold their arms and feel that they need have no enterprise since everything will be provided for them. It is surely a psychological error.

This discussion ultimately led to her writing Harold a letter that belatedly answered his unhappy one written the weekend that Virginia died. 'Of course I think, with you, that the war and after-the-war matters,' she reassured him on 9 December. But she did not have the coolness and the courage he attributed to her:

My calm is merely my cabbagy nature. Luckily for you, you have never seen the more tempestuous side of my nature. You have only seen an occasional bubble rising to the surface . . . but as you do not like that sort of bubble you have always wisely looked the other way. The emotions which I give to you are deep and strong; I love you more than anything on earth; you are about the only person in whose love I trust.

Not the least of Harold's gifts to her, though she never put this into words, was his unalterable loving belief in the powerfully 'good' Vita; it helped her to believe in that too. And in spite of her violent dislike of the welfare-state idea in general, when it came to a particular case she reacted quite differently. When the Coppers' child had rheumatic fever and the doctor was overcasual in his visiting, Vita was angry 'that they should treat poor people like that. Luckily Mrs Copper has got me to turn to, and I have telephoned; what does the ordinary cottage person do? Just bears it. It makes me go all democratic.'

Vita's diary, 8 January 1943: 'Think of writing a book of four sketches – of Leonard, the 2 St Theresas, and a fourth unworldly person.' The next morning, she unearthed her notes on 'the 2 St Theresas', as she always called them, collating the French and the Spanish spellings, and began writing what was to be *The Eagle and the Dove*, her best non-fiction book. (Leonard Woolf and the 'fourth unworldly person' dropped out at once.) The work took off immediately and restored Vita's equilibrium and her grip on life. Bomb-blast overturned everything in the big room and 'alas alas' broke her purple glass plates; but apart from her regular visits to Mrs Drummond the new routine was quickly established. 'Alone all day. Garden and St Theresa – mostly St Theresa.' (Some narcissus bulbs that she had dug up in Persia sixteen years before suddenly flowered for the first time that spring – 'it shows that one should never lose hope.')

Vita predictably preferred the 'eagle', the earthy, energetic Teresa of Avila – 'really irresistible, so very unbedint and autocratic and unnun-like', 'a grand woman' – to the 'dove', the Little Flower of Lisieux. She struggled through Teresa's autobiography in Spanish, with difficulty and a dictionary; she had a useful correspondence with the distinguished Abbess of Stanbrook, Dame Laurentia McLachlan, who belonged to an enclosed order but was the confidante of many lay people. Vita wrote to Harold on 3 February, after less than a month of intensive reading and writing:

> I think that I am dimly beginning to understand the saints and what they were after, far better than I did when writing about Joan of Arc; it is rather like trying to grasp relativity and every now and then getting a flash of understanding. It is such a totally different world, and the first point to understand is that all the ordinary values are reversed.

Her regular companions, she said, were 'saints and landgirls'; she carried out her responsibilities for the local branch of the Women's Land Army, including their transport from farm to farm, and she lent Vass's cottage for the accommodation of one group – plus a housekeeper, who irritated Vita a great deal:

> What I dislike most about bedint women is the absolute gusto with which they fling themselves into practical difficulties; to them, a missing pie-dish is as much of an excitement as if the entire contents of the British Museum disappeared during the night.... The housekeeper person ended up by asking me what should she give the girls for dinner: did I think boiled turnips would be nice? Oh my God! There are times when I really hate the English.

Vita's division of activities into those that were and those that were not worth consideration was a limitation – and not saintly. St Teresa of Avila, whom she admired so much, would have flung herself with 'absolute gusto' into the problem of the missing pie-dish however much she wished she need not.

Nevertheless, Vita, at the age of fifty-one, was doing some of her own housework for the first time in her life. 'I am still polishing with great effect,' she wrote to Harold on 24 March, 'but it is hell doing the brass hinges on the Coromandel cabinet. I now get up early and do it for an hour before breakfast. I am beginning to see what housemaids mean, when they talk of "dust-traps".'

In April 1943 Vita took part in the poetry reading organized by Osbert and Edith Sitwell at the Aeolian Hall in Bond Street, in the presence of the Queen and the young princesses. Vita lunched first at Sibyl Colefax's house, and then picked up Dorothy Wellesley at the Hyde Park Hotel. The poets were to read from their own work in alphabetical order, which meant that Dottie was last. Harold was in the audience, and told Ben and Nigel in his weekly letter (he used a carbon, and sent the same letter to each) that 'Mummy sat there looking like Pallas Athene in a brown hat.' When her turn came she read 'Moonlight' ('you know, the bit about the coral taffeta trousers') and then the final section of *The Land* : 'Not a tremor in her voice until she came to "That moon, that star" when there was an appropriate wabble. Wild applause.'

Then Vita left the platform to look for Dottie, who had already created a noisy diversion during the interval. She found her in the lobby, in no fit state to perform but determined to do so. Harold came out to Vita's aid, and got hit by Dottie for his pains. Edith Sitwell, according to him, wept to see the occasion spoilt ; both she and Osbert behaved with 'exemplary kindness and discretion'.

Vita got Dottie into a taxi and back to the Hyde Park Hotel, where Violet Trefusis was staying, and between them they escorted Dottie to her room. Vita came home that night 'shattered', and there were repercussions. Poor Dottie telephoned Vita repeatedly, denying that she had been drunk, and speaking of suicide. 'In spite of her violent and apparently genuine denials,' Vita wrote to Harold, 'I do not feel that we can possibly have been mistaken. I do not for a moment think she will commit suicide ... but I do feel dreadfully sorry for her.' ('How happy you and Harold must be together,' lonely Dottie had said on the telephone.) Duff Cooper sent Vita a note : 'You were so much the best – in voice and verse and beauty. Osbert and Edith were amusing and audible. The rest was silence.'

Violet Trefusis came for the first time to Sissinghurst that May, and stayed the night. Vita had mixed feelings about the visit. 'I do want her to see Sissinghurst, but I would rather she just came for luncheon.' Violet, on arrival, said she would be terrified to sleep alone in the dining-room cottage, in Ben's room, so Vita gave her her own bedroom, 'but did not share it with her' : she slept in Harold's room. 'It was all very odd and we were both acutely aware of the oddness. Luckily we were able to say so, which eased it into amusement instead of embarrassment.'

Earlier, while Violet was having a bath before dinner, Vita wrote to Harold about what it was like being alone in a house with Violet again. 'It is rather like speaking a foreign language that one has once known bilingually, and has not used for years : idiomatic phrases, and even bits of slang, come back to one suddenly, yet one finds that the foundation has gone.' Having Violet to stay was 'a shattering experience' that she took several days to get over.

They heard in early July that their neighbour Victor Cazalet had been killed in the aeroplane crash that killed the Polish general Sikorski. 'I will not pretend,' wrote Vita of Cazalet, 'now that he is dead, that I liked him better than I did, but I do think it is awful to die so unnecessarily like that. I hope also that it will be a further warning to you against those dreadful machines' – i.e., aeroplanes. Vita was terrified by the idea of flying, and tried to stop her near and dear from ever doing so. When they defied her ban, she went through agonies of apprehension.

Working fast and with excitement, she finished *The Eagle and the Dove* in six months ; afterwards, she worked in the garden by moonlight until midnight. As she wrote in *The Garden* :

> Strange were those summers ; summers filled with war.
> I think the flowers were the lovelier
> For danger.

She acquired yet more land – Brissenden Farm, with 109 acres, for £4,000. 'Mr Venning [her solicitor] will just have to produce the money somehow.' Harold, with no government office and uneasy about his other main extra-parliamentary activity, his governorship of the BBC, was less buoyant. He had a crisis of confidence in the House of Commons, and confided in Vita his fears of failure. She wrote him a strong letter of advice. He should take stock ; he was dispersing his energies into too many non-essential channels ; which was his mainstream ? She urged him to give up some committees, speaking engagements and articles for newspapers. 'My idea of heaven on earth', she wrote to him that summer, 'would be for Hadji to live here and bury himself morning and evening in his room and write – with perhaps one very interesting job that took him to London once every six months.'

He would have hated it ; but he enjoyed his weekends, in summer. They were happy together trimming the limes and clipping the Rondel in the evenings – while 'bombers stream overhead incessantly in huge formations.' 'We have managed to cope with the actual bones of the garden,' Harold told Ben and Nigel, 'and the hedges are in good trim. But I sometimes feel that Mummy works too hard. . . . She is dreadfully thin.'

She got flu and moved over to Ben's room, with Martha, so that Mrs Staples would not have to carry trays over the garden. On 25 July, at eleven o'clock at night, she heard on her wireless that Mussolini had resigned. She got out of bed, snatched up an old Eton sweater of Ben's, and ran across the dark garden to the South Cottage to bring Harold the good news. On 8 September, when she got back from visiting Gwen who was ill in the London Clinic, she found the station master at Staplehurst 'announcing the unconditional surrender of Italy to everyone coming off the train.'

*The Land* was suddenly bringing in royalties again ; Vita gave the cheque to Harold for a new suit. It was not a flash in the pan ; *The Land* enjoyed a prolonged revival during the war, and in May of 1944 was adapted as 'a sort of litany' to be spoken in Liverpool Cathedral on Rogation Sunday : 'It really reads like something out of Scripture.' Vita, always depressed after a while when she was not writing, was fired to get on with her garden poem ; she did not count the propaganda book she had undertaken for the Women's Land Army as real writing.

The circumstances under which this last commission was arranged opened Vita's eyes to the way some people – particularly those who did not live in an inconvenient 'encampment' like Sissinghurst – were managing to maintain pre-war standards. On 1 October she cleaned up a crocodile suitcase she had bought in Munich in 1921 and drove through 'poor damaged East Grinstead' to Balcombe Place, the home of Lady Denman and her headquarters as supreme head of the Land Army's 800,000 girls. Vita found Lady Denman 'surrounded by innumerable women all rather reminiscent of Hilda Matheson', and they discussed the book she was to write. Vita stayed the night, as she described to Ben, who was now in Egypt :

> I had Lord Denman's bedroom (minus Lord D.) and amused myself very much by opening all the large cupboards and admiring his array of suits, hats, shoes, and hunting-crops. So that is how the rich live! A glass of milk, two biscuits, and a jug of orangeade were put out on what is politely called the night table beside my bed, and there was a lovely writing table with stacks of note-paper and new Relief nibs in the pens.

(Vita herself had started using brown ink, a habit she retained for years : Violet called the resulting script her 'little chocolate crawl'.) Lady Denman apologized to Vita for the shortage of staff 'and said she was afraid I would find everything "very badly done". I thought of Sissinghurst.' Breakfast was brought to her in bed, 'with a carefully folded copy of the *Times* ; I felt sure it had been ironed, and opened it to discover that Gerry [Wellesley] had become Duke of Wellington. This meant that Dottie, with whom I had an appointment to luncheon that day, had become the Duchess of ditto.' (The Wellesleys, in spite of years of complete separation, had never divorced.)

There were changes for her own family too. Negotiations had been going on for more than four years to have Knole taken over by the National Trust, with an arrangement by which it should remain the home of the Sackvilles. Vita and Harold had close contacts with the administration of the National Trust, chiefly through James Lees-Milne who had become a friend of Harold's in the early 1930s. Vita knew that under the control of the Trust, Knole would be not only properly kept up but preserved from change or desecration, though she hated the whole business. She had been irritated by the slowness of her Uncle Charlie and Eddy in making up their minds: 'Eddy is as floppy as an unstaked delphinium in a gale.'

She used a similar garden image in *The Eagle and the Dove*, when writing about the comfort and support found by some temperaments in the authoritarian structures of the Roman Catholic Church:

Only the misfit, the rebel, lonely in a world with different values, perhaps can estimate the consolation of finding himself at last with a company whose aims are entirely similar to his own. No longer a plant blown this way and that by the gale, his precarious roots loosened as he roughly sways, a strong stake now holds him fast, implacable wire engages his tendrils, and above his roots a mulch centuries-old in richness keeps him fed and cool.

Vita did not like authoritarian institutions. But the sense of the passage goes some way to explain her own metamorphosis from would-be vagabond, 'the misfit, the rebel', to the 'pre-1792 Tory' and traditionalist. Equally, her later position, in an England undergoing rapid social change, preserved her status as misfit and rebel.

*The Eagle and the Dove* came out from Michael Joseph in early November. The initial printing of 8,000 copies had to be repeated within three days; between that and October 1947 there were five more reprints, and cheap editions followed. The intensity and absorption with which the book had been researched and written transformed a minority subject into one that interested a wide public. Some of the speed with which it had been written was probably benzedrine. When Harold's doctor prescribed the drug for him that autumn, Vita was already an authority: 'It really is a marvellous stimulant, rather like champagne only less expensive. It makes your brain work like fun.'

Harold gave a sample of her handwriting to an Austrian graphologist, Dr Strelisker. ' "This is", he said, "a woman of great gifts who is extremely nervous but manages to control her nerves. She is afraid of entering into emotional relationships with anyone. She has been much influenced by her childhood." I was amused by this.' Vita replied that 'extreme nervousness well controlled' was only too true. She was nervous with all visitors, even someone as familiar and welcome as Gwen:

> You know, Hadji, it disconcerts me so much having somebody to stay that I am not at all nice at first ... and then I adjust myself and it gets all right; I knew I was horrid and aloof on Monday, but had recovered by Tuesday and could get at the real Gwen whom I know and can talk to *real*; and then this morning she goes away and I find little coffee cups [i.e., reminders of her] which twist my heart and all my irritation goes and I wish I could have it all over again and be nicer.

It was worse with the 'clever' friends. She wrote to Eardley Knollys on 21 December that she thought 'complete simplicity often expresses better than any amount of cleverness the things we all feel.' She said in the same letter, speaking of religion, that 'there are aspects of life which are very rum, – far rummer than the intelligentsia of this world would choose to realize.' She had dedicated *The Eagle and the Dove* to 'Maria-Teresa' – the name Gwen had taken on her baptism into the Roman Catholic Church – and quoted on the dedication page Newman's 'There is a God, – the most august of all conceivable truths.' Harold suspected that she was considering becoming a Roman Catholic herself (as had Eddy, the 'unstaked delphinium'). No, she said, no, never.

> But I do not see how you cannot believe in God at all. Call him 'Thing' if you like, and if the word God puts you off because of all its connotations. But I do not see how you can get out of the idea of a creator and inventor, if everything is not to be utterly senseless. ... You see there *must* be some explanation, some solution, and that is God.

Harold was to spend the new year of 1944 with Gwen in Cornwall; the day he was to leave, he fell down the marble steps on the way to the cloakroom at the Reform Club and fainted. He proceeded to travel just the same, and Guy Burgess, who had been with him at the club, telephoned to Vita to tell her what had happened, and that Harold was all right. Harold was fifty-eight; it was the Nicolsons' first *memento mori*. Edwin Lutyens died in January 1944; Ethel Smyth died in May. Rosamund (Grosvenor) Lynch was among those killed when a bomb fell on the Savoy Chapel in July. Her husband sent Vita a telegram, though she and Rosamund had met only rarely in recent years. 'It has saddened me rather', Vita wrote, 'that somebody so innocent, so silly and so harmless should be killed in this idiotic and violent way.'

The deadly V1 and V2 bombs had begun falling, in Germany's last bid to change the course of the war. Harold described what it was like at home on 6 February in one of his joint weekly letters to Ben and Nigel : 'Mummy and I were in the little cubby hole off the dining-room fiddling with the wireless when there was a yell in the air ... thereafter came a double bump and the house shook. Martha leapt out of the cubby hole panting with fear and with saliva dripping from her jaws.' Mrs Staples had seen the German bomber on fire hurtling past the tower, missing it by a few yards. It fell near the moat, making a deep crater. 'Nothing was damaged but our nerves. I do not think that Kent is a safe place. I think it is very dangerous indeed.'

Vita had begun writing down her dreams in a book. She recorded her recurring childhood dreams about Knole, and also her more disturbing wartime dreams. In general, she dreamt of houses or of empty land-scapes of 'unearthly beauty'. These were happy dreams. She recorded also, in her 'little chocolate crawl', but undated, 'I dreamt I was given a lioness as a present, for a pet – but though her head was normal her body had no hide, and was just raw red meat – sloppy when I patted it – and she kept rubbing herself affectionately against my legs like a cat which disgusted me although I was ashamed of being disgusted because I felt I ought to be fond of her.'

On 4 February 1944, when the air battles had begun, she wrote down in the book not a dream but a real experience. It was a couple of days before the events described by Harold to the boys ; he was in London, and Vita alone in the South Cottage when the siren woke her. Unusually for her, 'I became so frightened I could not control my limbs from trembling.' She lay in bed listening to the planes droning overhead and waiting for the crash. At last she got up and went downstairs with Martha. The doors rattled with the gunfire and she heard bombs falling. She tried to think about other things so as not to be frightened, but failed.

> I tried to *think* phrases like 'You are in God's keeping', but that didn't work because I didn't know how God intended his keeping to work out, so then I tried to *see* God – staring at a knot in the wood of the door, and of course I saw nothing at all, but in about two minutes in the midst of my alarm a complete peace came to me – my limbs ceased from trembling and indifference to my fate took the place of terror. This is all quite true and so striking that I must record it.

A week later, Knole was damaged – not seriously – by a bomb. Eddy rang up to tell Vita, who was so upset that Elvira Niggeman (Harold's secretary at King's Bench Walk, who spent some days at Sissinghurst working for Vita) contacted Harold. Vita wrote to him too.

> I mind frightfully, frightfully. I always persuade myself that I have finally torn Knole out of my heart, and then the moment anything touches it every nerve is *à vif* again. I cannot bear to think of Knole wounded, and me not there to look after it and be wounded with it.
>
> Those filthy Germans ! . . . Oh Hadji I wish you were here.

She went with him to a tea party at Buckingham Palace. It was not an unqualified success. They stood with the other guests gazing at the King and Queen 'like cows looking at a train', as Harold put it. He himself was flatteringly borne off to talk to Princess Elizabeth ; Vita was not, and she found no opportunity to thank the Queen for allowing her to dedicate the Land Army book to her. Then Harold was so anxious that Vita should not miss her train home that he hustled her away a little prematurely. Apologizing for this, he told her afterwards that she had looked 'so lovely and distinguished and wonderful' and that he had been 'so deeply proud' of her. This was undoubtedly true. Equally, he had for so many years been conducting his social life independently, in bachelor fashion, that responsibility for his distinguished, ill-at-ease wife was perhaps not easy for him to handle. And Vita was happier next day, lunching with Ozzie Beale ('Oh how much I like that man !') and his wife ('I had a *delicious* pudding at the Beales') at the Castle Farm. The Government had put a temporary ban on all non-essential movement in the south coastal area of England, which took in Sissinghurst, so Vita's freedom from London visitors was briefly secure. 'If Sibyl [Colefax] comes she will get put in prison or have to pay £100.'

Vita kept up her visits to old Mrs Drummond, a loving tyrant. It was as if Mrs Drummond elicited all Vita's warm, positive feelings towards motherly women, whereas the demands of Lady Carnock, Harold's mother, drove her to fury. Vita resented Lady Carnock's dependence on Harold and her constant requests to be visited in distant Cornwall, where she was living near Gwen. 'She is a damned selfish grasping old woman, that's what she is. . . . I hate your mummy, I hate her, I hate her, I hate her. I don't care if she *is* 84. I wish she was dead. . . . I am furious, and you are just as weak as a cup of tea with too much milk in it.' Harold himself found his mother's demonstrativeness distasteful, and was glad when Gwen managed to whittle one of his visits down to one night. 'She understands more than anyone what I feel about the physical side of it all. That is the way homosexuals are formed. My sweet sweet Mar.' 'I don't think it *entirely* explains the making of homosexuals,' Vita retorted cheerfully. 'What about orphan homosexuals ?'

Vita decided to sell Long Barn. She held a sale of its contents, after having taken some pieces over to Sissinghurst. The most profitable item was a Chippendale armchair that fetched £102 (the reserve price was twenty-five pounds); but an oak wardrobe 'believed to have belonged to Queen Anne Boleyn and formerly at Hever Castle' (presumably wheedled out of William Waldorf Astor by B.M.) was left unsold. Large quantities of Jacobean oak furniture fetched risible prices. The total sum raised was £1,471 15s 6d, which included the sale of some 3,000 books.

It was not a good time to be selling antiques; within the week, the Allied invasion of Normandy had begun. 'No sleep last night from aeroplanes,' wrote Vita on 7 June. She saw her first doodle-bug (flying bomb) shot down at dawn that morning. It was hardly worth going to bed. 'It is like sleeping in the Piccadilly Underground.... We listen intently to the wireless at all hours.' Even by day, 'shadows of aeroplanes keep winking across my paper as I write. Once it used to be the shadow of white pigeons.' The greenhouses were smashed, and a window in Vita's abandoned tower. On 27 June, while Vita was reading her mail in the dining-room, a doodle-bug was blown up in the air by a Spitfire just over the Beales's barn. 'Mrs Staples and I clutched each other with excitement.'

Then on 1 August they heard on the one o'clock news that Paris had been liberated. They were having Sunday lunch; Harold was there, and Elvira Niggeman – who was 'so excited that she manufactured a tricolour flag out of some old envelopes of Christopher St John's and stuck it on top of the greengages on the dining-room table'.

On their wedding anniversary, 1 October, Vita handed Harold a poem she had written for him, which began

> I must not tell, how dear you are to me,
> It is unknown, a secret from myself
> Who should know best. I would not if I could
> Expose the meaning of such mystery.

Harold, as he told Ben and Nigel, 'became embarrassed and did not know what to say – so moved was I and so pleased. I loathe myself when I get tongue-tied. It is strange that someone so voluble as I am about incidental matters should be totally unable to express myself when something important happens, which I really care about.' A man of letters if ever there was one, he compensated for it, on paper.

They had been painfully anxious about their sons, who were both in Italy in 1944. Ben had given Vita's name as his next of kin; Nigel had given Harold's. Vita wrote to Elvira Niggeman about the eventuality of Nigel being killed. 'What I am writing to ask is : should a hand-delivered telegram come to KBW [King's Bench Walk] while you are there, could you open it? and if it is about Nigel, suppress it from H. and telephone to me? I would then come up to London and break it to him.... I should not like H. to have this shock by himself.'

Harold, who was passionately devoted to both his sons, saw in Nigel someone who would follow him into public life. Just as Ben had to free himself from Vita's projections, so Nigel needed to free himself from Harold's. In October Nigel wrote to his mother from Perugia. Like Ben, he was often irritated by his mother's prejudices, illogicality, slowness, and passion for tradition and the Royal Family; but on this occasion he wrote to her 'because I look on you as an ally'. Not that he looked on his father as an opponent, but 'I think that you, in a way, have a better idea of the sort of person I am, could be more sympathetic with what I want to do, and will argue my case for me.'

He knew his father wanted him to go into the House of Commons; but Nigel felt that he had led 'too soft a life'. No children, he told Vita, had had greater advantages than he and Ben: 'parents such as God provides for one in a million', the best education, encouragement, no pressures or restrictions, money of their own, independence, and 'always Sissinghurst to come back to'. The trouble was, he said, that he had never had to 'struggle for anything', and did not want to move on after the war to a series of similar 'feathered nests' such as the House of Commons, which he felt would not suit him. He had a 'passion for independence' and dreamed of building his own life in some remote country area. He also wanted to marry – 'For I no longer have this strange distrust of married life – strange because you both have provided me with such a flawless example.'

Nigel's distrust of married life was not so strange. He was aware – not always comfortably – of the complexity of his parents' private lives. While he had not had the unpleasant experience that Ben had had with B.M., neither had he had the reassuring sequel, Ben's long truthful conversation with Vita.

The Nicolsons' marriage was a 'flawless example' of something that few people could sustain, or would aspire to sustain. Vita and Harold were indeed 'parents such as God provides for one in a million', and in their adolescence the boys met many older people of quality and intellect who took them seriously and became their friends. Yet although the bonding between the four Nicolsons was very strong, there was a sense in which it seems to have been notional. The platonic ideals of relationship, however dearly held in the heart, are not a substitute for reality. Vita had no talent or taste for the commonality of family life. Sissinghurst itself was a world apart; the boys could not easily or casually bring friends there. Although everyone had that necessity, 'a room of one's own', there was never a commonly used family sitting-room, nor any desire on anyone's part to make one. The often tiresome noisy day-long intimacy of family life was unknown to Ben and Nigel; intimacy was something that came in the morning mail. Harold, who liked fun and found his own, was maybe looking for some expression of the family's singularity when he wrote to Nigel in May 1944: 'I think both you and Ben have missed actual gaiety in your lives. You have had much of interest, many adventures, much study, and full lives. You have had deep affection from Mummy and me. But we have not been able to give you that gaiety which young people should have.' (Not that Nigel and Ben were so young any more as to expect to depend on their parents for gaiety or anything else: Ben had his thirtieth birthday in 1944.) Vita was less aware of the effects on her sons of their unusual upbringing, because the family style had been established chiefly to meet her own needs. She was astonished when Eddy Sackville-West said of Ben and Nigel in 1945, 'How inhibited they are, those two!'

Vita's back was giving her serious trouble. Her doctor diagnosed arthritis. 'Depressed, feeling that my youth is now really behind me and nothing but a crippled age before me,' she wrote in her diary on 14 November. Evelyn Irons, who was now a war correspondent (and was awarded the Croix de Guerre), came to tell them about the excitement in Paris, where she had been. But when troops with tanks encamped in the grounds of Sissinghurst shortly before Christmas, Vita's depression engulfed her again.

> I have lost all pleasure in the lake, and indeed in the woods, since soldiers invaded them and robbed them of the privacy I so loved. . . .
>
> I wish I could sort out my ideas about this new world. I feel one ought to be able to adapt oneself, and not struggle to go back to, and live in, an obsolete tradition.
>
> All this makes me very unhappy, Hadji. And my back worries me too. I don't mind its hurting, but the *weakness* it brings to my limbs worries me. You see I used to be so strong. . . .
>
> I feel that I, and the lake, and the wood, are all damaged and spoilt for ever – and I mind very much. Our lost youth, in fact. . . .
>
> If only I thought I could write good poetry I should not mind anything. But even over that I have lost my convictions.

One of her dreams that year was that she 'could write poetry', and 'wrote and wrote till I nearly died. . . . It was one of the happiest dreams while it lasted but quite the most miserable on waking.' But her Nativity poem 'It was right, it was suitable', which was to be part of *The Garden*, was broadcast on the BBC on Christmas Eve. With Harold, she heard Hitler 'gabbling' on the wireless as 1944 became 1945. On that last night of the old year she had another animal dream: she was trying in the dream to identify 'my own cow', but was approached by the wrong one:

> This wrong cow was intractable, so I gave her a leather glove to chew to keep her in a good temper. Another cow then pushed me aside, and in a rage I hit her on the nose. She then looked at me with an expression of (unbearable) reproach, and exposed her udder which was bleeding with dark blood. . . . The dominant impression left by this dream was that the other cow was trying to take advantage of my cow, and that the bleeding udder of my cow was unendurably pathetic.

That winter, Mrs Staples was laid up with a poisoned leg. The pipes froze, and so did the lavatories. The acute discomfort of his home became almost more than Harold could bear. Just before Christmas, having walked through the snow to the Priest's House (where the pipes were unfrozen) to shave, he found himself without a razorblade and had to go all the way back to the South Cottage. 'And this convinces me how bitter it was to inhabit a house which was so cold and draughty and which entailed having to shave in a distant cottage . . . Sissinghurst is almost intolerably uncomfortable in winter.' He wished Vita had for herself 'a sitting-room, dining-room, bathroom and bedroom all opening into each other and most centrally heated.' But he minded the cold and the inconvenience much more than she did, in spite of her arthritis. She sat writing in the boys' old school sweaters and a mothy rabbit-skin coat, and if her work went well she was content.

She was unpredictable. It was she who suggested giving a party in London at King's Bench Walk for her birthday in March. 'Mar would of course pay: I have heaps of money at the moment, as Elvira will tell you.' She boasted cheerfully about her party to Evelyn Irons – 'a lovely party, crammed with every kind of celebrity'. It was a pre-dinner drinks party; earlier in the day she had recorded three broadcasts. James Lees-Milne wrote in his diary: 'Eardley [Knollys] and I walked to King's Bench Walk to a party Harold and Vita gave together, a very exceptional occasion. Harold in a gay and frolicsome mood; Vita very beautiful, regal, tall and thin, wearing a wide-brimmed hat over her eyes and smoking from a long cigarette holder. She is never frolicsome.'[1] Ten days later Captain Nicolson – Ben – came home from the war. 'Haven't seen him since October 1942. He looks quite extraordinary,' Vita wrote in her diary. He had been hit by a lorry in Italy, and was encased in plaster, with a filthy dressing on his head. 'Mummy puts bandages round it to hide the stains,' Harold wrote to Nigel (was she recreating

'Julian'?); 'Ben regards this as fuss on her part.... Thin and enormous he stalks through the streets of London arousing pity and terror.'

With the war over bar the shouting, on 23 April 1945 the blackout was lifted, and Vita turned on the garden lights for the first time in five years. Next day, she took possession once more of her tower room and 'scribbled a little verse straight off':

> There is a padlock on my door
> And 'Private' writ beneath my stair.
> Oh stranger, wander everywhere
> Within the garden that I made,
> But come not here, oh come not here,
> Where I am shy but unafraid.

Sending this to Harold, she said: 'It isn't true about the garden that *I* made, because Hadji made it really, with his design, but Hadji wouldn't scan. I only planted things. The credit is entirely yours.' The lifting of fear enabled her to write poetry fluently again – too fluently, she thought. She distrusted the 'appalling virtuosity' that had descended on her. 'My fear is that facility may damage quality.... I also feel that flatness has come with increasing competence.'

On VE Day, the day of Germany's unconditional surrender, 12 May, Ben and Harold were sitting in the garden in the afternoon when they heard the great news on the wireless. Harold wrote to Nigel: 'With great dignity Ben and I rose from our seats and walked across the garden to find Mummy. She was fiddling with aquilegias against the wall. Solemnly we climbed the tower steps and out onto the worn parapet. We tied the flag to its ropes. We hoisted it. And there after five sad years it fluttered in the spring breeze.' Vita, thinking to see London celebrating victory, went up by train with Ben and Harold in the morning. But the people did not come out on the streets until the evening; nothing was happening; impatient, she caught the train home to Martha, and the garden, and the tower. The next 'great day', as Vita called it in her diary, was 17 June. The other Captain Nicolson – Nigel – telephoned. 'He breakfasted in Naples and reached London by tea-time.' The war was over, and both the boys back safely.

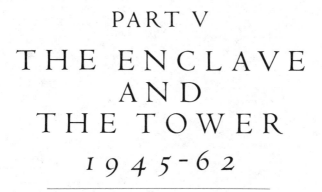

PART V

# THE ENCLAVE
## AND
## THE TOWER
*1945-62*

# CHAPTER 30

ITALIAN prisoners of war were cutting the grass at Sissinghurst in the summer of 1945. Gradually Vita's pre-war staff reappeared. Jack Copper came to ask if they wanted him back as chauffeur. 'I said yes of course we did, but realized that he could now command far better money than as a private chauffeur. "I don't care about that, madam; if you want me, I want to come. . . . You've been good to me, and you understand me; I'd come anywhere with you."'

Vita was glad too to have Mac back – 'though it wasn't so much fun trying to clean her room which hadn't been swept or dusted for three years'. Her relationship with Mac, her 'Anna', was in an equal disarray. Mac had written to her in late 1944 saying that she was now fifty, but looked sixty, 'and sometimes feel 70, so what have I to do with love? Anyway I shall always value your friendship (trite but true).' Mac settled in little by little as secretary and confidante, playing the role (given her lesser calibre and capability) that Hilda Matheson had played.

Jack Vass was back as head gardener by the end of the year. He had been in the RAF, and was reported missing after his plane was shot down in the south of France. But he survived and made his way north through occupied France and back to England on his own.

There was a general election in the summer of 1945. While Harold (standing as an independent, supported by the Conservative Central Office) nursed his West Leicester constituency, Vita put in order the poetry anthology they were compiling together. They called it *Another World Than This*, from a line in Vita's *The Garden*. Her attitude had changed since the last election. This time, she was not only concerned but involved. No longer did she disassociate herself. 'Oh my Hadji. I love you so desperately, more than I ever loved you before, more than I loved you when we were young and made such a muddle of being "in love".' She even went up to Leicester, spoke at a women's meeting and attended two evening meetings at which Harold spoke.

She still hated party politics, but wanted 'to help you if I can'. Turning her attention to these matters for the first time, she judged the mood in England with a possibly greater shrewdness than Harold himself. Churchill had been a great war leader; but was a tired, ageing Churchill, or the Conservative Party, right for the post-war world? She wrote to Harold on 22 June:

> You know I have an admiration for Winston amounting to idolatry, so I am dreadfully distressed by the badness of his broadcast election speeches. What has gone wrong with him? They are confused, woolly, unconstructive, and so wordy it's impossible to pick any concrete impression out of them. If I were a wobbler, they would tip me over the other side.

She urged Harold to hold meetings in factories, to catch the floating voters among the manual workers. She felt the Conservatives were going to need all the 'wobblers' they could pick up: 'Seriously, Hadji, if I wasn't a Conservative I shouldn't be, if you see what I mean, and I am afraid I think the argument "Churchill won the war" a bad argument. . . . I do not think that Winston has the temperament to deal with the immediate difficulties *at home.*' Nor did the British electorate. Vita and the boys were with Harold in Leicester on the day of the election to hear that he had lost his seat and that the Labour Party, under Clement Attlee, had a clear majority in the country. Back at Sissinghurst, Harold went to bed with two aspirins, sad that he would no longer have a place in his beloved House of Commons.

Two days later, Vita had to give him another piece of bad news. For months Harold's brother Eric had been urging that Lord Carnock (Freddy), their eldest brother, should take over the flat at King's Bench Walk, with a permanent attendant. Vita had been militant on Harold's behalf. 'This must be prevented at all costs. If necessary, I am prepared to murder F[reddy], but I won't have you become a displaced person and lose your lovely rooms which you love.' King's Bench Walk was in the Inner Temple, one of the Inns of Court; Freddy was a non-practising barrister, and Harold had only been able to lease the rooms by using his brother's name. Now there was a new ruling, that only practising barristers might reside there, so Harold had to move in any case.

Elvira Niggeman broke this to Vita, who told Harold. They found him a house in Neville Terrace, South Kensington, which he disliked cordially. It was also to be Ben and Nigel's London home: their company made it tolerable. On the day Harold moved into Neville Terrace, Mac moved out of her old bed-sitting-room at Sissinghurst to the less intimate proximity of Horse-race: thus two eras chanced to close on what Vita called a 'nasty painful day' just before Christmas.

It was after the loss of his seat in the House of Commons that Harold set his heart on having a peerage. To be a member of the House of Lords would solve his career problem, give him a permanent place in public life, and be the realization of an old dream – almost, of an old assumption, dating from the days when he imagined himself ending up as an ambassador, if not Viceroy of India.

But it was not so easy. There was after all no overwhelming reason why his name should be put forward. His apparent anxiety in the matter did little to recommend his case. Vita's advice to him was injudicious. 'I thought over what you said about my not having made myself clear about the House of Lords,' he wrote to her on 19 September, 'so I decided to write to William Jowitt.' Vita approved of this letter to the Labour Lord Chancellor, which expressed his ambivalence about the Labour Party as well as his willingness to go to the House of Lords. 'It is clear, dignified, and all that it should be,' she told him. 'Now we wait to see what happens.' They were both optimistic, thinking up possible titles. Vita hoped 'quite absurdly' that he would become a Lord:

> I wish I could analyze why. It certainly isn't for snobbish reasons, although I would like the babies to be the Hon. (Isn't that odd?) And it isn't because I would like to put 'Peeress of the Realm' instead of 'Householder' on the various forms I have to fill in. (I would rather put 'Author' or 'Poet', but ... it is some consolation to me to be able to put 'Householder' instead of 'Married Woman'.)
>
> But above all I would like you to have a platform on which to speak with authority, and not have to worry about elections or constituents.

In October Harold escaped to Greece for a holiday. Vita hated his going. 'Anyhow, there it is and life is now utterly black. It is terrifying, isn't it, the power that people have to hurt one another?' Harold pointed out that he had given up a great many trips to appease her neurotic fears about his travelling. He hated it when she was cross. 'When she scolds me I feel like a clematis which has been torn from its wires.'

Ben was publishing art-history articles in the *Cornhill* and the new periodical *Contact* set up by George Weidenfeld. In some ways he adjusted more quickly to civilian life than Nigel, who had had the more distinguished war career, emerging with an MBE. Harold thought Ben was their 'problem child' and needed, clematis-like, more support than Nigel. Vita was not so sure. No longer so close to Ben, she focused more clearly on Nigel. She wrote to Harold on 5 December:

I wonder if Niggs is right in thinking Ben is eccentric. I confess I do not quite get the hang of Ben. What is the middle of his mind really like ? . . . I do agree about never letting him down, but at the same time I think that the tough in the Grenadiers [Nigel] needs affection quite as much. I think he is *very* fond of us both ; and I think that under his assurance he is more [touching, pathetic] how than you would believe. . . . I wish to God Ben would marry, it would do him all the good in the world, even if it was only a Platonic sort of marriage.

She disliked and distrusted Philip Toynbee, Ben's closest friend, who she thought encouraged Ben in his 'irresponsible', bohemian, anti-establishment attitudes.

Harold had looked on his projected peerage, he told her, as 'a retirement, a consolation prize' for unfulfilled ambition. But now that it might be out of reach, 'I realize that I had come to desire the consolation prize even more than the prize itself.' Vita gave him her second piece of bad advice. In a letter of 6 January 1946, marked by her 'This is a very serious letter', she advised him to 'take the Labour whip' – in the hope of becoming a Labour-nominated peer. 'I see that you are in a jam, and the only satisfactory solution I can see is for you to do what I have suggested.' Harold was infinitely more versed in the politics of politics than she, and need not have taken her advice ; but in this matter he had lost his bearings.

Harold duly told the Lord Chancellor, in April, that he might be prepared to take the Labour whip. Vita advised him to press his case, this time with the Prime Minister : 'I think – if I may say so – that you make a mistake in not mentioning Cranfield [they had decided on 'Lord Cranfield' as his future title] to Attlee now that you have the chance. It may well be that the whole suggestion has gone out of his head . . . and a reminder would do no harm.'

But Harold's 'reminders' resulted only in disappointment and some loss of dignity. He did not formally join the Labour Party until spring 1947. By this time Vita was backtracking slightly – 'though not wholly hostile especially if it leads eventually to Lord Cranfield. Of course I do not really like you being associated with these bedints.'

Vita, having despatched at last her manuscript of *The Garden*, turned her attention to the real garden. She wanted to obliterate all traces of the neglect of the war years. 'Oh dear kind God, please let Vass live strong and healthy until he is eighty at least, and never let him be tempted away to anyone else's garden.' She concentrated on flowering plants ; growing vegetables was part of the discarded wartime mentality, though they always grew enough to supply the needs of the house.

She dashed off a murder story, commissioned for a desirable £3,000, with ease and pleasure. This was *Devil at Westease*, published by Double-day in the United States (but never in Britain). Set in a tranquil West Country village, it involves a Jekyll-and-Hyde double identity on the part of the murderer; there is no motive, only the desire to commit the undetectable crime. The novel also poses a moral problem: if a great artist is guilty of a crime, should he be punished like anyone else, or should he be protected from justice for the sake of his art? It is, as Vita herself considered, an 'ingenious' story – but far-fetched and ama-teurish in execution.

In February 1946 she got the proofs of *The Garden* from Michael Joseph, and wrote in her diary, 'Depressed by these. It is worse than I feared, – not a patch on *The Land* though that's not saying much.' She had been anxious about it all along, writing to Harold the previous October:

What worries me a bit, is being so out of touch with poetry as it is being written today. I get so many volumes sent to me by the *Observer* and also by would-be poets themselves, and I see that the influence of Tom Eliot and the Stephen Spender-Auden school is paramount – yet I can't get into gear with it at all. It is just something left out of my make-up. I think perhaps it has something to do with my dislike of politics ... I mean just a lack of interest in what must always be *temporary* things.

She loathed, she said, her virtuosity, 'my skill, – it's just like a pianola reeling off.... Why, then, should it make me so unbearably happy to write poetry, when I know that it is all out-of-date rubbishy words that mean simply nothing at all to Ben's generation? Will it ever mean any-thing to anybody's generation? I doubt it.' Her misery over the proofs provoked a return to what Harold, with an equal misery, called her 'muzzy moods'. Waiting for *The Garden* to come out, she worked franti-cally in her own garden – 'You see, I am prepared to devote all my energies to the garden, having abandoned literature.' The day before the poem was published, she went and hid herself in the wood 'from sheer misery'.

There was a particular reason for her despair. In March she went to a meeting of the Poetry Committee of the Society of Authors, chaired by Denys Kilham Roberts at his rooms near Harold's old apartment in King's Bench Walk. The committee – which included Edith Sitwell, Walter de la Mare, Henry Reed, Dylan Thomas, Louis MacNeice and George Barker – was to plan a poetry reading to be held at the Wigmore Hall in the presence of the Queen. Vita made no comment in her diary at the time; only in 1950, in depression, did she write: 'I don't think I will ever write a poem again. They destroyed me for ever that day in Denys Kilham Roberts' rooms in King's Bench Walk.'

What had happened is explained in a letter she wrote to Eddy Sackville-West in 1951, consoling him for his exclusion from the National Book League's exhibition of the 100 best books by 'representative authors' since 1920. (Harold's *Some People* and Vita's *The Land* were in.) Vita told Eddy about 'something which hurt me so much that I have never told it to anyone, – not even to Harold.' It was that at the meeting Vita's name had not been put forward by any of her fellow committee members as one of the poets to read their work at the Wigmore Hall.

> Now I don't set myself up to read poetry very well; but I know that I am audible, which is more than can be said for some of them; so the only inference to be drawn is that they didn't think me worth putting up on the platform – in other words, my poetry wasn't good enough. It had the effect on me that I have never written a line of verse since then.[1]

The aspiration of Vita's life had been to be a poet – and to be known and acknowledged as a poet of lasting significance. As a young woman her work had met with acceptance and acclaim; she had never had to struggle against neglect. That is perhaps why this rejection, this loss of ratification, seemed so absolute and damning.

The sad irony is that *The Garden* is a more interesting and a finer poem than *The Land*. In *The Garden*, which is a little shorter than the earlier poem, there are many occasions when, as she wrote in it, 'Martha's garden turns to Mary's cell'; it is not a gardening treatise in verse so much as a long meditation exploring her personal metaphysic in time of war. She dedicated it to old Mrs Drummond:

> The weeds in my garden remain as green,
> And I cannot tell if I bring you pleasure,
> But the one little patch I have cleared for you
> That one small patch of my soul is clean.

In the dedication she wrote of the loss of ardour that ageing brings, of the 'deathly rest' sought

> By a heart gone weak and a spirit tired
> By the long delusion of things desired.

Yet in the poem she quotes four lines from Eliot's *The Waste Land* – 'April is the cruellest month ... ' – only to refute their pessimism with passion: 'I will believe in Spring':

> Would that my pen like a blue bayonet
> Might skewer all such cat's-meat of defeat.

She does not offer a facile optimism in exchange :

> There is nothing to add but the fact that we had the vision
> And this was a grace in itself, the decision
> We took between hope and despond ;
> The different way that we heard and accepted the call ;
> The different way
> We tried to respond.

The 'vision' is, in part, the garden and its flowers :

> You dreamed us, and we made your dreams come true.
> We are your vision, here made manifest.
> You sowed us, and obediently we grew,
> But, sowing us, you sowed more than you knew
> And something not ourselves has done the rest.

Vita's 'something not ourselves' is not the loving God of the New Testament. Here she writes of hungry birds :

> It is not you they fear, but one another.
> Christ would have said that bird to bird was brother,
> But Christ and Nature seldom speak alike.

It is a fierce, lonely universe outside the paradise garden, the 'little perfect world' :

> For our life is terribly private in the end,
> In the last resort ;
> And if our self's a stranger, what's a friend ?
> A pretty children's game of let's pretend !

The inner landscape is as much in focus as the garden vista. A note in her manuscript headed 'General Themes' begins : 'Courage in Adversity. Determination to find pleasure and not to succumb. No sentimentality. Struggle. Weeds. Death and Loss. Success and rewards.'[2] The seasons in *The Garden* are the seasons of life as well as of the year. *The Garden* is a poem of menopause, in which the horticultural lists and litanies of species and processes are as much the occasion as the purpose of writing. The art of making a garden, she wrote here, is to 'Marry excess with an adroit repose' – a balance she vainly tried to maintain in her life, threatened not only by war from outside but by

> The rabble in the basement of our being,
> Ragged and gaunt, that seldom rush to light

> But in a cellar with the scurrying rats
> Live out their bleached existence till the cry
> Whistles them up the stairs, the curs, the beggars,
> And sets them running in a pack released
> To chase the frightened rabbit of the soul.

*The Garden* won the Heinemann prize; Vita spent the whole £100 on azaleas for the moat walk, and remained unconvinced about the poem. She was grateful for an encouraging letter about it from Nigel, to whom she wrote in reply saying how much she liked his new friend Shirley Morgan (daughter of the novelist Charles Morgan) – 'and I should be delighted if you married her, though please don't think, "Oh, if ever I produce a girl at Sissinghurst Mummy will instantly jump to the conclusion that I am in love with her."' This time, Vita would have been right; by August 1946, Nigel was telling his mother that he would like to marry Shirley. 'I hope only that he will not be too reticent,' Vita wrote to Harold. 'I told him that women were apt to misunderstand diffidence in such matters, and to interpret it as indifference.... She will be an ass if she doesn't marry him.'

Her unease about her poem made any praise of it, from any quarter, precious to her. She was pleased when her old adversary Edith Sitwell wrote her a praising letter – now, Edith's opinion seemed 'one of the few worth having'. But Vita was 'hurt and puzzled' because Desmond MacCarthy had not reviewed *The Garden* in the *Sunday Times*, and tried to persuade herself that the copy specially sent to him had never arrived.

Vita had not had a holiday abroad since before the war. Eardley Knollys and Raymond Mortimer asked her if she would like to go to France with them, and she said she would – provided they went in her car, and that she did all the driving. They planned to go through Paris and visit Harold, who was there covering the Peace Conference for the BBC, and then drive as far south as Albi. 'Oh I'm so excited.... Oh Hadji what fun.' She had to get her passport renewed :

> This [the form-filling], as always, has flung me into rage and indignation. You know I love you more than anybody has ever loved anyone else, but I really do resent being treated as though I were your dog.... One is allowed no separate existence at all, but merely as dependent on whomever one marries. Why not get me a collar with your name and address engraved on it, straight away ?

Never, for as long as she lived, did she become reconciled to the patriarchal attitudes of bureaucracy. There was also a slight mishap when she went to the hairdresser and asked if the nicotine stains could be taken out of her hair. The hairdresser gave it 'a rinse' – 'and the result is a pleasing shade of navy blue'. He also cut it extremely short at the back; Vita was reading *L'Education Sentimentale* and not paying attention.

With her navy-blue shingle, she set off on her holiday. She was happy to see Harold – they had a large luncheon party at the Café de Paris – but had little patience with the Peace Conference. Preceding her remarks to Harold with the statutory 'You know I am no feminist, but ... ', she said: 'just suppose this Conference were being conducted by women instead of men, – wouldn't you say, and wouldn't everyone say, "What can you expect of women?" Women get blamed on account of their sex – but surely men are just as silly and short-sighted. Q.E.D.'

She drove Eardley and Raymond south through the Loire valley, the Auvergne and the Dordogne. She 'outcoppers Copper', as Raymond wrote on a postcard to Harold. From Souillac Raymond wrote again:

> Vita seems wonderfully well, and after long days at the wheel not tired, and full of response to everything. We chatter and giggle incessantly, we don't read the papers.... Each has his duties: Vita drives and is pushed forward when charm is required to obtain something – and the charm always works; Eardley is Chancellor of the Exchequer, expending from a common purse; I am cicerone, poring over guidebooks and maps.

He wrote to Vita, when they were all home again:

> The journey was your notion, the motor was yours, the strain of driving was yours. We were the idle, luxurious friends and passengers. I don't know when I've enjoyed a fortnight so much. Perhaps after all friendship is usually a more trustworthy foundation for such expeditions than l'amourrr [*sic*] – no rifts of exasperation, no earthquakes or thunderstorms or collisions. I think we made an interesting trio.

Vita had come home fired by Raymond's idea that she should write a book about la Grande Mademoiselle (Anne-Marie Louise d'Orléans, first cousin to Louis XIV and the greatest heiress in France).

But a month later, when Vass and Neve were planting 'thousands of narcissus' in the orchard, she was unable to work with them. 'My back is worse. Think seriously about killing myself.' In November, Harold found her propped against a lime tree 'and crying because she could do no gardening'. On another November evening, he found no Vita waiting when he went over as usual to the dining-room cottage for dinner. He waited twenty minutes, then went out to look for her; and found her sitting on the bench under her tower, unable to move. 'Her back had cricked. She is alarmed and in pain. Eventually she struggles across [to the South Cottage] and goes to bed. But she is unhappy and fears she will be a cripple. My heart is wrung in two on her behalf and I sleep badly for once.' In between these two incidents, he had written to her about what he obliquely called the 'attendant complications':

> What distresses me also is that your own alarm about your back is bad for your nerves and seems to produce moments of giddiness or muzziness. I know you have always been subject to these nervous phases when you become not awake. ... I am not so distressed by the dread of your becoming lame as I am by the dread of your not grasping this nettle in good time.

There is something very sad and sympathetic about Harold's own inability to 'grasp the nettle' and talk to Vita directly about her drinking.

Vita's back improved again; and Ben, to his parents' delight, took the position of editor of the *Burlington* magazine. Nigel was soon to start as assistant editor of *Contact*, his leanings towards isolation and independence satisfied by the purchase of an island in the Hebrides. Vita's plans for the garden were stimulated by visits to Bodnant in North Wales, the house of Lord and Lady Aberconway. Harry Aberconway was a serious gardener and Bodnant impressed even Vita. In the late summer she had specially admired its 'masses of eucryphias', and told Harold that they should plant eucryphias instead of cherries on top of the azalea bank at Sissinghurst. 'We have so many flowering things in the spring and so little in summer, and they are very lovely, a greenish-yellowish-white. There are other things which have given me ideas, – thalictrum in masses.'

She did not have everything her own way in the garden. For all her appreciation of 'masses', when it came to the point she was not as uncompromising as Harold. On 29 December he wrote in his diary:

> In the afternoon I moon about with Vita trying to convince her that planning is an element in gardening. I want to show her that the top of the moat-walk must be planted with forethought and design. She wishes just to jab in the things which she has left over. The tragedy of the romantic temperament is that it dislikes form so much that it ignores the effect of masses. She wants to put in stuff which 'will give a lovely red colour in autumn'. I wish to put in stuff which will furnish shape to the perspective. In the end we part, not as friends.

It was this perpetual tension that made Sissinghurst so satisfactory as a garden.

Vita, depressed about her achievement as a writer, began in this first post-war year the weekly gardening articles in the *Observer* that were, whether she liked it or not, to make her more widely known and more eagerly read than anything else she ever wrote. That is not all the *Observer* articles were to achieve. They did more, as Anne Scott-James has written, 'to change the face of English gardening than any other writing since Robinson's *The English Flower Garden*'. The Sissinghurst style was copied everywhere. 'Thousands of climbing roses were planted at the feet of apple trees all over Britain. Hybrid tea roses were discarded in favour of shrub roses.' As Anne Scott-James says, the Sissinghurst disciples 'were mostly of an upper social class, for gardening has its social strata like everything else.'[3] Any amateur gardener becomes aware very quickly of the truth of this : gardening snobbery in Britain is the subject of some knowing horticulturist's unwritten dissertation. In so far as the Sissinghurst style insists on the purely architectural quality of plants and plant-groupings, the influence is Harold's. The grace and the magic of the Sissinghurst style is Vita's.

# CHAPTER 31

VITA's new friends, after the war, were Violet Pym and Edith Lamont. Vi Pym was married with children, and farmed with her husband at Barnfield, near Charing, about twelve miles from Sissinghurst. She was a good friend of the old 'Trouts' at Smallhythe, and Vita got to know Vi through Christopher St John. 'I do so want you to meet her,' Vita wrote to Harold. Vi was 'so nice and has a lovely voice. She is like a cornfield, or a loaf of bread, or a brown egg, or bracken in autumn.' Her husband was 'a tall handsome ex-Irish Guards Major – attractive and typical. Stupid, popular, likes watching cricket, – that sort of thing.'[1]

Edith Lamont – Mrs Newton Lamont – lived at Chart Sutton and was a painter: she and Vita met in the garden at Sissinghurst on an 'open' day. Bunny Drummond was a more established friend. Her mother-in-law, Vita's mother-substitute, died during 1947, and Bunny and her publisher husband Lindsay took over Sissinghurst Place. Bunny was already more attached to Vita than friendship generally allows. When she came to tea one day in March 1947 Vita advised her 'not to play with fire'; but Bunny Drummond could not keep away.

Women continued to fall in love with Vita, and to declare their love, notwithstanding her age and arthritis. (Nigel wrote to Harold that Ben and Vita shared the gift 'of concealing beneath outward slovenliness the capacity to look, suddenly, like a God. While you and I never look like Gods, we always look like human beings: which is duller.') Vita's reputation had something to do with it, and her fame as a writer, and the romance of Sissinghurst, and her seclusion, which made her friendship seem a special privilege – exciting, exotic and irresistible. She was always more herself in the intimacy of a *tête-à-tête* than in company; her powerful personality and physical presence, her deep caressing voice, her patient way of encouraging people to talk about themselves, all contributed to her spell-binding quality, touching a nerve in women of little sexual sophistication who had never before been attracted to other women. Her conventional, upper-middle-class, middle-aged friends in Kent were, in their simplicity, more susceptible than might have been women with greater self-knowledge and experience of sexual complexity.

Edy Craig died in the spring of 1947, leaving Christopher St John – who had lived with her for forty-eight years – and Tony Atwood, now over eighty, at their wits' end. They had almost no money. Vita gave them enough to carry on while negotiations went ahead for the Ellen Terry house to be acquired by the National Trust, so enabling Christopher and Tony to finish their lives in their old home without having to pay for its upkeep.

Vita broke her own rule and invited Christopher to come and stay at Sissinghurst for a couple of nights : 'I think I am probably the only person who can pull her out of the rut of sorrow she has got herself into.' Christopher, despondent and infirm, managed to rejoice that Vita had 'friends who can share your joy in life, that my melancholy devotion is not your only nourishment'.

Vita was writing a new guidebook to Knole for the National Trust – quite 'coldly and unmovedly' as she said, until she suddenly woke up to the fact that 'this is MY Knole which I love more than anything else in the world except Hadji.' Leonard Woolf was reissuing *Pepita*, and Vita would have liked to have her *Knole and the Sackvilles* reissued for the benefit of the new influx of tourists to Knole ; and was angry to discover that Heinemann, the publishers, had destroyed the metal blocks of the illustrations. But as she said she was 'not litigiously minded', unlike her mother.

Both she and Harold were increasingly involved with the National Trust – Harold as vice-chairman of its Executive Council, and Vita on the Gardens Committee, chaired by Lord Aberconway. Later, she too was on the Trust's Council. In the summer of 1947 they both went on a tour of National Trust properties with James Lees-Milne : they covered 1,200 miles and saw forty houses and gardens in ten days of beautiful weather. 'Dear Jim, I grew so fond of you,' Vita wrote afterwards. 'You must forgive the un-Englishness of my saying this.'

Jim Lees-Milne and Eardley Knollys were two men whom she genuinely loved and liked. Of her two sons, she was closer now to Nigel, who talked to her about Shirley Morgan, and about his personal anxieties, and whose confidences she respected. With some difficulty and embarrassment Ben was trying to extricate himself from his father's ménage at Neville Terrace to take a flat of his own, 'like an old bird flopping with heavy unpractised wings out of the nest', as he told his parents. He was, after all, thirty-three years old – but Harold was hurt nevertheless, and Ben did not go.

Vita, prepared to take on the public service aspect of country life, had put her name forward as a Justice of the Peace, and was sworn in in October. Her fellow magistrates on the Cranbrook bench included Sir George Jessel, whom she did not like, and 'a certain Major Robson from Tenterden, who reminds me *so* much of Dada'. She also joined the Committee for the Preservation of Rural Kent, which met at Maidstone in the County Hall, where a portrait of her father in his coronation robes looked down on the meeting. The one country activity to which she was violently opposed was any kind of blood sports, particularly stag-hunting. She was rooted in local activities and local life – not only as magistrate and conservationist, but in the Cranbrook Poetry Society presided over by Richard Church, and as a speaker to Women's Institutes – as Harold was not. His active life was always based on London.

She had no book on hand; she had a sudden fancy – after a visit from Gwen – to write the life of Cardinal Newman, but discovered that two biographies of him were already in progress. The 'gross materialism' of the age of Louis XIV made her reject, for the moment, her plan to write about la Grande Mademoiselle. All she published in 1947 was an 'essay', *Nursery Rhymes*, illustrated by Philippe Jullian in a limited edition published by the Dropmore Press. (It was republished by Michael Joseph in 1950.) Dedicated 'For Anna', it was a strained effort, written in the whimsical, mock-scholarly manner that Harold could carry off to perfection but she could not. In the 'Three Blind Mice', for example: 'One bright-eyed, entirely caudate mouse is apt to be more than enough for many people. Besides, grievous speculations may further harass the imaginative mind: how, for instance, did their cecity come upon them?'

The *Observer* articles were another story. A piece about the strawberry grape on one October Sunday brought her over 500 letters, requiring a special mail-van since the postman could not carry them.

At a cocktail party at Buckingham Palace in early December Vita enjoyed herself; she wrote to Evelyn Irons that she 'saw all the nobs, Molotov, Winston, and so on. I seldom go to parties but like them to be slap-up when I do. I wore a little Russian bonnet, which I made myself out of an old hat and some furry stuff I bought by the yard at the village haberdasher's.' At the party she was introduced to the Prime Minister, Mr Attlee – from whose office she had a letter two days later inviting her to become a Companion of Honour in the New Year Honours List. She showed the letter to Harold, who was surprised at her lack of excitement. 'But somewhere inside herself she is pleased, I think.'

Harold heard later that it was his old friend Alan Lascelles, the King's

Private Secretary, who had suggested that Vita be given the CH, and that Attlee himself had 'a passionate admiration for *The Land*'. It was ironic that it was the leader of the Labour Party who had honoured Vita, instead of her husband who had joined the party with honours on his mind. 'Mr Attlee is a nice man,' Vita wrote to Harold, 'and will be nicer still if he behaves as he should over Cranfield.'

Harold reacted with untarnished generosity. What he did, however, was to accept the nomination as Labour candidate in the coming by-election at North Croydon – which had had a small Conservative majority in the general election. To stand again for Parliament was the one thing Vita had begged him not to do when he joined the Labour Party; to contest an election would, she thought, 'hurt and wound you more than you imagine.'

Harold made it clear to the authorities on Vita's behalf that the CH was to be announced as to 'V.Sackville-West' and not 'Mrs Harold Nicolson'. He was sad that she did not enjoy the publicity – and that she was so annoyed when her name was linked with his. 'I never quite understand why,' he wrote in his diary, 'when *I* am so proud of being associated with her. Anyhow the whole business has made her, not happy, but irritable and nervous.' He was relieved she would be away – 'Thank God!' – when his by-election came up: she had agreed to undertake a British Council lecture tour in North Africa. Vita's lack of excitement over her CH was connected with her belief that her writing days were over. She replied to Eddy Sackville-West's letter of congratulation saying that it was 'the paucity of ideas, the drying-up', that was so worrying.

She also dreaded the election for Harold. She felt his experience of life had not equipped him for the social problems he would be expected to discuss. She described to him in late January 1948 a case that had come up before her bench: 'Two naughty mars, a brother and sister aged 10 and 11, who had been stealing bicycle lamps by the dozen.' It turned out that the children, who had streaming colds, came from a family of nine who lived in 'just *two rooms*':

> They have been trying to get a cottage, and of course they can't. Now this is the sort of thing I should be interested in if I were you – as a potential MP.
>
> How can kids like that get a decent moral upbringing?
>
> I hate to add any suggestion which would increase your many activities, but I am not at all sure that you wouldn't get a low-down on the life of the lower income-groups if you joined the Cranbrook bench. You would see aspects of life which I don't think you've ever really taken in.

Stealing bicycle lamps was the standard crime of young Kentish offenders – in addition to worse problems. A pompous official from the

NSPCC whispered to Vita, apropos of another eleven-year-old lamp-stealer: 'And it is my duty to add that this little girl has had carnal knowledge.' Vita was not happy when she was the only Justice on the Bench, as sometimes happened:

[I] have to sit in a large armchair behind a table, while the wretched delinquent stands before me, and the room is full of police officers and the Clerk of the Court and his Clerk and the Detective Superintendent, all bringing charges and evidence against the prisoner, and all the ponderous weight of the Law and its apparatus of which I am part. I always feel that here is a wild animal trapped and caged, and that if it sprang suddenly at my throat it would be seized and restrained by a dozen strong hands – and above all I feel 'There, but for the grace of God and B.M.'s marriage settlement, go I' – or, indeed, go Catalina and Pepita.

Vita went to North Africa in February. She suffered from chyluria while she was there. 'I've been very homesick all the time,' she wrote to Nigel. 'I hate being fêted and entertained; and I just long to be at home with all three of you once more.' She heard on the radio at the British Consulate at Tunis that Harold had lost at North Croydon. His telegram came soon after: 'Beaten by twelve thousand oh my.' Vita wrote to him:

Personally I know what I feel: I am *delighted* you got so many votes, and I know you will feel you have done well, but I am frankly relieved (taking the long view) that you can now go to the Other Place with an absolutely free conscience. My only worry is that they may let you down over this, but surely Frank Pakenham will now do something about this?

Frank Pakenham was Lord Longford, a member of the Labour Party and at that time Chancellor of the Duchy of Lancaster. Harold had a word with him in September, and was given some bleak news:

Frank Pakenham tells me that I was on the list for peerages last December, but then the P. M. found that Viti was getting the C. H. and this was awkward. At the King's Birthday I might have come up again had it not been for the recency of Croydon. Do I really care? Yes I do. I want to be back in public life in an easy indolent way. That is not disreputable.

Vita left Africa chiefly pleased by the purchase of 'the sort of garden hat I've been looking for for years', and on her way home went to stay with Violet Trefusis at La Tour de Saint-Loup, her house near Provins, not far from Paris. Saint-Loup was Violet's equivalent of Sissinghurst, and Vita wrote in her journey notebook that she had 'the oddest feeling of familiarity' there.

She saw Violet again in London in June, and wrote to Harold: 'She is lonely and unhappy, I think, but it is not easy to get at people's feelings in ½ an hour in the lounge at the Ritz.' In the autumn she wrote Violet a letter beginning 'My darling dear' – the endearment, she said, by which Dame Julian of Norwich 'supposed our Lord to have addressed her sometime during the Middle Ages – I forget the exact date – but no matter, it will serve me now as a pretty endearment for my Lushka.' She told Violet again how much she had liked Saint-Loup; a 'curious bond' between them was their 'intense sense of the character of places. We both have it so strongly that it becomes a pain.'[2]

Vita's dearly loved dog Martha began to suffer from a series of heart attacks. Harold described how in April Martha had collapsed panting on the lawn, 'and Vita collapses beside her. Mac arrives and takes Martha away. I find Viti pacing by the lake in an agony of tears.' She wrote to him, on 17 June:

> I don't know if you realize how miserable I have been, and still am, about Martha. I know I must kill her – but when she comes and rests her nose on my knee and looks up at her [sic] with her golden eyes, so trustful, it makes me feel a traitor. She took the opportunity last night, just after I had been to see a puppy for sale. She seemed to know. It was such a sweet puppy, too. I loved it at sight; and have bought it. The people will keep it till I send for it. But when I send for it, it will mean that Martha is dead, – killed by my orders. . . . You see, I am essentially a lonely person, and Martha has meant so much to me. She was always there, and I could tell her everything.

Her companion of thirteen years died three days after and was buried in the wood – 'A nightmare day.' Vita went to collect Rollo the puppy, another alsatian, that same evening. 'He is so soft and innocent and unaware of the blank he is meant to fill.'

While Martha was still ill, Sissinghurst Place, the Drummonds' house, burned to the ground. Bunny and her husband were in London. Vita and Harold, awoken by a telephone call, drove over at 2.30 a.m. to find a 'blazing furnace'. Harold's diary: 'We come back at 5.30 while the dawn is creeping over the woods. It is very cold. I go to bed, but Viti stays up and gardens. She then goes to meet Bunny and Lindsay by the train at 8 a.m. and takes them to the ruin of their house.' Before her faith in herself as a poet had left her, Vita had thought of following *The Garden* with a long poem about fire. This she never wrote; but the 'blazing furnace' that she watched that night, and her preoccupation with poor Martha, were the twin inspirations for a novel she was to write, *The Easter Party*.

The perfection of Sissinghurst seemed even more precious after this disaster, and Harold, during a June of 'hay and roses', told Vita that he thought he did better out of Sissinghurst than anyone else. His sitting-room and bedroom were the nicest in the castle, he said, and 'M.L.W. is the finest part of the whole garden.' 'M.L.W.' stood for 'My Life's Work' – otherwise the Lime Walk, whose spring border was Harold's special responsibility and creation. Vita liked Vass, her head gardener, more and more: 'His keen-ness is so endless, and nothing is too much trouble.' Vass had 'a sort of instinctive good taste ... besides, he's so nice to look at, so decorative.' They developed the flat rockery area at the side of the Priest's House and called it Delos. Vass's only fault was that he tried to make it too tidy, with neat brick edgings along the paths, 'But then he hasn't ever seen the real Delos lying out in the Cyclades.'

That August, while Sibyl Colefax was staying, they had a visit from the young writer Denton Welch, who was very ill; his account of Sissinghurst is the last entry in his published diaries. He found the Nicolsons difficult to talk to: 'Her manner was a little withheld, a little torpid. It was not quite social or bright enough to make a first meeting really easy; but, on the other hand, it would be wrong to call it boorish or neglectful. Can I describe it as sluggishly dignified? Her voice was slow and rather sleepy too – almost drawling.' Awkwardly, the party straggled across the garden to the Priest's House for tea

and I saw a long Spanish table with pointless spikes and curves of wrought iron running along its stretcher close to the floor. The table was only laid with a large farmhouse cake and cucumber sandwiches, but there was an air of richness and profusion. Perhaps this was caused by glasses [for cider] as well as cups being at each place. There was also a large old silver shell, rather beautiful, holding about half a pound of butter patted and spanked nicely with ridged wooden boards. At our approach a manservant retreated behind a curtain. The room had a mullioned window, an arched brick fireplace, brick floor, high beamed ceiling, Oriental rugs, fragments of tapestry behind a little medieval wood carving of a saint. Our chairs were William and Mary with high caned backs.[3]

Almost everything, Denton Welch noted, 'stopped short at the seventeenth century'. He died at the end of the year; and when Jocelyn Brooke, editing his diaries for publication, came to show Vita the account of the visit to Sissinghurst, she asked him to put in a footnote to the effect that their awkwardness had been due to their extreme awareness of his frailty, which made them 'embarrassed as how best to entertain him'.

Harold was happier, because he had been commissioned to write the life of King George v. Provided he was given a free hand, it was an interesting task – although, as he conceded, it would put him out of politics for at least three years, which probably meant for always, because of his age.

Both the boys were going through personal crises. Nigel had been seeing a lot of Shirley Morgan, and she had been down to Sissinghurst several times. On 30 July Vita wrote in her diary : 'Niggs rings me up after dinner to say Shirley's engagement will be announced tomorrow. . . . Oh dear oh dear !' Her engagement was not to Nigel but to the Marquess of Anglesey. Nigel went straight up to his Hebridean island on his own. From there he wrote to his mother : 'Thank you so much for your marvellous sympathy, both in your letter and on the telephone. I burst into tears when I had finished speaking to you on Friday night. It was partly you and partly Shirley that brought it on, and I was very surprised.'

Shirley was married in October – 'Nigel has disappeared' Vita wrote thankfully in her diary on the day. (But the friendship between the two survived, and was to be lifelong.) During this difficult autumn, Nigel asked Vita to lend him £4,000 to help to capitalize the new publishing house of Weidenfeld & Nicolson. This she did willingly : 'As it will be my own money, i.e. not Trust, I can do as I like. . . . It represents what I got for Long Barn.' The money was repaid with interest within ten years. Nigel's letter of thanks was written at Sissinghurst. True child of his parents, he could write what he could not say, and had too the need to make a durable record of his appreciation. He added to his gratitude, with unspoken reference to his personal life : 'I think there is nothing that I could not tell you.' Like Ben, he perceived the insulating effects of his upbringing : 'I grew up so slowly, met the real difficulties of life so ridiculously late, and still remain – I think this applies to Ben as well – strangely immature in some ways.'

In reply to his letter of thanks, Vita wrote :

But, my darling, you mustn't be so grateful : you know quite well that I would do anything for you, and only wish it were more. (By the way, it may have occurred to you that I sold Long Barn for more than £4000 ; yes, I did, – for £6,500 in fact, – but there was a £2000 mortgage that I had raised to buy Daddy's yacht. . . . )

You may think that with the vast sums I make by writing I ought to have invested more – but you see I have always spent my so-to-speak pocket money on Sissinghurst, either on extravagances, or else on supplementing the running expenses, which couldn't possibly be paid out of the income I get from the Trust money and rents.

She gave a more detailed account of her finances to Harold soon after. She received £2,243 a year net from the family Trust, and about another £1,000, before tax, from rents :

And as the wages alone come to £45 a *week*, or £1340 a year, you will readily see that there is not much balance left for such things as house-books, electric light and heat, rates, insurance, the motor-car, coal and coke (I have just had a bill for £149 for these), telephone, and the thousand things involved in the upkeep of a house.

She kept her literary earnings in a separate account – 'I bought the tractor and the trailer, and the Barford Atom cultivator and hedge-clipper, the two water-softeners, and lots of other things out of that – and of course my personal expenses ... all of which mount up in a surprising way.' The garden was open to the public nearly every day now during the summer; Vita had a box into which every visitor put a shilling, and these shillings – only a few pounds a week in 1948 – went into her wages' fund. Harold paid the wages of Sydney Neve, who looked after the Lime Walk for him. Harold was supportive to Vita in every possible sense except financially. It was her money that ran Sissinghurst and maintained their whole way of life. Yet Harold told her that he felt much better off than Gerry [Wellington] in spite of Gerry's ducal wealth. 'Yes,' replied Vita, 'I would rather have our untidy busy ramshackle life, irradiated by the love we have had for each other for thirty-five years now, so indestructibly, than all Gerry's titles and possessions.'

Ben, like Nigel, had also been in love for the first time. He had written to 'My darling Mummy' to explain the position in May:

> I write this, instead of saying it all, partly because I have had no opportunity during the last 24 hours, partly because it is less embarrassing so. I will give you the facts as baldly as possible. I have fallen desperately in love with the young man you may have heard Daddy mention as he met him ... an undergraduate at Christ Church.... It is much the most overwhelming experience I have ever had, and ever expect to have again. They say these things are wicked, they put you in prison for it: but this experience has brought out in me qualities (kindness, generosity, consideration for others) that I never believed I possessed. It has also killed growing cynicism. It has driven me back to poetry and the Italian Renaissance.

The point of the letter was to ask whether he might bring David Carritt to Sissinghurst for the weekend. Vita was to answer 'yes' or 'no' and to impose no conditions. 'But if "no", I should prefer to discuss it no further. Nigel must not know yet.'

Vita said 'yes', and David came to Sissinghurst with Ben several times during the rest of the year. Ben made another bid to leave Neville Terrace: he told Harold he wanted to share a flat with David in George Weidenfeld's house in Chester Square. Harold and Vita were afraid of scandal for Ben, which at that time was not unreasonable; but more than that, they seemed loth to grant Ben his independence. They talked of Ben as if he were an adolescent, not a man in his middle thirties. Nor did they ever fully appreciate his achievement as a scholar, or his personal qualities. Vita wrote to Harold about the flat-sharing:

> Of course I agree with you that this is a pity, almost a disaster. You see he is bound to fall out with D. again, and meanwhile there may have been a scandal which might involve both his jobs, the Palace and the *Burlington*, – and there he would be stranded, having lost his career for the sake of a clever little boy who is not worth the sacrifice.
>
> I will talk to him at the weekend, whether he likes it or not. After all, he knows I am not *hostile*, which is a great thing. . . . Poor little Ben, – so naïf, so sensitive, so fastidious, so much himself, and in such a muddle!

Ben was persuaded to give up the idea, and remained with his father and brother at Neville Terrace. He also gave up his work with the royal picture collection to concentrate on the *Burlington*. 'How I wish', wrote Vita, 'that he, of all people, could marry and have children. . . . It is all a great pity, and really my heart aches for him sometimes.' The affair with David Carritt, who was to become a distinguished art historian and art-dealer, was over in another six months.

# CHAPTER 32

IN February 1949 Vita embarked on another lecture tour for the British Council, this time in Spain. Mac went with her. On the way, she met Violet in Paris – 'with plumes waving all out of her hat, looking like a dowager duchess on two sticks' – and went with her to Saint-Loup for a night. Vita was appalled by the way Violet treated her old maid, Alice: 'it reminds me of B.M. It's really more than a little mad. . . . It is a sort of lust for power, I think: she must have someone she can bully.'

Vita was delighted with Madrid – 'Society here is like Paris for smartness and luxury and amusingness' – and lectured twice at the Ateneo. Someone obligingly assured her that 'it has always been assumed' in Spain that the Duke of Osuna, and not the obscure barber, was Pepita's father. The Irish hispanist Walter Starkie took her and Mac to Toledo, and on her birthday she was in Seville, 'really rather bewildered though very happy'. It was Harold's turn to be lonely, at home. 'But I know that I could not endure at my age to be separated from her for very long. I just could not bear it, and will not consent to it.' He wrote to her: 'You cannot imagine how empty the place feels without you.'

Vita went on to Malaga, her grandmother's birthplace. 'Now supposing Pepita, as a little muchacha in Malaga, could have had a glimpse of the future and foreseen her granddaughter . . . as a lecturer on a platform, – wouldn't she have been incredulous and surprised? How Virginia would have appreciated this!' The poet Muñoz Rojas took her to the street where Pepita was born. 'Oh such a slum it is – very narrow, you could almost shake hands from one little balcony to the other overhead, crowded with people and children, but there can be no doubt at all that it was exactly the same when Pepita was a little girl.'

When she got back from this expedition to the *parador* where they were staying, Vita found she was racked with a hard dry cough. She felt very ill and went to bed. It was a good thing that Mac was with her, and Vita clung to her 'Anna' – especially when after a few days her symptoms were no less severe, and the rest of the lecture tour had to be abandoned. They drove back to Madrid along the Jaen road, hoping to identify a house that Pepita had lived in at Atarfe, but failed to find it. 'This is the last straw, and I feel like bursting into tears,' Vita wrote in her disappointingly short 'Spanish Diary'. With a high temperature, she spent a 'nightmare night' in the Sud Express to Paris, and then the boat home. On the way, she lost both her purse and her spectacles.

The influenza, if it was influenza, strained her heart, and convalescence was long and slow. Her pulse rate soared if she got up for more than a couple of hours. It was June before she was well again, and the episode aged her and put an abrupt end to her enthusiasm for travelling without Harold. Towards the end of the year, Violet asked her to go with her to Spain to make up for the disaster. Vita replied that she would not even go to Paris : 'Cities are not for me. Sissinghurst and St Loup are my spiritual homes – and of course Knole, which is denied to me for ever, through "a technical fault over which we have no control", as they say on the radio.'[1]

Knole was on her mind particularly when she wrote to Violet, because Harold had told her that the Sackville Settled Estates Trust was being reconstituted, and that Nigel and young Lionel Sackville-West (son of Vita's Uncle Bertie, her father's youngest brother, and heir to Knole after Eddy if Eddy died childless) were taking over as trustees. 'She is pleased by this, but breaks down afterwards. Poor darling, she hides in the dark of my book-room and sobs and sobs into the corner.' Because of her sex, the 'technical fault', not only could she not inherit Knole, but she saw Knole removed further and further away from her, her sex – and now her age – debarring her from any institutional connection with it at all.

Saint-Loup was also particularly on her mind when she wrote to Violet, who had summoned her to London in June to say she would like to leave the place to her in her will. Vita demurred ; Saint-Loup should go to Violet's sister Sonia and her children. Only when Violet said that under no circumstances would she leave the property to Sonia did Vita accept – provisionally : 'You are younger than I am ... and a dozen things may arise to make you change your mind which anyhow I know isn't really made up, so nothing may ever come of this.'[2]

Vita knew her Violet – who, as she grew older, used the promise and withdrawal of legacies as emotional weapons. Violet was also writing her memoirs, and Vita was excited by this : 'Oh Duntreath ! How that is mixed up with my own memories. The owls ... the armoury ... and our own young innocent loves. I think you ought to dedicate this book

to me ? ... yes ? no ? I should be so flattered and gratified if you did'
[the suspension marks are Vita's].³ But Violet dedicated *Don't Look
Round* to the memory of her mother.


Vita was having a clock with a deep chime installed in the top of the
tower. 'Darling this is too exciting! I went down to have a look, and
they have got the dial out. It looks *superb*.... The gilt *is* a bit bright
perhaps, but that won't last long.' Her pre-war idea for a White
Garden had also been revived – by Harold: 'I think of it as *cineraria* in
masses, Rabbit's Ears [*stachys lanata*] in masses, Lad's Love a good
deal, some *Santolina* – the whole background being predominantly
grey. Then out of this jungle growth I wish regale [lilies] to rise.' Vita
forbore to point out that the idea had been hers in the first place
(though she had imagined it as white with touches of pink): 'My own
Hadji darling – what nice days – how happy we always are together. I
think your idea of a grey and white garden is lovely and I will work in
terms of what to plant.'

Vita could not and did not cook and when Mrs Staples – 'the rock on
which the whole edifice depends' – was ill, as she was in the autumn of
1949, life was very austere. Vita did not welcome casual visitors but
only those whom, she felt, needed to come. Harold was particularly
attached to James Pope-Hennessy, who had been Nigel's contemporary at Balliol; when James's mother died, he came down to Sissinghurst and Vita gave up her bedroom to him. Harold was grateful to
her for this.

Another friend who needed help and was an increasingly frequent
week-day visitor when Harold and the boys were in London was Vi
Pym. When Vita was recovering from her Spanish illness, she told
Harold that apart from himself there was only 'one other person I
would rather have here than not have, but will tell you verbally who it
is, in case this letter falls into wrong hands. I expect you know,
anyhow, but remind me to tell you in case of misunderstandings.'

In October, Vi's eighteen-year-old daughter was killed in a riding
accident. Vita went to stay at Barnfield to support her friend in this
grief. 'My precious – my darling – I hold on to you, and you alone, in
this agony. What you have been – are – to me, you know,' Vi wrote to
Vita. She wrote to Harold as well:

I never knew Vita could be so wonderful. I loved her before, but now – since
she has come through this with me – how much more. Often I have thought
it was nice of you not to mind us being friends, *mais on ne dit rien*. Well now
perhaps I can tell you, in thanking you, and that always I will try and take
care of her for you.

Mac had been on holiday in Canada, and when she returned to Horse-race it was agreed that she would work for Vita only part time. Harold suspected that what Vita would really like would be an even deeper solitude – 'if all the servants and gardeners and farm hands were all thrown into a trance like the sleeping beauty and she and Rollo and the little robin by the dining-room left as the only 3 moving things at Sissinghurst.' He liked and trusted Vi Pym and agreed with her that Vita needed looking after. Vita had written to him one day in June : 'Last night at dinner I looked up at you suddenly and I caught you looking at me down the table with such a funny loving expression – what were you thinking ?'

He may have been worrying about her. On the last night of 1949 he wrote in his diary that the year had been darkened for him by her illness. 'She seems to have recovered completely and her back is certainly much better. But I do not think her nerves are in a good state, poor darling. She gets easily flurried and falls into moods of confusion and inattention. She forgets things badly, and is not able to concentrate on her work. This makes her restless and unhappy.'

'Confusion and inattention' may have been responsible for the strange incident of 'The Novice to her Lover'. This was a poem that Vita had sent off to the *Poetry Review* in February 1949, just before she set out for Spain. It was published in the June/July issue. In November, Vita included *Poems 1935–48* by Clifford Dyment in her shortlist for the King's Medal for Poetry, of which she was one of the judges. In Dyment's book she found a poem strikingly similar to her own 'Novice' poem. The two were almost identical. Both were of twelve lines ; his, called 'St Augustine at 32', began :

> Girl, why do you follow me
> When I come to the threshold of this holy place ?

And Vita's :

> Why must you follow me
> When I come to the threshold of this holy place ?

The similarity was equally close for the following ten lines – as Vita saw with astonishment, and wrote to Clifford Dyment. He reminded her of a letter she had written to him in 1944 about his book *The Axe in the Wood*, which had also contained his 'St Augustine' poem, singled out by her then for special praise. The editor of the *Poetry Review*, John Gawsworth, wrote to the *New Statesman*, which followed up the story. Vita felt mortally depressed'. 'I am like a motor-car that has been standing in a cold garage and refuses to give out even one little *pétard* of a firing-spark.... The odd story of Clifford Dyment's poem and mine has suddenly blown up into life. I wondered why nobody had spotted it.'

Arthritis had reached her hands : she had to have deep-ray treatment at Pembury Hospital. Harold's ceaseless activity, in comparison with her involuntary inactivity, sometimes seemed an outrage. Her diary, 11 January 1950 : 'He works too hard. He has a timetable mind, which will not allow him any relaxation. It is becoming an obsession with him. I am beginning to dread the moment after luncheon or dinner when I know he will say, "Well, I must go and work now."' And on 14 January : 'I wish I could write. I ought to write a novel, to make some money. I am worried about money – awful surtax demands and the expense of running Sissinghurst. I don't see how I can go on keeping it up.' She went to London to see her lawyer about anticipating her income, had lunch with Violet at the Ritz and went with her to *Gigi*. Seeing Violet comforted her, giving her a sense of continuity :

> Isn't it odd, how we have come together again after all our *péripéties* – and are as fond of each other as ever we were, when we sat on your Papa's leather-covered seat before the fireplace in Portland Square [*sic*, for Portman Square], and I went home to Hill Street shouting to myself 'I've got a friend ! I've got a friend !'... There is a very odd thing between you and me, Lushka. There always was.[4]

Three days after this the story of the two similar poems was told in the *New Statesman* under the heading 'A Question of Inspiration'. Letters from both poets were printed alongside the poems. Dyment wrote : 'All I know is that my poem was first published in January 1943, in the *St Martin's Review*, and subsequently reprinted in book form in 1944 and 1949 and that it is not a translation.'

Vita had written that she wrote her version in 1942 or early 1943, when she was writing about St Thérèse of Lisieux, the 'novice' she had in mind. She had sent her poem in a letter to 'a recently converted Catholic and a devotee of St Thérèse', who said she had neither shown it to anyone nor copied it. When *Poetry Review* later asked her for an unpublished poem, she found it in her manuscript book and sent it.

The weakness of Vita's position was that she could not or did not prove that her poem really was sent to her Catholic convert friend (Gwen ?) 'in 1942 or early 1943', i.e., before she could have seen Dyment's in print. 'It is of course unthinkable', she wrote, 'that either I or Mr Dyment should have "lifted" a poem from one another. ... But what, then, is the explanation ? I have none to offer.'[5] Vita had long ago acknowledged to Harold that she was in general very bad at 'remembering whether a line is by me or somebody else'; Harold had reason to feel uneasy about the whole affair :

> Anybody reading the facts will be certain that you found Dyment's poem somewhere and scribbled it down; that you then put your scribble in a file and finding it there years later, thought it was a draft poem of your own, took it out and started to improve it and then, some further years later, sent it to the *Poetry Review*. Nobody will believe it was due to the marriage of true minds and a chance.... And the dates seem to make it more probable that you copied from Dyment than that he copied from you.

Nigel, in spite of what he had written to his mother towards the end of the war, was standing for Parliament after all in the 1950 general election – as a Conservative, in his father's former constituency of West Leicester. The fact that his father was now a member of the rival party was the cause of some comment. Vita was as proud and as fussy as the most traditional of mothers, writing to him during his election campaign :

> I have sent some honey for your breakfast, and a cake, and some ginger biscuits. It is your supper which worries me, so I am also sending a tin of turkey, which you can fall back on if you feel specially hungry one evening and can't get anything to eat at the hotel. But once you have opened it, you must turn it out of its tin on to a plate and *not keep it in the tin*.
>
> And put the plate somewhere cool, i.e. on a window sill, *not* on top of a radiator. I have sent a tin opener with it.
>
> A little butter for breakfast; and will send more later in the week. Some chocolate, and some cheese. . . .
>
> The moat is overflowing. The ducks are blissful. They sail triumphantly over what ought to be, and once was, a bed of irises.

After signing, she added in pencil : 'Remember that I would come up at any moment if you wanted me to, if I could be any use.' She had already been up to Leicester once and faced photographers, playing the 'candidate's mother' with a good grace. She told Harold that, next to him, Nigel was 'closest to my heart' : 'Ben is too difficult for me to cope with, – I have made a failure over Ben, and I often feel unhappy about it. But Niggs is my darling and my joy and my pride; as he is yours.' Copper fixed a Labour Party poster on the garage door; Vita tore it down in a rage. But Copper was one of the majority. Labour were in again, and Nigel did not win West Leicester.

The response to her *Observer* articles went a little way to restore Vita's own self-esteem. Letters still arrived by the van-load. People told her they changed from the *Sunday Times* to the *Observer* simply for her weekly pieces. Her confident, confidential style invited correspondence. 'How does one protect the choicer sorts of primroses from the attacks of sparrows? . . . This is a real S.O.S.' she wrote in her column that spring; and 'Have you got a *Viburnum Carlcephalum*? If not, please get it at once'; and 'What, I wonder, do you feel about rock gardens?' She advised boldness about taking cuttings of roses, she was robust about the unimportance of fuchsias being struck by frost; and in flooded the letters, week after week.

There were many letters too after she broadcast on 'Walking Through Leaves' in a series on the pleasures of life: 'You know, when I have heard my voice on records, I have never liked it. It always strikes me as rather monotonous and schoolmarmy, so I have been surprised by how many of the letters allude to it in complimentary terms. . . . "Your incomparably lovely voice" says one letter (from a stranger). Idiot. But nice idiot.' None of this made up for the worsening arthritis in her hands, nor for the fact that the doctor, after a cardiograph, warned her to be careful.

In late March, when the clematis macropetela was almost out in the Italian oiljars, making her unwilling to leave home, Vita went on a short visit to Violet at Saint-Loup. She wrote to Harold from Violet's garden room, decorated with murals by Philippe Jullian – 'very gay and charming, and completely fantastic. . . . Violet is very sweet to me, – she really is, – and the food is divine, but *how* I want to come home.' When James Pope-Hennessy met Violet in London in June, she was 'amusing' about Sissinghurst and boasted that Vita was so impressed by the comfort of Saint-Loup that 'she was going to try and make Sissinghurst habitable.'

Vita had no such intention; but she did, shortly after her return, begin a new novel, which was to be *The Easter Party*. She also received an Honorary D.Litt. from Durham University; and many old friends came to see Sissinghurst – Leonard Woolf, Lord Salisbury (in a wheelchair), Margaret Irwin the historical novelist, Ozzie Dickinson, Cyril Joad the philosopher and broadcaster, Ivy Compton-Burnett, and Sibyl Colefax (now very frail, also in a wheelchair, but still talking incessantly).

It was Sibyl who procured the black lace dress that Vita wore at a party at Hertford House to celebrate the fiftieth anniversary of Seery's Wallace Collection. (Vita had no evening dress of her own.) She draped a black lace shawl over the borrowed dress, and wore, for the last time, her diamond and emerald chain and earrings – she had that morning arranged to have them sold. She wrote enthusiastically to Harold afterwards, 'Wasn't it a lovely party last night? I think it is an awfully good plan to go to a party once every four years. . . . My red nails look all wrong here!' This crossed with a letter from Harold: 'I wish Mar would get a dress just like Betty Hussey to wear. It suits you so well to have black and you can always wear it with different shawls etc. But you looked so splendid last night with your dingles and dangles that I should like to feel you could come oftener to parties and not have to scrounge round for dresses with Sibyl as entrepreneur.'

For the next important party, at Buckingham Palace the following February, Vita again borrowed the black dress belonging to Mrs Hussey; then she acquired one of her own, costing eighteen pounds, 'which is cheap for these days. As it will have to last me for the next twenty years, if I live as long, it will work out at under £1 a year!'

James Pope-Hennessy, who had been at the Hertford House party, thought that Vita had looked 'very blue and ill' that evening. He came down to lunch at Sissinghurst the Sunday following: 'Harold in an orange shirt drinking sherry, Violet Trefusis ebullient in white cotton, and Vita looking amazingly, frighteningly ill.... It was a strained, unsatisfactory day.'[6] At lunch Violet suggested that Harold and Vita should drive out to Florence in her Fiat in September, since she wanted to sell it in Italy, and they could stay with her at l'Ombrellino, the house on the hill of Bellosguardo, above Florence, that had belonged to her mother.

Vita's doctor told Harold that her heart was still dilated, and she must share the driving with Copper and not get tired. Her arthritis was spreading to her right elbow ('Breaking up, that's what I am!' she wrote in her diary) and she worried privately about the £2,814.6s.4d. that she still owed in surtax. 'Where on earth am I to get it?' Only at the end of August did she say anything to Harold about the novel she was writing, and the news did nothing to reassure him. 'Oh dear! ... You were not at all in a good state last Sunday and I dread the burden of a novel making you all strained and anxious again.'

They set off with Copper in Violet's car in mid-September. They drove through Val d'Isère, where Vita had been with Hilda Matheson over twenty years before – 'there are now 28 hotels!' Driving now, not walking, over the Col d'Iseran, she stopped to take some seeds of gentian *acaulis*.

In Rapallo Harold discovered he had left his satchel 'with all his money, passport, and 3 chapters of his book' behind them at Alessandria. The satchel was not recovered, and 'poor H. much cast down'. Vita was at her best in such a crisis; Harold told her afterwards how much he had appreciated her gentleness, 'It was like the Lac des Cygnes instead of a horrible turmoil.' From that moment on they began to enjoy themselves and one another, and to talk. 'And how happy we were my sweet sweet mar! So happy. Our youth seemed to come back to us.' At Lerici that evening, they sat by the sea and Vita told him more about the novel she was writing. On the way to Lucca they dug up wild cyclamen to plant at home. (Vita kept roots damp by putting them in her sponge-bag; she kept cuttings alive by sticking them in a raw potato.) They reached l'Ombrellino in the evening. 'Go out on the balcony and absorb the incredible beauty of Florence framed between cypresses.'

Bernard Berenson, aged eighty-three, was at his summer villa at Vallombrosa, not far away. He was determined to entertain Violet's distinguished visitors; he sent his jeep and his Welsh chauffeur to collect them. At Vallombrosa Vita had a long talk with Berenson's companion Nicky Mariano about Geoffrey Scott, who had loved them both; and she briefly met Luisa Vertova, a young art historian working with Berenson. Berenson was a patron of Ben's – and five years later, Ben was to marry Luisa.

The only sorrow of the holiday was a considerable one: they heard, while with Berenson, that Sibyl Colefax had died. 'Shocked.'

Back with Violet at l'Ombrellino, they drove round Florence with her other guest, Gaston Palewski, and lunched with Harold Acton at La Pietra, where there were 'the finest zinnias I have ever seen,' noted Vita. They went home by train, restored and reunited. 'There are days and moments I shall never forget,' Vita wrote to Harold, 'all things to add to our store of memories. Bless you for being so sweet to me always – my perfect companion, my dearest friend, my love.'

# CHAPTER 33

BEFORE Vita and Harold had gone to Italy together, Ben had at last succeeded in moving out of Neville Terrace to a shared flat in St George's Square, Pimlico. Harold went to see him there: 'Much gayer than Neville Terrace. I fear that we have failed rather in providing our sons with "gaiety". That I suppose is what Sibyl means when she says that we have been bad parents.'

Ben, although he had craved to be out of Neville Terrace, loved his father uncritically. Towards Vita, he remained every bit as ambivalent, even hostile, as she feared he was. Sometimes he was 'charming' with her, and she was touched and delighted. Sometimes he was silent, coldly ignoring all her conversational efforts at meals, so that in her extreme nervousness she lost her temper with Harold – 'His calmness half soothes and half enrages me.' After one weekend in December 1950 when Ben had for once been charming, she wrote to Harold:

I go such a see-saw over him: he gets me into a state when he arrives in one of his moods, and then when he is in a good mood I *love* him. I often feel I should be nicer to him, and I long to be, but he makes me so dreadfully shy sometimes. I can't feel at ease with him, I feel like a motor-car with a clutch that won't go into gear – it grinds and grinds and nothing happens.

But in the aftermath of the happy holiday Vita was a new person. The novel was 'going fine', and Michael Joseph had given her an advance. Being able to write again made 'the whole difference to life':

I have been so miserable the last two or three years, not being able to write; really worried I have been, thinking it was gone from me for ever. I don't mean by this that I think my novel will be any good, – you know I am not a good novelist, – but at any rate it is exciting doing it, and it keeps me alive, living in an imaginary world which seems more real than the ordinary world.

Of course I would rather write poetry, and perhaps that also will return to me
some day.

All my depression is gone.

Nigel told her that he and Lionel Sackville-West had been negotiating for
the National Trust to take over the park at Knole, in addition to the house,
so as to prevent speculative building. Vita had been having dreams about
Knole – about 'the deer galloping down the stable passage, their hooves
rattling on the wooden boards' – and after hearing from Nigel she wrote to
Mason, the agent at Knole, to ask for a key to the garden gates. She had
been given one after the death of her father; it had been kept in a green
leather box, along with the key of the gate of the Villa Pestellini, and left at
Long Barn. When the contents of Long Barn were being sorted and sold,
the green box disappeared. She did not imagine she would ever again use
a key to Knole, but 'If I had a key I wouldn't feel locked out', as she told
Harold, with the old lament – 'If only I had been Dada's son, instead of his
daughter.'

Lord Sackville, her Uncle Charlie, sent her a new key. He spoilt her
pleasure by telling her he hoped she would not lose it again; just in case,
he had had the engraved word 'Knole' erased from it. She did not tell
Harold, but determined to ask Copper to 'put back the word Knole on my
key'. This humiliation she scribbled in her dream-book. To Harold, she
simply said: 'I am so happy, writing, with my key to Knole in my pocket.'

Unprecedentedly, the Nicolsons asked someone to stay for Christmas
– Rose Macaulay – and, unprecedentedly, Vita was sorry when her guest
left. They even gave a cocktail party during her visit, in the big room. The
guests were not literary, but local friends, with a core of Beales, Pyms,
Lamonts and Drummonds.

After Christmas Harold's mother, aged ninety, was taken seriously ill at
her London house in Tedworth Square. Soon after Vita's birthday in
March it was clear the end was coming. Vita put Rollo in the car and drove
up to join Harold and his family: 'It is all pretty grim, – Freddy drunk
downstairs, and his mother dying upstairs.... Glad I went.' She took
Harold to the Victoria and Albert Museum to take his mind off it all, and to
Kew, 'but it pours with icy rain'. There was nothing she could do at
Tedworth Square; she had never been close to Lady Carnock, who died
on Good Friday, 23 March 1951. Harold went to her cremation, which
worried Vita, 'as apparently he fainted in his bedroom last night, and has
bruised his back and elbow.' Lady Carnock's death brought about Vita's
first and only visit to Gwen and Sam St Levan at St Michael's Mount; she
and Nigel joined Harold's assembled family there for the interment of the
ashes.

Harold felt he had to offer his eldest brother Freddy a home at Neville Terrace. Vita was hotly against it; she said it was too much for him, not fair to Nigel, and that the Parrotts – the couple who looked after the household – would leave. She had no sympathy for Freddy, although she felt acute sympathy for the sorrows of people less close to her – such as Ivy Compton-Burnett, who had just lost her friend and companion Margaret Jourdain. She wrote to Harold, while the discussions about Freddy's future were in progress, that she had offered Ivy a 'refuge' at Sissinghurst if she cared to come. 'I really cannot bear to think of people's sorrow and grief and loneliness. I cannot bear it, Hadji. Think if it was you or me! and so one translates one's own feelings into the feelings of other people.' Harold was not impressed by this. Nor did he see any alternative to his looking after Freddy at Neville Terrace:

> Mar has no sense of family obligation. I suppose it is a bedint rather than an aristocratic feeling.... Anyhow I do not think Freddy will live for long. I want to feel if he dies that I have done something at least to render the last stage of his life less horribly miserable than it threatens to be. But why does Mar get into such a state about Ivy Compton-Burnett; why is she such an angel to the Trouts, Mrs Carey, Mrs Lamont, and old Mrs Drummond; why does she fuss about sending flowers to Elvira's Mum: – when she has no feeling at all about Aunt Cecilie and never thought for one moment of sending flowers to my Mum?... But I love you for it none the less, in the way one loves the looniness of someone who is everything in the world.

Harold's problems were augmented in June when news broke of the defection of Guy Burgess and Donald Maclean to Russia. Guy Burgess had been a close friend of Harold's in his Foreign Office days; they had worked together on propaganda in the war, and met frequently at clubs and parties. Harold found him amusing company. He worried about Guy's fate on the other side, writing in his diary on 8 June – a night when Vita, alone at Sissinghurst, noted in hers how 'the young moon and Venus came quite close together, a beautiful and romantic sight' – that the Russians would probably only use Guy for a month or two, 'and then shove him quietly into some salt-mine. During my dreams, his absurd face stares at me with drunken, unseeing eyes.' At the weekend, Vita was puzzled by Harold's silence and depression. Her diary, Saturday 9 June:

> The irises are coming out rapidly. H. is still worried about Guy Burgess and Maclean. It seems to be obsessing him. It is curious and interesting how things absorb his interest suddenly. I shall never understand him, – i.e., although he is a health-fuss, he never asked me about my [arthritic] hands which are a real worry to me. So I said nothing.

He was still 'morose' on the Sunday. 'I hope it is the prospect of Freddy moving into Neville Terrace this week.' Or was it something more serious ? He wrote to her from London :

No my darling I am not hiding anything from you. I have not become involved in a spy ring nor have I become connected in any way with Guy's disreputable habits. I have not seen or heard from him for two years.

   If I was depressed this weekend it was due to a combination of circumstances.

He had had to think back over the whole course of his friendship with Guy, in the light of what he now knew had been going on. As Harold's biographer James Lees-Milne has written, 'There can be no doubt that Guy Burgess extracted from Harold [during the war] inside information which he passed on to his masters in Moscow.'[1]

   James Lees-Milne himself was married later that year. His wife was Alvilde, the daughter of a Lieutenant General and the former wife of Viscount Chaplin. Vita and Harold were witnesses at their quiet wedding at Chelsea Registry Office. Because of a religious difference between the couple, and because of her great fondness for Jim Lees-Milne, Vita had a special concern for this marriage.

The first collection of her *Observer* articles was being published in book form. In her column, Vita continued to air her gardening prejudices : 'I hate, hate, hate American Pillar and her sweetly pink companion [Dorothy] Perkins.' She condemned herbaceous borders, and the colour of ordinary terracotta flower-pots : these she advised whitewashing, or painting cream.

   More and more strangers came to see the garden : she made £550 from 'shillings' in 1951, and was proud of it : 'I do feel we have created something here ; something lovely and peaceful has grown out of dereliction, under our hands.' She lectured to the Royal Horticultural Society, and resented the fact that her prowess as a gardener, worse still as a writer, was so tied to the *Observer* articles. 'I get furious inside when people drag up *The Edwardians*, and of course the *Observer* is worst of all.' She felt that she got credit – in both senses – for the wrong reasons. She wrote away for some peat, and the firm replied saying, 'May we be allowed to supply the peat free to so great a gardener ?' 'Now that is nonsense,' Vita said to Harold.

   If the 'shillings' were people who knew her, they liked to call on her personally. With distinguished acquaintances to whom she had little to say, Vita would switch on the television and they would all sit watching *Muffin the Mule*, a children's programme that became something of a cult with Vita. 'How people pester one! Dottie telephones: will I come to Penns one day before she goes abroad? Violet telephones: will I go to London to see her? The Boy-scouts of Cranbrook: will I open their show? I don't mind doing that; it takes less time. .... But, really, Hadji, I want to *work*.'

She liked having Jacquetta Hawkes for a weekend, having greatly admired her book *A Land*; and she liked having Freya Stark – 'she has really lived up to the hilt'. Dorothy Bussy, the author of *Olivia*, came to tea and became a friend; when Vita visited her in London, 'Dorothy and I sat up talking till I don't know when – it was one of the things I shall never forget.' A Mrs Wilton came, claiming she was 'either B.M.'s daughter by Seery, or Dada's daughter by Constance Hatch.' Bunny Drummond's husband died, and Bunny's evening visits became even more frequent. Harold wrote to her in November: 'I do distrust all your parasites so – they are selfish about you. Except Vi [Pym] who is unselfish.' But Vita was capable of ruthlessness on occasion. One sentimental woman friend, forbidden to come to Sissinghurst any more, called Vita 'an angel with a flaming sword', barring her from Paradise.

The Nicolsons had reached the age when their names began to appear in the memoirs and biographies of eminent contemporaries. 'There is lots in it about us both,' Vita wrote to Harold about Rupert Hart-Davis's biography of Hugh Walpole. But 1952 opened with Harold's discovery that Roy Campbell's forthcoming biography *Light on a Dark Horse* contained a 'fiendish attack' on the Long Barn episode. Vita thought they might try and get an injunction against the publishers. Raymond Mortimer and Alan Pryce-Jones (editor of the *Times Literary Supplement*), both old and trusted friends, advised against taking any action at all. Harold was more upset than Vita who was, as he said, 'funny about it'. She had reviewed Campbell's *Talking Bronco* favourably and generously in 1946, calling him 'one of our most considerable living poets'; and she had every sympathy with vengeful love. Nevertheless she wrote in her diary that his autobiography was 'anything but agreeable'.

At the same time, Vita was sent a typescript copy of Dorothy Wellesley's memoirs, *Far Have I Travelled*, by the young woman, Ursula Codrington, who was acting as Dottie's secretary. (Miss Codrington was soon to do some secretarial work for Vita too, helping her answer some hundreds of letters in response to an *Observer* piece about slug-bait.) Vita found the book 'just too awful': 'Not indiscreet, or disagreeable about Gerry, or anything like that, but just so SILLY. A mixture of whining and boasting.' Then she had a telephone call from Mary Campbell, saying that Roy was the poet to be honoured at the Foyle's Literary Luncheon at the Dorchester to which Vita was invited as a guest of honour. Mary begged Vita not to go, 'lest Roy should make a scene'. Vita did not go. Instead, she lunched with Violet at the Ritz, bought herself a new pair of high boots from Poulson and Skone, and ordered a new coat and skirt at Burberry's.

Nigel was standing as Conservative candidate at a by-election in Bournemouth East. Vita and Harold went out with him on polling-day, touring the constituency, and were there to hear his victory announced : 'Vita is so proud of him, her eyes gleam gently. It is dangerous, but delicious, to love someone so deeply.' On 19 February 1952 they watched him take his seat for the first time in the House of Commons. Afterwards Harold went to Greece – 'And I stick here,' Vita wrote to Jim Lees-Milne, 'rooted like an old turnip in to the Wealden clay.'

King George VI died that spring ; his widow Queen Elizabeth, now the Queen Mother, expressed a wish to visit Sissinghurst, and to have luncheon, on 4 June. 'I shall have to put on a skirt,' said Vita. Lady Diana Cooper told Harold the protocol, which he relayed to Vita : 'She sits at the end of the table and I on her *left* hand. ... The reason is that when she enters a house it is technically *her* house, and she therefore takes the head of the table !'

Before the royal visit Freddy, Harold's brother, collapsed at Neville Terrace and went into hospital. On 27 May Vita had a disaster of her own. 'Before dinner I go out to snip some dead lilac heads and collapse. Heart. Finally I manage to crawl to the office and telephone to Anna [Mac] who is dining with Bunny.' She did not tell Harold what had happened, and tried to conceal her weakness, especially when Freddy died four days later. Freddy's ashes were buried at Sissinghurst.

In spite of these troubles the Queen Mother's visit was a success. She sat at the top of the table as etiquette required, with Harold on her right and Nigel on her left. (Ben was in Italy.) Vita sat at the other end. They had coffee out in the Erechtheum, and walked round the garden. The staff and the Beales were presented, the Pyms came with a basket of cherries, and there was tea in the big room. 'Everything goes *comme sur des roulettes*,' Vita wrote in her diary. 'Viti was splendid and serene,' Harold wrote in his.

She lost this serenity when a few days later Rollo was bitten by a visiting dog in the garden and became seriously ill. Harold now noticed that Vita herself was unwell too. Mac, under pressure, told him about her heart attack.

Harold and Vita were uncommonly nervous about one another's health and safety. Vita worried herself to the point of tears about what might happen to Harold not only in aeroplanes but in trains, taxis, thunderstorms, crossing roads. As she made Rose say about her husband in *The Easter Party*, 'I live in fear. . . . Not a day, not an hour passes without my imagining some disastrous happening.' Why was this? 'People say, don't they, that [fear] springs from a hidden feeling of guilt. But I am not aware of any guilt. I don't think I have committed any major wrong . . .,' says Rose. Whatever the sources of their shared anxiety, both Nicolsons would have agreed with Vita's fictional Rose. Harold was a 'health-fuss' on his own account. Vita was not. Yet in spite of their acute concern, they were of very little help to one another in illness, both of them being hopelessly impractical. When Harold had flu earlier in the year, Vita stuck a thermometer in his mouth and went away and forgot all about it. When she plumped up his pillows, they were more uncomfortable than before. 'She has wonderful and superb qualities but that of a sick nurse, bless her sweetness, is not among them.'

Now, paralysed by anxiety about Vita's health, Harold behaved as he said 'clumsily': 'she is such a difficult patient to manage, resenting all fuss, but not careful herself.' She spoke harshly to him, and then apologized; it was easier for them to talk about Rollo's illness than hers, and still impossible for Harold to talk openly to her about the drinking to which anxiety over Rollo had driven her. Lady Powerscourt (the poet Sheila Wingfield) came to luncheon during these unhappy days in June, and 'Viti is all confused and repeats herself the whole time. I am terribly embarrassed and sad.'

It was the same story when James Lees-Milne and James Pope-Hennessy came down one evening in August. She told Harold, who was in London, that the dinner had not gone well 'and I felt it was a dreadful failure. . . . I am sorry about it, and feel sore and inadequate.' James Pope-Hennessy, from concern for them both, told Harold that Vita had been 'in a muzzy condition'. A diary poem of Vita's, undated:

> There are times when I cannot endure the sight of people.
> I know they are charming, intelligent, since everyone tells me so,
> But I wish they would go away.
> I cannot establish contact with anybody;
> They are all unreal to me, the charming intelligent people,
> And I daresay I seem as unreal to them.

Harold left Neville Terrace for an apartment, C1 Albany, which made him happy and Vita happy for him. Albany is an elegant eighteenth-century building set back from Piccadilly, originally a mansion, converted into apartments arranged on each side of the arcaded Rope Walk. Harold could have had no finer London base. The rooms were John Sparrow's; he had been appointed Warden of All Souls, Oxford, and, retaining an attic for himself, offered the rest to Nigel, who accepted on the condition that Harold came too. Harold's room was downstairs, at the back. The weekend after the move, all trouble seemed put aside. Vita's diary, Sunday 29 June : 'Sit out in the white garden with H. till 10 p.m. planning improvements in the white garden which is getting better. L. regale coming out rapidly. Rose filipes lovely in an almond tree. A perfectly still, breathless evening, scented and warm.' They went on a garden tour together in August, through Wales and on to Ireland, where Vita had never been. They stayed at Clandeboye, a magical house to Harold in his childhood when he had stayed there with his uncle Lord Dufferin and Ava. Through Vita's eyes it was less magical. She wrote in her diary that she was not happy there. Humbly, Harold wrote in his : 'I had given Vita the impression that Clandeboye was one of the most stately houses of Ireland, packed with lovely furniture and beautiful pictures. She finds an ugly County Down house with relics of Burma in 1850 and bad copies of Reynolds and Gainsborough.' It was an anti-climax ; but Harold had grown used to the subordination of his family myths to Vita's. When Nigel told him he always felt more Sackville than Nicolson, Harold commented : 'It is quite true that neither of our boys regards any of my family as belonging in the way they regard Eddy, Lionel etc. as belonging. So there I am next to Sackville Street [at Albany] and imposed upon, crushed, humiliated by that gloomy melancholic breed.' It was a joke – just : an old resentment that no longer had power to hurt.

Arriving home, Vita found 'some colchicums still out, zinnias still very good. . . . Rollo sleek and fat, but sulky.' She abandoned Rollo again almost at once, to go alone to stay with Violet Trefusis at l'Ombrellino. Philippe Jullian, Harold's old flame Jean de Gaigneron, and Rolfe Faucigny-Lucinge, a long-standing escort of Violet's, were also staying. Philippe Jullian recalled driving in Florence with Vita and Violet : 'The two women indulged in a leisurely survey of the passers-by, their verdicts those of a pair of latter-day disciples of Oscar Wilde : "Ah, my dear, that profile : *pure* Donatello !"'[2] (Vita was an admirer of male beauty ; telling Harold that year about one of her court cases, she described the accused as 'one of the handsomest men I have ever seen, with tough grey curls like Alvilde [Lees-Milne] and a complexion like a ripe nectarine. He absolutely *glowed* with colour and beauty, as he sat in the dock.')

While the others went into Florence, Vita stayed up at the villa a good deal, correcting her proofs of *The Easter Party* and Violet's proofs of *Don't Look Round*. She wrote to Harold :

V. has just gone off in the usual *tourbillon* to Florence. Really I don't know why her servants stay with her. She never gives them orders, and then curses them for not having done what she wanted. She will never say how many people there are to lunch or dinner.... I simply can't make her out.... And yet she can be so sweet and tender-hearted. She really is an enigma.

Writing to Alvilde Lees-Milne a couple of years later, Vita said she thought Violet was 'a profoundly unhappy, even tragic person', which was why 'one loves her and tolerates a lot of things one wouldn't otherwise tolerate. She is *une âme damnée* ; Dance, dance, dance, little lady.'

Violet was an enigma, and so was the 'indestructible' bond between them. Home again, Vita thought on her thirty-ninth wedding anniversary on 1 October 1952 of the equally 'indestructible' way she loved Harold, and felt she wanted to investigate this equally great enigma. 'I am thinking out a new novel to write,' she wrote in her diary. 'It will be about marriage, and the problems associated with that sacrament. I can't get it to take shape in my mind as yet.' Picking apples in the orchard – Allington pippins, Coxes, Blenheims – with gentians at her feet 'like the Mediterranean', her thoughts 'wandered vaguely round and round my new book', a line of John Masefield's running in her head : 'The days that make us happy make us wise.'

That Christmas Harold noticed for the first time that Vita was becoming bent at the shoulders. 'Poor darling it is her arthritis.' She was sixty. In her diary, Vita wrote on 27 December : 'I feel that H. hates the idea of getting older (so do I too).' After fourteen years, Harold was giving up his 'Marginal Comment' column in the *Spectator*.

With the New Year Honours List, they became Sir Harold and Lady Nicolson : Harold had been offered the KCVO for his biography of George v. They were not very pleased ; they even thought of turning it down. It depressed them because the honour, so far from being an honour, seemed to them dreary and middle class. 'If I had never been given anything I should have retained my potential repute,' Harold wrote to Vita ; 'being assessed so low diminishes my prestige.' Vita forbade Mrs Staples to call her 'm'lady' ; they remained Mr and Mrs Nicolson to all the servants and gardeners, by order. Vita dropped the now superseded 'Hon.' on her envelopes to Harold and addressed him simply as Harold Nicolson. She remained V. Sackville-West wherever possible, and always hated to be called 'Lady Nicolson'.

Her novel *The Easter Party* came out in January 1953. The first review she saw was by Marghanita Laski in the *Observer* – 'contemptuous and wounding', Harold called it, amazed at the stoicism with which Vita took it. 'I fully expect it to be slashed to pieces,' Vita wrote of her book in her diary. Not all the reviews were unfavourable ; there was 'a lovely full-page article' in the *TLS*, which Vita suspected was by Alan Pryce-Jones. Harold liked the book. 'The triumph of course is that you have treated of a dog without one moment of sentimentality – that is an achievement and shames all the cat lovers and poodle fakers. I hope Rollo is flattered by the portrait.'

The alsatian in *The Easter Party* is called Svend and belongs to Sir Walter Mortimer, whose marriage to his wife Rose is unconsummated. Their incomplete union is contrasted with the living, loving marriage of Rose's otherwise dull sister. The novel sets romanticism against rationalism, revelation against reason. Rose loves her husband Walter, but he loves only Svend, his dog, and Anstey, his house. Sleeping alone with Svend on his bed, he is content as Vita was content with Rollo. Rose sees in him 'passion gone wrong', cynicism, and a cruel streak.

In a contrived ordeal, Walter loses both Svend – or so he thinks – and his beautiful house, which is burned to the ground. In extremity he turns to Rose, realizing that in his egotistic way he 'had built up throughout the years since marriage a system by which he could depend on her without cost to himself', by casting her – irrational, primitive as she was – in a role she would not have chosen.

*The Easter Party* is not a good novel, but for the student of Vita's life and nature it is a moving book to read. Her major set-piece of the fire at night at Anstey – based on the fire at Sissinghurst Place – is effective. But the source of the novel's moving quality is in the battle of temperament. It was Vita who loved solitude, and detachment; it was also Vita who, like Rose, experienced passion, irrationality and transcendence. The non-consummation of the marriage reflects her own unresolved duality, as well as the enigma of her sexless love for Harold. It is as if she herself longed for some apocalyptic happening that would fuse the separate parts of her life.

# CHAPTER 34

AT the end of March 1953 Nigel became engaged to be married. It was a complete surprise to his parents. His fiancée was Philippa Tennyson d'Eyncourt, twenty-four years old, cheerful, pretty and unbookish. Vita was very pleased, though she and Harold made jokes about 'the Tenniscourts' as they called the Tennyson d'Eyncourts. Vita liked Philippa: 'Really I couldn't have wished for a nicer daughter-in-law.'

Harold at first found the engagement harder to accept, not wanting to lose Nigel's company at Albany, but it was he who was to come to love and depend on Philippa most. He was sadly aware of his own fall from centrality in public life – he told Vita that the morning mail brought more letters for Nigel now than for him. Vita was immediately reassuring, writing dismissively that Nigel's letters must be 'mostly constituents bothering him, plus some wedding congratulations'. When Harold was made an honorary Fellow of Balliol, his old college, she wrote congratulating 'my only love, my true love, my Hadji, my curly-box, my darling, my life-long love, my silly clever Hadji'.

1953 was the summer that Everest was conquered – 'Furious about this', Vita wrote in her diary, resenting the violation of the unknown. It was also the summer of the coronation of the young Queen Elizabeth II. Vita was enthusiastic and 'immensely moved'; still secretly half-hoping to be appointed Poet Laureate in succession to John Masefield (who was to outlive her) she wrote a coronation poem, published in the *TLS*, which combined proper respect with an aristocratic familiarity:

> Madam, how strange to be your Majesty.
> How strange to wake in an ordinary bed
> And, half awake, to think 'Now who am I?' ...

Her arthritis spreading to her knee, Vita prowled miserably up and down Regent Street looking – unsuccessfully – for a hat to wear at Nigel's wedding. She bought her wedding garments in Tenterden, near Sissinghurst. Nigel and Philippa were married on 30 July at St Margaret's, Westminster. In October there was another family wedding: young Lionel Sackville-West was married to Jacobine Hitchens. 'My relations all look pretty dim,' Vita wrote in her diary afterwards, 'except Uncle Charlie who retains his elegance.' Later that month she heard that Philippa was expecting a baby – or that 'our little Niggs is going to have a mar of his own', as she told Harold: 'It has sort of upset and disturbed me, in the nicest possible way, but you know how unexpected one's reactions can be even to oneself, and I feel turned all upside down with pleasure.'

Leonard Woolf had edited a selection from Virginia Woolf's diaries under the title *A Writer's Diary*. Vita read it that autumn; it was, she wrote in her own diary, 'an event in the mind'. 'Oh God, how I wish I could get Virginia back! Reading her diary makes me regret her so poignantly; and also feeling that towards the end I might have done something to stop her from taking her life.' To Harold she said that she had made the unexpected discovery that Virginia 'minded about money':

> Now I should have supposed her to be quite indifferent. But I don't think it was a real minding; not natural to her; I think it was all due to association with Leonard, the Jew side of Leonard. He took all her earnings, and allowed her 13/- a week pocket money. ... And then she starts to make more money, and is allowed to keep some of it, 'so I can buy myself a new frock and a hat'!

Vita reviewed *A Writer's Diary* for *Encounter*, before getting back to her *Observer* article about hedges: 'I tried to squeeze too much into it, and must make two articles out of it. I am not sorry, as I do find it difficult to get subjects, having told the cycle of my country's gardens for so many years now. I sometimes wonder how much longer I can keep it up, but 15 guineas a week is not to be lightly foregone.'

Repetition was as she said inevitable. Her enthusiasms – for trough-gardening, one-colour gardens, old roses, climbers grown through trees, blue flowers and white ones, 'gloomy' hellebores and all small, subtle, quiet-coloured flowers – were reiterated year after year. Likewise her dislikes – for hybrid tea roses and most floribundas, most 'double' varieties of anything, and showy or outsize blooms such as giant chrysanthemums, 'shaggy things as big as an Old English Sheepdog's face'.

When she began gardening, she and Harold had uninhibitedly dug up wild flowers wherever they found them. In the 1950s, as the chemically treated fields and hedgerows became denuded, she began warning her readers against vandalism. Yet she defended her own actions in 'rescuing' rare white violets, or even pink windflowers, and transplanting them to the safety of her garden – at the right time of year, and in the right way. She maintained her relaxed style, as if talking to friends : 'I never say things I don't mean ; or at any rate, not in this column,' she told her readers. By 1957 she was telling them with some justification : 'I think I shall soon have to stop writing these articles, because they are becoming like a parody of my own style.'

Christmas 1953, with Nigel and Philippa elsewhere, was a strain. Vita and Harold's attempts at entertaining at Sissinghurst – a compromise for them both, since they had different friends – were generally strained and unsuccessful. Ben made little effort. Vita's own moodiness elicited a protest from Harold – and an apology from Vita on 23 February 1954 :

> Darling, you did upset me by saying I grumbled, and that you would make a list of my grumbles, and that Nigel said I was cross to you when Ben was there, and that I wasn't as easy-going as you were. This really upset me, because I hate people who grumble or who fuss over trivialities, which honestly I don't think I do. I try not to. I dare say it is true that I am not as easy going as you are, but then perhaps you go to the opposite extreme and are *too* easy going.

One source of Vita's moodiness was her bad relations with Mac, who with age had become increasingly demanding, often rude and sometimes indiscreet. Harold urged Vita to break with her once and for all and get an efficient new secretary. Vita bought a nursing-home in Deal called Channel View for Mac, who, after weeks of wrangling, went off to run it : it was what she had always said she wanted. 'You will be wholly glad,' Vita wrote to Harold in March ; 'my own feelings are mixed. I hate change, and new people, but I daresay it is for the best.' Mac had been part of Vita's life since before the war. She departed with Vita's blessing : whenever Vita parted, even temporarily, from someone she was fond of, she would mark a cross with her thumb on that person's forehead. It was a ritual she had learnt from her mother, who had learnt it from Pepita, who had learnt it from the gypsy Catalina. She was lucky to find a replacement for Mac, since the only accommodation offered was a bed-sitting-room, with no bathroom attached. A young divorcée, Betty Arnett, took the job.

Vita's first grandchild was a girl, who was named Juliet. The news of her birth caused a great stir at Sissinghurst, as Vita reported to Philippa : 'Mrs Staples nearly burst into tears, and Copper rushed up to the tower to pull the flag up, and returned half an hour later to say he'd forgotten to ask how much Mr Nigel's daughter weighed.' In her diary, Vita wrote : 'May God please be kind to Juliet all her life. And if she ever inherits Sissinghurst, may she love it and care for it. Amen.'

Nigel, later in the year, enquired whether his mother would ever consider making Sissinghurst over to the National Trust. Her reaction was passionately negative, as she reported in her diary :

> I said Never never never. *Au grand jamais, jamais*. Never, never, never. Not that hard little metal plate at my door. Nigel can do what he likes when I am dead, but so long as I live no Nat. Trust or any other foreign body shall have my darling. No, no. Over my corpse or my ashes ; not otherwise. It is bad enough to have lost my Knole, but they shan't take S/hurst from me. That, at least, is my own.
>
> *Il y a des choses qu'on ne peut pas supporter*. They shan't ; they shan't ; I won't ; they can't make me. I *won't*, they can't make me, I never would.

Sissinghurst was included in a *Country Life* book of gardens open to the public that year : 'It is funny, isn't it, that our own dear garden should be taking its place among the better gardens of England ?' The 'shillings' brought in £1,394 in 1954 ; there were traffic jams at the front of the house and a public lavatory had to be installed.

In August Vita and Harold took a holiday together in the Dordogne, at her suggestion ; it had become her favourite part of France. She took him in her little Austin car to the cave at Lascaux, where she had been with Raymond Mortimer and Eardley Knollys in 1946 ; then, it had only recently been discovered, and was untouched. By 1954 it had been 'developed' for tourists, with steps and a handrail, and the prehistoric paintings lit by electricity. When they were home and Harold re-established in his week-day routine at Albany, Vita wrote to him : 'I miss you ! It is dreadful, getting so used to your daily companionship, my most perfect companion, whether travelling or at home. But we were happy, weren't we ?' Harold wrote at the top, 'Keep this dear letter always.'

The departure of watchdog Mac meant that Vita was free to expand her companionship with other friends when Harold was in London. She got to know Alvilde Lees-Milne better. Christopher St John, nearly eighty, was a liability and as adoring as ever : 'My dearly loved Vita – my soul's joy.' Edie Lamont came to paint in the garden, and on an evening in July came to see Vita after dinner. 'Strange encounter', Vita wrote cryptically in her diary. For Harold's birthday in November, Vita gave him a painting of the White Garden by Edie. He did not like the picture – or Edie – very much.

Vita knew he fretted about getting old. 'He thinks he is getting deaf, but it is very slight, anyhow I love him even more than I did in 1913 when we

were married, and that is saying a lot.' One *memento mori* was Duff
Cooper's death, and another Ozzie Dickinson's. Her own increasing
age, isolation and arthritis made her always eccentric appearance more
extreme. Harold would not allow her to wear her breeches on holiday;
and just before they went to France, he had written to her:

I am glad you have had something done to your hair as it really was getting a
bit sheep-doggy, especially at the back, where Mar can't see it during those
three seconds when she scowls at herself in the glass. Of course it seems
strange for a bit to be tidy. ... But it did NOT look right my sweet, and I am
delighted you had that 1½ hour to spare.

In December, after buying a hat, she wrote to him:

Now that is where biographers go wrong. If ever any biographer undertook
to write our lives, yours and mine, using our letters as copy, he would say
'V.S-W could not by any stretch of the imagination be regarded as a well-
dressed woman, or indeed as a woman who gave sufficient consideration to
the smartness of her appearance, yet here we find her, at the somewhat
advanced age of 62, writing to her husband to inform him that she has got a
new hat. We may assume, therefore, that such feminine and frivolous interests occupied her mind far more urgently than has been supposed. ... '
   You just wait till you see my new hat.

It had been bought for a reading of her own poetry at the Royal Society
of Literature, but in the event she wore her old felt. As an encore, Vita
read the opening of *The Land*. She saw the word 'Boeotian' approaching
– it was a word she could never remember how to pronounce. When she
reached it she paused in agony and called out 'Harold!' 'So,' Harold
wrote in his diary, 'I say in a loud voice "Boeotian!" The audience were
much amused, but some of them thought it must be a put-up job.'
   The hat problem remained unsolved. When in February 1955 Vita and
Harold were asked to luncheon at Buckingham Palace to meet the
Shah of Iran, Harold warned her 'But now don't go and borrow
Bunny's hat with the huge feather in it. Get yourself a real nice one. Not
a beret or a toque.' Vita wrote in her diary after the party: 'The children
and corgis came in after lunch and ate coffee sugar. Talked to the Queen
Mother who says she has never got over being shy when she comes into
a room. Winston talked about history at lunch, and was charming.... I
did enjoy that party; it was worth going up to London for.'
   One evening in March, at Sissinghurst, Harold had a slight stroke. 'I
looked at him and saw that his poor mouth was all twisted, also his
speech was so thick I could only just understand what he said.' After the
doctor had gone, Vita lay in bed 'wondering how I could most tidily

dispose of myself if he died, as I should not care to go on living without him.' He made a good recovery. Ten days later Vita herself had a fall, and cracked a bone in her sacrum.

To his parents' surprise and delight, Ben told them in April that he was going to marry Luisa Vertova. Vita was particularly pleased: when she had first met Luisa at Vallombrosa, as she told Alvilde Lees-Milne, 'I took an enormous fancy to her and said [to Nicky Mariano] there's the person I would like Ben to marry.' Harold had another mild stroke in May and Vita worried constantly about him; she also worried because her book on la Grande Mademoiselle, which she had taken up again after nine years, was being preempted by another, by Francis Steegmuller.

Yet while Harold experienced the first serious intimations of mortality, Vita experienced a sudden new flare-up of life. It is hard to know what was cause and what was effect. She was happy about Nigel, and calmer about Ben. The White Garden was perfect, 'the roses in the almond tree just pure lace'; at the end of the year she heard she had won the Royal Horticultural Society's Veitch Memorial Medal: 'I say: I hope Vass will be impressed!' She bought a Jaguar car; and, at the age of sixty-three she was falling in love again. 'I can't see the future, it frightens me,' she wrote to Alvilde Lees-Milne at the end of May. But she was happy and excited.

The day after writing that she set off with Harold for Florence, for Ben's wedding – '*and* with a new dress for the wedding,' she told Alvilde (herself a most elegant woman):

> rather pretty, I think, though you mightn't agree, deep rose with black. I got an old one copied, and refused to be tried on, – can't stand women crawling round me with pins in their mouths. . . . I've got a huge lovely black straw hat I bought for a garden-party at Buckingham Palace before the war, and have never worn since except at Nigel's wedding, and perhaps at yours? I've also got a silk petticoat, Marks and Spencer, 7/6, so am well equipped.

Vita enjoyed the wedding at the Palazzo Vecchio more than Harold, who feared exhaustion and another stroke. Vita was 'so happy about Ben and Luisa', feeling not only that they were well suited 'but I like her being a Florentine, as Florence has always meant so much in my life, and indeed I think that Ben was probably conceived there, at Villa Pestellini.' (Before, when it had suited her fantasy, she had supposed Ben to have been conceived at Coker Court.)

When Luisa came by herself to stay at Sissinghurst, Vita had 'a long and very nice talk' with her in the tower room. 'She says she is terribly happy. I think she is really very much in love with Ben.' By Christmas Luisa was pregnant. Vita did not however underestimate the complexities of this marriage. Luisa had told her one evening 'all about Ben's courtship, if it may be given that name! Ben is even odder than I thought. . . . I hope he never makes her unhappy.'

Her own feeling for Alvilde set her writing poetry again that autumn – 'a doggerel I shouldn't like to qualify as verse'. She and Harold went to France again in October, in the Jaguar. At Aix-en-Provence, Vita began a new short story 'about a woman in a hotel'; this was 'Interlude in Two Lives', about a chance meeting in Provence between a middle-aged man and woman who had been friends in youth. They enjoy a month's idyll, but decide not to consummate their love, and to part – agreeing to meet again at the same time, in the same place, every year. The man is a bohemian and the woman a smart New Yorker; the story was in part inspired by Vita's inhibited love for Alvilde. Two days after she began the story, in Aix, she had a dream:

I dreamt I saw a mouse, obviously ill, so in order to give it a quick death I picked it up and threw it into a puddle of water. Somebody said 'Don't you see the water is not deep enough, it won't drown, it will just go on swimming about.' So I picked it out again, and as I did so it bit my finger. Somebody said 'That mouse has got a disease and you will get it.' I was terribly distressed by this, because I said 'Harold wants me, Harold needs me, and if I get a disease I can't look after him.'

Vita was uneasy about being disloyal to Harold in his weakened condition. In a letter to Alvilde, she described her relationship with him:

We have gone our own ways for about 30 years; never asked questions; never been in the least curious about that side of our respective lives, though deeply devoted and sharing our interests. I love him deeply, and he loves me; and as he gets older and has worries about his health ... he comes to depend on me more and more. In other words, I could never now go away from home, i.e. to stay with you at Roquebrune [in the south of France] ... because I know he would worry, and worry is the worst possible thing for a person in his rather precarious state of health.

I have treated him badly enough in the past and must make it up to him now.

Yet after a visit from Alvilde, her 'head and heart in a whirl', Vita wrote to her: 'Strange, how a few hours can transform life.'

The transformation of life did not drown Vita's anxieties. She went to sleep worrying about Harold, and woke in the night thinking that Rollo, sleeping on her bed, was dead. 'I know this all goes back to the time when I used to get frights about Martha. But really it is because I worry about H.,' she wrote in her diary. She was afraid of calling to him one morning and getting no answer – 'and then I should have to open his door and find – what? Oh dear, the approach of the end of life is so sad.' Her realization of the whole huge paradox of her marriage to Harold took strange forms. She wrote to him on 31 January 1956:

> I suddenly thought, supposing you were found poisoned one day when we were here alone together, and I was accused of poisoning you. Then there's an inquest, and it is discovered that I have been buying cyanide of potassium, ostensibly to destroy wasps' nests, but I cannot account for it: where did I put it? What have I done with it? . . . People aren't so careless as all that with a deadly poison, surely, Lady Nicolson? Come now! You can't expect us to believe that.
>
> And then my Counsel for the Defence produces our letters to each other, years and years of letters full of love.

It was as if her awareness of how much and how often she had hurt Harold – 'I have treated him badly enough in the past and must make it up to him now' – was oppressing her, and connected with her fear that he would die. The 'years and years of letters full of love' were an invest-ment, kept up in the bad times as well as the good; a huge testimonial – in spite of voluntary separation, compromise, incompatibility, infidelity and sometimes deception – to the love in which they both believed, and needed to believe. The letters are, in themselves, the counsel for the defence of their marriage.

In the hard winter of early 1956 the soda-water froze solid in the siphon at Sissinghurst, and Vita vainly tried to keep the icy draughts out of the dining-room by pinning blankets and towels over the doors and open staircase. Like her employers, Mrs Staples, now sixty-five, was slowing up. Dinner in the evening was simplified; Mrs Staples just left out plates of cold food and a thermos flask of hot soup which would wait until Vita, or Vita and Harold, were ready for it.

Alvilde came to stay at the end of February. 'We listened to Mozart on the 3rd Programme after dinner, and I read some poetry (Dylan Thomas' "Fernhill"). A nice evening. A. likes the things I like.' In July Vita and Alvilde went to the Cotswolds, to take a fresh look at the gardens at Hidcote, for which Vita was writing the National Trust guidebook. They stayed at the Lygon Arms in Broadway; while they were there, Vita received a telegram saying that Dorothy Wellesley had died. Later Vita described the funeral to Alvilde. Gerry Wellington and the two children had been there: 'It was rather moving – just a little hole in the ground, and a tiny wooden box containing her ashes. All that was left of those blue eyes and that wild spirit!'

Alvilde learnt of Vita's vulnerability. She was always miserably aware
of her lack of formal education ; even when it came to gardening she felt
unqualified still. The creator of Sissinghurst wrote to Alvilde : 'I am
taking a correspondence course in Horticulture. I shall have to fill in a
weekly examination paper and send it up for correction.' Harold was
always aware of her uncertainties. 'I love seeing Mar in London. It is like
a country-bred puppy on a lead, seeking to escape up some side-street
from the crowds upon the pavement and the fierce traffic on the streets.
Your hand was trembling with panic when we crossed Piccadilly. Oh
my dear dear Mar !'

Shortly before they left for a fortnight in France in October – the Suez
crisis was raging in England – Vita was stung on the neck by a wasp
while giving tea to Megan Lloyd George in the garden. Her neck, tongue
and gums swelled up and she had to spend a night in Pembury Hospital. She was allergic to wasps – and had devoted a section of *The Garden*
to her enemies, 'small samurai in lacquered velvet'. The danger of wasp
stings was partly why Harold was so glad that they had asked Philippa
to come with them on this holiday. 'Your presence was a delight to us,'
he wrote to Philippa afterwards, 'and for me a great release from
anxiety. I could not have coped with Vita singlehanded if a disaster had
occurred. You are so quick and so competent.'

On the drive south, Vita was intrigued to be in Carcassonne : 'I
haven't been here for thirty years,' she wrote to Alvilde, 'when I was
here with Violet. It seems like another life.' Vita still did all the driving,
very fast, sometimes going round roundabouts the wrong way. When
in France she, who hated shops at home, loved the most ordinary
Monoprix store. The climax of the holiday came in Beynac, a favourite
place for both Harold and Vita. At dinner, Philippa was puzzled by their
conspiratorial glances and mutterings. After dark they casually proposed a walk – and took her out to see the castle floodlit on the rock, a
treat they had planned for her with childish pleasure. On the night they
came home to Sissinghurst, Vita herself had a surprise pleasure : in the
October twilight, the closely planted gentian bed that had given her so
much trouble was in full bloom, a carpet of solid blue.

# CHAPTER 35

On his seventieth birthday in November 1956 a group of Harold Nicolson's close friends presented him with a cheque for £1,370 and a list of some 200 names of those who had subscribed to this birthday present. He was overwhelmed and embarrassed – and very glad to have the money. When Vita had suggested that they sell out capital to go on a winter cruise, he had ruefully replied that he had no capital and precious little income either. Now there was no problem. 'I am so glad that all his sweetness and kindness should be recognized,' Vita wrote in her diary. Just before they set out on the cruise ship *Willem Ruys* for Indonesia in January 1957, she wrote to him:

> My darling fellow-traveller; how oddly life turns out. . . . There were you and me, sitting on Angela Manners' hat box in the attics of Hatfield. And now we are going off to Djakarta, 40-odd years later, loving each other far more deeply and wisely than we did then, and with our sons and daughters-in-law, and grand-daughters [Ben and Luisa's Vanessa was born in August 1956] growing up and making their own lives for themselves.
>
> That is all very pleasing; but what pleases me more than anything is that you and I, after all the mistakes and infidelities and errors we have both made in our lives, should now be closer than ever we were. . . .
>
> It is rather nice to embark on a honeymoon again, after 47 years. Yes?

No one but the Nicolsons would have considered their routine aboard the *Willem Ruys* to have approximated to that of a second honeymoon. Except when they had meals and went on trips ashore, they spent the whole day apart. Harold swam every day; but Vita spent all morning and afternoon in her cabin writing *Daughter of France*, her Grande Mademoiselle book, with her notes spread over her bunk as Harold said 'like a picnic'. After dinner, they watched the dancing for a while, and were both in their separate cabins by 9.45. Vita was also going through the typescripts of her letters from Virginia Woolf – many of them undated – putting them in order. Leonard Woolf was considering some form of publication; he had been through them himself, and got them 'into a terrible muddle, damn him', as Vita wrote in her diary.

Her relations with Leonard had become strained. He had strongly objected to the first book about Virginia, *The Moth and the Star* by Aileen Pippett, which had drawn on the correspondence with Vita, and had bombarded Vita with what she called 'fulminating letters'. Harold suggested to Clive Bell that Leonard's anger 'was due in part to the feeling that his property was being dispersed and its value depreciated', and Clive did not contradict him.

In July 1956 Vita had learned that Leonard had been selling some of Virginia's manuscripts to America. 'What an odd man he is,' she wrote to Alvilde. 'Well, they shan't have *Mrs Dalloway* or *Orlando*; it would give me great pleasure to refuse some enormous offer, and to tell Leonard that I had done so.' She had been to see Leonard at Monk's House, 'rather sad, thinking of Virginia, and seeing Mrs Parsons more or less in her place.' (Mrs Parsons, a close friend of Leonard's, was the wife of Ian Parsons, chairman of Chatto and Windus, the publishers.)

The last straw, before they set out on their cruise, had been the publication of Virginia's correspondence with Lytton Strachey, edited by Leonard Woolf and James Strachey. Harold was appalled by their 'silliness, dirtiness and cattishness'. He and Vita thought that not only was Leonard avaricious, but he was seriously misrepresenting Virginia's character in the selection of what he published. Vita had written to him saying that what she would like best would be to have all Virginia's letters to herself published privately, at her own expense, in a strictly limited edition. This would not prevent his publishing them 'with the necessary omissions' later. Leonard, who owned the copyright, would not agree.

In the book Harold wrote about their first cruise, *Journey to Java*, he playfully caricatured both Vita and himself. When Nigel read the manuscript he, like Harold, was afraid that Vita might take the portrait of her amiss: 'I hope you don't mind being made comic relief. He was a little worried, I think, that he had pulled your leg too much. But I can't believe that anybody will miss the obvious affection with which he does it. Indeed, the contrast between you is one of the most charmingly effective things in the whole book.' Harold described Vita's travelling habits – her vast amount of luggage (mainly books), the importance she gave to her pile of mail picked up at every port of call, her love of souvenir shops, her argumentativeness. The portrait of Vita in *Journey to Java* is that of an irritable, eccentric, entertaining, independent-minded aunt, putting the author right on all topics, sometimes wrongly, and not suffering fools gladly. She did not mind at all; he wrote in the teasing, twinkling tone with which he had countered her 'difficultness' all their lives. And as far as suffering fools gladly was concerned, people meeting the Nicolsons for the first time in their later years often found Harold gruff, dismissive or intimidating, and Vita courteous, patient and kind, especially with children. But Harold, in his image of himself and in his relation to Vita, was amiably boyish, and he had a misleading way of writing about himself in both his books and his diaries that was humorously self-deprecating.

When they got home, they found a row going on between the Vasses and the other estate workers. The long idyll with Vass as head gardener was over; Vita suspected he was a Communist, and had quarrelled with him in the summer over strategy for the Sissinghurst Flower Show. Fresh and fierce from her cruise, she fired him. The qualities she had admired so much were now forgotten. 'Well, I never *loved* Vass, you know,' she told Alvilde,

> not as I love Mrs Staples or my wicked warm-hearted old Copper, or my simple slow William [Taylor] – so I don't really mind in my heart. . . . He was a convenient co-operator who shared my tastes and ideas in gardening, but I always felt he was a cold-blooded animal – a lizard, dry, rustling, shooting a long tongue – and would have strung me up *à la lanterne* as soon as not.

Alvilde was discovering what everyone who knew Vita well discovered. Vita wrote to her on 24 April: 'Was I always detached? Yes, I suppose so, only more mobile when young and certainly more irresponsible. I refer to escapades with Violet, much of which I now bitterly regret; I mean, I did behave very badly. I should never have listened to her.' Making it up to Harold for those early years was increasingly her priority.

On the day she wrote the above to Alvilde, Vita heard on the radio that Roy Campbell had been killed in a car smash and Mary badly injured. She wrote at once to Mary, who replied from Portugal:

> Thank you for your loving letter. I know that in spite of everything it is absolutely sincere and it comforted me.
>
> There is one thing I have always meant to ask you, although I am quite sure it is ridiculous and unnecessary – whether you still have any letters of mine? perhaps among old papers and forgotten? In any case will you be so very patient and kind as to tell me that you have not. It is rather a matter of conscience with me, so forgive me.

Vita kept Mary's letters, in spite of this heartfelt request.

Vass's departure left a problem in the garden; three under-gardeners were not enough to keep it going. Friends helped with weeding, watering and planting-out during the early summer. In July Vita engaged a new head gardener, Ronald Platt – an educated man, 'not a menial'. Her former maid Emily Booth came over to show the garden to old Jane Gay, the 'Giovanna' of Vita's childhood; Vita gave them tea, 'I was so pleased to see them.' 'Dear Miss Vita,' Giovanna wrote afterwards, 'I saw you a little girl again. I remembered the night you dined in the Great Hall with the grown-ups ... I took a peep at you from the Minstrel Gallery, and marvelled at the ease in which you were talking to I think it was Lord Balfour.'

Half a century had passed since those evenings of pomp and circumstance at Knole. Eddy Sackville-West, the ageing heir, had gone to live in Ireland; Alvilde, visiting him there, reported to Vita, who commented: 'Drip, drip, drip; and all so green, and Eddy mouldering away towards old age when Knole ... could be his – and he doesn't want it, and I who would have given my soul for it.' Yet when Eddy asked her 'if I would go and live there and look after it when his father died and he succeeded,' she said no. No bread was preferable to half a loaf; and perhaps Sissinghurst, though she might not realize it, had become as dear to her as Knole, and more real.

In August something happened at Sissinghurst that crystallized Vita's unease about continuing her friendship with Alvilde at its present intensity. 'I have made the most unpleasant discovery that my letters are being tampered with. I haven't the faintest idea who by, but it must be someone on the place, and I don't like it.' A letter Vita had written to Alvilde and left in the office to be posted 'was readdressed in a disguised illiterate hand to someone else; that's how I found out.'

The potential horror of what was happening made Vita's old, now safe relationship with Violet seem more precious; in the same month she wrote Violet a tender letter about the past. 'Odd that I should be writing you a love-letter after all these years, when we have written so many to each other. ... You said it would last for three months, but our love for each other has lasted for forty years.'[1] Perhaps Violet, like Harold, was someone to whom Vita wanted to make amends.

On 12 September, Nigel and Philippa's second child was born – a boy, Adam. It was the only cause for rejoicing that Vita had in those nervous weeks. On 4 September she wrote to Alvilde in 'muzzy' writing: 'I gather that there is a lot of talk.' She went away to Suffolk for a week with Edie Lamont, who knew her troubles.

The mystery of the intercepted letter seemed even more threatening on her return, when she learned of an incident at Sissinghurst concerning two men on the place; the word 'blackmail' was in the air. This was the year of the Wolfenden Report on Homosexual Offences, which Vita thought 'enlightened and sensible', but according to the extant legislation homosexuality between adult males was still a criminal offence. Vita was terrified of scandal, of indiscreet revelations, and most of all of Harold being drawn into the matter. The incident had nothing at all to do with her, but if, as she thought, people were saying 'Well, if Lady Nicolson herself...', it could become very unpleasant. For everyone's sake, she did not want any of her women friends to come and stay at Sissinghurst for the present.

James Lees-Milne came to see her. 'We sat and talked in my sitting-room till dinner, and after dinner in the dining-room – one of the most peculiar conversations I have ever had.' In his biography of Harold Nicolson, James Lees-Milne conveyed the quality of her presence and conversation in these confidential talks more vividly that any of her other friends, or any of her lovers:

> Conversation with Vita transcended all barriers. There were no reservations of any kind. No topics were barred. Her curiosity about and understanding of human nature in all its aspects were limitless. Her sympathy with every human frailty and predicament was all-embracing. This was the Vita I knew and dearly loved.[2]

He described her voice, 'deep, slightly quavering, gently-swelling', and her 'short, sharp laughter', like the sea, he wrote, breaking on shingle. In the morning, Vita wrote in her diary: 'I wish I could talk with Hadji as Jim and I talked last night, but it would only bore Hadji if I tried to, and he would just roll away – Gwen's Woolly Ball.' In any case, she wrote, she must sort out the problems of life for herself. Hadji 'would always roll away. It would be no good at all, – only an irritation to him and no help to me.' Instead, she went with him to see *The Bridge On the River Kwai*: 'Taking H. to see a film he likes is like taking a schoolboy: he enjoys himself so frankly.'

Alvilde could not help being sceptical about the rumours of scandal and blackmail. Perhaps Vita had a new interest? She meant Edie Lamont. 'No, not that,' replied Vita. 'The person you mean is a friend of eleven years standing – solid and indestructible – a rock in my life. The only intimate friend I have; I don't make friends easily, and she is about the only close friend I have.' Harold, Violet, Edie were 'indestructibly' dear to Vita now; it was the indestructible that she wanted and not, after all, the excitement of being in love. Luckily for everyone's peace of mind the Nicolsons departed in early December on their second winter cruise, aboard the *Reina del Mar*, bound for the West Indies and South America.

Vita fell ill, with a high temperature, on the first day out. The ship's doctor said she had a tired heart, 'but I can see he has no real idea of what is wrong with her,' Harold wrote to Nigel. After three weeks she picked up and enjoyed the rest of the trip ; they were not home until early February 1958. In Lima, Vita bought a rug made of llama fur – 'It is the softest, lightest thing, as though it were made of thousands of kittens,' she wrote to Alvilde. It kept her warm in the chilly tower as she worked on at *Daughter of France*, in which she had no confidence : 'Oh Hadji, my book is so bad. It really is. I am not imagining this : I *know* it is bad. I am writing to you late at night. I haven't been over to have my supper yet.'

In July Luisa told Harold and Vita that her marriage to Ben was far from well. Vita talked to them both ; what shocked her most was Ben's 'harsh attitude' to Luisa. He told his mother that he just wanted to be left in peace, on his own. Both Harold and Vita were anxious to patch up the marriage, and Luisa wrote long letters to Vita, confiding all the sad complications of her life with Ben, grateful for the 'reassuring, comforting love' of Ben's parents.

Vita's own reassurance and comfort came increasingly from her deepening intimacy with Edie Lamont. Vita did not bother Harold with the details of her personal life. Remembering her free, open conversations with James Lees-Milne, she told Harold with mild sarcasm that he never listened to anything she said, 'so it's not much use my saying it. As Gwen called you, "My Woolly Ball, because he just rolls away." How wise you are, and what a lot of trouble it saves you.' He replied sharply that he devoted far more time to thinking about 'wasps and Alvilde and Bunny' than to thinking about his own work, only 'I keep quiet about it.'

Just before Christmas 1958 Vita had what she dismissively called in her diary 'a sort of tiny heart-attack'. Harold, in London, was not told. 'It wasn't anything much, but made me feel rather rotten, so I just spent the day tidying papers etc up and going on with beastly index [for *Daughter of France*].'

Nigel and his partner George Weidenfeld were thinking of publishing Nabokov's *Lolita*. Vita read it in the Olympia Press edition over Christmas and was shocked. She sent Nigel a formal, typed letter begging him to abandon the project, which 'horrified and appalled' her. She saw little of value in *Lolita* and much that was disgusting and cynical. She was afraid it would damage Nigel politically, and 'tarnish the bright name' of Weidenfeld & Nicolson. In her own handwriting, at the end, she said, 'I *am* sorry to be so disagreeable and tiresome, darling, but I really do feel strongly about it.'

Harold wrote in the same vein to George Weidenfeld, even though he had not yet read the book – apart from a particularly 'lustful passage', as he put it, that Vita had shown him. Weidenfeld & Nicolson stood their ground ; *Lolita* was published, and the first edition of 40,000 copies was sold out before publication.

Vita, like Harold, was conservative about what came to be called 'permissiveness' in print. This was not so much hypocrisy as caution – an instinct for reticence, reinforced by a lifetime's experience. She very rarely intervened in the boys' lives as she did on this occasion. As she had written to Nigel, 'You know I have always gone on the line of never interfering with your liberty of action ... but there have been moments when I feared that you (or Ben) might interpret this loose-rein theory as indifference.' On the contrary – behind it was 'a very deep true love which never wants to interfere but which always would be there if you wanted to call on it ; like a huge bank-balance ready to meet an unexpected call.'

Their winter cruise had become an annual fixture. (Vita paid.) In early January 1959 they rather halfheartedly left for the Far East aboard the *Cambodge*. 'Our depression at leaving is surpassed only by Rollo's misery at being left,' Harold wrote to Philippa and Nigel. On board were Jewel and Philip Magnus-Allcroft (the author Philip Magnus), and Sonia Orwell, widow of George Orwell, with her second husband Michael Pitt-Rivers. Vita was fascinated by Sonia : 'Can't make up my mind if she is a bitch or a waif. She is certainly an intellectual snob, but deliciously ignorant,' she wrote to Alvilde. Letter-writing took up a great deal of Vita's time on shipboard : apart from all her other correspondence, she wrote twenty-six times to Edie Lamont. The port of call she enjoyed most was Macao : 'I don't think H. and I have ever spent a happier two days,' she wrote in her diary, and told Alvilde that she would like to live there, 'in an eau-de-nil housing among the banyan trees and tamarinds, looking out over the fishing fleet towards China.'

They were greeted at Colombo on their way home by a man from Reuter's who had, according to Vita's diary, 'a long cable from Guy Burgess who wants to come to England because his mother is dying, and who said that H. is the only one of his friends who has stuck to him and written to him regularly.' While Harold was proud of the fact that he did not desert friends in trouble, he dreaded further involvement and worried that the linking of his name with Burgess's might have an adverse effect on Nigel's political career.

The next day a cable came from Nigel to say that he had lost a constituency poll at Bournemouth East by ninety-one votes. (Harold made

Vita open the cable.) It was not *Lolita*, nor Guy Burgess, that had unseated him ; he was not conservative enough for his ultra-Conservative constituency, having been among the rebels who had abstained from the vote of confidence in the Government during the Suez crisis.

The next piece of bad news was waiting for them at Djibouti. Vita found letters from Bunny Drummond and her secretary Betty Arnett telling her that Rollo – who had been so sad to see them go – had died. Vita was badly upset. 'He meant so much to me,' she wrote to Alvilde. 'He was so beautiful, so good, such a gentleman, and such a companion.' On the ship, she had a horrible dream about Rollo :

> I dreamt B.M. was dead, and her body lay on one bed and her head on a pillow of another bed. I was looking at her body (covered by sheets, all decent) when I suddenly realized that Rollo had got her head off the other bed's pillow, onto the floor, and was gnawing the raw red stump of the neck.
>
> Her face was still beautiful – just like her face in life. It horrified me to see Rollo chewing at the raw stump.

When she got home, Vi Pym told her about a young border collie advertised in the local paper ; he had been found abandoned, tied up against a barn. Vita took him and called him Dan. 'He is silky, black and white, and 8 months old.' Dan comforted her for the fact that 'everything seems to be coming to pieces.' She began to make immediate plans for the next winter journey to the sun. 'We must go somewhere ... and damn the expense.' She sent four of Seery's urns from Bagatelle up to Sotheby's, where they were bought by the National Art Collections Fund and returned to the Wallace Collection. In March, she sold some of the rue Laffitte silver.

In early April 1959 she was seriously ill with virus pneumonia. Her friends vied with one another to take care of her, increasing the tension and irritating Harold :

> I am still puzzled by the way Alvilde scolded me for allowing people to see you and then Edie scolded me for letting Alvilde see you and then Vi scolded me for letting Edie see you (which I hadn't) and then Bunny said I was "so weak" about visitors and should prevent them coming and tiring you. That *franchement* was pretty stiff. I do so hate all this jealousy and crinkum crankum. All these women loathe each other.

He was not jealous, he said, like the women were. 'You say that jealousy is the symptom and concomitant of true love. But I disagree. It is an emerald eyed lizard.'

Luisa came to tell Vita about her unhappiness with Ben. Ronald Platt, Vass' successor, came to give in his notice. And *Daughter of France*, the book that had been so long in the writing and given her so little pleasure, was published, and reprinted twice within the year. She made a special acknowledgement in it to Raymond Mortimer, 'who said to me many years ago in a French vineyard, "Why don't you write the life of the Big Miss?"'

Nigel, writing to her about the book, said: 'I have always come to know you better through your books than in any other way. With Daddy it is the other way round. This one has shown me that what you admire most in a person is sympathy for other people.' He also said that la Grande Mademoiselle reminded him of Christopher St John. Vita had written of her subject – who had never married – that

> her friendships were always with women rather than with men, and that these friendships were apt to be deeper and more violent than is customary. ... Sour grapes may have entered into Mademoiselle's indifference to the opposite sex. We must – and why shouldn't we? – admit that she was very ugly, uncouth, hoydenish, and devoid of charm for men.

Old Christopher herself chose not to notice any parallel. She wrote in her diary that Vita's new book was 'boring' and that its central character 'never came to life'.

By mid-May Vita was raging against the slowness of her recovery. 'I am fed up with being a nuisance to everybody, and not being able to get out. Missing all these weeks of spring has nearly broken my heart, and I'll be damned if I miss all the summer as well.' She sobbed with rage at not being able to come downstairs to see visitors she liked. Harold could do little for her. 'She regards me as so incompetent in practical matters that she has no confidence in anything except my love.' It was July before Vita went out in her car again, to lunch with Edie Lamont. In another month she was well enough to write a jaunty letter to Evelyn Irons, now working for the London *Sunday Times* in New York: 'Sissinghurst is one long garden-party throughout the summer. It is rather fun: the most unexpected people turn up, sometimes old friends I haven't seen for years, and there is no obligation and no effort, they don't impinge, one just has an agreeable half-hour with them, and it's all very nice and easy.' When she was not in the middle of writing a book, Vita liked to be available to the garden visitors. Sometimes she and Harold stood together regally in the archway of the tower, answering queries. They kept no part of the garden for their private use; friends who were staying, hoping for a quiet read out of doors, were sometimes disconcerted by the impossibility of solitude.

Betty Arnett left to get married, and Ursula Codrington came part-time to give secretarial help. Vita also had to find a replacement for Ronald Platt. She picked two girls : they were friends, both highly qualified, holding the Diploma from the Waterperry Horticultural School. Their names were Pamela Schwerdt and Sibylle Kreutzberger. Vita called them 'the Mädchen', and approved of 'their youth, their keenness, and their workmanlike blue jeans'. Also, 'they do not stop working while one talks to them, which I like. No time wasted.' After the Mädchen had been in the garden a month, it was clear that the experiment was a success : 'Almost everything I had instructed them to do, after breakfast, was already done by 11.30. If only we can keep those girls, we might get something like a garden in time. And somehow I don't feel they are just new brooms sweeping clean. But I suppose they will go and marry and be lost to us.' Nearly a quarter of a century later, when Vita and Harold were long gone, Pamela Schwerdt and Sibylle Kreutzberger were still in charge of the garden at Sissinghurst.

# CHAPTER 36

AT the beginning of each week, Vita picked and packed flowers for Harold to take up to his room in Albany and arrange in the silver vase she had given him: it was a loving ritual dating from his years in King's Bench Walk. His 'scoop' – the basket in which he carried the flowers – would, said Vita, be 'the most poignant coffee cup ever made' if he was to die. 'I often think I have never told you how much I love you – and if you died I should reproach myself, saying Why did I never tell him? Why did I never tell him enough?' 'It is awful,' replied Harold, 'the way we are getting preoccupied by death.'

In London, he held open house at six every evening, the sherry hour, for his friends. Deafness and health worries had not lessened his pleasure in congenial company. The only concession he made to age was to go up to London on Tuesdays instead of Mondays. 'You've gone away again, into the different life you lead in London,' wrote Vita one Tuesday in November 1959:

> It is an odd sort of life we have evolved for ourselves – me here, and you in London, and then both of us in our real home over the ends of the week, so happy and quiet and busy. Few people would understand it, in fact people often think we are on the edge of divorce.
> How wrong they are.
> How wrong!

In August, Vita had had a visit from Frances Hamill and Margery Barker, the American dealers who had bought Virginia Woolf's manuscripts from Leonard. They offered her £600 for her manuscript of Virginia's *Mrs Dalloway*, which she turned down. But she liked the two women – 'We sat under the catalpa and I gave them Spanish Chablis' – and was relieved to learn that Vanessa's children Quentin Bell and

Angelica Garnett would inherit Virginia's copyrights from Leonard, and that they 'would then be willing and indeed anxious to publish V's letters to me.'

The question of her letters from Virginia was still sore. Leonard Woolf had said he was willing to include a selection of them in a volume of letters to various people. Vita had been against this, since it was 'the continuity that makes them more interesting, or so it seems to me.' In her final letter on the subject, on 25 September 1957, she had spoken her mind sharply :

> I was naturally very disappointed to get your letter saying that you did not feel inclined to publish Virginia's letters [to Vita]. I am afraid that I cannot resist saying that I feel they would go far towards undoing any harm to Virginia's reputation that may have been done by other books, as they are so gay and human and would surely undo any false conception of the grimness of Bloomsbury. . . . Meanwhile do by all means get copies made but please do ask your typist not to muddle my set, as it took me days to put them straight when you returned them to me before.[1]

There the matter had rested for two years. Now Vita was going to Rodmell to give a talk on writing biography, and to spend the night at Monk's House. 'I hope I don't get haunted,' she wrote to Harold, 'or would it be rather exciting to hear Virginia's voice suddenly addressing me in the middle of the night ?' When she woke up at Monk's House, as she wrote in her diary, 'I got up early and went out into the garden and looked across the valley and thought of Virginia walking off to drown herself. . . . Had breakfast with Leonard and his dogs and cats. We went round his garden and came on Stephen Tomlin's bust of Virginia – which was the only time her name was mentioned.'

The Nicolsons' next winter cruise, in the New Year of 1960, was aboard the *Europa* to South Africa, stopping at Aden, Mombasa, Zanzibar and Dar-es-Salaam. They boarded the ship in Venice, after seeing Freya Stark at her house in Asolo ('Her revolving table ; Greek vase ; marble bathrooms,' Vita noted in her diary). Vita resumed work on a novel she had begun the year before – it had a shipboard setting. At Durban they were met by Betty Arnett, who had married a South African ; Vita took the opportunity to ask her to type two *Observer* articles, 'quite like old times'. Conservative though she was, the sight of apartheid in practice horrified Vita. 'Mummy screams with rage,' Harold told Nigel. 'She says it is like Hitler all over again and that those nice newspaper people who came to see us last night will end their days in a concentration camp. Fists of execration are raised on high.'

The bad news that reached them on this cruise was the death of Newton Lamont, Edie's husband. When Vita came home, she and Edie became closer than ever. (Once Vita wrote 'Virginia' by mistake for 'Edie' in a letter to Harold.) Vita loved Edie and depended on her. Until her last days, Vita was never without love or the physical expression of love. Her great adventure was never over. Like so many of the people that Vita had been close to, Edie was Scottish – and more self-sufficient than most of Vita's other friends.

Vita was lucky too in Ursula Codrington, who was typing her new novel *No Signposts in the Sea* and was 'first-rate at typing intelligently, – she even comments on my prose and says do I realize I have used the same word three times in as many lines, and she is right.'

Harold was depressed about his lack of money and his flagging energy. Vita vainly tried to make him accept money from her, instead of undertaking a book on monarchy for Weidenfeld & Nicolson, which he did not want to write. Vita fretted about his low spirits and ill-health; but it was she who fell ill in July, with an apparent recurrence of virus pneumonia. From now on, Edie Lamont usually stayed at Sissinghurst during the week when Harold was in London. 'Edie has been a perfect angel to me, and I really *don't* know what I should do without her. It is the most wonderful friendship I have ever had.'

Vita was not well again until September, when she went with Edie to convalesce by the sea at Worthing. They drove over to Brighton and looked at B.M.'s old house in Sussex Square, and at White Lodge, 'terribly overbuilt now'. In October Christopher St John died, in her late eighties. Vi Pym, going through Christopher's papers, sent Vita some of her diaries – including what Vita called 'the shattering record of her friendship with me', Christopher's love-journal, which Vita had no idea she had written. Huddling under her llama rug on the sofa in her tower, Vita read 'Christopher's horrifying document'.

Emily Booth's husband 'Wuffy', Harold's valet on their long-ago wedding journey to Constantinople, had died too. Another funeral, another link with the past gone. A link with the future was Lionel Sackville-West, Vita's cousin and Eddy's heir. He came to see her just before Christmas 1960, and she wrote to Harold:

> I did like having Lionel here – pop-pop-pop at his pipe. You see I don't mind talking to him about Knole, because he loves and understands it as I do, and as Eddy doesn't. In fact I love talking to him about it, and when he and Jacobine go to live there I shall be able to go there again, – Moses descending from Pisgah, as poor Moses never did.

*No Signposts in the Sea* came out while Vita and Harold were on their fourth winter cruise, to South America. It was serialized in *Woman's*

*Own*: 'an awful paper', Vita said, but it paid well. This novel, her last, is dedicated 'For Edie'. It is the story of a man who knows he is terminally ill and as a last pleasure takes a sea-voyage on a cruise ship in the company of a widow, Laura, whom he likes and finds good company. Vita told Evelyn Irons that the character of Laura was an invention 'except in so far as she bore certain resemblances (mental not physical) to the Edie of the dedication'.

In this book Vita envisaged for the first time a synthesis between love and lust, mind and heart, love and 'in love' – a complete union, too late for her doomed hero Edmund. She wrote here too about what was important to her – writing, for example:

Ah, it is heavenly while it lasts. A sort of intoxication. . . . You *see* suddenly, as in a finished picture, the entire shape and design of what you want to do. I don't say that you ever carry it out to your satisfaction, but for one brief moment of illumination you have apprehended the unity of what you meant. That is . . . one of the few moments in life worth living. No matter if it only lasts ten minutes while you are soaking in a hot bath.

She wrote for the first time (in print), through Laura, about lesbianism:

Perhaps a relationship between two women must always be incomplete – unless, I suppose, they have Lesbian inclinations which I don't happen to share. Then, or so I have been given to understand, the concord may approach perfection. You see, there is a kind of freemasonry between women – and no doubt between men also – which makes up for the more elemental excitement of the sex war.

There was only one snag in the perfect concord of two women – jealousy. 'You see, if a man is jealous of a woman, he at least meets his rival on level ground, man to man; but if a woman is jealous of a woman, she enters into an unfair competition with the other sex; she is always afraid that the natural thing will conquer in the end.'

Edmund and Laura discuss 'the natural thing' – love between men and women. Edmund, before he falls too deeply in love with Laura, thinks there is 'a certain chic' in chastity. 'Monotonously repetitive, carnal delights all merge.' Laura's prescription for happy marriage, before she falls too deeply in love with Edmund, is that advocated so often on platforms, in print and in life by Harold and Vita: mutual respect, independence of movement and independent friendships, separate rooms – 'no bedroom squalor' – separate finances and 'the same sense of values'. Edmund points out that she has left out love.

They fall in love; though Edmund, ironically, fails to realize that it is he whom she is speaking of when she describes her feelings: 'Love, fondness, devotion, one can comprehend; but not this extraordinary nature of *in love-ness*; you see that I separate them. ... For the time being nothing matters but the one thing. *Parce que c'était lui*; *parce que c'était moi.'* That was a formulation Vita and Violet had often quoted to one another: and still did, in nostalgia.

Laura was speaking of 'an astonishing thing which comes on one in later life, when all such thoughts have been put away as an impossibility, and one believed rather sadly that fulfilment was to be found nowhere in this world.' If she really loved, said Laura, looking at Edmund 'with a severity that was almost a challenge', she would be utterly faithful, and presume the same fidelity in the other person – 'unquestioning'. But Edmund dies, and is buried at sea, without knowing that he was loved in that total way. *No Signposts in the Sea* is loaded with the if-onlys and what-ifs of Vita's divided life, divided love, divided nature, which had made total commitment and the luxury of faithfulness impossible.

Vita was bored on the South American cruise, and disliked Brazil when they arrived. 'I think it is a beastly country and I never want to see it again.' On the way home, off Lisbon, they heard that Lord Sackville's American wife Anne had died. Vita had always disliked her, and disliked what she did to Knole. 'We did not pretend to feel sorry except for Uncle Charlie' – who was ninety.

When she was home in February 1961 she had a bout of bronchitis, and, after twenty-five years, at last gave up her weekly *Observer* articles. 'Great relief.' Now that Uncle Charlie was alone at Knole, she felt able to go there for the first time in thirty years. She went to luncheon, taking Edie with her. 'It was heaven to be back there. ... I shall go again.' She went again in May, when Eddy was there, and again with Harold in July. The spell was broken.

She ordered plants for the autumn – 'we may not live long enough to see them come to maturity' – but the grandchildren would. She visited Alvilde's new house in Gloucestershire and gave her advice about what to plant in a north-facing flowerbed: 'Peonies would not mind. Hydrangeas? the lace-cap sort.... Lily of the Valley. Polyanthus. Trilliums. *Mertensia virginice* (a lovely forget-me-not blue). Omphalodes. Phlox.' She had Violet to lunch – 'really very sweet, though inaudible' – and wrote to Evelyn Irons, her 'Darling Scrape', telling her how 'Cecil Beaton and Princess Margaret and Cyril Connolly and Clive Bell' had been to see the garden – 'it's really like having a *salon*. ... Oh, and I've got a new friend: Elizabeth Bowen. She came to stay a weekend. I like her so much. So you see I am enjoying life, although I don't racket about in the exciting way you do. ?Remember Les Baux?' Uncharacteristically, Vita tended to adopt a tone of self-assertive bravado whenever she wrote to Evelyn – perhaps because it was Evelyn who had left her, and not the other way around.

Harold's book on monarchy turned out to be inadequate. It was his seventh book since the war, and he also wrote the lead book review for the *Observer* every week. He was tired. Nigel consulted Vita when he had read the manuscript. 'I'm worried, and I want your help.... Don't tell him that I have written to you, but he is almost certain to raise the subject this coming weekend,' he wrote on 20 September. Vita, always protective of Harold, did not protect him from the truth. 'Vita consoles me, as always,' Harold wrote in his diary. 'She is not in the least annoyed with Nigel for ticking me off, and agrees that he is perfectly right.' The book was revised and made acceptable.

The following weekend was more problematic. Dan, the young collie, had become hysterical and started biting people. As if in anticipation of his fate, he became ill, and Vita frantic. Harold was – in his view and hers – inadequate. He wrote to her when he returned to Albany :

I know you think I abandoned you when little Dan collapsed on the tower staircase. But in fact I had gone and sat in the porch, a draughty place, in order that you could get hold of me if wanted. I know you hate being stared at when you are crying. But I got scolded none the less. I felt dreadfully sorry about you and little Dan but I am bad at expressing these things.... I never was good at that sort of thing and now that I am becoming senile I have got worse than ever. I do love you so and I do suffer when you suffer. In fact it was a ghastly weekend.

Having Dan put down 'cracked my heart', Vita wrote to her American correspondent Andrew Reiber.[2] But her heart was not broken, as it had been over Martha and Rollo. She replaced Dan with two golden retriever puppies; Glen became Vita's own dog, and his brother Brandy ended up belonging to the Mädchen.

Vita published *Faces: Profiles of Dogs* that autumn – one-page essays on forty-four different breeds, opposite photographs by Laelia Goehr. She amused herself by making special references to dogs she had known personally : the saluki given her by Gertrude Bell in Baghdad, 'without exception the dullest dog I ever owned'; Pippin, her golden cocker spaniel; Ethel Smyth's series of Old English sheepdogs, all named Pan. In her piece on 'The Alsatian' she 'saluted the memory of Rollo'; Brutus, 'the only Great Dane I ever intimately knew', had belonged to Dorothy Wellesley; she mentioned Canute, her elk-hound in Long Barn days; True, who was Edie Lamont's golden labrador, and Dan himself, 'who tries to herd the clumps of daffodils in the orchard'.

To publicize the book she appeared – for the first and only time – on BBC television's *Wednesday Magazine.* Harold was an experienced television performer, but she had stoutly refused all invitations to appear.

The patching-up of Ben and Luisa's marriage was wearing thin. Vita conceded to Harold, unwillingly, that she felt there was no solution but separation. There was no failure in communication, except between Ben and Luisa: they both talked and wrote freely to Vita and Harold. Nicky Mariano, knowing Ben and Luisa of old, was involved, and letters flew hither and thither. His parents' sympathy melted Ben's reserve; he wrote to them on 11 September: 'You are really – both of you – the nicest, kindest and most sympathetic of parents. In every crisis of my life you have risen wonderfully to the occasion and I have never been sufficiently grateful.' 'Poor Luisa. Poor Ben. Poor Vanessa. My heart and sympathies are torn to rags between the three of them,' Vita wrote in November. But it was Ben who had to come first for her. She agreed to tell Luisa that he wanted a divorce, since he seemed unable to do so himself. Luisa found this connivance between mother and son hard to accept. Vita had her difficult forty-seven-year-old 'dark boy' back at last – or so Luisa hoped, since there was very little else to be salvaged from what had happened. On the last day of 1961, Vita wrote in her diary:

> Horribly cold. It starts to snow. By evening it is inches deep. Ben sits in the dining room, reading. I stay there with him some time, but have to go back to the tower, and creep under the llama and listen to the 6 o'clock news, which is of more snow and frost everywhere.
> We have champagne for dinner, and I hope that 1962 will be nicer than 1961.

Thirty years earlier, she had had a dream that she had made into a poem. She dreamt that she was setting plants in the garden in the winter dusk as the snow fell round her. She knew she must not stop, she had to finish her task. As she worked on, she seemed to be surrounded by candles that the falling snow buried but did not extinguish, and by fallow deer with flames on the tips of their antlers:

> And she knew that she neared the end of the garden path,
> And the deer and the buried candles travelled with her,
> But still she knew that she would not make an end
> Of setting her plants before the shroud came round her.[3]

Vita sold eight of her own manuscripts to Miss Hamill, the American dealer, for £1,500. This was to pay for their fifth winter cruise, to the Caribbean. Edie Lamont was going with them this year – 'if either you or

I got ill,' Vita told Harold, 'she would be a rock of help and comfort.' They set off in the New Year of 1962.

Having breakfast on the boat train from Waterloo to Southampton, Vita had a haemorrhage. She was very worried and confided in Edie. She spent the next day in her cabin on the *Antilles*, reading Agatha Christie. Harold was told nothing, but sensing disaster or resenting Vita's obvious dependence on Edie, began to feel ill himself.

Off Martinique, Vita had a high temperature and bronchitis. After injections from the ship's doctor she was well enough to go ashore at their next ports of call, and to write deceptively normal letters to friends in England – with anecdotes about Evelyn Waugh, who was on board with his daughter Margaret.

All Vita wanted was to get home. On the return train journey from Southampton to London, 'H. and Edie and I have a nice little compartment to ourselves, but I go into the Pullman car and see that dreadful tell-tale stain on the seat.' At Sissinghurst the puppy, Glen – 'perfectly beautiful, grown a lot' – was waiting. 'The orchard is misty-mauve with Tomasinianus ; parrotia flowering as never before ; witch hazel arborea still out ; a few specie crocuses. . . . I feel really ill, and try to hide it from Hadji.'

She saw a specialist in London – 'Edie my own darling came' she added in pencil to this diary entry – and went into the Royal Free Hospital for tests on 23 February. Then home again for a few days ; she answered a letter from Evelyn Irons, with no attempt this time at bravado : 'I send you my love darling Scrape as ever. We did have fun didn't we ? I still have the pottery dish I bought at Tarascon on the way to Les Baux.' She went back to London to undergo a hysterectomy. Edie Lamont went with her to the hospital. Harold, who now knew what had happened, wrote to Vita : 'Edie's tact and discernment and reticence about the tragedy on the boat train has wiped out all trace of jealousy. It was ridiculous of me to feel jealous and Edie I know suspected it and was wonderfully considerate. But I *was* jealous, idiot that I am.' He went on feeling jealous of Edie to the end, and fighting against it. He had always believed that jealousy was not a necessary component of love. But sitting beside Vita's bed at the hospital he felt useless, and wrote to James Lees-Milne that 'Mrs Lamont is deft and competent. I am the most incompetent man since Noah.' When Vita came home from the hospital there was little that he – old, clumsy, reticent, frightened – could do for her. Edie was usually there.

Vita's friends misunderstood his attitude. 'I feel,' he wrote to Vita from London, 'that Edie, Vi, Bunny, Gwen and Dorothy [Beale] are under the impression that I don't know how ill you have been, or that, if I know, I don't care. How little they understand !' The surgeon had told him that Vita had cancer. But he was slow to face the truth; he had to be told, in so many words, by their own doctor, that Vita was not going to get better.

Vita heard that Mac had died; and then, in May, her Uncle Charlie. Eddy Sackville-West was at last Lord Sackville.

On 11 May Vita wrote to Alvilde Lees-Milne, 'I can just totter downstairs and have a chair that Copper wheels me about in, but although I suppose I am getting better I can't say that I *feel* much difference.' She wanted to go and see what Alvilde had done with her new house – 'but when? the future looks very dark.' She was too weak to keep up the treatments that had been arranged at Pembury Hospital. She lay in the Priest's House, in Ben's old room, so as to be near the kitchen and not to cause extra work for Mrs Staples and Quinlan the manservant. She had been told so many lies about when she would feel better, she wrote to Harold, 'that I no longer believe anything.' She was too tired to see more than one visitor each day. 'Edie doesn't tire me because I don't have to talk.' Alvilde came to see her; and she managed to scribble a note to Jim Lees-Milne, whose mother had died, on 18 May: 'Jim, dear, I'm so sorry. I know you will mind.'

Harold, who had been keeping up his routine of spending the week in London, came home on 25 May for 'a whole week', as he wrote to Vita: 'That will be agreeable indeed.' He knew now that there was not much more time.

Vita's last morning, 2 June, was warm and sunny. Edie sat with her until lunch-time. Then Ursula Codrington took over. The last words Ursula heard Vita speak were to the golden retriever, Glen, who came nosing in at her door.

Harold was in the South Cottage writing a review when Ursula, soon after one o'clock, after opening Vita's bedroom windows wide to the Weald, went across the garden to look for him. 'Ursula comes to tell me. I pick some of her favourite flowers and lay them on her bed.'

Vita had not had time to tell Harold that she had asked Edie to take Glen when she died. A day or two later Edie, anxious to fulfil Vita's wishes, returned to Sissinghurst to collect him. Harold was sitting with his sons and Philippa in the garden. When Edie told him why she had come, his temporary calm deserted him. In tears he stumbled up from where he sat under the catalpa tree to fetch Glen's lead.

In the deserted tower room everything has remained just as Vita had left it, the hours measured by the clock's bell high in the tower – a bell that thuds as well as rings, to the ears of the person working below. Vita had not redecorated the tower room in the thirty years that she had used it.

The strips of fringed velvet on the surfaces were already faded and worn in 1962, as were the apricot velvet curtains. Throughout Sissinghurst, the old embroideries, bits of tapestry, tassels, brocades, silks and velvets were dusty, discoloured, worn, irreplaceable.

The walls of the tower room are lined with books. Three steps down, through the archway into the turret, they reach the ceiling. Here are the books on the psychology of sex that she had read with Violet, and then with Harold: six volumes of Havelock Ellis, with 'V. N.' written in each. In the volume *Sexual Inversion* Harold had inscribed a quotation from Verlaine, '*On est fier quelquefois quand on se compare.*' There is Edward Carpenter's *The Intermediate Sex*, and Otto Weininger's *Sex and Character*, with 'V. N. Polperro 1918' on the flyleaf, and passages about male and female characteristics heavily annotated. 'When [women] marry they give up their own name and assume that of their husband without any sense of loss,' wrote Weininger. 'I disagree,' scrawled Vita in the margin.

On the right in the turret are her gardening books. On the left is a low carved cupboard; inside it is a black hide Gladstone bag, initialled 'V. N.' There is now a long slash in the thick leather, where Nigel, unable to find the key, cut it open – and discovered the 1920 manuscript about Violet and Vita that he published in *Portrait of a Marriage*.

There are old Persian rugs on the floor, and the beads, pebbles, shells, shards, pots that Vita collected on her travels ranged on the windowsills. On the chimney piece across the corner of the room are two Chinese crystal rabbits – she described one of these as having belonged to Sebastian in *The Edwardians* – a photograph of Rollo, Persian blue ceramics, and framed poems and prayers illuminated on vellum by Christopher St John. Near Vita's sofa are the English poets and Shakespeare. On the other side of the room, all Harold's books, and Virginia's, history and travel books – and her own books, unobtrusively arranged at floor level in the shelves under the big window.

On her worm-eaten oak writing-table are photographs of Harold, Virginia, Luisa and Vanessa, Ben, a reproduction of Branwell's painting of the Brontë sisters, and small engravings of Knole. Ranked at the back are the memoirs of La Grande Mademoiselle. In a rack at right angles to the table are her reference books – dictionaries, the *Thesaurus*, *The Rhymer's Lexicon* (in which she had written on the title page, 'A rhymer – that's what I am') – and her address book, garden accounts book, a 'books lent' book, and the book in which she wrote down her dreams.

Everything is as she left it, down to the letters stuck in her blotter. Only the lamp is different; the utilitarian one that she used has been replaced by something prettier. A wrought-iron door now bars the entrance to the tower room, enabling visitors to see, but not to enter and touch :

> Oh stranger, wander everywhere
> Within the garden that I made
> But come not here, oh come not here
> Where I am shy but unafraid.

There are flowers on her writing table, as there always were when she was there. One thing is missing : the small pink marble sarcophagus that had held her two ink-wells, from Long Barn days. It contains her ashes, which lie in the Sackville family crypt at Withyham with her ancestors.

Vita had long ago told Harold that she did not want a memorial service. There was just a simple funeral service for her in Sissinghurst church. When Harold died, a joint memorial service was held for them both in London. Vita had repeatedly said that she would not go on living if Harold died. He did not echo this but, as Nigel wrote after his death in 1968, 'He was never the same again. He really died with her.'[4] He went into a physical and mental decline. He had written to her once, 'I simply cannot contemplate life without you and I just dismiss the thought from my mind. . . . When I feel something deeply I am totally unable to express it. You understand that, but who will understand anything when you are gone ?'[5]

Vita had once asked him whether he would marry again, if she died first. He replied vehemently that he would not. He would devote his declining years to 'thinking about you and remembering all our happy days together. . . . No, my angel – no stranger either in this world or the next shall come between you and me.'[6] He hoped that 'every leaf' at Sissinghurst would be a link between them. But not even the garden could solace Harold.

Eddy Sackville-West, now Lord Sackville, wrote to Evelyn Irons : 'Well, dear Evelyn, it is all very sad, and one wonders what on earth will happen to that lovely garden. As long as Harold lives, I suppose it will continue the same . . . but people's gardens are apt to die with them, even if the status quo is kept – or perhaps just because of that.' He supposed that something was 'bound to be done to keep it going . . . but it can never be the same'.

He was right on both counts. The year before Harold died, Sissinghurst passed into the ownership of the National Trust, and its future was made secure. Nigel and Philippa converted the staff quarters in the south wing of the gatehouse into a home for their growing family and their descendants. (Nigel and Philippa were divorced in 1970.) The garden continued to be run by the 'Mädchen' whom Vita herself had initiated. It is the garden that Vita made, though it 'can never be the same'.

Vita had fought a losing battle with her gardeners over the use of weed-killers; she had a liking for the random flowers that appeared from nowhere. She encouraged self-sown wild flowers, heart's ease, and the tiny dark viola, Bowles's Black. 'Rollo's path' – a diagonal of bricks across Delos – has gone; the rather harsh red and yellow flowers in the urns at the entrance, grown from seeds brought back from the war by Vass, have gone. The wayward, mysterious, lordly air that Vita gave the garden is less felt. Delos itself has been changed from a rock garden to a shrub garden; it was always a difficult corner and this is an improvement. Constant experiment and renewal are part of the life of the garden, which is visited by tens of thousands of people every year. Grass paths have been replaced by York stone, to take the tread of so many feet.

But the white roses dangle from the apple trees, and the loveliness she made is there in the shelter of the rose-coloured walls, in the flowers that bloom and die year after year and are her memorial:

> They cannot break the heart, as friend
> Or love may split our trust for ever.
> We never asked them to pretend :
> Death is a clean sufficient end
>     For flower, friend or lover.[7]

# NOTES AND SOURCES

MOST of the material from which this book was built was, at the time of writing, at Sissinghurst Castle: Vita's mother's diaries, letters and scrapbooks; Vita's diaries, cuttings books, notebooks and many manuscripts, published and unpublished; letters to Vita from childhood friends, from Rosamund Grosvenor, and Violet (Keppel) Trefusis; the huge correspondence between Vita and Harold Nicolson; copies of Harold Nicolson's diaries; and a mass of letters to Vita from publishers, strangers, fans, friends, family and lovers. Harold and Vita's letters to each other, Vita's early diaries and the diaries of her mother are now (1983) in the safe-keeping of the Lilly Library, Bloomington, Indiana.

To give a separate reference for every item quoted from the Sissinghurst material would encumber these pages unprofitably. Where no source reference is given, it is to be assumed that the document quoted was at Sissinghurst. Particularly important letters or diary entries are dated in the narrative; all others can be dated by month and year from the context. If a letter is quoted out of chronological context, a reference is given. References are given for letters from other sources, quotations from printed books, and for material from university or library collections. The letters from Vita to Evelyn Irons, Eardley Knollys, Alvilde Lees-Milne and James Lees-Milne were, at the time of writing, in the possession of the recipients.

PROLOGUE

1 For the facts of Vita's mother's background I am indebted to Susan Mary Alsop, *Lady Sackville*, 1978

2 VSW, *Pepita*, 1937

PART I KNOLE

CHAPTER I

1 VSW, *The Edwardians*, 1930

2 VSW, 'Leopards at Knole', *Collected Poems*, 1933

3 VSW, *Knole and the Sackvilles*, 1922

4 idem

5 VSW, 'To Knole', *Poems of West and East*, 1917

6 VSW, *Nursery Rhymes*, 1947

7 VSW, 'Shameful Reminiscence', *Little Innocents*, ed. Alan Pryce-Jones, 1932

8 VSW, 'Autobiography of 1920', in Nigel Nicolson, *Portrait of a Marriage*, 1973

9 idem
10 idem
11 *Pepita*
12 *Portrait of a Marriage*
13 *Pepita*
14 idem
15 idem

CHAPTER 2

1 VSW to HN, 11 May 1960
2 *Portrait of a Marriage*
3 *Pepita*
4 *Portrait of a Marriage*
5 VSW ms, no date
6 *Portrait of a Marriage*
7 VSW, 'Country Notes', *New Statesman*, 24 June 1940
8 Violet Trefusis, *Don't Look Round*, 1952
9 idem
10 *Portrait of a Marriage*
11 *Knole and the Sackvilles*
12 *Portrait of a Marriage*
13 *Pepita*
14 8 April 1947
15 idem
16 *Pepita*
17 *Portrait of a Marriage*
18 VSW, 'Shepetovka', *Spectator*, 25 February 1944

CHAPTER 3

1 *Portrait of a Marriage*
2 VSW, Centenary Poem for Ellen Terry, *The Times*, 27 February 1947
3 *Portrait of a Marriage*
4 idem
5 James Lees Milne, *Harold Nicolson*, vol. 1, 1980
6 *Portrait of a Marriage*

CHAPTER 4

1 *Portrait of a Marriage*
2 Violet Trefusis, *Don't Look Round*
3 VSW to HN, 23 November 1960

4 James Lees-Milne, *Harold Nicolson*, vol. 1
5 *Portrait of a Marriage*

CHAPTER 5

1 VSW to Alvilde Lees-Milne, 14 April 1957
2 *Poems of West and East*
3 VSW, ms 'Marian Strangways'
4 I have been unable to identify this quotation – VG
5 A. E. Housman, *A Shropshire Lad*, 1896
6 'Marian Strangways'
7 *Poems of West and East*
8 'Marian Strangways'

PART II  CHANGE AND CHALLENGE

CHAPTER 6

1 *Portrait of a Marriage*
2 VSW, *Passenger to Teheran*, 1926
3 *Portrait of a Marriage*
4 *Poems of West and East*
5 *Portrait of a Marriage*

CHAPTER 7

1 'The Garden', *Poems of West and East*

CHAPTER 8

1 VSW in *Beginnings*, ed. L. A. G. Strong, 1935
2 *Portrait of a Marriage*
3 idem

CHAPTER 9

1 *Portrait of a Marriage*

CHAPTER 10

1 *Portrait of a Marriage*
2 idem
3 idem
4 Rupert Hart-Davis, *Hugh Walpole*, 1952

PART III EXPLORATIONS

CHAPTER 11

1 *Collected Poems*
2 Charleston Papers
3 *The Diary of Virginia Woolf*, vol. II, ed. Anne Olivier Bell, 1978. 15 December 1922
4 idem
5 *The Letters of Virginia Woolf*, vol. 4, ed. Nigel Nicolson, 1978. 8 August 1931

CHAPTER 12

1 *The Diary of Virginia Woolf*, vol. II, 19 February 1923
2 idem, 17 March 1923
3 Mary Lutyens, *Edwin Lutyens*, 1980
4 VSW, *The Land*, 1926
5 *The Diary of Virginia Woolf*, vol. II, 21 August 1929

CHAPTER 13

1 University of Sussex Library, 16 July 1924
2 *The Letters of Virginia Woolf*, vol. 3, 19 August 1924
3 University of Sussex
4 *The Letters of Virginia Woolf*, vol. 3, 5 September 1924
5 *The Diary of Virginia Woolf*, vol. II, 21 December 1924
6 *The Letters of Virginia Woolf*, vol. 3, 26 December 1924
7 Leonard Woolf, *Downhill All the Way*, 1967
8 *The Diary of Virginia Woolf*, vol. III, 5 June 1925
9 *The Letters of Virginia Woolf*, vol. 3, 24 August 1925
10 Berg Collection, New York Public Library, 18 September 1925
11 'Sometimes When Night', *Collected Poems*
12 *The Diaries of Virginia Woolf*, vol. III, 7 December 1925
13 *The Letters of Virginia Woolf*, vol. 6, to Ethel Smyth, 22 August 1936

14 Berg, 17 January 1926
15 Berg, 8 January 1926
16 Berg, 17 January 1926

CHAPTER 14

1 Berg, 21 January 1926
2 Berg, 29 January 1926
3 University of Sussex, 20 February 1926
4 Berg, 23 February 1926
5 University of Sussex
6 *Passenger to Teheran*
7 Charleston Papers, 19 March 1926
8 Berg, 8 April 1926
9 *Passenger to Teheran*

CHAPTER 15

1 Berg, 16 June 1926
2 Humanities Research Center, University of Texas, 18 June 1940
3 *The Diary of Virginia Woolf*, vol. III, 30 October 1926
4 Berg, November 1926
5 *The Letters of Virginia Woolf*, vol. 3, 19 November 1926
6 'Year's End', *Collected Poems*
7 University of Sussex
8 *The Diary of Virginia Woolf*, vol. III, 23 January 1927
9 Berg, January 1927
10 Berg, 29 January 1927
11 *The Letters of Virginia Woolf*, vol. 3, 2 February 1927
12 University of Sussex
13 Berg, 23 February 1927
14 Berg, 4 April 1927
15 Berg, 30 March 1927

CHAPTER 16

1 *The Letters of Virginia Woolf*, vol. 3, 22 May 1927
2 University of Sussex, 17 September 1926
3 Charleston Papers, 2 June 1927
4 Berg, June 1927
5 *The Letters of Virginia Woolf*, vol. 3

6 *The Diary of Virginia Woolf*, vol. III, 18 June 1927
7 Berg, 23 June 1927
8 *The Letters of Virginia Woolf*, vol. 3, 24 June 1927
9 23 June 1927. Published by courtesy of Sir Rupert Hart-Davis
10 *The Diary of Virginia Woolf*, vol. III, 4 July 1927
11 *The Letters of Virginia Woolf*, vol. 3, 4 July 1927
12 Berg, 11 July 1927
13 *The Letters of Virginia Woolf*, vol. 3, 2 September 1927
14 Berg, 11 October 1927
15 Unpublished
16 Unpublished

### CHAPTER 17

1 Berg, March 1928
2 Charleston Papers, 14 March 1928
3 Berg, 14 March 1928
4 *The Diary of Virginia Woolf*, vol. III, 21 April 1928
5 *The Letters of Virginia Woolf*, vol. 3, 27 April 1928
6 *The Diary of Virginia Woolf*, vol. III, 7 July 1928

### CHAPTER 18

1 Berg, 31 August 1928
2 *The Diary of Virginia Woolf*, vol. III, 7 November 1928
3 Berg, ?24 June 1933
4 *Encounter*, January 1954
5 Berg, 5 October 1928
6 Berg, 11 October 1928
7 *Portrait of a Marriage*
8 Leonard Woolf, *Downhill All the Way*, 1967

### CHAPTER 19

1 VSW, 'Hilda Matheson', *Spectator*, 22 November 1940
2 Berg, 6 January 1929
3 Berg, 5 February 1929

4 Berg, 21 February 1929
5 Berg, 25 February 1929
6 Berg, May 1929
7 University of Sussex
8 *Listener*, 26 June 1929
9 *The Diary of Virginia Woolf*, vol. III, 5 August 1929
10 *The Letters of Virginia Woolf*, vol. 5, 18 October 1932

### CHAPTER 20

1 *The Diary of Virginia Woolf*, vol. III, 4 September 1929
2 *The Letters of Virginia Woolf*, vol. 4, 3 November 1929
3 Berg, 16 September 1929
4 *The Diary of Virginia Woolf*, vol. III, 25 November 1929
5 *The Letters of Virginia Woolf*, vol. 4, 25 April 1930
6 *Journal of the Royal Horticultural Society*, November 1953
7 Berg, 16 September 1929

## PART IV  SISSINGHURST

### CHAPTER 21

1 'The Garden at Sissinghurst Castle', *Country Life*, 11 September 1942
2 Berg, 18 August 1933
3 Texas, 6 September 1930
4 Leonard Woolf, *Downhill All the Way*
5 *The Diary of Virginia Woolf*, vol. III, 2 September 1930
6 idem, ?11 November 1930
7 Christopher St John, *Ethel Smyth*, 1959
8 idem
9 *Country Notes* (New Statesman articles), 1939
10 *The Diary of Virginia Woolf*, vol. IV, 23 January 1931
11 Texas
12 Evelyn Irons to author, 9 September 1981
13 *Country Notes*

CHAPTER 22

1 With ms of *The Garden* in the Huntingdon Library, California. Quoted by Elizabeth W. Pomeroy in her unpublished paper 'Within Living Memory: Vita Sackville-West's Poems of Land and Garden', 1981
2 'Tess', *Collected Poems*
3 *The Diary of Virginia Woolf*, vol. IV, 13 January 1932
4 Berg, 24 April 1932
5 *The Letters of Virginia Woolf*, vol. 5, 8 May 1932
6 *Collected Poems*
7 *The Letters of Virginia Woolf*, vol. 5, to Hugh Walpole, 17 August 1932
8 *The Letters of Virginia Woolf*, vol. 5, 8 November 1932

CHAPTER 23

1 To Virginia Woolf. University of Sussex
2 VSW, diary
3 Berg, 28 March 1933
4 University of Sussex, 9 April 1933
5 *Portrait of a Marriage*
6 *The Letters of Virginia Woolf*, vol. 5, 1 June 1933
7 University of Sussex, 'Whit Monday' 1933
8 *Portrait of a Marriage*
9 Berg, 17 May 1933

CHAPTER 24

1 Berg, 17 May 1933
2 Berg, 18 August 1933
3 Berg, September 1933
4 Berg, 3 November 1933
5 *The Letters of Virginia Woolf*, vol. 5, 26 November 1933
6 Berg, 6 February 1934
7 University of Sussex, 2 March 1934
8 *The Diary of Virginia Woolf*, vol. IV, 17 July 1934
9 *The Letters of Virginia Woolf*, vol. 5, 23 September 1934
10 Berg, 18 November 1934

CHAPTER 25

1 *Letters on Poetry* from W. B. Yeats to Dorothy Wellesley, 1940
2 *The Diary of Virginia Woolf*, vol. IV, 11 March 1935
3 *The Letters of Virginia Woolf*, vol. 5, 26 November 1935

CHAPTER 26

1 Peter Quennell, *Customs and Characters*, 1982
2 Berg
3 Berg, 2 December 1937

CHAPTER 27

1 Berg, 19 December 1938
2 Berg, 22 February 1939
3 *Country Notes*, 1939
4 Berg
5 'Other People's Gardens', *Country Notes*
6 Anne Scott-James, *Sissinghurst: The Making of the Garden*, 1974
7 Berg, 16 September 1939
8 Yale, 31 August 1940
9 Yale, 31 August 1940, published in Philippe Jullian and John Phillips, *Violet Trefusis*, 1976
10 idem, 25 September 1940
11 Yale, 5 December 1940

CHAPTER 28

1 Yale, 5 December 1940
2 Yale, 16 March 1941
3 Berg, 10 October 1940
4 Mitchell Leaska, *Pointz Hall: The Earlier and Later Typescripts of Between the Acts*, 1983
5 Nigel Nicolson, Introduction, *The Letters of Virginia Woolf*, vol. 6, 1980
6 15 April 1942

CHAPTER 29

1 James Lees-Milne, *Prophesying Peace*, 1977

PART V THE ENCLAVE AND THE TOWER

CHAPTER 30
1 Berg, 6 November 1951
2 Huntingdon Library
3 Anne Scott-James, *Sissinghurst: The Making of the Garden*

CHAPTER 31
1 To Eddy Sackville-West, 30 June 1950. Berg
2 Yale, 13 October 1948
3 Denton Welch, *Journals*, 1952

CHAPTER 32
1 Yale, 19 December 1949
2 Yale, 4 October 1949
3 Yale, 5 July 1949
4 Yale, 18 January 1950
5 *New Statesman*, 21 January 1950
6 James Pope-Hennessy, *A Lonely Business*, ed. Peter Quennell, 1981

CHAPTER 33
1 James Lees-Milne, *Harold Nicolson*, vol. II
2 Philippe Jullian and John Phillips, *Violet Trefusis*

CHAPTER 35
1 Yale, 3 September 1957
2 James Lees-Milne, *Harold Nicolson*, vol. II

CHAPTER 36
1 University of Sussex
2 *Dearest Andrew* (VSW's letters to Andrew Reiber), 1979
3 'A Dream', *Collected Poems*
4 To Hamish Hamilton, 8 May 1968
5 20 August 1957
6 25 November 1952
7 VSW, *The Garden*, 1946

# BOOKS BY
# V. SACKVILLE-WEST

1909  *Chatterton* (verse drama), privately printed in Sevenoaks
1915  *Constantinople: Eight Poems*, privately printed in London
1917  *Poems of West and East*, Bodley Head
1919  *Heritage* (novel), Collins
1921  *The Dragon in Shallow Waters* (novel), Collins. *Orchard and Vineyard* (poems), Bodley Head
1922  *The Heir* (short stories), Heinemann
      *Knole and the Sackvilles*, Heinemann
1923  *Challenge* (novel), Doran, New York (1st British ed., Collins, 1974)
      *Grey Wethers* (novel), Heinemann
      *The Diary of the Lady Anne Clifford* (ed.), Heinemann
1924  *Seducers in Ecuador* (novel), Hogarth Press
1926  *The Land* (long poem), Heinemann
      *Passenger to Teheran* (travel), Hogarth Press
1927  *Aphra Behn* (biography), Gerald Howe
1928  *Twelve Days* (Persian travel), Hogarth Press
1929  *King's Daughter* (poems), Hogarth Press
      *Andrew Marvell*, 'The Poets on the Poets' series, Faber
1930  *The Edwardians* (novel), Hogarth Press
1931  *Sissinghurst* (poem), Hogarth Press
      *Invitation to Cast Out Care* (poem), Faber
      *Rilke* (translations), Hogarth Press
      *All Passion Spent* (novel), Hogarth Press
1932  *The Death of Noble Godavary and Gottfried Kunstler* (stories), Benn
      *Thirty Clocks Strike the Hour* (stories), Doubleday, Doran, New York
      *Family History* (novel), Hogarth Press
1933  *Collected Poems*, vol. 1, Hogarth Press
1934  *The Dark Island* (novel), Hogarth Press
1936  *Saint Joan of Arc* (biography), Cobden-Sanderson
1937  *Pepita* (biography), Hogarth Press
      *Some Flowers* (gardening), Cobden Sanderson
1938  *Solitude* (poem), Hogarth Press

1939   *Country Notes* (*New Statesman* articles), Michael Joseph
1940   *Country Notes in Wartime*, Hogarth Press
1941   *English Country Houses*, 'Britain in Pictures' series, Collins
1942   *Grand Canyon* (novel), Michael Joseph
1943   *The Eagle and the Dove* (biography), Michael Joseph
1944   *The Women's Land Army*, Michael Joseph
1945   *Another World Than This* (poetry anthology, with H.N.), Michael Joseph
1946   *The Garden* (long poem), Michael Joseph
1947   *Nursery Rhymes*, Dropmore Press, limited ed. ; also Michael Joseph, 1950
       *Devil at Westease* (detective story), Doubleday, Doran, New York
1951   *In Your Garden* (*Observer* articles), Michael Joseph
1953   *In Your Garden Again*, Michael Joseph
       *The Easter Party* (novel), Michael Joseph
1955   *More For Your Garden*, Michael Joseph
1958   *Even More For Your Garden*, Michael Joseph
       *A Joy of Gardening*, Harper & Row, New York
1959   *Daughter of France* (biography), Michael Joseph
1961   *No Signposts in the Sea* (novel), Michael Joseph
       *Faces : Profiles of Dogs*, Harvill Press

*Collected Poems*, vol. 1, Hogarth Press, 1933 (No vol. 11)
*Selected Poems*, Hogarth Press, 1941

*Posthumous*
1968   *V. Sackville-West's Garden Book*, ed. Philippa Nicolson, Michael Joseph
1979   *Dearest Andrew* (Letters to Andrew Reiber, 1951–62), Michael Joseph

# INDEX